A Companion to the Works of J. M. Coetzee

Studies in English and American Literature and Culture

A Companion to the Works of
J. M. Coetzee

Edited by
Tim Mehigan

CAMDEN HOUSE
Rochester, New York

First published 2011
by Camden House

Camden House is an imprint of Boydell & Brewer Inc.
668 Mt. Hope Avenue, Rochester, NY 14620, USA
www.camden-house.com
and of Boydell & Brewer Limited
PO Box 9, Woodbridge, Suffolk IP12 3DF, UK
www.boydellandbrewer.com

ISBN-13: 978-1-57113-507-0
ISBN-10: 1-57113-507-3

Library of Congress Cataloging-in-Publication Data

A companion to the works of J. M. Coetzee / edited by Timothy J. Mehigan.
    p. cm. — (Studies in English and American literature and culture)
    Includes bibliographical references and index.
    ISBN-13: 978-1-57113-507-0 (hardcover : alk. paper)
    ISBN-10: 1-57113-507-3 (hardcover : alk. paper)
    1. Coetzee, J. M., 1940– — Criticism and interpretation. I. Mehigan,
Timothy J. II. Title. III. Series.
PR9369.3.C58Z6368 2011
823'.914—dc23
                                                                    2011022484

A catalogue record for this title is available from the British Library.

This publication is printed on acid-free paper.
Printed in the United States of America.

Contents

Acknowledgments

VOLUMES SUCH AS THESE are the labor of many hands and many minds. I would like to acknowledge, first and foremost, the skill, dedication, and constant good humor of the scholars who have participated in this project. I thank Brittany Travers and Helen Churchman, who helped me locate sources and organize the final state of the manuscript. The volume has profited from comments provided by two anonymous reviewers. I thank these reviewers for their suggestions. I am grateful to the University of Chicago Press for permission to reprint part of Derek Attridge's 2004 study, *J. M. Coetzee and the Ethics of Reading: Literature in the Event*. I thank the Art Gallery of New South Wales and Adam Chang for permission to use Adam Chang's portrait of John Coetzee on the cover of this volume. I am indebted to Jane Best and Edward W. Batchelder for their production expertise and copyediting assistance. I also acknowledge the generous support and encouragement extended to me by Jim Walker at Camden House — it was he who first suggested this project to me. Thanks, finally, to the University of Otago for providing a supportive environment in which to conduct this project.

T. M.
July 2011

Abbreviations of Works by J. M. Coetzee

Chronology of Main Writings by J. M. Coetzee

NOTE: First publication of these writings only is listed. Significant essays and book reviews not included in Coetzee's book publications are listed separately.

"The Works of Ford Madox Ford with Particular Reference to the Novels" (Master's thesis, U of Cape Town, November 1963)

"The English Fiction of Samuel Beckett: An Essay in Stylistic Analysis" (PhD diss., U of Texas at Austin, January 1969)

Dusklands (Johannesburg: Ravan Press, 1974)

Translation of *A Posthumous Confession* by Marcellus Emants (Boston: Twayne, 1976)

In the Heart of the Country (Johannesburg: Ravan Press, 1977; London: Secker & Warburg, 1977); *From the Heart of the Country* (New York: Harper & Row, 1977)

Waiting for the Barbarians (London: Secker & Warburg, 1980; Johannesburg: Ravan Press, 1980)

"Die Skrywer en die Teorie," *SAVAL Conference Proceedings* (Bloemfontein 1980), 155–61

Translation of *The Expedition to the Baobab Tree* by Wilma Stockenström (Johannesburg: Jonathan Ball, 1983)

Life & Times of Michael K (London: Secker & Warburg, 1983; Johannesburg: Ravan Press, 1983; New York: Viking, 1983)

Truth in Autobiography: inaugural professorial address at the University of Cape Town (Durban, South Africa: U of Cape Town P, 1984)

Foe (London: Secker & Warburg, 1986; Johannesburg: Ravan Press, 1986)

A Land Apart: A Contemporary South African Reader, ed. with André Brink (London: Faber and Faber, 1986)

White Writing: On the Culture of Letters in South Africa (New Haven, CT: Yale UP, 1988)

"The Novel Today," *Upstream* 6, no. 1 (1988): 2–5

Age of Iron (London: Secker & Warburg, 1990; New York: Random House, 1990)

"Breyten Breytenbach and the Censor," *Raritan* X, no. 4 (Spring 1991): 58–84

Doubling the Point: Essays and Interviews, ed. David Attwell (Cambridge, MA: Harvard UP, 1992)

"Homage," *Threepenny Review* 53 (1993): 5–7

"The Heart of Me," *New York Review of Books* (22 Dec. 1994): 51–54

The Master of Petersburg (London: Secker & Warburg, 1994; New York: Viking, 1994)

Food: The Vital Stuff, with Graham Swift, John Lanchester, and Ian Jack (New York, NY: Penguin, 1995)

"Meat Country," *Granta* 52 (Winter 1995): 41–52

Giving Offense: Essays on Censorship (Chicago: U of Chicago P, 1996)

Boyhood. Scenes from Provincial Life (London: Secker & Warburg, 1997; New York: Viking, 1997)

What Is Realism? (Bennington, VT: Bennington College, 1997)

Disgrace (London: Secker & Warburg, 1999; New York: Viking, 1999)

The Lives of Animals, ed. Amy Gutmann (Princeton: Princeton UP, 1999)

Introduction to *The Vivisector*, by Patrick White (London: Penguin, 1999)

William Kentridge, with Dan Cameron and Carolyn Christov-Bakargiev (London: Phaidon, 1999)

Introduction to *The Confusions of Young Törless*, by Robert Musil (London: Penguin Classics, 2001)

Fifty-One Years / David Goldblatt, with texts by J. M. Coetzee (Barcelona: Museu d'Art Contemporani de Barcelona: ACTAR, 2001)

The Humanities in Africa = Die Geisteswissenschaften in Afrika (Munich: Carl Friedrich von Siemens Stiftung, 2001)

Stranger Shores: Essays 1986–1999 (New York: Viking, 2001)

Letter of Elizabeth: Lady Chandos, to Francis Bacon (Austin, Texas: Press Intermezzo, 2002)

Youth (London: Secker & Warburg, 2002; New York: Viking, 2002)

Elizabeth Costello: Eight Lessons (New York: Knopf, 2003; New York: Viking, 2003)

Lecture and Speech of Acceptance, Upon the Award of the Nobel Prize, delivered in Stockholm in December 2003 (New York: Penguin Books, 2004)

Introduction to *Brighton Rock*, by Graham Greene (London: Penguin Classics, 2004)

Translation and introduction to *Landscape with Rowers: Poetry from the Netherlands* (Princeton: Princeton UP, 2004)

Slow Man (London: Secker & Warburg, 2005; New York: Viking, 2005)

Introduction to *Samuel Beckett: The Grove Centenary Edition*. Vol 4. Ed. Paul Auster (New York: Grove Press, 2006)

Introduction to *Dangling Man*, by Saul Bellow (London: Penguin Classics, 2006)

Inner Workings: Literary Essays 2000–2005 (New York: Viking, 2007)

"Roads to Translation," *Meanjin* 64, no. 4 (2007): 141–51

Diary of a Bad Year (Melbourne: Text Pub., 2007; London: Harvill Secker, 2007)

Summertime. Scenes from Provincial Life (North Sydney, NSW: Knopf, 2009); *Summertime: Fiction* (New York: Viking, 2009)

Foreword to *Second Nature: The Inner Lives of Animals* by Jonathan Balcombe (New York: Palgrave Macmillan, 2010)

Introduction

Tim Mehigan

J. M. COETZEE IS ONE OF THE MOST IMPORTANT writers in the world today. He is also one of the most distinguished: he was the first writer to win the Booker Prize on two occasions (1983 and 1999),[1] and the second South African writer, after Nadine Gordimer, to receive the Nobel Prize for Literature (2003). He is the recipient of numerous other literary awards including the Prix Femina Étranger, the Commonwealth Writers' Prize, and the Jerusalem Prize for the Freedom of the Individual in Society.

Although he writes in English and was raised speaking English at home in his native South Africa, Coetzee's parents were of Afrikaner descent and his family origins date back to the arrival of the first Dutch settlers in South Africa in the seventeenth century. While later to spend significant periods of time abroad in England and the United States, Coetzee spent his early life in Cape Town and the nearby town of Worcester in the Western Cape. After a Catholic schooling with the Marist Brothers in the Cape Town suburb of Rondebosch, he matriculated to the University of Cape Town in 1957, successfully completing honors degrees in English and mathematics in 1960 and 1961. From 1962 to 1965 he worked as a computer programmer in England while undertaking research for a master's thesis on the English novelist Ford Madox Ford. He was awarded the degree of Master of Arts by the University of Cape Town in 1963. From 1963 to 1980 he was married to Philippa Jubber, a bond that produced two children: Nicolas, born in 1966, and Gisela, born in 1968. Nicolas died in an accident in 1989.

In 1965 Coetzee traveled to the United States, beginning graduate studies in linguistics at the University of Texas with the support of a Fulbright scholarship. His doctorate on the early fiction of Samuel Beckett[2] was completed in 1968. He was appointed an assistant professor of English at the State University of New York in Buffalo in the same year, staying in that post until 1971. During this period his first work of literature, *Dusklands*, was begun, although not published until 1974. In 1971 he applied for permanent residence in the United States, an application that was denied on account of his involvement in a campus protest at Buffalo in 1970 against the Vietnam War. Returning to South Africa in 1972,

Coetzee took up the first in a series of positions at the University of Cape Town teaching English literature. He retired from the university as Distinguished Professor of Literature in 2000 and emigrated with his partner Dorothy Driver to Australia two years later. He now lives in Adelaide, South Australia.

Coetzee's biography is closely connected with some of the most momentous events to have taken place since the Second World War. These events include the period of apartheid and white minority rule in South Africa from 1948 to 1994, the tumult of the antiwar movement in the United States in the late 1960s and early 1970s,[3] the transition to democracy and black government in South Africa in 1994, and the emotively charged period of reconciliation between whites and blacks after the abolition of apartheid in South Africa in 1994 and the establishment of the Truth and Reconciliation Commission in 1995 (the Commission did not present its final report until October 1998). Despite his proximity to events of geopolitical significance and the ever-present factor of censorship[4] during the years of apartheid, Coetzee has repeatedly been subjected to the criticism, notably from fellow South African writers Nadine Gordimer and Athol Fugard, that his fiction neither engaged directly with the ravages of apartheid nor took a clear stand against the Nationalist government during the apartheid years.[5] Since the advent of democratic rule, these critics further contend, his apparent gloominess about post-apartheid South Africa — as sketched, for example, in his novel *Disgrace* (1999)[6] — has only served to undermine the fragile process of reconciliation underway in that country. Against this predominantly South African opinion must be weighed the sheer number of international plaudits he has received and, among them, statements such as those of the Swedish Academy in its 2003 citation for the Nobel Prize. In this citation Coetzee is praised for portraying "the surprising involvement of the outsider" in his works — a statement that recognizes the profound nature of his moral, if not also his political, commitments in relation to the postwar history of his homeland.

This divergent opinion about Coetzee's political responses[7] suggests something of the complexity with which his writing speaks to readers. It equally highlights the important role of the critics and literary criticism in throwing light on the literary-aesthetic and political-moral assumptions that inform his writing. In developing an understanding of these assumptions and the complicated narrative strategies at work in Coetzee's fiction, the present volume aims to consider Coetzee's contributions to literary criticism as an important body of work alongside his creative output. A focus on both the criticism and the imaginative literature of the author is accordingly brought to bear in most of the chapters in this volume; Carrol Clarkson directs attention exclusively toward the criticism in the last chapter of the volume.

Despite a well-known reluctance to speak directly about his work, Coetzee has by no means left the task of evaluating his intentions entirely to others. In his Nobel lecture to the Swedish Academy in 2003, for example, he talked, albeit elliptically, about his motives and the general task of the writer. In this lecture, to which he gave the title "He and His Man," he returned to a subject already explored in an earlier work *Foe* (1986), an enigmatic novel whose literary point of departure is Daniel Defoe's 1719 novel *Robinson Crusoe* (*Foe* represents one of the most interesting contributions to the literary genre of the Robinsonade, the desert island story). James Joyce called the figure of Crusoe "the true prototype of the British colonist." Joyce went on to note Crusoe's "manly independence, the unconscious cruelty, the persistence, the slow yet effective intelligence, the sexual apathy, the calculating taciturnity."[8] Coetzee's decision to engage a second time with the figure of Crusoe, his creator Defoe, and a novel that has been considered one of the important literary works of the European Enlightenment in the eighteenth century seems to have been made with similar thoughts in mind. Defoe, it could be said, extending from Joyce's insights as well as from Coetzee's *Foe*, stands at a point of evolution of European civilization when the spirit of adventure began to lose its innocent allure, when to travel out into the world was to subdue that world, often violently, when the talk of foreign parts was, among other things, a commercial enterprise designed to enrich those (writers) practiced enough to command such talk with eloquence and to turn it to profit. These themes are touched on in Coetzee's lecture, itself perhaps ultimately a parody as much as a portrayal of the acute self-consciousness of the (great) writer, but also a writer who is prepared to acknowledge his place in a morally ambiguous history of ideas.

Still another element can be found in Coetzee's Nobel lecture. It connects with the idea of literary inheritances and the nature of authorship — a theme of many of his novels, and, as Chris Prentice indicates in this volume,[9] an important topic in *Foe*. As Coetzee (with *Foe* again in mind) might be taken to suggest in the lecture,[10] the writer today cannot write — if s/he ever could — outside a literary tradition and the assumptions about authorship that helped chisel that tradition into being. Writing, in other words, is obliged to make use of the constructions, notions, and mannerisms this inheritance of authorship has brought into being. This leads to the following conclusions about the nature of writing: there can be no naïve language of address toward readers, no "view from nowhere" with regard to moral intention, and no political position that the writer can assume when speaking publicly (even publicly when receiving a major literary award) that is able to disavow or otherwise be elevated beyond this literary tradition. As he pointed out in an interview with David Attwell shortly after receiving the Nobel Prize for Literature,[11] this is also a matter of historical record, this is what history teaches us about the conditions that bear upon every speaking position, every writerly utterance. In his own case, these historical circumstances turn Coetzee — whose family origins, as already mentioned, reach back to the first Dutch settlement of the Cape — "into a late representative of the vast movement of European expansion that took place from the sixteenth century to the mid-twentieth century of the Christian era, a movement that more or less achieved its purpose of conquest and settlement in the Americas and Australasia, but failed totally in Asia and almost totally in Africa." The epithet "postcolonial" has been coined to describe literature, of which Coetzee's writing is a prominent example, that has been crafted in deep awareness of this prior history of conquest.

To some extent, then, the Nobel lecture provided a belated response to those who had criticized Coetzee for failing to issue overt statements in his writing condemning the oppressive and racist white minority government of the apartheid era and its policies, and for offering an allegedly bleak view of postapartheid South Africa since that time. His response in the Nobel lecture seems to have been to remind these critics about the problematical nature of writing, that writers can find no sanctuary in any speaking position that is oblivious to its own moral blind spots, that writing — should it wish to be honest and truth-seeking — must first engage with the difficult question of what it means to speak politically in a time of social and political crisis, if such engagement with the political is to be considered meaningful. As many of the contributors to the present volume suggest,[12] Coetzee's writing can be understood as an attempt to ask this question about the speaking position of the writer before any other question.

There are two direct consequences arising from a literature that acknowledges the primacy of this question. First, writing is turned into an open process of interrogation of the writer's conscience as s/he seeks to speak. A potentially limitless questioning of the truth of narration and of the capacity of the writer to speak such truth results. Coetzee's fiction accordingly betrays several points of contact with postmodernist assumptions about writing. These assumptions highlight the constructed, and to this extent "artificial," nature of truth-directed discourse. They also underscore the fact that there is no alternative to discursivity, that, to speak with Jacques Derrida, there is "nothing outside the text"[13] and its immanently constraining truth-conditions. Secondly, Coetzee's interest in the position of the outsider — an interest highlighted by the Swedish Academy — would appear to constitute a response to the vexed question of how to assume a position from which to speak politically through imaginative literature. The perspective of the outsider, in other words, effectively emerges as a political choice for the writer who has difficulty sustaining any position at all from which to speak. A growing interest in the outsider, for this reason, is visible in his novels. Many of these outsiders become his protagonists: from the farmer Magda, a "spinster with a locked diary" who resists becoming "one of the forgotten ones of history" (*In the Heart of the Country*, published in 1977) (*IHC*, 3), to the vagrant, and later orphaned, Michael K in *Life & Times of Michael K* (1983),[14] the aging, mortally ill Mrs. Curren in *Age of Iron* (1990), the eccentric, morally wayward English professor David Lurie in *Disgrace* (1998), through to the tongueless, silent Friday of *Foe* (1986), who, though not the novel's main character, illustrates more than any other of the outsiders of Coetzee's fiction that the true outsider is the one who does not speak and, moreover, cannot under any circumstances be brought to speech. In this sense, Friday is the vanishing point of the literary enterprise that, in Gayatri Chakravorty Spivak's well-known phrase, asks whether the subaltern speaks.[15]

Coetzee's references in his writing to the underlying constraints that condition the political act of speaking therefore must be considered programmatic. They give this writing a postmodern appearance, in that the act of writing is utterly infused with consciousness. This is not just the "false consciousness" highlighted by theorists such as Georg Lukács in the tradition of Marxist critique, but also the problem of consciousness as such, since every moment of consciousness must be considered in some ways "false," must to some extent be ethically compromised in ways unknown to speakers, and at any rate appear as the product of the discursive conditions of power that emerge historically. The literary production of Coetzee that faces directly onto a problematic of postcolonial consciousness, and that penetrates deeply into this consciousness at every turn, is certainly that of the period prior to his emigration to Australia. This is the fiction that extends from *Dusklands* (1974) to *Disgrace* (1999), the criticism that encompasses the extended reviews and readings gathered under the title *White Writing* (1988), and includes *Giving Offense* (1996), a study of literary censorship; the essays and interviews with David Attwell published (or, in the case of the essays, republished) in *Doubling the Point* (1992); the later essays on literature (*Stranger Shores*, 2001), and, finally, the fictionalized memoirs *Boyhood* (1997) and *Youth* (2002). This literary production gives evidence of what might be thought of as a distinctive temper relating not just to Coetzee's fairly continuous residence in South Africa during this period, but to the themes and topics this production is mainly concerned to discuss: themes of postcoloniality, as already mentioned; general problems that afflict rational consciousness in the manner first raised and discussed by the Frankfurt School theorists Adorno and Horkheimer and others;[16] and, in this same vein, political and intellectual questions arising from the underlying dialectic of master and slave, first discussed by Hegel and Marx, and also alluded to by Coetzee in the Nobel lecture.

In the period following Coetzee's emigration to Australia, these themes and topics persist, but they are widened beyond the ambit of the postcolonial and betray a general concern to set out what might be called a comprehensive project of ethical understanding of self and world, of ethical thinking in general. A key, enabling figure of this disposition in his writing is Elizabeth Costello, an aging Australian writer who travels the world on lecture tours, providing disquisitions on topics such as censorship, vegetarianism, and the proper treatment of animals. Yet despite her propensity to make weighty pronouncements — and this remains typical of Coetzee's writing overall — Costello is not allowed to occupy any position of final authority.[17] In fact, the work in which these disquisitions (which take the form of separate lectures) occur, *Elizabeth Costello* (2003), is notable for the presence of countervoices that, coming for the most part from a skeptically minded son, gnaw away at every utterance and unmask any pretension these utterances might conceal to command knowledge and to speak with clarity and certainty.[18] To this extent, Coetzee's ethical project might be termed "anti-Cartesian." It can be characterized as an attempt to set out a "postrational" manner of thought grounded in the conditions of an embodied, suffering understanding that acknowledges the prior material fact of the body.[19] Such a project would eschew preconceived rational commitments and extend to all living beings as a matter of definition as well as conviction — not just the human beings in Descartes's account who are privileged to maintain the reflective ground of the *cogito*. As Clarkson points out in the last chapter, this project would gesture toward a space where the "accents of anguish" arising from embodied understanding exceed anything that could be contained within the confines of authorial consciousness alone.[20]

In a later work, *Slow Man* (2005), in which Costello appears as a famous writer, the interest in staking out the ground of a thinking lying outside the separation of mind and bodily "extension" ordained by Descartes reappears. Interestingly, it is now Costello herself who takes on something of the perennially doubting quality of a Mephistophelean spirit, pricking the conscience of her host, Paul Rayment, and, thereby like Mephistopheles himself in Goethe's drama *Faust*, in which the "double thoughts"[21] of conscience are memorably played out, perhaps also achieving something positive for her client without really intending to.[22] In the two most recent works that Coetzee has published, *Diary of a Bad Year* (2007) and *Summertime* (2009), the latter of which constitutes the third part of his fictionalized autobiography, the ethical disposition again appears at the forefront of his concerns, whether in pursuit of a politics "that, impossibly, does not want to be political," as Johan Geertsema argues in this volume, or, as Sue Kossew maintains in regard to *Summertime*, to cultivate a type of literary confession that confronts head-on "the betrayal of self and others." The interest of Coetzee's more recent writings, therefore, is to explore the metaphysical dimensions of an ethical outlook and type of thought where to write in the mode of confession is to acknowledge the prior claim of the other to be heard and to be honored.[23] And this might mean, in the final analysis, to find and follow a manner of living beyond the terms of the strictly political.

Notes

[1] For *Life & Times of Michael K* in 1983 and *Disgrace* in 1999.

[2] Chris Ackerley assesses Coetzee's study of the early Beckett in relation to the development of his writing style in chapter 2 of this volume.

[3] In chapter 3 of this volume, David James discusses this period in relation to *Dusklands*, Coetzee's first novel.

[4] The issue of the writer and the censor is discussed extensively in this volume. See especially the discussion of *The Master of Petersburg* by Michelle Kelly and *Diary of a Bad Year* by Johan Geertsema.

[5] Dominic Head evaluates these criticisms in *The Cambridge Introduction to J. M. Coetzee* (Cambridge: Cambridge UP, 2009), 26–27.

[6] Simone Drichel considers these criticisms of Coetzee in chapter 10.

[7] For a summary of this opinion, see Eva-Marie Herlitzius, *A Comparative Analysis of the South African and German Reception of Nadine Gordimer's, André Brink's and J. M. Coetzee's Works* (Münster: LIT VERLAG, 2005), 23–32.

[8] "Daniel Defoe by James Joyce," edited from Italian manuscripts and translated by Joseph Prescott, *Buffalo Studies* 1, no. 1 (December 1964): 5–25; here, 24–25.

[9] See Chris Prentice's discussion of *Foe* in chapter 7. In chapter 9 Michelle Kelly also considers the factor of literary inheritances on *The Master of Petersburg*, a novel whose main character is the "master author" Dostoevsky.

[10] Others, of course, might see the Nobel lecture as being about nothing more than decoy ducks. See Rachel Donadio's essay "Out of South Africa" in the Sunday Book Review of the *New York Times*, 16 December 2007.

[11] See David Attwell, "An Exclusive Interview with J. M. Coetzee." *Dagens Nyheter*, 8 December 2003, 1–4; www.dn.se/kultur-noje/an-exclusive-interview-with-j-m-coetzee-1.227254 (accessed 31 March 2008).

[12] See, for example, Mike Marais's discussion of *Waiting for the Barbarians*, Kim Worthington's chapter on *Age of Iron*, and Simone Drichel's chapter on *Disgrace*.

[13] Jacques Derrida, *Of Grammatology* (Baltimore: Johns Hopkins UP, 1976), 158.

[14] Engelhard Weigl, in his discussion of *Life & Times of Michael K* in chapter 6, discusses the outsider in relation to the influence of Kafka on Coetzee's writing and thinking.

[15] Gayatri Chakravorty Spivak, "Can the Subaltern Speak?" in *Marxism and the Interpretation of Culture*, ed. Cary Nelson and Lawrence Grossberg (Urbana: U of Illinois P, 1988), 271–313.

[16] In this context, Mike Marais, in his analysis of *Waiting for the Barbarians* in this volume, speaks of "an ethic grounded in bewilderment rather than rational control."

[17] Carrol Clarkson discusses Coetzee's renunciation of the speaking position of the "subject supposed to know" in chapter 14.

[18] See James Meffan's discussion of *Elizabeth Costello* in chapter 11.

[19] As Coetzee told David Attwell in an interview reproduced in the volume *Doubling the Point*: "Whatever else, the body is not 'that which is not,' and the proof that it *is* is the pain it feels. The body with its pain becomes a counter to the endless trials of doubt" (*DP*, 248).

[20] See chapter 14.

[21] Coetzee's expression in his essay "Confession and Double Thoughts: Tolstoy, Rousseau, Dostoevsky" (see *DP*, 251–93).

[22] See my discussion of *Slow Man* in chapter 12. Another noteworthy aspect of the period since Coetzee's emigration to Australia, as Johan Geertsema points out in chapter 13, is the author's movement away from the genre of the novel as it is traditionally understood.

[23] Several contributors in the present volume underscore the proximity of such thought to the mental horizon of the French-Lithuanian thinker Emmanuel Levinas. See, in particular, Simone Drichel's discussion of Levinas in chapter 10.

1: *Scenes from Provincial Life* (1997–2009)

Sue Kossew

J. M. COETZEE'S TRILOGY OF FICTIONALIZED MEMOIRS, or *Scenes from Provincial Life* as he has subtitled them, provides readers with a quirky and peculiarly Coetzee-like perspective on the genre of autobiography.[1] While some reviewers were confused as to the genre of *Youth* in particular, it is clear that these three texts — *Boyhood* (1997), *Youth* (2002) and *Summertime* (2009) — form a continuum in Coetzee's life-writing or, as David Attwell puts it, a "life-of-writing."[2] This most recent text, *Summertime*, is narrated by a "biographer" supposedly after Coetzee's death. Covering the years 1972–77 of the writer's life, and comprising interviews with people who apparently knew the writer, this third volume is even more distanced from the subject of the memoirs than were the previous two, narrated as they were in the third person. Literary techniques such as the blurring of narrative boundaries between the biographical and autobiographical subject and the betrayal of self and others that inevitably form part of writing a memoir draw attention in this text — as other texts by Coetzee have done — to the question of "who speaks" in any literary work. This teasing textual instability and the crossing of narrative borders and genres have increasingly become features of Coetzee's later works.

This chapter will consider *Summertime* both within Coetzee's own elusive life-writing (alongside the previous two memoirs) and in the context of his own critical writing on autobiography. In particular, it will suggest that Coetzee's writing of the self-as-other obsessively draws attention to the generic conventions of writing a life and to the ethical implications of such writing. In doing so, it both exposes the impossibility of representing "truth" in any genre, whether history, fiction or life-writing, and engages with the problem of authority that has haunted all of Coetzee's work.

Throughout his fictional *oeuvre*, and in his commentaries on writing, Coetzee has scrupulously insisted on the constructed discursive nature of both fiction and history, or what is usually understood as either imaginative or factual writing. He has drawn attention to the notion that "everything you write, including criticism and fiction, writes you as you write it" (*DP*, 17). In addition, as he has suggested in an interview with David Attwell, "all autobiography is storytelling, all writing is autobiography" (*DP*, 391). At the heart of his concern with discourses of self is the notion of "truth" and, alongside that, of writerly authority. Indeed, his inaugural professorial lecture at the University of Cape Town in 1984 was entitled "Truth in Autobiography," signaling the longstanding and ongoing importance of this issue to Coetzee. In this lecture, he considers Rousseau's autobiographical text *Confessions* in terms of what he terms "the *cost* of telling the truth" (*TA*, 4). He identifies Rousseau's own autobiographical mode as that of *making* the truth rather than finding and telling the truth — not just representing the past but also representing the "present in which you wrestle to explain to yourself what it was that *really* happened that day" (*TA*, 4). The resulting account "may be full of gaps and evasion" but at least represents the mind trying to understand itself. In a post-Dostoevskian world, however, even such self-questioning "merely lands one in an endless regression" (*TA*, 4). It is clear that this lecture contains the seeds of the argument Coetzee presents in more detailed form in his seminal essay, "Confession and Double Thoughts" (*DP*, 251–93).

If all writing is a form of writing the self, it may be assumed that there is a certain truth-value in all writing. Yet Coetzee distinguishes between the personal narrative of autobiography and narrative *fiction* in two ways: by the intentionality of truth-telling on the part of the writer as well as by the readers' assumptions of "certain standards of truthfulness" when reading an autobiography. Thus, he suggests that autobiography has the *intention* to be "a kind of history rather than a kind of fiction."[3] However, he points out that any verifiability to which autobiographical narratives may be subject is limited as only their author is able to vouch for their reliability. He continues, in the same piece:

> For that reason, the element of trust on the part of the reader has to be strong: there has to be a tacit understanding, a pact, between autobiographer and reader that the truth is being told.
>
> Such a pact is, I would guess, rarely observed to the full. . . . There may be actions or thoughts which he [the writer] feels it is simply too shameful to make public, or that he feels could destroy the reader's good opinion of him. . . . There may be things he simply does not understand about himself, or has forgotten, or suppressed. (FT, 12)

Citing Freud's paper entitled "Therapy Terminable and Interminable," Coetzee suggests that autobiography is "bound up with soul-searching and the confession of sins." As such, its ultimate reader is God from whom there can be no secrets. Thus, he suggests, following Freud, any story about the self will have within it a mixture of historical and poetic truth, resulting in a "fiction of the truth" (FT, 12). This seemingly paradoxical notion informs the narrational strategies of all three of his fictionalized autobiographies in a process that Frank Kermode, in his recent review of *Summertime*, has labeled "fictioneering" (the term "fictioneer" is used by Coetzee's fictional biographer in *Summertime*).[4]

Most obviously, it is the use of the third person and the present tense in the first two volumes of Coetzee's memoirs that engaged the attention of reviewers, critics, and readers. For example, in a review entitled "Third Person Singular," William Deresiewicz in *The New York Times* calls the deployment of a third-person narrative perspective and of the present tense "bizarre choices" for a writer of a life, signaling that Coetzee has "turned his back on the entire autobiographical tradition."[5] As Margaret Lenta points out, though, this is clearly not the case, as numerous other memoirs have been written both in the third person and in the present tense.[6] For Lenta, Coetzee's use of the third person, which converts autobiography to *autre*biography, has a number of writerly and readerly effects, including "the apparent separation of narrator from embryo artist, the love-hate relationship of narrator and reader with protagonist, [and] the remoteness in time" (A, 168). She continues: "Free indirect discourse, borrowing for the most part from the thought habits and vocabulary of the protagonist, but capable of moving into those of his associates or of a narrator, is the effective substitute for what in a more conventional account would be the first person" (A, 168).

It is particularly appropriate, Lenta argues, that this artist-figure (most particularly figured in *Youth*), who is self-absorbed, lonely, proud, and uncompromising, should be constructed through the narration as separate, distant, and different from the author/narrator. This is narrating the self *as* other, or *autre*biography, a term Coetzee himself introduces in an interview with David Attwell (*DP*, 394). This perspective of otherness, however, does not *just* produce a distancing effect: as Dirk Klopper points out, these narrative devices of third-person and present-tense narration construct a "contradictory *simultaneity* of intimacy and distance, directness of observation and emotional detachment, access to the textured impressions of consciousness and its ironic displacement."[7]

For both Lenta and Hermione Lee, it is James Joyce's *Portrait of the Artist as a Young Man* that provides a close comparison with these two Coetzee memoirs. Lee suggests that Coetzee is "even harsher towards his younger self than Joyce is to Stephen's high aspirations" and that *Youth* is "the ultimate alienated and alienating autobiography; not an inward exploration, or an ethical indictment of the author/subject, but a self-parody."[8] The self-deceptiveness of any seemingly truth-telling act exposed and addressed in these two volumes returns one to the issue of "double thoughts" in the confessional mode. For, as Coetzee points out, "the only sure truth in autobiography is that one's self-interest will be located at one's blind spot" (*DP*, 392). Thus, for Coetzee, it is likely that "getting to the core of yourself may not be feasible, that perhaps the best you can hope for will not be the history of yourself but a story about yourself, a story that will not be the truth but may have some truth-value" (FT, 12). By using narrative strategies that draw attention to the constructed nature of writing a life, then, and to the impossibility of "sincerity" or "authenticity" (words he uses in relation to Rousseau's *Confessions*), Coetzee mobilizes a self-referential autobiographical mode that holds out the promise of intimacy and revelation, and occasionally approaches it, while simultaneously keeping the self at arm's length.

Thematically, the notion of being a provincial, evoked in the subtitle *Scenes from Provincial Life*, is inevitably linked to Coetzee's apartheid-era South African identity. This subtitle itself could ambiguously echo William Cooper's little-known 1950s autobiographical trilogy (*Scenes from Provincial Life, Scenes from Metropolitan Life*, and *Scenes from Married Life*, and its sequels, *Scenes from Later Life* and *Scenes from Death and Life*) or Honoré de Balzac's *Scenes from Provincial Life*, one section of his *Comédie Humaine*. Clearly, there is some reference, too, to Tolstoy's fictionalized autobiographical trilogy, *Childhood* (1852), *Boyhood* (1854), and *Youth* (1856).[9] The provincialism of *Boyhood* lies both in the physical isolation of its setting in a new housing estate in the town of Worcester ("between the railway line and the National Road": *B*, 1) and in its protagonist's uncertain identity: as neither English nor Afrikaner South African, as of the farm but not on the farm, as an outsider shut out of the comfort of belonging to a designated group in his own motherland. In *Youth* it is the painful and shameful nature of his South Africanness ("like an albatross around his neck": *Y*, 101) as well as his apparent sexual ineptitude that mark him as a provincial: a colonial other in swinging London of the 1960s. *Summertime* presents the shame of his enforced return to the provincialism of South Africa after having failed to secure a green card in the United States, a return from the relative freedom of living overseas to a place of restriction from which he has grown apart and a return to living with his father in unwanted domestic intimacy.

If, for Coetzee, double thoughts and self-interest are inevitably linked to the confessional mode as explicated in the "Confession and Double Thoughts" essay, betrayal of the self and others is an inevitable aspect of autobiography as, indeed, of all writing. As one critic has pointed out, Coetzee's "cynical ethics of the self" produces a "self in Coetzee's fiction [that] is irredeemably self-interested, fails to transcend itself to engage with the other as other, and, in effect, is caught in an interpersonal aporia between self and other."[10] There are many examples of how this sense of betrayal is played out in Coetzee's life-writing trilogy, both in his representation of interpersonal relationships and in the very practice of writing the self and others.

Boyhood begins with betrayal. The ten-year-old narrator tells of his mother's desire to escape the confines of their house on a newly built bleak housing estate outside the town of Worcester — a "restlessness" he shares with her — by buying a bicycle. Her initially fruitless attempts to ride the heavy bicycle are met with ridicule by the narrator's father: "Women do not ride bicycles, he says" (B, 3). Replicating the child's logic, the narrator tells of how he "begins to waver" in his support of his mother's cycling as she struggles to learn to ride, asking "What if his father is right? . . . Perhaps women are indeed not supposed to ride bicycles" (B, 3). From that point, it is only a matter of a paragraph until "His heart turns against her. That evening he joins in with his father's jeering. He is well aware what a betrayal this is. Now his mother is all alone" (B, 3). The childish notion of his taking sides, ganging up with the men against the woman to keep her in her place, is counterbalanced by a sophisticated awareness of the way this behavior has defeated her and that he "must bear part of the blame." The betrayal of his mother continues with his keeping his life at school "a tight secret" from her, despite his awareness of her strong need to protect him. Similarly, his rages against his mother and the "torrents of scorn he pours upon her," conduct that is kept "a careful secret from the outside world" (B, 13), form part of a self-acknowledged pattern of abusive behavior. By conceding that this turning-away from his mother reinforces that he "belongs with the men," he is showing a consciousness of gender roles and their Freudian implications well beyond his years. The revelation to the reader of this previously closely guarded secret of what he terms his "shameful" behavior comes close to the confessional mode that Coetzee has identified as an inevitable element in autobiography.

Similarly, he shows an awareness of the painful nature of his strong emotional attachment to his father's family's farm. While confessing through his life-writing his fierce love for the farm, he is also aware of it as a source of contention in the tug-of-war between his parents and thus of the need to keep it secret. Thus, "he cannot talk about his love [for the farm] . . . because confessing to it would be a betrayal of his mother . . . not only because she too comes from a farm, a rival farm . . . but because she is not truly welcome on this farm" (B, 80). The idea that a place in and of itself can lie at the heart of both belonging and contestation is played out in the text both in the context of his parents' rival family backgrounds, as in this quotation, and also in the context of apartheid South Africa, where "his people" are "uneasy guest[s]" (B, 79). His instinctive awareness that "one day the farm will be wholly gone, wholly lost" and that he is already "grieving at that loss" (B, 80) signals a distinctly unchildlike perspective. Thus, the theme of betrayal is linked not just to his fluctuating loyalties to his parents ("He is her son, not his father's son": B, 79) but to the wider issue of disputed national belonging. It is also, inevitably, located on the site of the body. The narrator, undergoing the changes to his body that signal adolescence, "feels like a crab pulled out of its shell, pink and wounded and obscene" (B, 151). Betrayed by his own body, the writing self, the thirteen-year-old boy of *Boyhood*'s ending, turns to the life of the mind, taking on responsibility for being the only one to "do the thinking" (*B*, 166). It is he who has to keep in his head "all the books, all the people, all the stories" for, if he does not remember them, "who will?" (*B*, 166). The duality of this heavy writerly responsibility coupled with the awareness of the inevitability of betrayal through writing ends this first installment of the life-of-writing and points the way to the second installment.

Indeed, betrayal of women and the sense of his leading a double life in which he has to bear the "burden of imposture" (*B*, 13) that often takes the form of an excruciating self-consciousness extends from *Boyhood* into *Youth*. It is the genre of the memoir that enables the double life to be exposed; the secrets and silences of his troubled family life evoked so painfully in *Boyhood* are relentlessly returned to in *Youth*. The betrayals in *Youth* are twofold and linked: the floundering of his quest for poetic creativity and the failure of his sexual encounters. John, the "he" of the text, is sure that he is destined to be a writer but is instead working for IBM, desperately trying to "burn with the sacred fire of art" (*Y*, 66) while living out a mundane and unfulfilling daily life and keeping secret his desire to become a poet. If, as "everyone says," "sex and creativity go together," and if women instinctively locate "the fire that burns in the artist" (*Y*, 66), he believes that it is through sex that he may be able to access this creative spark. However, he is unable to attract attention from any English girls on the train, despite his ostentatious flourishing of various books of poetry (*Y*, 72), attributing this to their awareness of his "colonial gaucherie" (*Y*, 71). The sexual, and indeed social, encounters he does have are marked by a coldness in his own responses, a lack of reciprocity that he attributes to his own meanness and "poverty of spirit," what amounts in his estimation to a "moral sickness" (*Y*, 95). Yet, amusingly and ironically, in tendering his notice at IBM, he cites lack of friendships as one of the reasons for his resignation.

His inability to escape his provincial South Africanness (his first prose story is, for him, disappointingly set in South Africa, a "handicap" that he would prefer to leave behind: *Y*, 62), is a failure of his programmatic plan of "turning himself into a different person that began when he was fifteen" (*Y*, 98) and that will not end, he asserts, until "all memory of the family and the country he left behind is extinguished" (*Y*, 98). This is, it appears, a significant shift in thinking — from that of the thirteen-year-old narrator at the end of *Boyhood* to what the narrator of *Youth* suggests is the need to assert distance from his past self and all that marks him as South African. Despite his desire to escape his prior identity and assume that of his new surroundings, he is still a foreigner in London: "Not in a month of Sundays would Londoners take him for the real thing" (*Y*, 102). His romantic notion of being remade in London and of getting rid of his old self to reveal a "new, true, passionate self" (*Y*, 111) is, of course, itself couched in the language of fiction, revealing through ironic distancing the naiveté of the narrator. By the end, though, he believes he is "on his way to becoming a proper Londoner" (*Y*, 113) by becoming emotionally hardened as a result of his ongoing misery. But he also experiences a rare moment of positive and even transcendent belonging, transformed by a moment of "ecstatic unity" with the green earth on Hampstead Heath (*Y*, 117). Even this, however, is couched in Lawrentian language that signals the bad faith of self-conscious romanticism. The pull of his South African past is reawakened with the arrival in London of his cousin Ilse, for whom he still harbors a secret erotic desire. As Ilse has flu, John takes her Afrikaans-speaking traveling companion Marianne back to his flat and has sex with her, at which point he discovers she is a virgin. The blood from this encounter soaks through his mattress that he "guiltily, angrily" turns over, aware that it is only a "matter of time before the stain is discovered" (*Y*, 129). The stain of his provincial identity, and the guilt associated with it, like the stain of Marianne's blood on his mattress, can be hidden for a while but not for long.

His own reflections on his writing self and his fear of the "confrontation with the blank page" (*Y*, 166) that stands for the failure of his poetic ambitions are confronted in his contradictory attempts to come to terms with the shame of his "caddish behavior" (*Y*, 130) towards Marianne. While admitting to himself his dishonorable behavior in seducing his cousin's innocent friend, he is both seeking to punish himself and to fit the episode "into the story of his life that he tells himself" (*Y*, 130). He can only hope that the story "will not get out" (*Y*, 130) but is humiliated by his cousin's letter that accuses him of behaving badly. He recognizes the bad faith of his excuse that an "artist must taste all experience, from the noblest to the most degraded" (*Y*, 164) in order to justify himself, as well as the sophistry of the paradox that the poet needs to tell self-justificatory lies in order to experience "moral squalor." In this self-recognition of an impasse that is at once personal and writerly, the text draws towards an ending with the twenty-four-year-old John still awaiting a visit from destiny: "he would rather be bad than boring, has no respect for a person who would rather be bad than boring, and no respect either for the cleverness of being able to put his dilemma neatly into words" (*Y*, 165). This paradox is one that "goes to the heart of all his writing" (*Y*, 9) and that he expresses much earlier in the text, when he is still living in South Africa, in relation to his diary. He deliberately leaves this diary lying around so that Jacqueline, the nurse with whom he has an affair and who moves into his flat in Cape Town, can read about his resentment of her intrusion on his privacy. When she confronts him with this writerly betrayal of their life together, he wonders whether he should record in his diary all his emotions, even the ignoble ones, or keep them "shrouded."

He continues: "Besides, who is to say that the feelings he writes in his diary are his true feelings? Who is to say that at each moment while the pen moves he is truly himself? At one moment he may be truly himself, at another he might simply be making things up. How can he know for sure?" (*Y*, 10) The double bind of "truth in autobiography" is brilliantly encapsulated in these paradoxes of the writing self.

The notion of self-punishment through confession is evoked in both *Youth* and in *Summertime* by the repetition of the phrase "*Agenbite of inwit*" (*Y*, 130 and *S*, 4). Meaning literally "a prick of conscience," it is also the title of a confessional prose work written in Middle English and referred to by James Joyce in *Ulysses*. In *Youth*, it is referred to in the context of the narrator's suggestion that he "will gnaw away at himself" as penance for his "caddish" behavior (*Y*, 130) and Coetzee takes up the question of bad faith and conscience again in the first pages of *Summertime* in the context of South African border killings recorded in the notebook entry of 22 August 1972 that opens the text: "How to escape the filth: not a new question. An old rat-question that will not let go, that leaves its nasty, suppurating wound. Agenbite of inwit" (*S*, 4). In this entry, it becomes clear that the writer has come back to South Africa[11] after living abroad, to be again under the "dirty thumb" of the ruling Nationalist Party government (*S*, 6).

The eight notebook entries that make up the first section of the text cover the dates from August 1972 to June 1975 and appear in the text with additional italicized writer's comments that were — we are told by the biographer, who is known only as Mr. Vincent and who has purportedly put together this book — written by Coetzee as "memos to himself, written in 1999 or 2000 when he was thinking of adapting those particular entries for a book" (*S*, 20). The self-judgmental nature of these comments (for example: "*To be expanded on: his readiness to throw himself into half-baked projects; the alacrity with which he retreats from creative work into mindless industry*": *S*, 8) recall the idea of his using writing to punish himself for his perceived misdeeds that we encountered in *Youth*.

They also set the tone for the increasingly distanced and self-critical portrait of the artist that will emerge in this text. The next six sections of the text bear the names of the people being interviewed by Mr. Vincent about the person, J. M. Coetzee, under whose name, of course, the text appears, and the final seventh section is titled "Notebooks: undated fragments." Thus, while the opening and closing sections of the text, the "Notebooks," are written in the by-now-familiar third-person present-tense narration of the previous two volumes of the memoirs, the remaining material is presented in interview form, with questions from Mr. Vincent and answers from those who have known the by-now-famous but dead author, J. M. Coetzee. These interviewees include five women and one man, and the interviews are conducted in Canada, South Africa, Brazil,

London, and Paris, in the chronological order in which the interviewees entered Coetzee's life and sometimes with a hinted association with particular works of fiction. That Mr. Vincent has never met "Coetzee" means that what his interviewees tell him is unverifiable. Thus, the truth-value of autobiography is doubly displaced in the major part of this text: firstly, onto Mr. Vincent, the biographer, who is supposedly transcribing but also editing the interviews, and, secondly, onto the interviewees whose own memories make up the text. The literalness of this "making up the text" is evident when Dr. Julia Frankl warns the biographer (and reader) of the truth-status of her recollections: "So let me be candid: as far as the dialogue is concerned, I am making it up as I go along. Which I presume is permitted, since we are talking about a writer. What I am telling you may not be true to the letter, but it is true to the spirit, be assured of that" (*S*, 32). At the same time, Julia warns Mr. Vincent not to try to manipulate her story in which, contrary to what she believes to be his expectations, she is the main character and John the minor one (reminiscent of Susan Barton in *Foe* who is trying to keep control of her own story): "if you go away from here and start fiddling with the text, the whole thing will turn to ash in your hands" (*S*, 44). And her final words to him are that she is "just telling the truth. Without the truth, no matter how hard, there can be no healing" (*S*, 84). She refuses to answer Mr. Vincent's final brief question and the reader never finds out what that question might have been. The inclusion of the request for another question and its refusal, along with the place and date of the interview, adds a level of believability to the text, emphasizing the reality effect that pretends to be using unedited, unmediated material.

In contrast, the editor admits to his next interviewee, Margot Jonker, Coetzee's cousin, that he has indeed fiddled with the interview material collected in a first interview with her a year previously. His editing of the interview includes his having cut out his questions, having "fixed up the prose to read as an uninterrupted narrative spoken in your voice," and having "dramatized it here and there, letting people speak in their own voices" (*S*, 87). Additionally, he has used the third-person and present-tense narration of Coetzee's other memoirs, explaining that "the *she* I use is like *I* but is not *I*" (*S*, 89), a convention that Margot finds confusing. It is, of course, appropriate that many of the memories are of the family farm, Voëlfontein, so poignantly described in *Boyhood* and of Coetzee's early and later association with it.[12] Despite Mr. Vincent's assurances that he will change anything she doesn't like — and that Margot's sister is unlikely to read "an obscure book put out by an academic press in England" (*S*, 91) and so will not object to the description of her as "hard-hearted" — when he reads Margot his "recast" narrative version of her first interview, she interrupts with objections, suggesting that his version doesn't sound like the one she originally narrated (*S*, 91). By the end of the narration, she is adamant that it cannot stand as it is: "I want to go over it again, as you promised" (*S*, 152). That the narrative does indeed appear to "stand as it is" in the version we read suggests either that she did in the end agree to the changes or that the editor betrayed her trust by not making them.

While the interview in the section entitled "Adriana" and conducted in Brazil maintains its conventional transcribed form, the interviewee suggests that her ability to "change the record" of the interview is extremely limited. This is because she is aware of her status as "one of Coetzee's women," a label that she is doomed to wear because of his infatuation with her, which was, she confirms, totally unreciprocated. Mr. Vincent suggests that she was the original for Susan Barton in *Foe*, a Brazilian woman in the first draft — attractive, resourceful, and with "a will of steel" (*S*, 200). In this way, the reader is offered yet another version of how writers betray their subjects: by turning them into fictional characters.

It is in the interview with Martin, a fellow academic at the University of Cape Town and rival for an academic position for which John has applied, that the biographer is called on to account for the methodology of his biography. While Martin is ultimately not particularly forthcoming about details of John's personal life (it is the shortest interview in the book and he parries the biographer's question about John's personal relations by replying: "You are the biographer. If you find that train of thought worth following up, follow it": *S*, 211), he does comment on their shared sense of discomfort at living in apartheid South Africa, their shared academic interests, and John's "strain of secretiveness." It is predominantly the interviewee, though, who here asks questions of the interviewer, questioning Mr. Vincent's desire to hear "stories" about his subject, his choice of interviewees, and his decision to interview those with an emotional investment in their relationship with him. Thus, Martin queries, in choosing only five sources for his work, whether the biographer is "inevitably going to come out with an account that is slanted towards the personal and the intimate at the expense of the man's actual achievements as a writer" (*S*, 218). The biographer's responses include his belief that a biography has to "*strike a balance between narrative and opinion*" (*S*, 216) and that he is "*not interested in coming to a final judgment on Coetzee*" which he leaves to history. He continues: "*What I am doing is telling the story of a stage in his life, or if we can't have a single story then several stories from several perspectives*" (*S*, 217; emphasis in original). The silence with which the biographer meets some of Martin's comments about his biographical method signals a subtle shift in power. The biographer himself is being asked to justify his approach.

In the final interview, that with Sophie Denoël, a former colleague and lover of John Coetzee's, the ethics of writing a life and the connections between a writer's private life and his work are brought even more strongly to the fore. In challenging the biographer about his "authorization" to write a book on Coetzee (and the word "authorization" is both a play on the notion of an "authorized" biography and on the slipperiness of authorship and authority), Sophie elicits a response from him that goes to the heart of the text's instability. Mr. Vincent admits that his efforts to speak to people in South Africa who had known Coetzee were largely unsuccessful (some who had claimed to know him had mistaken him for another Coetzee). When Sophie asks why he does not rely more on the diaries, letters, and notebooks, the usual raw material for biography, he cites their unreliability: they "*cannot be trusted . . . as a factual record . . . because he was a fictioneer . . . making up a fiction of himself*" (*S*, 225; emphasis in original). He himself would rather hear "*the truth . . . from people who knew him directly in the flesh*," which will provide a range of "*independent perspectives*" than rely on the writer's own "*self-projection comprised by his oeuvre*" despite the risk that these people may also be "fictioneers" (*S*, 226; emphasis in original). It is, though, clear to the reader by now that Mr. Vincent's own collection of interviews has an equally end-directed intentionality, particularly his desire for more personal stories from his interviewees that would dispel the image of Coetzee as "a cold and supercilious intellectual" (*S*, 235). It is also clear from the interviews that he has failed in this regard, as most confirm his character as wooden, without special sensitivity and as bordering on the autistic in matters of the body. So to whom is the reader to turn for a more nuanced version of Coetzee the man?

The final undated fragments from the notebooks provide a very different tone, even from the dated entries provided at the beginning of the book, which tend to a more political perspective on the writer's reporting of events on his return to South Africa. These final entries project more deeply personal and emotional material that centers on the father/son relationship. If the biographer has failed to produce an image of Coetzee that is warm and personable in the interviews, these final notebook entries, despite their italicized commentary that suggests they may be used later for other purposes, come closer to it. For it is here that we return to the realm of guilt and confession. In explaining, for example, his accompanying his father to a rugby match at Newlands, the writer of the notebooks records his feelings as follows: "He goes with his father . . . because sport . . . is the strongest surviving bond between them, and because it went through his heart like a knife . . . to see his father . . . go off to Newlands like a lonely child" (*S*, 245).

The compassion of the son for the father's loneliness and the way it pierces his heart speaks more about the man and his emotional life than anything the reader has encountered previously in the text. Similarly, his awareness that he would be a better son if he knew what his father cared about or wanted, in the absence of his talking about himself, or keeping a diary, or writing letters, is made even more poignant by the fact that his only insight into his father's state of mind is provided by a quiz entitled "Your Personal Satisfaction Index" that his father has perhaps deliberately left lying around. In it, his father has scored a total of 6 out of 20, suggesting a less than fulfilled life. Thus, the sense he has that his father's family is without passion extends also to his own assessment of himself as a "gloomy fellow; a wet blanket; a stick in the mud" (*S*, 248).

The adult son's memory of his "mean and petty deed" as an adolescent of scratching his father's favorite Renata Tebaldi record is one that has haunted him with a remorse that has "grown keener" with time. This returns us to the "Agenbite of inwit" (*S*, 4) reference at the beginning of the text, the prick of conscience that demands confession. Trying to atone for this misdeed by replacing the record was, he insists, his way of seeking his father's forgiveness "*for countless acts of meanness. . . . In sum, for all I have done since the day I was born, and with such success, to make your life a misery*" (*S*, 250; emphasis in original). The directness of this first-person address marks a significant shift in the text, making it seem less mediated, more *felt*. But there is no response from his father. It is equally heart-wrenching to read of the son's inability to reach out, physically or emotionally, prior to his father's operation, an operation that will render the father forever wordless. The son's inability to interpret his father's needs is even more tragic now. The dilemma of the ending of the text, where the son is trapped either into responsibility for his father or into abandoning him, is clearly not really a choice at all.

So, as readers, we do after all gain some insight into the emotional life of the writer through these final notebook entries. But, again, we are warned of the "double thoughts" of confession as well as the intentionality, the fictioneering, of all writerly material, whether diaries, letters, notebooks, autobiographies, or biographies. In the end, there is no one version, only versions, of a life, and the more lasting impression, apart from rare moments when "true confession" seems momentarily attainable, is that the subject of the life-writing will inevitably both betray and/ or be betrayed.

In his preamble to reading one of the notebook entries to Martin in *Summertime*, Mr. Vincent suggests that he suspects that the entry "was intended to fit into the third memoir, the one that never saw the light of day" (*S*, 205) and refers to its use of the same third-person convention as in *Boyhood* and *Youth*. This teasing self-referentiality (the book we are reading is, of course, the third memoir that never saw the light of day disguised as a partial and perhaps even unfinished biography) is in keeping with the ironic humor deployed throughout *Summertime*, particularly in Coetzee's use of the distancing effect of biography to make comments on himself through the words of others. An example is when Julia says: "I know he had a reputation for being dour, but John Coetzee was actually quite funny" (*S*, 63). In writing the self as other, Coetzee is able to draw attention both to the constructed nature of any version of the self and to the ethical implications of such writing. In doing so, he emphasizes the impossibility of representing "truth" in any genre and the double bind of self-interested confession that is an inevitable part of autobiography. But, as Derek Attridge points out, even such doubts about verifiability or the status of a "true confession" do not preclude the work encapsulating, for the reader as well as the writer, what Attridge calls a "certain form of truth" (ER, 161) and what Coetzee calls, perhaps more circumspectly, the "aura of truth" (*Y*, 138).

Notes

[1] While *Boyhood* (1997) was published with the subtitle *Scenes from Provincial Life*, *Youth* (2002) did not have this subtitle at the time of publication, although it was clearly the next stage in the series of autobiographical texts by Coetzee. Most recently, the dust-jacket notes of *Summertime* suggest that it "completes the majestic trilogy of fictionalized memoir begun with *Boyhood* and *Youth*," and Coetzee has referred to it as the "third installment" of *Scenes from Provincial Life*. Hermione Lee points out that while *Youth* was published without a subtitle in the United Kingdom, the US edition was indeed subtitled *Scenes from Provincial Life II*; see Hermione Lee, "Heart of Stone: J. M. Coetzee," in *Body Parts: Essays on Life Writing* (London: Chatto & Windus, 2005), 167. Coetzee's description of *Summertime* as the third "installment" of *Scenes from Provincial Life* suggests that he would have preferred to have had this subtitle in all editions of *Youth*, thereby avoiding the confusion caused to some reviewers.

[2] David Attwell, "Coetzee's Estrangements," *Novel* (Spring/Summer 2008): 237.

[3] J. M. Coetzee, "Fictions of the Truth," *The Age*, 13 May 2000: 12 (attributed to *The Telegraph*, London, no date). Subsequent references appear as FT with the accompanying page number.

[4] See p. 225 of *Summertime* and Frank Kermode's review, "Fictioneering," in *London Review of Books*, 8 October 2009: 9–10.

[5] William Deresiewicz, "Third-Person Singular," *New York Times*, 7 July 2002: 6.

[6] Margaret Lenta, "Autrebiography: J. M. Coetzee's *Boyhood* and *Youth*," *English in Africa* 30, no. 1 (May 2003): 157–69. Subsequent references appear as A with the accompanying page number. Lenta gives the examples of Caesar's Gallic War and the Civil War, Lord Hervey's eighteenth-century memoir, and Christopher Isherwood's memoir, *Lost Years: A Memoir 1945–51*. She also points out a number of parallels in subject matter between Coetzee's first two memoirs and Joyce's *Portrait of the Artist as a Young Man*. Others have pointed out that there are further precedents for this third-person autobiography. These include Dirk Klopper's example of Henry Adams's *The Education of Henry Adams* (Dirk Klopper, "Critical Fictions in J. M. Coetzee's *Boyhood* and *Youth*," *scrutiny2: Issues in English Studies in South Africa* 11, no. 1 [2006]: 22–31: 30n6). Derek Attridge refers to both Adams and Joyce as "two obvious precursors," but points out that they both

use the past tense, a choice that introduces "adult irony to complicate" childhood naiveté: Attridge, *J. M. Coetzee and the Ethics of Reading: Literature in the Event* (Chicago: U of Chicago P, 2004), 141. Subsequent references appear as ER with the accompanying page number.

[7] Dirk Klopper, "Critical Fictions," 24; my emphasis.

[8] Hermione Lee, "Uneasy Guest," *London Review of Books*, 24, no. 13 (11 July 2002): 14–15; here, 15.

[9] Derek Attridge also mentions Turgenev and George Eliot's works as possible sources for Coetzee's subtitle, particularly Eliot's *Middlemarch: A Study of Provincial Life* (ER, 155n20).

[10] Gilbert Yeoh, "J. M. Coetzee and Samuel Beckett: Ethics, Truth-Telling, and Self-Deception," *Critique* 44, no. 4 (Summer 2003): 331–48; here, 345.

[11] Also referred to in *Youth* as a "wound" — "South Africa is a wound within him" (*Y*, 116).

[12] It is interesting to compare the account given on page 97 of *Summertime* with the parallel account on page 94 of *Boyhood*. In both, John unburdens himself to his cousin (she is called Agnes in *Boyhood*, Margot in *Summertime*) and in *Summertime*, the John-figure admits to being in love with her. An episode that is not mentioned in *Boyhood* but is given prominence in *Summertime* is John's cruel treatment of a locust, when he pulls off its rear leg and leaves Margot to put it out of its misery by mercy-killing it. In *Summertime*, this is represented as a shameful memory — a violation of the mantis god — which he remembers with pain and for which he "asks forgiveness every day." The more detailed confessional account given in *Summertime* underlines the theme of remembered betrayals and the earlier suppression of this guilty memory.

2: Style: Coetzee and Beckett

Chris Ackerley

A S PLENARY SPEAKER AT THE 2006 Samuel Beckett Symposium in Tokyo, J. M. Coetzee presented a tantalizing "what might have been" had Samuel Beckett in 1937 succeeded with his half-hearted application for a lecturing position in Italian at the University of Cape Town and been appointed to that university where Coetzee was subsequently to spend much of his professional academic life. Rewriting the account for a set of reminiscences,[1] and again for the volume of essays from the Tokyo occasion,[2] Coetzee documents the circumstances leading to the application: a job vacancy advertised in the *Times Literary Supplement* and seen by T. B. Rudmose-Brown of Trinity College, Dublin, who prevailed upon his star pupil to apply; the laconic letter that Beckett ("M.A., T.C.D.") wrote on his own behalf (presented in facsimile: IH, 76) to support a brief CV on which *More Kicks than Pricks* was discreetly rechristened *Short Stories*; and his failure to get the job, which instead went to a specialist in the Sardinian dialect. Coetzee then offers the fantasy of a young academic trapped by the war at the southern tip of Africa, married (with children) to a South African belle ("some sweet-breathed, bronze-limbed Calypso capable of seducing an indolent Irish castaway who found it hard to say no into the colonial version of wedded bliss"; EW, 29); promoted to a professorship in the Romance languages; and still in residence in 1957 when Coetzee enrolled at the institution, the two perhaps meeting when Professor Beckett consented now and then to conduct the Wednesday afternoon creative-writing class to which students brought their work. Under this scenario, some things emphatically could not have been: Beckett, in this multiverse no longer hiding out from the Gestapo in Roussillon, would not have written *Watt*, and Coetzee could not therefore have done his PhD (1968) on the manuscripts of that novel at the University of Texas at Austin, where they recently had been archived.

A more convincing, albeit ostensibly still-fictional account of what led Coetzee to Beckett is offered in the former's *Youth* (2002), a *nel mezzo del cammin* reflection by the recent recipient of his second Booker Prize (for *Disgrace*, the furor over which, in South Africa, might have clinched the decision to leave the land of his birth), taking stock of the forces and processes that had shaped his destiny as a writer. *Youth* invokes the years

(1962–64) when Coetzee was working, mostly as a computer programmer, in London, having left South Africa (as he believed, for good) in the wake of the 1960 Sharpeville Massacre, but there are frequent, sustained flashbacks to the more recent South African experience. During these years, Coetzee, like his fictional alter ego, "John," researched and wrote his master's thesis on Ford Madox Ford, and the degree was awarded by the University of Cape Town in 1963. The title, *Youth*, echoes self-referential works by Tolstoy and Conrad; like that of the former, it presents the protagonist's earlier self in a searching and largely unfavorable light; unlike that of the latter, it does not romanticize the formative experiences, instead reworking these so as to puncture the illusions and acknowledge the ambivalence embedded in the colonial experience.[3]

While *Youth* ostensibly chronicles the political and sexual ambiguities as well as the indiscretions of the protagonist in the 1960s, the book's literary theme is intimated by its mildly ironic epigraph: "Wer den Dichter will verstehen / muß in Dichters Lande gehen" (Whoever wants to understand the poet must go into the poet's land). This is drawn from Goethe's dictum in "Noten und Abhandlungen zu besserem Verständnis des Westöstlichen Divans" (1819), his representation of the Oriental tradition, these lines being preceded by "Wer das Dichten will verstehen / muß ins Land der Dichtung gehen" (Whoever wants to understand the poetry must go into the land of poetry).[4] The irony arises in part because John's stated theme is very much the rejection of his South African family and heritage, from which he cannot entirely escape, however much he might wish to do so, but also because, as the book itself will testify, the land of the poetry may well be (or wish itself to be) something quite other than the land of the poet. *Youth*, in this sense, and as its title also indicates, becomes the allegory of one assaying literary traditions (here, modernism rather than Orientalism) that are not obviously his own.

John is uncertain of his motives for writing, of what his "true thoughts" might be, or how his emotions will ever be "transfigured and turned into poetry" (*Y*, 10). To clarify his dilemma, he reads the *Letters* of another writer in self-imposed exile, Ezra Pound, who quit America because he was infuriated by its provincial small-mindedness (*Y*, 19). John admires Pound's craftsmanship, the sacrifice of his life to art, his suffering, and even his likely fate of being — despite all his sufferings, then and later — minor (*Y*, 20). He absorbs from Pound (and Chaucer) the impulse to follow "the flexions of the ordinary speaking voice" (*Y*, 21), he learns how to smell out and avoid the "easy sentiment" of the Romantics and the Victorians (*Y*, 21), and he is attracted to precision: in his case, that of mathematics and computational analysis. Following Pound's recommendations, he reads Flaubert, Henry James, Conrad, and, eventually, Ford Madox Ford (*Y*, 24). He reads the world around him (including the women therein) as signatures of these and other authors, and when the time comes to formulate a topic for his thesis, he naturally accepts Pound's endorsement of Ford as a stylist par excellence. Like other would-be modernist scholars, he is at first convinced that Pound is right in calling Ford the greatest prose stylist of his day; he is dazzled by the complicated, staggered chronology of Ford's plots, the magnificence of *The Good Soldier* and (yes, almost) the four books that constitute *Parade's End*, and the cunning with which a note casually struck and artlessly repeated will stand revealed, at the end of the piece, as a major motif (Υ, 53). If Ford could write five such works, he tells himself, there must be among "the sprawling and only just catalogued corpus of his writings" other masterpieces that he, John, can bring to light. And so he embarks on a reading of the Ford oeuvre, in the Reading Room of the British Museum (where else?), and though the early works prove somewhat disappointing, he "presses on" (Υ, 54), with the oblique consolation, given his solitary occupation, that the life of the mind will be its own reward (Υ, 55).

Ford, however, proves to be increasingly tedious, and the "unrecognised masterpieces" (Υ, 56) that he, John, was going to uncover fail to materialize. Still working as a programmer for IBM, he ventures into the writing of prose. He "sets himself exercises in the style of James" (Υ, 64), but these prove less easy to master than he had thought, and, besides, he is less convinced than he had been previously that a fine sensibility and "cleverness" (Υ, 65) is what matters most; he simply cannot "feel the ghostly hand of James extended to touch his brow in blessing" (Υ, 67). Nor do Joyce and Lawrence, for all their admirable qualities, quite fit his bill: Joyce is too bound up by Ireland and Irish affairs "to be in his pantheon" (Υ, 67), and he is too scared and inexperienced to enact the Lawrentian ethic, to the effect that only by bringing a woman to her dark core can a man reach his own (Υ, 68). The time finally comes for him to "deliver his judgment" (Υ, 112) — that is, to bring his thesis on Ford to conclusion — but he feels that he has nothing new to say. He still trusts Pound (Υ, 133), but is now beginning to doubt that Ford, on whom he has lavished so much time, is truly an "authentic master" (Υ, 136); if he were, then why is there so much rubbish mixed in with the five good novels? Nevertheless, out of deference to Ford's assurance that the civilization of France owes its lightness and grace to a diet of fish and olive oil and garlic, he buys fish fingers instead of sausages, fries them in olive oil instead of butter, and sprinkles garlic salt over them (Υ, 136). Somehow, the thesis gets written, hundreds of pages of notes finally reduced to "a web of connected prose" (Υ, 136).

The ironies are exquisite, but they compose a portrait of the artist manqué, destined to be unexceptional, heartless, pretentious, shortsighted. Then, something happens, unexpectedly, but in such a way as to constitute the emotional and aesthetic heart of Coetzee's memoir. John sees in the window of a second-hand bookseller off Charing Cross Road "a chunky little book with a violet cover" (*Y*, 155). That book is *Watt*, by Samuel Beckett, published by the Olympia Press in Paris. He knows of Beckett as the author of *Waiting for Godot* and *Endgame*, but not as a novelist: "What kind of a book, then, is *Watt?*" He buys it, pages through it, knows from the first page that he has hit on something, reads and reads, and when he comes to the end he starts again at the beginning. *Watt* is quite unlike Beckett's plays: "There is no clash, no conflict, just the flow of a voice telling a story, a flow continually checked by doubts and scruples, its pace fitted exactly to the pace of his own mind" (*Y*, 155). And *Watt* is also funny, so funny that he rolls about laughing. Why did people not tell him that Beckett wrote novels? And how could he have imagined that he wanted to write in the manner of Ford when Beckett was around all the time? In Ford, there has always been "an element of the stuffed shirt" (*Y*, 155); but Beckett is classless, or outside class, as he himself would prefer to be.

Not unlike Stephen Dedalus's vision of the wading girl in *A Portrait of the Artist as a Young Man* (a text not directly invoked, but never very far from *Youth*), the moment is epiphanic, both in the protagonist's life and in the aesthetic of the book itself. There had been earlier mentions of Beckett: in Cape Town John had argued the merits of Beckett (among others) with a girl named Caroline; Beckett, she said, was too gloomy (*Y*, 68). Then, on Hampstead Heath, one Sunday afternoon, John stretches out on the greensward and sinks into "a sleep or half-sleep in which consciousness does not vanish but continues to hover"; he experiences an intimation of "ecstatic unity with the All!" and awakes to find himself, if not utterly transfigured, then "at least blessed with a hint that he belongs on this earth" (*Y*, 117). This is a moment that combines, not without irony, Murphy's experience in Hyde Park in chapter 5 of *Murphy* with the Faustian experience of the Easter bells as invoked in the addenda of *Watt*: "die Merde hat mich wieder."[5] Shortly before this climactic moment, John has been reading *Burchell's Travels*, which invokes in him a recognition of the need in writing to make things real; he would like, he says, to write a book as convincing as Burchell's, one with its sense of particularity, so that the creaking of the grease pot and the trilling of the cicadas will be convincing (this, he imagines, he can do), but that will also have "the aura of truth" (*Y*, 138); yet to bring that off, he will need to know less than he knows now (*Y*, 139). Where, then, will he find what he needs to know, or perhaps not to know, "a knowledge too humble to know it is knowledge?" The answer comes fifteen pages later with the discovery of *Watt*, and its aesthetic of impotence and failure that is precisely what he is seeking, that aesthetic in retrospect having shaped the structure of *Youth* and, by implication, much of the writing that has preceded this fictional memoir.

Youth does not elaborate the consequences of John's epiphanic moment, but Coetzee has frequently testified to the importance of this unattended discovery. In an interview with David Attwell, where he discusses the problematic "truth" of autobiographical writing, he admits to having written "nothing of substance" before he was thirty, but points out that he had been reading and making notes for many years (*DP*, 19). The account he gives in this interview squares neatly with that in *Youth*, with reference to his coming to Ford through Pound and being attracted to Ford because, as well as being a consummate stylist, Ford wrote as an outsider. Coetzee adds, revealingly, that what perhaps attracted him to Ford was as much the ethics of Tietjens as the aesthetics of *le mot juste*. As for Beckett: he had read *Waiting for Godot* in the 1950s, but the encounter that meant more to him (as *Youth* would later testify) was that with *Watt*, and thereafter *Molloy*, and, to a lesser extent, the other novels: "Beckett's prose, up to and including *The Unnamable*, has given me a sensuous delight that hasn't dimmed over the years. The critical work I did on Beckett originated in that sensuous response, and was a grasping after ways in which to talk about it: to talk about delight" (*DP*, 20).

At the time, Coetzee was seriously interested in stylistics and stylostatistics. As David Attwell notes in his 1992 interview, interest in the quantitative branch of stylistics has waned over the years, and while Coetzee seems to have been drawn to its elements of positivism, he nevertheless had remained (Attwell's questioning reveals) suspicious of some of the consequences of this kind of analysis (*DP*, 21). Coetzee in reply admits to perhaps a "wrong turning" in both his career and in the history of stylistics (*DP*, 22), and comments that as stylistics gave up the ideal of mathematical formalization that had at one point inspired it, and started looking for more pragmatic models, he lost interest in it (*DP*, 22). However, he insists, Beckett's prose, being highly rhetorical in its own way, "lent itself to formal analysis" (*DP*, 23); as Attwell then makes clear, Coetzee's time at Texas in the mid to late 1960s coincided with the moment in American linguistics when the power was shifting from the structuralism associated with Leonard Bloomfield towards the generative-transformational grammar of Noam Chomsky, and, in European linguistics, with the rise of continental structuralism (Roland Barthes and Claude Lévi-Strauss). In other words, Coetzee's linguistic studies coincided, "quite dramatically it seems, with the emergent moment of linguistics in the West, both as method and as model for the analysis of culture" (*DP*, 23).

Coetzee came to America in 1965, he told Attwell, because he felt that in England he was going nowhere, that he needed to change direction, and because he felt that there was "something in the air" (*DP*, 25): the possibility that linguistics, mathematics, and textual analysis might be brought together in some meaningful way. He chose Texas because they offered a reduction in fees and $2,100 for teaching freshman composition part-time, and because they had "a good reputation in linguistics and a big manuscript collection" (*DP*, 26). His proposed doctoral dissertation was to be on stylistic analysis, but despite the recent *Watt* epiphany he did not know that the Beckett manuscripts of that novel (another "corpus of recently catalogued writings") were in Texas until after he arrived. But in the "manuscripts library," better known as the Harry Ransom Humanities Research Center and containing the world's largest holdings of twentieth-century literary and manuscript materials, he found the six exercise books in which Beckett had written the first drafts of *Watt* while hiding out from the Germans in the south of France.[6] He spent weeks pursuing these, finding it "heartening" to see from what unpromising beginnings a book could grow: "to see the false starts, the scratched-out banalities, the evidences of less than furious possession by the Muse" (*DP*, 25). For the scholar of Beckett, and perhaps equally for the scholar of Coetzee, what matters most about the doctoral dissertation that eventuated in 1969 was less the "Essay on Stylistic Analysis," as it was subtitled, than the almost incidental literary response to the false starts and scratched-out banalities, and Coetzee's recording of such demented particulars as the image of the prototypical writer, penniless and decrepit, fading out in a room lit feebly by "a snippet of his last underpants floating in rancid dripping,"[7] or Watt's semiotic, nominalist creation of a fish out of words (SA, 247–48; with reference to *Watt*: W, 102).

The *Watt* manuscripts in the Harry Ransom Humanities Research Center have been described by Carlton Lake, past curator of the collection, as the "white whale" of Beckett studies: "magnificently ornate, a worthy scion of the Book of Kells, with the colors reduced to more somber hues. The doodles, cartoons, caricatures, portraits *en cartouche* include reminiscences of African and Oceanic art, the gargoyles of Notre Dame, heraldry, and more."[8] There are six handwritten notebooks, the first dated "11/2/41" and the last signed off on "Dec. 28th 1944 / End";[9] there is also an early typescript that has been erratically combined with a later retyping, and several loose sheets, some interpolated within the notebooks but others not. In all, there are almost a thousand pages of materials, belonging to various stages of composition and revision, those categories by no means separate (Beckett tended, for instance, to write on the rectos only, leaving the versos free for insertions and often undated rewriting). One of the lasting legacies of Coetzee's thesis was to have restored the amorphous materials into some kind of order. Coetzee recognized three different "levels" of the drafts (SA, 96): A — a first holograph draft, 282 pages, itself a compendium of four stages (A1 to A4); B — a typescript recension with holograph corrections, 269 pages, incomplete (but coherent); C — a conflation of part of B with a new holograph draft of 163 pages (mostly notebooks 5 and 6). The work required to complete this overview was meticulous and demanding, and the ordering is, by and large, reliable; this is all the more creditable given that Coetzee had no access to the final typescript of *Watt* (still missing) nor to the galley proofs (now at Washington University, St. Louis, but not then available). This pioneering work has laid the foundation for a number of subsequent genetic studies, including my own.

Some of Coetzee's findings were published in "The Manuscript Revisions of Beckett's *Watt*," in the *Journal of Modern Literature* 2 (1972), a piece of scholarship that has withstood the test of time. Some elements of his thesis have not fared so well, however radical or contemporary they might have seemed at the time. His Abstract perhaps suggests why: it defines a mode of statistical analysis that will set itself at odds with the mathematical (statistical, computational) assertion of "style" as an object of scientific thought — that is, he will demonstrate that "frequency-distributions" are not the same as meaningful configurations (SA, 1). This is a statement that few today would seriously question, and hence the hypothesis advanced to arbitrate what Coetzee calls "a crisis in the relation of form and content" (SA, 3) in Beckett's fiction seems, in a postmodernist (or post-Mauthnerian) era, no longer to reflect any genuine crisis; this, however, was not the case at the time, when computational stylistics as advanced (for example) by Archibald Hill at the University of Texas at Austin were very much state of the art.[10] The thesis, then, is somewhat mired in the aesthetics of outmoded linguistic and theoretical concerns, such as whether there can be in a literary work "a content which exists as in some sense prior to its expression" (SA, 5), or whether a literary work can use the language of daily life, as addressed by the Prague School Formalists with their sense of poetical language as deviation from the norms (SA, 14).

The value of Coetzee's thesis lies elsewhere: for example, in his sense of the way that Beckett explores "the resources of pity and terror" that lurk in the abstractions (SA, 9); his recognition that a "starting point" for the parody of *Watt* is the prose of the seventeenth century (SA, 147), words that might apply readily to his own writing; or the acute scrutiny that he brings to bear on Beckett's narrational stances, in *Watt* and elsewhere, through the use of *oratio obliqua* and *style indirect libre*, but equally the varied use of *oratia recta*, and disconcerting mixtures of tense allied with the putative authorial statement (see, for example, Coetzee's first scholarly article, "The Comedy of Point of View in Beckett's *Murphy*" [1970]). In one of the few scholarly articles to acknowledge the importance of this thesis, Stephen Kellman notes that Coetzee is animated by Beckett's "challenge to verbal determinism: does the language we use necessarily define the thoughts we have?"[11] Kellman draws attention to the multilingual heritages of both writers, and thus to the way that a complexity of tone arises from what he calls the "translingual" elements of language, the sense of echoing and reflexivity implicit in the disjunctions between concept and the fragmented modes of possible articulation.[12] Coetzee has an excellent sense of Beckett's control over the variety of vocal elements; he appreciates that *Watt* is not "an extended doodle in words" nor "an exercise in symmetry and ritual" (SA, 30), but rather a tonal masterpiece, controlled yet various. Coetzee's intense appreciation of Beckett's tonal variety, even (or perhaps especially) with respect to apparently bland or unexceptional passages of prose, is eerily prescient of a quality that will later be found in his own writing, with its curious reliance upon the present continuous, or what Molloy might call "the mythological present": "I speak in the present tense, it is so easy to speak in the present tense, when speaking of the past. It is the mythological present, don't mind it."[13] This is what in Greek might be called the Middle Voice, the voice of one's talking to oneself, experiencing in the present past trauma, or bearing witness, in a manner that anticipates the disembodied, ghostly voices of Beckett's later fiction and plays.[14] Of all Beckett's gifts to Coetzee, this is perhaps the most insistent and enduring.

Coetzee's interest in stylistic and computational analysis may have faded after the submission of his thesis, but it by no means entirely disappeared. David Attwell begins his introduction to *Doubling the Point* with an account of how the *New York Times* Sunday Book Review in August 1973 devoted its regular The Last Word column to a report that had recently appeared in *Scientific American*, concerning an experiment at the University of Cape Town in which "someone" had produced a computer-assisted reading of Samuel Beckett's short work, *Lessness* (1970) (*DP*, 1).[15] Computer analysis identified the rules of construction in Beckett's text, which, as Attwell correctly notes, has a "structure of repetitions" in which all the phrases appearing in the first half of the work are repeated in a different order in the second.[16] *Lessness* is a text built around six families of images, combined into sixty sentences, each originally written on a separate sheet and drawn from a container one by one, the outcome recorded as an aleatory sequence, with further paragraphs built upon similar processes. The compositional strategy suggests an experiment with pure chance on what Beckett called a set of variations on disorder; however, although chance or the aleatory intervenes in the creative process, all the parameters and structures were controlled by Beckett (the words, the arrangement into sentences, the motifs, the number of sentences, and the paragraph structure).[17] Other than the long permutations of *Watt*, which Coetzee had earlier discussed in his dissertation, this was and would be Beckett's only sustained experiment of this kind, and Attwell is probably correct to state that Coetzee's analysis (both here and in that thesis) reflects his long involvement in what would turn out to be "the relatively unrewarding, technical branch of modern stylistics" (*DP*, 1). Coetzee has often insisted that Beckett's later short fictions have never seriously held his attention: "They are, quite literally, disembodied. . . . The late pieces speak in post-mortem voices. I am not there yet. I am still interested in how the voice moves the body, moves in the body" (*DP*, 23). Again, in the interview conducted with Attwell after the Nobel Prize in 2003 (Beckett had been thus honored in 1969, but did not go to Stockholm and gave no interviews), Coetzee again stated that with Beckett it was the work before 1952 rather than the work after 1952 that engaged his attention.[18] Derek Attridge qualifies this, but only somewhat, when he suggests that Coetzee by 2006 was "less likely" to place *Watt* among Beckett's finest works,[19] given the comment he made in his 2006 introduction to volume 4 of the Grove Press centenary issue of Beckett's works, to the effect that Beckett did not truly find himself as a writer until he switched to French.[20] Whatever the force of this qualification, Attwell in the earlier interview is surely right to insist on what the *NYTBR* columnist failed to note with his dismissive "Ah, Beckett! Ah, Cape Town!": that Coetzee's analysis of Beckett's curious text reflects a "rigorous inquiry into the ontology of fictional discourse" and thus an attempt to "locate a position from which Coetzee himself might some day begin to speak" (*DP*, 1–2).

Indeed, Coetzee himself has implied as much. In "Samuel Beckett and the Temptations of Style" (1973), he had examined the tension between "nothing" and "fiction," and the apparent paradox of the generation of an entire contingent world from an initial segmentation of a set into classes X and not-X (*DP*, 43).[21] Having described Beckett's "progression" (Beckett would have said "gress") from *The Unnamable* to *Lessness* as that "toward a formalization or stylization of auto-destruction" (*DP*, 45), Coetzee returned to the roots of that process in *Watt* to offer the detailed analysis of one sentence, assumed to be entirely typical of that volume, in which the paragraph grows out of one rhythm (A), set against another (B), to submerge the narrator "in its lulling plangencies" (*DP*, 47), the effect being finally that of "narcissistic reverie" (*DP*, 47), and "the impasse of reflexive consciousness" (*DP*, 49). Much of his own future prose would be marked by a similar rhetorical impulse towards reverie and reflexivity.

One of the more important acknowledgements of the influence of Beckett (among others) on the development of his own prose style is to be found in the essay entitled "Homage" (1993), in which Coetzee pays tribute to some of the writers without whom he could not have been the person (let alone the author) that he is/was.[22] He admits to having devoted years of his life to Beckett, "as both academic and aficionado" (H, 6), finding in his prose of the 1940s and early 1950s "an energy of quite a savage order," and a "rhythm and syntax not only of words but, so to speak, of thought too" (H, 6), the "deeper lessons" being, quite properly, those of rhythm (H, 6–7). Even more than Nabokov, Beckett used a language in which "each word, each phrase, each idiom" had to be "held up, weighed, inspected, approved, before being dropped into place in the sentence" (H, 7); Beckett was, he concludes, one whose "sensitivity to the nuances of weight, coloration, provenance, and history of individual words" was superior to his own (H, 7), and thus (he implies) one who set in such matters the standard that he would himself aspire to.

In a brief recapitulation before a final coda, Coetzee identified in particular "Rilke and Musil, Pound and Faulkner, Ford and Beckett" (curiously, not Tolstoy nor Dostoevsky, let alone Kafka), before asking: "do I acknowledge no South African paternity?" His short answer was that in 1960 there was no South African writer to whom he as a young writer might turn, were he to write about his own country, and that the few "versions of the land" that South Africa had produced were "false and corrupt" (H, 7). This points towards the crucial notion that the ethical, so marked in Coetzee but more recondite (yet very much present) in Beckett, is essentially embedded in *style*. Twenty years later, in the 2003 interview with Coetzee, after the Nobel Prize, David Attwell alluded to this earlier essay, then commented: "What is striking, though, is the almost visceral relationship you have to these influences, if I may put it that way. 'The deepest lessons one learns from other writers,' you say, 'are, I suspect, matters of rhythm, broadly conceived.' And later, you say, it is not 'ideas' that one picks up from other writers, but (I simplify here) style: 'a style, an attitude to the world, [which] as it soaks in, becomes part of the personality, part of the self, ultimately indistinguishable from the self'" (EI).[23]

Coetzee in response acknowledged the broad truth of this comment, admitted that his intellectual allegiances were clearly European rather than African (in Attwell's words, that the aesthetics of the early to mid-twentieth century seem to have been especially influential), but he urged caution, saying that he could see no marks of Wordsworth's style or thinking in his own writing, and yet (he insisted) Wordsworth is a constant presence whenever he writes about human beings and their relation to the natural world. He then commented directly on Beckett:

> Beckett as a formative influence on my writing, let me say something about Beckett. Beckett can certainly be called a high modernist or even a proto-postmodernist. Beckett was an Irishman and a European with no African connections at all. Yet in the hands of a dramatist of the sensitivity and skill of Athol Fugard, Beckett can be transplanted into South African surroundings in such a way that he seems almost native there. What does this show? That the history of the arts is a history of unceasing cross-fertilization across fences and boundaries. (EI)

Given that Beckett is acknowledged so often and so openly by Coetzee as a "formative influence," it is perhaps the more surprising that so few direct evocations of Beckett appear in the South African fictions. *Dusklands*, despite its obsessive rationality and the presence of narrators who "play out the failure of the Cartesian self," did not emerge "from a reading of Beckett," Coetzee insisted, but rather from the spectacle of what was going on in Vietnam and his gathering sense, as he read back in South African history, of what had been going on there (*DP*, 27). This might imply that Beckett's influence is, like that of Wordsworth, a constant but invisible presence, or rather than that Beckett had been transplanted into the "South African surroundings" in such a way as to seem native there. Curiously, however, this latter statement may be true, and unexpectedly so, with respect to three later fictions, two of them set in South Africa and the third, while nominally in Australia, drawing heavily upon the South African experience. None of these fictions, *Boyhood: Scenes from Provincial Life*, *Life & Times of Michael K*, or *Elizabeth Costello*, assumes the deliberate voice of a known author — as, for example, that of Defoe in *Foe* or Dostoevsky in *The Master of Petersburg* — yet Beckett is a presence in all three, and this despite the obvious echoes of Tolstoy and Balzac in (respectively) the title and subtitle of *Boyhood*, or the deliberately marked imitations of Kafka within the other two works.

Boyhood (1997) is perhaps the most deliberately Beckettian of Coetzee's fictions, even though the Irish writer is never mentioned or alluded to. The "memoir" could not have been written without the example of Beckett's *Company* (1980), not because both texts dramatize the plight of a loveless childhood and recount embarrassing incidents in the early years of a sensitive child, but rather because both are not so much autobiography as what Coetzee, in a further interview with David Attwell, has termed *autre*biography (*DP*, 394). That is, the narrative voice, rather than simply recounting formative events, accepts that there can be no ultimate truth about oneself (*DP*, 392), and instead enacts a submerged dialogue between two persons — the one he desired to be and was feeling his way towards, and the other that he then was (and perhaps still is). Beckett's *Company*, similarly, is neither memoir nor autobiography but rather a set of devised images,[24] a fugue between one imagining himself into existence and an external voice, recounting memories ill-seen and ill-heard, the past not so much recaptured (in the Proustian sense) as devised, conjured out of memory and imagination. Coetzee, I suggest, has deliberately avoided echoes of *Company*, but the common rhythm is marked.

This might be considered "proof by assertion," for tone and rhythm, like all aspects of the auditory imagination, are not otherwise easily defined (what is needed is another "Essay in Stylistic Analysis," an application to the works of Coetzee of the principles that he had brought to bear on Beckett), yet they can be compelling. Coetzee's *Life & Times of Michael K* (1983) has obvious overtones of Kafka, as Coetzee in another interview with David Attwell (1992) readily admitted, saying with what he hoped was a "proper humility" that he had no regrets about the use of the letter *K* in his own novel (nor, presumably, about the book's many references to "the Castle" as the center of military police power: *DP*, 199).[25] Coetzee acknowledged the common forms of alienation between the experiences of Josef K and Michael K (*DP*, 199), but did not draw attention to the equally compelling presence and tragedy of *Watt* as part of that experience. Like Michael K, Watt is an innocent more sinned against than sinning, one who suffers both passively and impassively, one who lacks the means to articulate his plight but serves his inexplicable calling as best he can. *Life & Times of Michael K*, perhaps more directly than any of Coetzee's other novels, reflects and refracts the complex tonalities of *Watt*, even to the extent of imitating its narrative form by having one part of the narrative told by another voice: in *Watt*, that of Sam; and in *Life & Times of Michael K*, that of the medical officer of the work camp in which Michael is detained. *Watt* is "transplanted" unobtrusively into the South African world with such sensitivity and skill that it becomes almost "native" within that landscape, and testifies to what Coetzee, with respect to the appropriation, noted above, of Beckett by Athol Fugard, called in his post-Nobel interview the "unceasing cross-fertilization across fences and boundaries." A minor curiosity: in his speech at the Tokyo Symposium, having invoked the unlikely spectacle of Beckett as a South African academic, Coetzee then cited Kafka as a "misfit of higher order than other artists," implicitly likening him to Beckett, with images of one behind a lectern, or the counter of a butcher shop, or "punching tickets on a tram," a specialist in how not to fit in (*EW*, 30). The final image was not chosen randomly: as Coetzee would have known, and as Lucky's speech in *Waiting for Godot* asserts and the French translation of *Watt* confirms, "Puncher" (one who punches tickets on a tram) and "Watt-man" (one who changes the points and settings) are inextricably bound.

The most unexpected presence of *Watt* in Coetzee's later writings may be in *Elizabeth Costello* (2003). Elizabeth is familiar with the university world as the recipient of literary prizes and invitations to speak as an honored guest, and much of the novel consists of the speeches and discussions she gives on campus. Her world seems (unlike that of Michael K) to have little in common with that of *Watt*, but Watt, it will be recalled, was once a university man (*W*, 17), and he shares with Elizabeth not only a sense of the world's suffering (of which he is himself a mute and poignant emblem, likened to a bear, the baiting of which Elizabeth also contemplates), but also a deep distrust of what his creator (Sam, or Beckett) calls "anthropomorphic insolence" (*W*, 175). Elizabeth's inner being reaches more deeply into *Watt* than into the ostensible point of reference cited in her novel — the character of Molly Bloom in her bestseller, *The House on Eccles Street* (1969). The Beckett connections arise only gradually, and by no means obviously: a sustained consideration of Wolfgang

Köhler's *The Mentality of Apes* (1917) that is an important point of reference in *Murphy* and the source of his later dramaticule, "Act without
Words, I" (1958), which is directly invoked without being named (*EC*,
72); a weighted comment of "Anthropomorphism" in the margin of
Köhler's book (*EC*, 74), the word unmistakably evocative of *Watt* (*W*,
64, 175); Elizabeth's hatred of the Cartesian arrogance (one of Beckett's intense dislikes) implicit in the assumption that we have souls but
animals (despite the etymology of that word, from Latin *anima*, "soul")
are mere machines; an innocuous reference to "anthropology" (*EC*, 86),
in a context of both the Greek ideal (that the measurement of mankind
is man) and the dominion granted by God to man in Genesis over the
beasts of the field and fowl of the air, these constituting for Beckett as
much as for Coetzee the conditions of anthropomorphic insolence in the
Western tradition; the "divine *apathia*" (*EC*, 188) from Lucky's speech
in *Waiting for Godot*; and finally, but unmistakably, the image of changing from one belief to another, "as often as a woman changes her hat
(now, where does *that* line come from?)" (*EC*, 223). The answer to *that*
question is, unequivocally, part 2 of *Watt*, in the midst of Watt's anthropological speculation, where his need of "semantic succour" is at times so
strong that he sets to trying names on things, and on himself, "almost as
a woman hats" (W 68).

The image is innocuous, a note "casually struck and artlessly repeated"
that becomes a major motif, but it invites an interpretation of the final
(more precisely, the penultimate) sequence of *Elizabeth Costello* — the
imitation of Kafka's short story, "Vor dem Gesetz" ("Before the Law"),
in which a man waits endlessly before a door through which he finally can
never enter, in terms drawn equally from the suffering of Watt. This is not
to force an interpretation upon the ending of Coetzee's novel, but rather
to make the simple claim that, given these tiny intimations of Beckett's
enigmatic work, Elizabeth's reference to the song of the little frogs (in
terms of what she can believe) is colored by Watt's experience of the Frog
Song (*W*, 117–18), and its sense of an aesthetic harmony that is finally
(and distressingly) without any epiphantic meaning. In like manner, her
"vision" (the first that she has had for a long time) of the old dog near the
gate (*EC*, 224) that invites the obvious GOD-DOG anagram and elicits a "curse on literature," in some obscure way intimates the satire in
Watt, where the saga of the famished dog critiques the entire doctrine
of preestablished harmony, and thus, in Coetzee's novel, subtly undermines the precarious edifice of Elizabeth's belief. These are not allusions,
in the ordinary sense of that word, but rather unobtrusive testaments to
how the stylistic sensibilities of the Irish writer, Samuel Beckett, have infil-
trated those of his South African imitator (with the "proper humility" of
that word). They suggest, claiming much without appearing to claim anything, that Coetzee's early discovery of *Watt* and the laborious translation

of the euphoria associated with that discovery into a disciplined essay on stylistic analysis has become, imperceptibly and in the words of Coetzee's tribute to Beckett, part of the personality, part of the self, and ultimately indistinguishable from that self.

Notes

[1] J. M. Coetzee, "Samuel Beckett in Cape Town: An Imaginary History," in *Beckett Remembering / Remembering Beckett*, ed. James and Elizabeth Knowlson (London: Bloomsbury, 2006), 74–77. Subsequent references appear as IH with the accompanying page number.

[2] J. M. Coetzee, "Eight Ways of Looking at Samuel Beckett," in *Borderless Beckett / Beckett sans frontières: Tokyo 2006* [*Samuel Beckett Today / Aujourd'hui* 19], ed. Minako Okamuro et al. (Amsterdam: Rodopi, 2008), 28–30. Subsequent references appear as EW with the accompanying page number. The circumstances are further discussed in Coetzee's review of the first volume of Beckett's *Letters* (2009), "The Making of Samuel Beckett," *New York Review of Books* 56, no. 7 (30 April 2009), http://www.nybooks.com/articles/22612 (accessed 30 June 2011).

[3] Dominic Head, *The Cambridge Introduction to J. M. Coetzee* (Cambridge: Cambridge UP, 2009), 11.

[4] Cited by David Bell, "Goethe's Orientalism," in *Goethe and the English Speaking World*, ed. Nicholas Boyle and John Guthrie (Rochester, NY: Camden House, 2002), 199, with the comment that the epigraph is sufficiently well-known for it to be cited out of context, as if it were a statement claiming general validity; my suggestion is that Coetzee critiques this assumption.

[5] Samuel Beckett, *Watt* (1953; rpt. London: Faber and Faber, 2009), 214. Further references to *Watt* are to this edition; subsequent references appear as *W* with the accompanying page number. The macaronic echo is of Goethe's *Faust* 1:784, when Faust, about to take poison, hears the Easter bells and obeys their summons to return to life: "Die Erde hat mich wieder" (The earth has me again).

[6] J. M. Coetzee, "Remembering Texas (1984)" (*DP*, 51). The best treatment of Coetzee's PhD thesis and of its impact on his own style is that by Derek Attridge, "Sex, Comedy and Influence: Coetzee's *Beckett*," in *J. M. Coetzee in Context and Theory*, ed. Elleke Boehmer, Katy Iddiols, and Robert Eaglestone (London: Continuum Press, 2009), 71–90, with which my account is substantially in agreement, though we develop our respective arguments in different directions. Attridge, for instance, makes the point (74) that Coetzee was less attracted by Beckett's "famous negativity" than by the Irish author's handling of language, which he affirms (in a passage that I have also cited) as "a sensuous delight"; however, he goes further than I would in seeing this (and particularly its sexual tonalities) as a source of comedic art.

[7] J. M. Coetzee, "The English Fiction of Samuel Beckett: An Essay in Stylistic Analysis" (PhD diss., U Texas at Austin, 1969), 99–100. The detail did not survive into the final text. Subsequent references appear as SA with the accompanying page number.

[8] Carlton Lake, ed., *No Symbols Where None Intended: A Catalogue of Books, Manuscripts, and Other Materials Relating to Samuel Beckett in the Collections of the Harry Ransom Humanities Center* (Austin: Harry Ransom Humanities Research Center, U of Texas at Austin, 1984), 76.

[9] Details concerning the *Watt* manuscripts have been drawn from "The *Watt* Manuscripts: An Overview," in my *Obscure Locks, Simple Keys: The Annotated "Watt"* (London: Faber and Faber, 2006), 22–24.

[10] I was engaged, a decade later, on my own PhD dissertation on the (linguistic) ambiguity of Joyce's *Ulysses* (U Toronto, 1978), and had to deal in a similar manner with several studies (now outdated) of ambiguity that were essentially computational in both their analysis and with respect to the conclusions that their authors or programmers drew from that analysis.

[11] Stephen Kellman, "J. M. Coetzee and Samuel Beckett: The Translingual Link," *Comparative Literature Studies* 33, no. 2 (1996): 165.

[12] Despite the felicity of the author's surname, I find Daniel Watt's study of fragmentation in Beckett and Coetzee (*Fragmentary Futures: Blanchot, Beckett, Coetzee* [Ashby-de-la-Zouch, UK: InkerMen P, 2007]) less compelling than Kellman, precisely because it is grounded in the abstractions of postmodernist theory rather than in the empiricism of Coetzee's linguistic work.

[13] Samuel Beckett, *Molloy*, in *Three Novels* (New York: Grove Press, 1959), 26.

[14] See C. J. Ackerley and S. E. Gontarski, *The Grove Companion to Samuel Beckett: A Reader's Guide to His Works, Life, and Thought* (New York: Grove Press, 2004), 397.

[15] That "someone" was, of course, Coetzee.

[16] J. M. Coetzee, "Samuel Beckett's *Lessness*: An Exercise in Decomposition," *Computers and the Humanities* 7, no. 4 (1973): 195–98; as cited in *DP*, 1 and 397.

[17] Ackerley and Gontarski, *Grove Companion*, 317–18.

[18] David Attwell, "An Exclusive Interview with J. M. Coetzee," *Dagens Nyheter*, 8 December 2003, 1–4; www.dn.se/kultur-noje/an-exclusive-interview-with-j-m-coetzee-1.227254 (accessed 31 March 2008). Subsequent references appear as EI. Derek Attridge makes the further point ("Sex, Comedy and Influence," 76) that Coetzee was by now "less likely" to place *Watt* among Beckett's finest works, given the comment he made in his introduction to volume 4 of the Grove Press centenary issue (2006) of Beckett's works, to the effect that Beckett did not find himself as a writer until he switched to French.

[19] Attridge, "Sex, Comedy and Influence," 76.

[20] J. M. Coetzee, introduction to *Samuel Beckett: The Grove Centenary Edition*, vol. 4 (New York: Grove Press, 2006), x. In this occasional piece, Coetzee is called on to honor the later short prose (about which he is elsewhere less respectful) as well as the earlier poetry and fiction. He argues that with *Company* (1980), *Ill Seen Ill Said* (1981), and *Worstward Ho* (1983) "we merge miraculously into clearer waters" (xii). The point may be as much rhetorical as ethical (see footnote 27), or it may signal (for Coetzee, as much as for Beckett) a change of emphasis.

Only the churlish would quibble that *Worstward Ho*, like *Watt*, was written first in English, and that Beckett regarded it as untranslatable.

[21] Compare the comment above about Watt's creation of a fish (to say nothing of a famished dog and a family to look after it) entirely out of words, as further discussed in my *Obscure Locks*, 122.

[22] J. M. Coetzee, "Homage," *Threepenny Review* 53 (Spring 1993): 5–7; 5. Subsequent references appear as H with the accompanying page number.

[23] A similar point is made by Gilbert Yeoh in "J. M. Coetzee and Samuel Beckett: Ethics, Truth-Telling, and Self-Deception," *Critique* (June 2003).

[24] Ackerley and Gontarski, *Grove Companion*, 106.

[25] The "Castle" is the Castle of Good Hope (the irony is telling), the oldest structure in Cape Town, which long acted as the headquarters of the military forces.

3: *Dusklands* (1974)

David James

MODERNISM HAS OFTEN CAUSED COETZEE to do a double take. "I have never known how seriously to take Joyce's — or Stephen Dedalus's — 'History is a nightmare from which I am trying to awake'" (*DP*, 67). But the fact that Coetzee does look again at the ambivalence of modernism's message, questioning how seriously one should regard its most emblematic and solemn pronouncements, suggests that he hasn't been willing to think of modernism as finished. While he is adamant that "an unquestioning attitude toward forms or conventions is as little radical as any other kind of obedience" (*DP*, 64), Coetzee's dynamic ways of responding to the modernist legacy exemplify how he has sought to realize the promises of his formally radical precursors — even, and especially, if those responses amount to deliberate acts of disobedience, deliberate avoidances of pastiche. For Coetzee has never been passive in the face of literary heritage. And in returning to his earliest novel, the purpose of this chapter is not simply to paint a portrait of Coetzee at a stage in his career when he was most influenced by modernism, but rather to explore how this text might be considered as a deliberate meditation on the political implications of reviving modernist aesthetics. Insofar as this novel — which, incidentally, some prefer to regard as two novellas, even though both narratives rely upon their thematic correspondence with each other — is aware of the modernist conventions it redeploys, I don't mean to imply that *Dusklands* (1974) is simply a metafictional account of its own indebtedness to early twentieth-century literary history. If anything, it anticipates Coetzee's eventual diffidence toward "self-referentiality," that hallmark of *post*modern narration whose attractions, for him, "soon pall," because "writing-about-writing hasn't much to offer" (*DP*, 204). Instead, what this early novel shows us is that Coetzee hadn't given up on the possibilities of modernism even as he was breaking new ground. Coetzee's utilization of the technical accomplishments of what could still have been perceived, at the time of this novel's release, as a Eurocentric movement, drawing upon its resources to narrate interracial violence in colonial South Africa, is unquestionably controversial.[1] It highlights the ethical ramifications of Coetzee's choices in responding to and reemploying modernist methods to tell horrific stories of colonial dominance. This apparent disjuncture between the formal virtuosity Coetzee exhibits and the imperial legacies that he relentlessly examines could be seen as part of the "double paradox" that according to Simon Gikandi lies at the heart of Anglo-American modernism's confrontation with social customs and artistic formations beyond its own domain. As Gikandi contends, "modernism represents perhaps the most intense and unprecedented site of encounter between the institutions of European cultural production and the cultural practices of colonized peoples." And yet, despite the impulse of postcolonial critics to situate "modernism as the site of Eurocentric danger," Gikandi shrewdly suggests that in fact "without modernism, postcolonial literature as we know it would perhaps not exist."[2]

To suggest, therefore, that a formally adventurous text like *Dusklands* is somehow compromised by its own kinship with modernist innovation — reproducing through its style the very structures of power that Coetzee seeks to expose in the events he plots — would be to dismiss the potential for understanding modernism's capacity for the sort of critique that we associate with, and indeed expect from, postcolonial fiction. In *Dusklands* he further complicates matters, for the book suggests that a reengagement (at the level of narrative description) with the history of modernist aesthetics is entirely compatible with a sustained interrogation (at the level of its diegesis) of the limits historiographic authority and the brutalities condoned by those who assume that discursive authority for themselves. In the course of exploring that compatibility as way of opening up relations between style and content, aesthetics and politics, in this text, I remain sympathetic to Derek Attridge's[3] notion that "whatever else the 'modernist' text may be doing . . . it is, through its form, which is to say through its staging of human meanings and intentions, a challenge that goes to the heart of the ethical and political" (ER, 12).[4] In turn, he writes, we need to approach Coetzee's modernist inheritance not as an object of narratological investigation, but as a working practice, a revitalization of his literary past whose results elicit our emotional as well as analytical responses. Hence, Coetzee's "reliance on the resources of modernism," insists Attridge, should not be explained "as a technical feature to be assessed and interpreted . . . but as a moment in the reader's experience of the work" (ER, 17, 18). What this implies is that questions to do with how Coetzee's novels unfold, how they're textured, how they impact affectively upon us — whether it's across the discrete space of an arresting paragraph or more gradually over the course of a series of episodes — are as crucial as what they literally show. Such a fruitless exercise it would be, then, to evaluate *Dusklands* merely as an (over)stylized account of empirical history. Arguing against the prospect of "instrumentalizing" Coetzee's narratives as allegories of colonialization and its late twentieth-century afterlives, Attridge avers that the "importance of *Dusklands*" lies less in its ostensible "critique of colonialism and its various avatars." While colonial violence could be read as the novel's foundation and ultimate horizon, the text itself "provide[s] no new and illuminating details of the painful history of Western domination." Rather, what makes *Dusklands* so "singular" is precisely *how* it unfolds when "otherness is engaged, staged, distanced, embraced," when the formal and figurative effects of which are "manifested in the rupturing of narrative discourse" (ER, 30). By paying close attention to the reprise of modernist aesthetics in this early novel, I want to demonstrate not only how Coetzee orchestrates these affective and ethical dynamics at the level of form, but also the extent to which *Dusklands* reveals a more effective alliance with modernism than with the era of postmodern writing on whose cusp Coetzee published his first fiction yet with which he would subsequently never remain in tune.

This gesture toward Coetzee's recalcitrant position in the face of postmodernism's acceleration through the 1970s is more than a matter of debating literary-historical labels. From the outset of his career, Coetzee was more alert to the pitfalls of postmodernity than to its artistic or political potential. We might expect this reticence from someone who wrote a synoptic master's dissertation covering the majority of Ford Madox Ford's oeuvre, before proceeding to doctoral work on Beckett.[5] But Coetzee was also thinking in terms of his own writing practice when predicting the declining appeal and eventual exhaustion of postmodern strategies. Saying that postmodernist fiction could, from its earliest days, never really abandon or surpass the modernist ideals it sought to lampoon is something of an old chestnut for criticism of the postwar era. Thus Coetzee was not simply concerned with classifying trends, but also with what postmodernism's move against psychological realism might or might not mean for his own craft. In this practical sense, he intimated that "in the end there is only so much mileage to be got out of the ploy. Anti-illusionism is, I suspect, only marking of time, a phase of recuperation, in the history of the novel" (*DP*, 27). It's perhaps no coincidence that Coetzee echoes the forecast of another then-emerging writer, who was limbering up for his first novel: Ian McEwan. In the year after *In the Heart of the Country* (1976) appeared, McEwan announced that "experimentation in its broadest and most viable sense should have less to do with . . . busting up your syntax," than with what is effectively a matter of "content" — what McEwan called "the representation of states of mind and the society that forms them."[6]

How it is that an individual's mental states become so horrifically shaped either by society or as a result of the actions carried out in the name of cultural supremacy becomes the dramatic focus of *Dusklands*. Those shaping forces in turn affect not only the novel's "content" but also its manner of address, as each of its two sections employs a first-person register that disturbingly blends cruelty and confession. It's this register that initiates some of Coetzee's most audacious — and most recognizably modernist — simulations of interiority, simulations that give us perceptions of the world refracted by monomania and derangement. Divided into two sections, *Dusklands*'s first part, "The Vietnam Project," tracks the production of a report on psychological warfare written by Eugene Dawn, whose reach for a rational analysis of military conflict is matched by his own increasing irrationality and the eventual insanity that leads him physically to harm his own son. The second part of the novel, "The Narrative of Jacobus Coetzee," is an explorer's account of imperial domination and revenge. For this, Coetzee drew material from researching the colonial history of South Africa as a graduate student in Texas in the mid-1960s, reaching "further back in time," as he recalls, to trace "the fortunes of the Hottentots in a history written not by them but for them, from above, by travelers and missionaries, not excluding my remote ancestor Jacobus Coetzee, *floruit* 1760" (*DP*, 52). Intersecting circumstances therefore inspired a novel that reenters, in part two, the historical moment of Afrikaner brutality and control in a way that invites the reader to reconnect events there with the contemporary moment of US military warfare. The world-historical events of an accelerating bombing campaign against the North Vietnamese and Coetzee's personal investigation of "the earliest linguistic records of the old languages of the Cape" (*DP*, 52) thus coincided to structure the alternate contexts of colonial power as they are depicted in the novel's two halves.

If *Dusklands* was to a significant extent born out of Coetzee's fascination with vernacular discourses, it would seem appropriate for any discussion of his affinity with modernism to consider how particular features of his narrative language enable his interrogation of imperial self-interest. In so doing, we need also to consider this language on its own terms rather than sift it for signs of inherited methods. Pertinent here is Coetzee's insistence that *Dusklands* "didn't emerge from a reading of Beckett" (*DP*, 267), a disclaimer that reflects his broader skepticism about "questions of influence" (Beckett's or otherwise) and about the limits of speculatively tracing his literary inheritance — both of which "entail a variety of self-awareness that does me no good as a storyteller" (*DP*, 105). His reticence toward self-revelation has turned into a hallmark of his persona, of course, such that it's tempting to see Coetzee's famous reserve as synonymous with his fiction's rhetorical economy. But where the job of the literary historian is concerned, there's a more substantial upshot of this antipathy for influence. It suggests that we would be doing better justice to the style of his psychologically forbidding work — as well as to the sensibilities that inform its response (or not) to Coetzee's more obvious precursors — by approaching *Dusklands* as a modernist enterprise in itself rather than as one of modernism's heirs. By this I mean we should treat it as a narrative that refuses to rehearse past modes — as though modernism were a period style — precisely in order to counteract the "rejection," in Angus Wilson's phrase, of "overexploited devices still rich in promise."[7] As I indicated above, that Coetzee sets out to realize modernism's surviving promises in this way is hardly unproblematic, in view of the kind of journey into the colonialist psyche that he undertakes. But if we accept that modernist devices might actually facilitate that journey into interior dimensions of imperialist violence, we can begin to appreciate how Coetzee's extensions of earlier twentieth-century formal strategies advertise "precisely . . . his ability," as Attridge sees it, "to test" his own "absorption in European traditions in the ethically and politically fraught area of South Africa" (ER, 20).[8]

Such a self-reflexive process of testing the politico-ethical ramifications of reanimating literary heritage might not sound conducive to the project of retaining modernist aesthetics for a postcolonial age, as I'm suggesting Coetzee does, if that level of reflexivity is understood as merely metafiction, playing a postmodern game of undermining the viability of historiography. As I've indicated, we would only get so far in reading his work as a self-conscious meditation on, or admission of, its own "absorption in European traditions," for Coetzee is all too aware that "there is no hope of successfully arguing the political relevance of what, in the present South African context, must seem Eurocentric avant-gardism of an old-fashioned kind" (DP, 64). What he achieves instead is what my following close readings intend to show: that formal innovation — at its most responsible, at its most ethically attuned — reaches beyond "mere prose reverie," proving in contrast to any indulgence in style-for-style's-stake that "every element of the novel must be extremely 'justified.'"[9] This was Coetzee writing in 1963, making a convincing case for the way Conrad and Ford revealed that modernism was not all about technical mastery because "the ultimate demands were those of the artistic conscience" (FMF, 2.27). It is these early observations that would lead Coetzee to value modernist writers who were able "to disengage technique from intuition sufficiently to make statements of principle about narrative procedures" (FMF, 2.63), concerned as they were (and as Coetzee continues to be) with the ethical ramifications of using certain narrative methods rather than others. In the novel he completed some ten years later, these lessons in disengaging artistry from instinct came to fruition. *Dusklands* negotiates the distinction between craftsmanship and political commitment in order not merely to enlist features of modernist style that are appropriate to postcolonial critique; it could also be read as a novel about its creator striving to show that he knows the difference between passively depending upon modernist conventions — however seductive and influential they may be — and understanding how conventions can instead be remade "new in their *relation* to a past," exemplifying that "what is 'new now' emerges from an active, contestatory remembering of the defeated or forgotten."[10]

What Coetzee took away from his time studying *The Good Soldier* (1915) was Ford's brilliantly handled conceit of allowing the novel's "scheme" to remain "depend[ent] solely upon the mental tactics of the narrator" (FMF, 5.23). Much the same could be said of *Dusklands*, since a similar kind of conceit is in play from the opening page. "I deserve better," complains Dawn, reflecting on the fact that his mentor "Coetzee" has instructed him to "revise" his draft report of psychological warfare (*D*, 1). In this mixture of plangency and resignation we hear echoes of the man whose surname is Dawn's phonetic neighbor, John Dowell who, in the unforgettable opening stages of Ford's "Tale of Passion," poses to the reader the question of "why I write." While his "reasons," we learn, "are quite many," they are united by the belief that recollection will at least memorialize — even if it doesn't entirely make sense of — relations that have become "unthinkable." As Dowell attests, "it is not unusual in human beings who have witnessed the sack of a city or the falling to pieces of a people, to desire to set down what they have witnessed for the benefit of unknown heirs or of generations infinitely remote; or, if you please, just to get the sight out of their heads."[11] Though Dawn shares his introspective tone as well as his propensity for occasional divagation, the first part of *Dusklands* hardly endorses Dowell's logic of getting destruction out of sight and out of mind. In place of Dowell's hesitation and doubt, Coetzee introduces us to a narrator who seems to have taken quite literally Ford's famous advice from "On Impressionism" (issued a year before *The Good Soldier* appeared) that to write in this mode is to articulate "a frank expression of personality":[12]

> Here I am under the thumb of a manager, a type before whom my first instinct is to crawl. I have always obeyed my superiors and been glad to do so. I would not have embarked on the Vietnam Project if I had guessed it was going to bring me into conflict with a superior. Conflict brings unhappiness, unhappiness poisons existence. I cannot stand unhappiness, I need peace and love and order for my work. I need coddling. I am an egg that must lie in the downiest of nests under the most coaxing of nurses before my bald, unpromising shell cracks and my shy secret life emerges. Allowances must be made for me. I brood, I am a thinker, a creative person, one not without value to the world. I would have expected more understanding from Coetzee, who should be used to handling creative people. (*D*, 1)

What sounds at first like an indulgent exercise in self-pathologization turns out to be a commentary on the need for such an exercise to be carried out in the first place. It's as though Dawn is standing at some distance from the subject of his own self-dissemination. This same distance invites or indeed coerces us to pay more attention to *how* he recounts that "conflict" with the supervisor from whom he "would have expected more understanding," than to what it is, professionally, that this clash involves. Consequently, in place of a measured recollection of the causes of dispute, we get a performance of rhetorical prowess, a performance that unfolds at some remove from the stuttering confessions and frustrations we might expect from a genuinely unsettled mind. What *does* potentially unsettle the reader, however, is the insinuation that the intimacy of candid reflection here is fabricated, and that the emotional economy from which Dawn's complaints stem has already been exhausted. That is, his words sound like they've been rehearsed, which gives the impression that he's merely offering an emotive reprise rather than an emotional response — replaying a sense of indignation that's already evacuated of its original sentiment. This notion of an affective state being recycled finds verbal expression in Dawn's repetitions, "unhappiness" being a case in point, as he repeats the word in order to theorize its consequences rather than feel its repercussions. Despite the dehumanizing side effects of having worked on "The Vietnam Project," Dawn speaks in creamy prose that objectifies "unhappiness" as something less to be experienced than to be observed as a link in a causal chain, leading from "conflict" to "poison[ed] existence." Similarly, Dawn's identification with "an egg" has the effect of replacing his own ontology with an abstract analogy, so that he starts to reveal less about his disappointment with his "superior" than about his agility as a rhetorician in the face those hideous images of US imperialism he has dissected. At the level of this idiom, Coetzee draws our attention, at this early stage, to the quasi-rational language that will later characterize Dawn's dehumanized responses to images of brutality inflicted upon the Vietnamese. We will see that in his description of such images, as in the passage above, Dawn is all the more disturbingly revealed to us, when Coetzee has him nimbly negotiating metaphors that screen and divert the scrutiny of his own culpability as a mythographer of military tactics — tactics that rehearse, and are indeed dependent upon, the self-legitimating logic of Western domination.

Beckett's "stories," says Coetzee, often "become the fictional properties of their narrators" (*DP*, 44). Dawn's solipsistic disorientation emerges as both his property as well as his experience when he attests that "it is only recently that I have begun to falter. It was been a bewildering experience, though, being possessed of a high degree of consciousness, I have never been unprepared for it" (*D*, 5). Like the subject of "unhappiness" in the novel's opening, bewilderment here is posited as a theme for rumination, one that Dawn can mull over theoretically as much as he endures it viscerally — providing him with yet another cerebral lens through which to observe and applaud his own susceptible "consciousness." We might detect something here of the perpetual and self-perpetuating cycle of knowledge and uncertainty that besets the eponymous character of Beckett's 1945 novel, *Watt*, a cycle that implies that insofar as "there seemed no measure between what Watt could understand, and what he could not, so there seemed none between what he deemed certain, and what he deemed doubtful."[13] Certainly, hesitation and unease are present enough for Dawn to affiliate him with the eternal doubt that afflicts Watt. But the difference is that we watch Watt at a distance, with a pseudo-comic third-person commentator as our guide, whereas in *Dusklands* the first-person narration creates a more collusive and unstable mood, giving us the suspicion that Dawn is entirely in charge of his own demise, both literally and rhetorically, in a way that few of Beckett's displaced characters can ever hope to be.

Objectifying one's own grievances is one thing; doing the same to the grief of others is quite another. Coetzee highlights this unsettling transition when Dawn imaginatively projects himself into a "12" X 12" blowup" of a caged Vietnamese prisoner taken on Hon Tre Island:

> I close my eyes and pass my fingertips over the cool, odorless surface of the print. Evenings are quiet here in the suburbs. I concentrate myself. Everywhere its surface is the same. The glint in the eye, which in a moment luckily never to arrive will through the camera look into my eyes, is bland and opaque under my fingers, yielding no passage into the interior of this obscure but indubitable man. I keep exploring. Under the persistent pressure of my imagination, acute and morbid in the night, it may yet yield. (*D*, 16–17)

The moment is not only an account of the imperious desensitization of images of war victims, an account that Dawn gives as a kind of testimony whose confessional idiom nonetheless bears no trace of compunction. It is also a demonstration by Coetzee — facilitated by the coolly handled, sibilant inflections with which he renders Dawn's self-observations — of the maintenance of discursive power over the imagined victim, when that victim becomes the fantasized possession of "morbid" Western pleasure. Sinuous yet unnervingly elegant, the present-tense narration facilitates a palpable degree of immediacy — expressive of the extent to which atrocity is pornographic for Dawn — that is directly at odds with the separation that comes with Dawn's incomprehension: the separation that characterizes his failure to identify with, in the very process of fetishizing, this "obscure but indubitable man." Instead of attempting to bridge that void, Dawn orients his empathy towards the aggressor, ventriloquizing the self-legislating policy of invasion but in a manner that gestures ahead to the brutalities of part two, as he adopts the anachronistic language of wonderment akin to early colonial explorers:

> Our nightmare was that since whatever we reached for slipped like smoke through our fingers, we did not exist; that since whatever we embraced wilted, we were all that existed. We landed on the shores of Vietnam clutching our arms and pleading for someone to stand up without flinching to these probes of reality: if you will prove

yourself, we shouted, you will prove us too, and we will love you endlessly and shower you with gifts." (*D*, 17)

With its grandiloquence, Dawn's condescension anticipates the self-mythologizing discourse of Jacobus Coetzee, who pontificates about "the effective meaning of savagery" as a condition defined by "enslavement to space, as one speaks obversely of the explorer's mastery of space" (*D*, 80). In each case, the righteous process of categorizing populations to be encountered, penetrated, and idealized, if only thereafter to be fought and suppressed, is conducted in self-congratulatory terms. Both Dawn and Jacobus have conversations with themselves, despite their outward gesture to the communities or individuals subjected to imperial domination whom they expect — hypothetically in Dawn's case, literally in Jacobus's — to contain either within the imaginative retelling of events, which is nonetheless conducted (in another tonal affinity between their perspectives) in tangibly paranoiac terms. It is in the interests of accentuating the manner and ethical consequences of both characters' tendency toward introverted self-justification, then, that Coetzee enlists the modernist device of interior monologue, tracking from the inside out the perpetuation of imperial worldviews that gestate and flourish in states of moral and epistemological insularity.[14]

More perversely, such states breed a sentimentality that coexists with violence:

> From tears we grew exasperated. Having proved to our sad selves that these were not the dark-eyed gods who walk our dreams, we wished only that they would retire and leave us in peace. They would not. For a while we were prepared to pity them, though we pitied more our tragic reach for transcendence. Then we ran out of pity. (*D*, 18).

This warped logic of "pity" emerging from military ferocity is one that we will see again in Jacobus's nostalgic view of the Hottentots, a people he desires at once to preserve as a living monument to his explorer's authority and to destroy in a demonstration *of* that authority's endurance. In the episode above, though, the important point to recognize is not simply that the scene of annihilation is vicariously imagined rather than historically located, or that Dawn is empathizing with the lost consciences of combat soldiers who will go to commit those atrocities against civilians that he romanticizes more avidly than he researches. Rather, what's key is also the form in which this violence is anticipated: while the exhaustion of pity is aptly registered in dispassionately staccato syntax, the very stylistic features that influence the tenor and perspective of Coetzee's narration "cannot satisfactorily be contained in interpretation," as David Attwell aptly maintains, "for the aggressiveness [of his prose] remains a *social* fact that readers have and will continue to give witness to."[15]

Being a witness is very much in keeping with the position that Coetzee, via the testimonial idioms of his two narrators, wants his readers to assume throughout *Dusklands*. This invitation also disproves the assumption that the modernist difficulty of Coetzee's early fiction serves more to estrange than to immerse his audience. For, if anything, this prose — written though it was after he had absorbed so formidable a precursor as Beckett — complements the way recent literary historians have come to regard modernism as an intensification, rather than repudiation, of the emotionally involving strategies of realist fiction. As Stephen Mulhall points out, "one cannot intelligibly reject realistic novels as necessarily failures simply on the grounds that they rely on representational conventions of some kind." In this model, Coetzee's work exemplifies how a "faithfulness to the realist impulse that is so deeply embedded in the genre of the novel may be precisely what pushes a writer into the condition of modernism."[16] Conventions of depiction, of course, enter the very action of *Dusklands*, as Coetzee thematizes questions of knowing and showing, perception and articulation, in the most climatically disturbing of scenes:

> something which I usually think of as my consciousness is shooting backwards, at a geometrically accelerating pace, according to a certain formula, out of the back of my head, and I am not sure I will be able to stay with it. The people in front of me are growing smaller and therefore less and less dangerous. They are also tilting. A convention allows me to record these details.
>
> I have missed certain words.
>
> But if I am given a moment I will track them back in my memory and find them there still echoing.
>
> ". . . put it down . . ." Put it down.
>
> This man wants me to put it down.
>
> This man is still walking towards me. I have lost all heart and left the room and gone to sleep even and missed certain words and come back and here the man is still walking across the carpet towards me. How fortunate. They are indeed right about the word *flash*.
>
> Holding it like a pencil, I push the knife in. (*D*, 42)

A twin register that Coetzee has identified in Beckett as "the impulse toward conjuration, the impulse toward silence" (*DP*, 43) directly informs this episode, especially in the way it hovers between what Dawn is able to "track" down in words and those seconds that his rearward "shooting" "consciousness" fails to capture. Most explicitly, Beckett's dual emphasis on conjuring and silencing is also played out in Dawn's admissions about omission that sit alongside his desire to "record these details" despite his difficulty in apprehending them. A further pair of twinned yet seemingly opposed devices are revealed in aspects of tone:

Dawn's heinously impersonal displacement of accountability toward the injuring of his son is nonetheless accompanied by a distinctly personal series of concessions about what he can and can't recall "echoing" from his "memory." Like much of the novel's dissonance between its modes of telling and what is told, Coetzee deliberately contrasts the inhumanity of Dawn's actions with the apparent candor and collusiveness of his testimony.[17] In such cases as these, "tonal undecidability," notes Molly Hite, "defamiliarizes, not only for aesthetic purposes . . . but to open up spaces for ethical questioning without necessarily guiding readers to a definitive conclusion."[18] Hence, the episode above could legitimately be read as the expression of encroaching psychosis, but we could also see it as part of Coetzee's effort to simulate a desensitized vision of imperial violence that will reappear in part 2, sanctioned by colonial expansion, in the monomaniacal adventures of Jacobus Coetzee. What is evidence, for Dawn, of insanity will be for Jacobus a statutory "convention," as he exercises white authority in ways that are nothing *other than* conventional, just as the severity of imperial control is predictably decided according to racial ascriptions.

Conventions of acting and telling are therefore dramatized and stylistically embodied by *Dusklands*, as much as they are interrogated or subverted. Susan VanZanten Gallagher suggests that by narrating from the perspective of "the all-powerful chronicler of history, Jacobus can construct his story in any way he pleases, and we are helpless before his narrative power" (SSA, 66). One consequence of that power is the frequent transcription of violence, remembered or anticipated, into a kind of aesthetic category, one that Jacobus then manipulates and romanticizes at will: "I might, yes, I might have enjoyed it, I might have entered into the spirit of the thing, given myself to the ritual, become the sacrifice, and died with a feeling of having belonged to a satisfying aesthetic whole, if feelings are any longer possible at the end of such aesthetic wholes as these" (*D*, 82). The repetition here of the modal verb *might* ushers in a forward-lilting rhythm, so that the sentence emulates in its appetitive steps the masochistic relish with which Jacobus speculates about his heroic fate. Such is his commitment to idealizing violence that Jacobus rapturously embellishes the prospect of his own sacrifice in terms akin to understanding how an artwork might be organically composed, the appreciation of which rests on the assumption that concept and execution, matter and manner, remain fused in a "satisfying aesthetic whole." This aestheticized equation of violence with artistic integrity has a rhetorical counterpart in Jacobus's florid meditation on the return journey he intends to make from physical vulnerability to renewed superiority:

> In the blindest alley of the labyrinth of my self I had hidden myself away, abandoning mile after mile of defences. The Hottentot assault

had been disappointing. It had fallen on my shame, a judicious point of attack; but it had been baffled from the beginning, in a body which partook too of the labyrinth, by the continuity of my exterior with the interior surface of my digestive tract. The male self has no inner space. The Hottentots knew nothing of penetration. For penetration you need blue eyes. (*D*, 97)

The labial adjectives and verbs (blindest, abandoning, baffled, beginning) might not simply be construed as expressions of frustrated revenge, but also as a cluster of words whose phonetic kinship links them to that central noun of the novel: the body. For *Dusklands* may well be "about the dangers of discourse" (SSA, 79), but it is also concerned with the recalcitrant body, when the dangers Jacobus face are less discursive than they are physiological — shamed as he eventually is by his own infections. This reversal occurs after Jacobus has commanded what he perceives to be a deity-like authority over the Namaqua, when in fact they treat him and his soon-to-defect servants with little reverence, taking charge of his oxen and wagonload of commodities. His phallocentric self-promotion as a demigod then falters when he becomes increasingly weak with dysentery. Following his confinement by the Namaqua beyond the boundary of the camp, Jacobus's condition gradually improves. After he attempts to bath his inflamed anal carbuncle and a group of Namaqua children gather to mock him, he takes vengeance upon them by biting off a child's ear. The act leads to banishment by the Namaqua, and his expulsion into the desert sets in motion his plans for renewed vengeance, relishing as he does the rapine and destruction of the village — a totalizing return-defeat that, in the erratic manner of its projection, marks Jacobus's monomaniacal desire to rewrite the iconicity of his position as colonizer back into his own mythology of imperial control.

To convey the volatile combination of mock rationality, derangement, and self-deification through which Jacobus articulates these plans, Coetzee adapts the "narcissistic reverie" he admired in *Watt* to his own purposes when evoking the prolonged self-aggrandizements of Jacobus's excited resolve (*DP*, 47):

About tasks there is always something dreary, the taskmaster and the taskmaster's alien will; whereas games, my games, I played against an indifferent universe, inventing rules as I went. From this point of view my expulsion by the Hottentots was merely the occasion for a contest in which, primitively equipped, I was required to walk across three hundred miles of scrub. The selfsame occasion might at another time initiate an entirely different contest between myself and the circumjacent universe in which I might be required to call up an expeditionary force and return in triumph to punish my depredators and recover my property. (*D*, 98)

"Inventing rules" as he goes, Jacobus designs alternative games by assuming the heightened, proleptic language of expectancy and adventure. If, as Coetzee claims, the novel as a form "allows the writer to *stage* his passion" (*DP*, 61), then in turn what happens in *Dusklands* is that the stage becomes co-opted by Jacobus for the purposes of his own rhetorical exhibitionism. His "universe" is one that demands variance and agility from him as a chronicler. Alternative prequalifiers (indifferent, circumjacent) serve as intensifying adjectives that do less to illuminate for his implied audience the sort of world he inhabits than to reveal the extent to which he perceives the merciless conquest *of* that world to be inherently heroic. The ominous nature of his undertaking is highlighted by Latinate epithets, invoked here to describe his environment as animate if not adversarial. He personifies an inhospitable rural terrain, revealing in part his aptitude for topographical documentary, but rather more about his contribution to what Rita Barnard calls "the codes that have shaped the representation of the South African landscape."[19] While he is at the mercy of this territory, he turns that vulnerability into an "occasion for contest" rather than the rationale for reporting factually on the threat of his surroundings. Jacobus thus exploits the conventions of the adventure yarn over the more impartial register of anthropological travelogue, proving that what is "at stake" in Coetzee's writing — here, as in later novels — "is not place as an empirical and inert object of mimesis, but rather the discursive, generic, and ultimately political codes that inform our understanding, knowledge, and representation of place" (AB, 21).

In keeping with this response to landscape as a discursively and culturally mediated site of representational conventions, the same could well be said of Coetzee's response to modernism, as he utilizes its techniques without uncritically accepting his alignment with what could potentially (though reductively) be regarded as a Eurocentric heritage of literary prestige.[20] The question I've broadly tried to respond to in this chapter, then, is one that Peter Hitchcock poses to Nuruddin Farah's fiction and that's equally applicable to *Dusklands*: namely, how can Coetzee utilize the resources of modernism — both early and late, drawing upon predecessors as different as Ford and Beckett — while making the very text in which he does so "answerable," at the same time, "to the novel as inexorably colonialism's success, a narrative form writ large in modernity's reach?"[21] The answer *Dusklands* gives is contained in what it formally *does*: providing an exposé — through its stylized renditions of interior states where self-absolution coexists with the ferocious denial of personal and ethical culpability — of two disturbingly linked mindsets, minds separated by centuries yet "develop[ing] a direct analogy," as Attwell suggests, "between mythography and colonial exploration" (PW, 40).

Far from perpetuating the notion of modernism as "the art of exclusiveness" (to recall Gikandi's phrase), or as solely the provenance and reflection of the ideals of advanced, metropolitan, Western nation-states, Coetzee capitalizes on modernism's capacity for highlighting linguistic or generic conventions while remobilizing the politics of its methods. Such methods that have proved especially effective, as we've seen, for correlating (and thereby condemning) the pseudorationalization of military tactics of psychological suppression with that "indifferent universe" in which the reign of colonial imperatives at the level of discourse and deed is heinously restored. If this sounds like a self-conscious contemplation, on Coetzee's part, about his own position in and towards literary history, he is careful not to take this exercise too far. Despite its more obviously metafictional apparatus — and despite its self-interrogative treatment of the very possibility of providing an adequate historiography of colonization and its late twentieth-century reconstitutions in war — *Dusklands* ultimately refuses to inhibit the reader's involvement in the simulation of the characters' most brutal thoughts, as Coetzee refuses to sacrifice his most involving descriptions of hideous mental states in favor of postmodern self-reflexivity. This is a delicate balance for Coetzee to maintain: between his general reflections about literary conventions (modernist or otherwise) open to appropriation by any contemporary writer, and his more specific reflections about his own complicity — confronting what it means to assume the authority to write about imperial projects in such a historically comparative framework as that provided by *Dusklands'* two novellas. But he sustains that balance, and places certain limits on the degree to which he calls our attention to it, in order to sustain for his readers the intense discomfiture of shadowing the volatile perspectives and deleterious actions of figures like Dawn and Jacobus.

Yet it's a balance that also strikes to the heart of his endeavor to present, in Michael Vaughan's words, "a modernist challenge to liberal aesthetics." For Coetzee, that challenge cannot be realized merely by recycling some latter-day version of modernist opacity, where interpretive difficulties overtake the pleasures of passive reading — though this is partly what Vaughan implies when he praises Coetzee for bringing "limpid prose," as one of the "basic premises" of liberal discourse, "into question."[22] Rather, the very *mode* of resistance built into that challenge is a longstanding one, drawn from Beckett, in whom Coetzee has admired the refusal of "style as consolation, style as redemption" (*DP*, 47). Beckett may be difficult, but impenetrability is not his bequest; rather he showed that it is possible for a writer to work as a late modernist — with all the weight of inheritance that such an act of *following-on* implies — and yet still be inimitable. *Dusklands* sets the standard for the way Coetzee never allows his stylistic dexterity to console for the traumas he so unflinchingly conveys, let alone to redeem the dilemma of his own authorial decision to use modernism for entering the psychic fabric of the colonial legacies he surveys. What this debut novel realizes is the aim he would define over a decade later: to write "a novel that evolves its own paradigms and myths," one that's not "checkable by history."[23] A narrative that equally refuses to be checked against the historical achievements and political shortcomings of modernist fiction, *Dusklands* nonetheless epitomizes how, from the beginning, Coetzee's work needs to be regarded both in sensibility and in style as a part *of* rather than *apart from* modernism. For us, the ongoing critical challenge is to account for whether, in that process of taking part, he is demonstrating a stronger case for modernism's recrudescence than for its repetition alone. It's in relation to this very distinction that *Dusklands* inaugurated the paradox that would punctuate the reception of Coetzee's ensuing development: his readers continue to negotiate the fact that gauging precisely what makes him so original is itself dependent on the kind of dialogues we're willing to hear between his work and the literary past.

Notes

[1] The transnational "turn" in the new modernist studies has facilitated the redefinition of modernism as cosmopolitan in scope and reception, and as a phenomenon that has always been geopolitically implicated. In opposition to what she calls "the early days of the field," when "modernism was understood primarily in formalist terms as a loose affiliation of movements coalescing around certain aesthetic rebellions," Susan Stanford Friedman has drawn attention to the widely recognized shift in the discipline toward the study of modernism's multiplicities. While this might arouse fears in some of an endless, and critically vague, process of enlargement, Friedman instead "advocate[s] a *transformational* planetary epistemology rather than a merely expansionist or additive one, one that builds on the far reaching implications of the linkage of modernism with modernity." Friedman, "Planetarity: Musing Modernist Studies," *Modernism/Modernity* 17, no. 3 (September 2010]: 471–99; here, 474.

[2] Simon Gikandi, "Modernism in the World," *Modernism/Modernity* 13, no. 3 (September 2006): 419–24; here, 421.

[3] Derek Attridge, *J. M. Coetzee and the Ethics of Reading: Literature in the Event* (Chicago: U of Chicago P, 2004). Subsequent references appear as ER with the accompanying page number.

[4] Following this idea of performative and dynamic nature of modernist narration, we can appreciate Coetzee's interest in how fiction can invite, if not demand, what Richard Walsh calls that "conceptual shift" that readers of genuinely inventive writing have to make, the shift from seeing "narrative as object to narrative as activity: narrative as an intentional, communicative, sense-making process." Walsh, "How to Explore a Field," *Modernism/Modernity* 14, no. 3 (2007): 569–72; here, 570.

[5] I have written elsewhere on the somewhat underappreciated importance that Ford (and earlier modernist aesthetics in general) has had for Coetzee's development. It was Coetzee's early engagement with the compositional ideals of spareness,

selection, and precision, which Ford upheld, that paved the way for his later — and longer-standing — intellectual and creative conversation with Beckett's legacy. See David James, "By Thrifty Design: Ford's Bequest and Coetzee's Homage," *International Ford Madox Ford Studies* 7 (October 2008): 243–65; esp. 260–63.

[6] Ian McEwan, "The State of Fiction: A Symposium," *The New Review* 5, no. 1 (1978): 50–51; here, 51.

[7] Angus Wilson, "Diversity and Depth" (1958), in *Diversity and Depth in Fiction: Selected Critical Writings*, ed. Kerry McSweeney (London: Secker & Warburg, 1983), 132.

[8] In his lecture "What Is a Classic?" Coetzee's awareness of his own implication in the acquisition, involuntary or calculated, of cultural capital via his extension of tradition becomes clear. Bach could well stand for Beckett in the following question that Coetzee asks himself: "is there some non-vacuous sense in which I can say that the spirit of Bach was speaking to me across the ages, across the seas, putting before me certain ideals; or was what was really going on at that moment that I was symbolically electing high European culture, and command of the codes of that culture, as a route that would take me out of my class position in white South African society and ultimately out of what I must have felt, in terms however obscure or mystified, as an historical dead end [?]" (*SS*, 10–11).

[9] J. M. Coetzee, "The Works of Ford Madox Ford with Particular Reference to the Novels" (Master's thesis, U of Cape Town, 1963), 2.29. As the thesis's pagination is sectionalized by chapter, subsequent references appear as FMF with their chapter number and page number.

[10] Peter Brooker, "Afterword: 'Newness' in Modernisms, Early and Late," in *The Oxford Handbook of Modernisms*, ed. Peter Brooker, Andrzej Gasiorek, Deborah Longworth, and Andrew Thacker (New York: Oxford UP, 2010), 1012–36; here, 1031, 1035. This idea of the reciprocity between literary heritage and formal innovation, whether "contestatory" or convivial, is not entirely unprecedented, of course. Coetzee himself draws T. S. Eliot's model of the artist's immersion in and responsiveness to tradition as a catalyst for new advancements in discussing what counts as inimitable art, those artworks whose aura survives. Gauging their present and future impact requires an acute attention to history: "Historical understanding is understanding of the past as a shaping force upon the present. Insofar as that shaping force is tangibly felt upon our lives, historical understanding is part of the present. Our historical being is part of our present" (*SS*, 15).

[11] Ford Madox Ford, *The Good Soldier*, ed. Martin Stannard (New York: Norton, 1995), 11.

[12] Ford Madox Ford, "On Impressionism," *Poetry and Drama* 2, no. 6 (June–December 1914): 167–75; here, 169.

[13] Samuel Beckett, *Watt*, in *Novels* (Grove Centenary Edition), vol. 1 (New York: Grove Press, 2006), 275.

[14] Discussing the parallels between the novel's parts, Susan VanZanten Gallagher notes that "in their respective roles as government servants, Dawn explores the psychological interior of the Vietnamese rendered in their mythology, and Jacobus journeys into the physical interior of Africa. As explorers, both are driven to

know the unknown, to encompass that unknown both mentally and physically." Gallagher, *A Story of South Africa: J. M. Coetzee's Fiction in Context* (Cambridge, MA: Harvard UP, 1991), 59. Subsequent references appear as SSA with the accompanying page number.

[15] David Attwell, *J. M. Coetzee: South Africa and the Politics of Writing* (Berkeley: U of California P, 1993), 55. Subsequent references appear as PW and page number.

[16] Stephen Mulhall, *The Wounded Animal: J. M. Coetzee and the Difficulty of Reality in Literature and Philosophy* (Princeton: Princeton UP, 2009), 160. Chris Baldick makes a similar argument in concluding his survey of "the modern movement," by contending that "much of what we call modernism was indeed realism in a new manner, modulated by symbolist or expressionist devices, inflected by new psychological emphases, but still dedicated to puncturing false idealisms and to telling the truth about the world as it is." Baldick, *The Oxford English Literary History*, vol. 10, *1910–1940: The Modern Movement* (Oxford: Oxford UP, 2004), 401.

[17] Samantha Vice detects a comparable duality in the timbre of *Age of Iron*. "There is," she writes, "on the face of it a rather strange cohabitation between the elements of Coetzee's style: On the one hand, there is the scrupulous, unadorned recording of events and mental states, which rewards the reader with a sense of impartiality. On the other hand, the channeling of events and meaning through one consciousness is just as much a feature of Coetzee's style. The particular socially and historically embedded consciousness is precisely what is supposed to be the cause of distortion, partiality, and moral blindness. Both these modes . . . carry their moral dangers." Vice, "Truth and Love Together at Last: Style, Form, and Moral Vision in *Age of Iron*," in *J. M. Coetzee and Ethics: Philosophical Perspectives on Literature*, ed. Anton Leist and Peter Singer (New York: Columbia UP, 2010), 293–315; here, 299.

[18] Molly Hite, "Tonal Cues and Uncertain Values: Affect and Ethics in *Mrs. Dalloway*," *Narrative* 18, no. 3 (October 2010): 249–75; here, 250.

[19] Rita Barnard, *Apartheid and Beyond: South African Writers and the Politics of Place* (Oxford and New York: Oxford UP, 2007), 21. Subsequent references appear as AB with the accompanying page number.

[20] Debra Castillo implies that there need not be any discrepancy between Coetzee's modernist allegiances and his self-reflexive critique of white European privilege; indeed, it's the modernist style, in the form of penetrating interior monologue, that enables and intensifies that critique: "One function of Coetzee's frankly brutal monologues is precisely to provide a necessarily mediated glimpse of the other, effaced voice of European conquest, the inhuman counterhistory denied by the depersonalized colonialist narrative, the underlying motivations buried in the conventions of scholarly publication or hidden in eyewitness accounts." Castillo, "Coetzee's *Dusklands*: The Mythic *Punctum*," *PMLA* 105, no. 5 (October 1990): 1108–22; here, 1112).

[21] Peter Hitchcock, *The Long Space: Transnationalism and Postcolonial Form* (Stanford, CA: Stanford UP, 2010), 118.

[22] Michael Vaughan, "Literature and Politics: Currents in South African Writing in the Seventies," *Journal of Southern African Studies* 9, no. 1 (October 1982): 118–38; here, 126–27.

[23] J. M. Coetzee, "The Novel Today," *Upstream* 6, no. 1 (1988): 3.

4: *In the Heart of the Country* (1977)

Derek Attridge

T HE FIRST THING THE READER OF *In the Heart of the Country* notices is that every paragraph is numbered. This simple device announces from the outset that we are not to suspend disbelief as we read, that our encounter with human lives, thoughts, and feelings is to take place against the background of a constant awareness of their mediation by language, generic and other conventions, and artistic decisions. It is testimony to the power of fictional narration that it is not difficult to forget the numbering as we read; after all, the division of virtually all novels into chapters or sections is not something that interferes with the illusion of immediacy, and in every one of his novels Coetzee's intense prose can produce a readerly involvement that overrides all markers of fictionality. It is, however, always possible to shift our attention to the numbering and to its antirealist implications. The device also encourages the reader to treat each paragraph as having more self-sufficiency than is usually the case with fictional prose: each one a little mininarrative or speculation or diary entry, something like the stanzas of a long poem.[1]

The novel exists in two forms, the 1977 British and American version (differing only in the title — the American publisher preferred *From the Heart of the Country*) and the 1978 South African version.[2] The latter presents the reader with another defamiliarizing surprise: the dialogue is in Afrikaans. For most South African readers, the shift into Afrikaans would not hinder comprehension — there is nothing very complex in the utterances — but to encounter the juxtaposition between the two languages is to be made aware of the main narrative's mediation via English, and via the European fictional tradition. This mediation becomes particularly evident when Magda on two occasions (paras. 203 and 226) addresses one of the servants in what are effectively soliloquies, and provides both English and Afrikaans equivalents for many of her phrases — usually the English first, as if this were the language that comes naturally to Magda, then the Afrikaans, as if for the benefit of her ostensible addressee. Thus, to give a short example: "But that is not the worst, dit is nie die ergste gewees nie. Energy is eternal delight, I could have been another person, ek kon heeltemal anders gewees het, I could have burned my way out of this prison, my tongue is forked with fire, verstaan jy, ek kan met 'n tong van vuur praat" (para. 203).

The question of the use of English and Afrikaans — is Magda really an English speaker, for whom Afrikaans is a necessary instrument in practical matters? — is, however, never addressed in the text. (It becomes an important issue in *Boyhood*, reflecting Coetzee's own complicated linguistic background.) Yet the question of language choice is foregrounded toward the end of the novel, when Magda, alone on the farm, hears voices speaking what she is convinced is Spanish, although her lack of Spanish doesn't prevent her from understanding them, and we read them as English. (In fact, we have already heard about her "voices" and been given an example — a sentence, in English translation, from Rousseau's "Discourse on Political Economy" [para. 76]. We might notice, too, that the Blakean proverb in the soliloquy just quoted, "Energy is eternal delight" — from *The Marriage of Heaven and Hell* — remains untranslated.) A final surprise is the speech of reminiscence Magda addresses to her father (with whom she has always used Afrikaans) near the end of the book: it is in highly conventional "literary" English (para. 262).

For the reader of the British and American versions of the novel, however, there is no switching of languages to disturb the process of comprehension. The disquieting unreliability of the first-person narrative is, however, something that emerges for all readers in the very first paragraph. The narrator (whom at this stage we do not know as Magda) gives two alternatives for the animals drawing her father's dogcart — a horse or two donkeys — as it brought him and his new bride back to the farmhouse earlier in the day,[3] and two alternatives for what she was doing when they arrived — reading or lying with a towel over her eyes. So the statement in the middle of the paragraph, "More detail I cannot give unless I begin to embroider," already reads ironically. In any case, it turns out in paragraph 36 (after Magda has apparently murdered both of them in their bed) that the father in fact arrived back without a bride (at least, if we give the second version priority over the first, as we are encouraged to do), and when the same words are used in paragraph 38 to describe the arrival back on the farm of Hendrik, the colored servant and *his* new bride Anna, we remain uncertain whether this arrival will be confirmed or retracted in our further reading.

What transpires is that Hendrik, like the father, lives on to play an important role in the strange narrative that follows. But once having read paragraphs 1 through 35 in the good faith of the novelistic consumer, only to find them a fantasy, we can never quite achieve the same confidence in the scenes presented to us thereafter. The question "What *really* happened?" becomes unanswerable, and, in a sense, unaskable, since we have been made conscious of what we usually keep out of our minds as we read: that novels, unlike histories, do not tell of what happened.[4] (Similarly, it makes no sense to ask of "The Narrative of Jacobus Coetzee": "How did Klawer *really* die?")

Unlike "The Narrative of Jacobus Coetzee," however, we do have an escape route that keeps us within the bounds of the realist tradition (apart, that is, from those numbered paragraphs): we can ascribe the inconsistencies and impossibilities in the narrative to Magda's disordered state of mind, and treat the unaskability of the question of what really happened as the inevitable result of a discourse that proceeds entirely from a mind that is breaking down. This is, of course, a common readerly or critical ploy in dealing with problematic fictions — Gregor Samsa, in Kafka's *Metamorphosis*, is held to be suffering from hallucinations, or the peculiarities of *Finnegans Wake* are explained away by calling the whole thing a "dream," — but it's one that we fall back on only at some cost: if everything we read could be the product of fantasy or insanity, the novel loses *any* grip on the real, and thus much of its narrative drive and engagement with the very real issues of family, gender, racial, and master-servant relations.[5] A more satisfactory approach is to assume, as we normally do in reading fiction, that the words are to be taken as referring to real events unless there is good reason, in a particular section of the novel, to take them as the outcome of fantasy or psychological derangement.

Of course, "real events" in fiction may go beyond the norms governing the world we are familiar with. "Magic realism" is based on this premise, and in the later stages of the novel, when Magda hears, delivered to her from aircraft passing overhead, her "Spanish" voices uttering quotations from European literature and philosophy, we might consider that Coetzee has entered this realm.[6] Fantasy or mental disorder on Magda's part seems out of the question now, as there is no suggestion that she could have read Hegel, Blake, Pascal, Spinoza, and Rousseau.

Coetzee's use of modernist techniques is just as prominent in this novel as in *Dusklands*, then, although the richer evocation of a mental world makes it easier for the reader to experience the mimetic power of narrative, the illusion of reality that enables us to be moved by the thoughts and feelings of an imagined character. All the novels and memoirs that follow in Coetzee's career possess this power, the power that the young John dreams of as he reads Burchell in the British Library in *Youth*. Magda, the spinster on an isolated farm in what appears to be the Great Karoo, is capable of vivid expression of her emotions, and we share, as the bare narrative unfolds, the modulations and eruptions in her anger, her bitterness, her self-pity, her hatred of her father, her attraction toward the servants Hendrik and Anna. When her father takes Anna to his bed, she kills him by shooting through the window with his rifle. In the aftermath of that event, drawn out by the father's slow death, she tries to achieve some intimacy with Hendrik and Anna, for both of whom she feels physical desire. The passage I want to focus on — for again I can best make the points I want to make in relation to a short segment of the work — occurs when Hendrik arrives back at the house from a two days' journey to the post office in a vain attempt to withdraw some money. (The passage is written in the "impossible" first-person-present narration we first encountered in "The Vietnam Project," though unlike Eugene Dawn, Magda does not break off to comment on the convention that allows her to write in this way.)

In paragraph 205, Hendrik, furious at his wasted journey, grabs Magda's arm as she tries to leave the kitchen. She stabs pathetically at his shoulder with a fork, and he throws her down and beats her. She crawls toward the door, he kicks her in the buttocks, and she rolls over onto her back and lifts her knees. "This is how a bitch must look; but as for what happens next, I do not even know how it is done. He goes on kicking at my thighs" (para. 205). The paragraph ends here, with Magda half-terrified of Hendrik, half-inviting him to have sex with her. The moment is one of powerful narrative expectation, but the reader's involvement is suddenly ruptured. Paragraph 206 does not begin where 205 left off, but reverts instead to the moment where Magda turns to walk out of the kitchen. The feeble stabbing is described again, in similar words, but in this telling Hendrik throws Magda against the wall and rapes her. The violation is described with painful vividness, and it's unlikely that any reader remains aware for long that the event is, like Klawer's second death, a narrative impossibility. It's as if the capacity of mimetic writing to overcome the metafictional apparatus is being demonstrated, though we aren't aware of it at the time of reading.

The paragraph ends with Hendrik's semen seeping out of Magda as she sobs in despair. The following paragraph, 207, once more reverses time, beginning at a moment that had been registered soon after the beginning of the previous paragraph. Hendrik again throws Magda against the wall and thrusts himself against her, but what follows this time is not the rape on the kitchen floor. Instead, we have a bitter monologue from Magda, ending, "Please not like this on the floor! Let me go, Hendrik!" The following paragraphs return to a normal temporal sequence, and describe a different sexual act from the one depicted in paragraph 206. Paragraph 208 begins with the couple in the bedroom: Hendrik has presumably taken Magda there after her plea that they not have sex on the kitchen floor. Magda undresses, accepting her "woman's fate"; in 209 she finds that in spite of that acceptance she "cannot help him" and he forces himself on her; in 210 through 212 he sleeps and, with something of a change of heart, she begins to caress his detumescent penis.

Twice in this sequence, then, the narrative backtracks to an earlier point and develops in a different direction; as a result, Hendrik's rape of Magda is described twice, or rather, two rapes are described, since there are significant differences between the two events (to which I shall turn in a moment).[7] The effect of these narrative anomalies is clearly related to that of Klawer's double death: we are made aware of the constructedness of the events and the craftedness of the descriptions, as well as of the author's sovereign power to do whatever he pleases with the narrative. The alterity that Hendrik, as colored, as servant, represents for Magda, could have been compellingly conveyed without the distortions, but these distortions produce a fuller sense of an unknowable other, unknowable to such a degree that the conventions of narrative accounting break down. We might compare this passage with the enigmatic final section of *Foe*, in which Friday's alterity, already powerfully suggested in the novel, is given even greater force when an unnamed first-person narrator ascends Foe's, or Defoe's, staircase and comes upon the black servant in mysterious circumstances — and then the account is repeated, with a quite different outcome. It is as if in its dealings with otherness, the main part of the story, for all its subversion of realist narrative, has been too conventional.

The realist narrative can be preserved, however, if we assume that the two rapes are another example of Magda's fantasizing. She has, after all, already imagined, in some detail, being raped by Hendrik. Paragraph 167 presents Magda's fantasy of a monologue uttered by Hendrik to Anna as they lie in bed — and it is notable that in conjuring up Hendrik's words, Magda at first converts what would be third-person references by Hendrik to her to first-person pronouns: "Someone should make a woman of me, he tells her, someone should make a hole in me to let the old juices run out." But then the pronouns switch to the third person, perhaps to achieve a safer mental distance, as she imagines Hendrik's speculations about sex with her and thus imagines the act itself (the "I" now is, of course, Hendrik): "Would she pretend it was a dream and let it happen, or would it be necessary to force her? Would I be able to fight my way in between those scraggy knees?" There is, therefore, some plausibility in interpreting the narrative inconsistencies in paragraphs 205 to 207 as the outcome of Magda's indulgence in two separate fantasies of rape.[8]

The differences between the two rapes certainly suggest two alternative ways of imagining the event. The first is presented as wholly undesired, with the emphasis on Magda's pain, disgust, and distress: "Something is going limp inside me, something is dying. . . . I am nauseous with fear, my limbs have turned to water. If this is my fate it sickens me. . . . I sob and sob in despair" (para. 206; ellipses in original). The second, though Magda is again violated, and feels humiliated and revolted, is more ambiguous: they have apparently walked to the bedroom, Magda undresses herself, she mentions her "fate" but this time not that it "sickens" her, she "sobs and sobs" but this time not "in despair." Whereas in the first rape her thoughts are dedicated to getting Hendrik to stop, in the second they range more widely: she realizes with some mortification that she has forgotten to take her shoes off, she reflects that Hendrik's ripping of her pants means "more womanwork" for her, she revolves in her mind his words "Everyone likes it" (para. 209).

Yet, as we have seen, there is nothing in the narrative from start to finish that, in the final analysis, could escape the possibility of being read as fantasy. A responsible reading procedure will keep the appeal to psychological explanations (like unbridled fantasizing) to a minimum. A different way of responding to these paragraphs is to read the first rape as a product of Magda's fears, and the second, with its moments of ambivalence and its unexpected details (the shoes, the thought of "womanwork"), as real. Supporting this reading is the fact that the narrative flows on in a coherent sequence after the second rape, just as it does after the revised version of the father's homecoming: Hendrik sleeps, Magda ruminates, she begins to feel some tenderness toward him, he leaves, and then in paragraph 213 she visits the servants' cottage and thinks to herself as Anna greets her, "So she knows nothing."

Hendrik is soon visiting Magda regularly during the night, and she is doing her best to learn the ways of physical love. We have already encountered this pattern of a corrective sequence — first a fantasized version that comes to an abrupt halt, then a more grounded one that carries the narrative on to the next stage. The account of the arrival of Magda's father and his new bride at the opening of the book (which is followed by Magda's murderous attack on them) is corrected, as we have seen, when we learn that he is alone; the fantastic sequence in which Magda and Hendrik seal up the room containing the corpse and watch it float into the night air (paras. 153–56) is corrected by the relatively more realistic sequence (realism here is distinctly a relative matter) in which the corpse is pushed into a porcupine hole in the graveyard (paras. 173–85). A short sequence with a similar corrective rhythm occurs in paragraphs 197 and 198, in the first of which Magda shoots Hendrik and in the second of which she shoots and misses — and the story goes on from there.[9]

But such a recuperation of these problematic sequences can never be secure enough to restore our faith in the realism of the narrative. The consistency of style, the lack of any overtly signaled transitions between what might be fantasy and what might be reality, the improbabilities that remain in the latter (culminating in the impossible final pages, in which Magda's father is once more alive — unless he has been alive the whole time): all these make clear distinctions highly problematic. As a result, Hendrik and Anna remain problematic presences, never wholly grasped by the machinery of the text, never securely "in their place." Although Magda's language for describing or speaking to them is relatively free of the conventional formulae that we noted in Jacobus Coetzee's discourse (a conventionality that is more evident in Magda's father's language, or what she imagines as his language, in addressing Hendrik, especially in the Afrikaans version), she cannot be said to achieve knowledge of them.

The pressure of Hendrik's unknowable otherness finally prompts an extraordinary outburst of questions from Magda:

What more do you want? Must I weep? Must I kneel? Are you waiting for the white woman to kneel to you? Are you waiting for me to
become your white slave? *Tell me! Speak!* Why do you never *say* anything? . . . How can I humiliate myself any further? Must the white
woman lick your backside before you will give her a single smile? Do
you know that you have never kissed me, never, never, never? Don't
you people ever kiss? (para. 228; ellipses in original)

But if we find ourselves responding to this tirade (and I have quoted
only a small part of it) as the climax in the (non)relationship between
Magda and Hendrik, the moment when the concealed truth is shaken
out by sheer emotional violence, we are soon disabused. The ironic self-
undercutting characteristic of Magda's narrative begins again in the following paragraph: "Where was it in this torrent of pleas and accusations
that he walked out? Did he stay to the end?" We may be reminded of
Klawer's apparent noncomprehension of Jacobus's philosophical speculations, and think ahead to the painfully self-reinventing speech made by
Mrs. Curren to Vercueil in *Age of Iron* during which he appears to be
asleep. There are no communicative breakthroughs in Coetzee's fiction,
just moments when a character talks himself or herself into a new mental
position, a new constellation of thought and feeling, with no guarantee
that the addressee will take the slightest notice — with the likelihood, in
fact, that the alterity of the addressee will be underscored all the more.
(Soon after Magda's tirade, Hendrik and Anna flee the farm by night.)

For the otherness that makes demands on us as we read Coetzee's
novels is not an otherness that exists *outside* language or discourse, it is
an otherness brought into being by language, it is what two thousand
years of continuously evolving discourse has excluded — and thus constituted — as other. Not simply *its* other, which would, as an opposite,
still be part of its system, but heterogeneous, inassimilable, and unac-
knowledged unless it imposes itself upon the prevailing discourse, or
unless a fissure is created in that discourse through which it makes itself
felt, as happens at some of the most telling moments in Coetzee's writing. Modernism's foregrounding of language and other discursive and
generic codes through its formal strategies is not merely a self-reflexive
diversion but a recognition (whatever its writers may have thought they
were doing) that literature's distinctive power and potential ethical force
resides in a testing and unsettling of deeply held assumptions of transparency, instrumentality, and direct referentiality, in part because this taking
to the limits opens a space for the apprehension of the otherness that
those assumptions had silently excluded.[10] Since it is language that has
played a major role in producing (and simultaneously occluding) the
other, it is in language — language aware of its ideological effects, alert
to its own capacity to impose silence as it speaks — that the force of the

other can be most strongly represented. The effect is one that I would want to describe as textual otherness, or *textualterity*: a verbal artifact that estranges as it entices, that foregrounds the Symbolic as it exploits the Imaginary, that speaks while it says that it must remain silent.

The importance of both *Dusklands* and *In the Heart of the Country* does not lie in their critique of colonialism and its various avatars; there needs no Coetzee to tell us that the white world's subjection of other races has been brutal and dehumanizing, for both its victims and for itself. These novels — unlike some — provide no new and illuminating details of the painful history of Western domination. All this brutality and exploitation is certainly there in the novels to be felt and condemned, but it is not what makes them singular, and singularly powerful. It is what they do, how they happen, that matters: how otherness is engaged, staged, distanced, embraced, how it is manifested in the rupturing of narrative discourse, in the lasting uncertainties of reference, in the simultaneous exhibiting and doubting of the novelist's authority. Whether we call this modernism or postmodernism is, finally, inconsequential; what is important is the registering of the event of meaning that constitutes the work of literature — the event that used to be called "form," and that was given new potential by modernist writers. In Coetzee's hands, the literary event is the working out of a complex and freighted responsibility to the other, a responsibility denied for so long in South Africa's history. The reader does not simply observe this responsibility at work in the fiction but, thanks to its inventive recreation of the forms and conventions of the literary, experiences, in a manner at once pleasurable and disturbing, its demands.

Notes

This material was first published in the chapter "Modernist Form and the Ethics of Otherness: 'Dusklands' and 'In the Heart of the Country,'" in Derek Attridge, *J. M. Coetzee and the Ethics of Reading*, pages 21–31. © University of Chicago Press, 2004. Used by permission of the University of Chicago Press and the University of KwaZulu-Natal Press.

[1] Coetzee himself has related his use of discrete paragraphs to the influence of film on modernist writers, who discovered that they could omit a great deal of "scene-setting and connective tissue" to speed up the narrative (*DP*, 59). However, the use of numbers is not a characteristic filmic device (except rarely, as in Peter Greenaway's *Drowning by Numbers*). As Coetzee himself observes, *Dust*, Marion Hänsel's film of *In the Heart of the Country*, makes little attempt to find an equivalent for the numbered paragraphs.

[2] Because the two editions have different pagination, I shall refer to the text by paragraph numbers.

[3] In the South African version of the text, the bride, unlike the other characters in the novel, is imagined as speaking English (para. 11); later, Magda discovers a love-letter written to her father in English (para. 121).

[4] Dominic Head provides a sensible account of the uncertainties of reference in the novel; see *J. M. Coetzee* (Cambridge: Cambridge UP, 1997), 56–58.

[5] In *Doubling the Point*, Coetzee — for all his reluctance to comment on his own novels — is clearly unhappy with the idea that Magda is sometimes taken to be mad, and stresses instead the intensity of her passion — a passion allied to the love for the country and its people — that he feels has been lacking among white South Africans (60–61).

[6] Yet a comparison of *In the Heart of the Country* with, for example, Etienne van Heerden's *Ancestral Voices* or *The Long Silence of Mario Salviati* — fine South African examples of magic realism, which has flourished especially in Afrikaans writing — forces the acknowledgment that Coetzee's fiction has little in common with this mode.

[7] The rape sequence is not repeated "several times," as David Attwell states (*J. M. Coetzee: South Africa and the Politics of Writing* [Berkeley: U of California P, 1993], 67), nor are there four "versions" of it, as Sue Kossew has it (*Pen and Power: A Post-Colonial Reading of J. M. Coetzee and André Brink* [Amsterdam: Rodopi, 1996], 65), nor is it "described five times in consecutive sections," as Dominic Head claims (*J. M. Coetzee*, 58). It was members of my graduate class on Coetzee at Rutgers University in 2001–2 that made me aware of the exaggeration in these assertions.

[8] Attwell, for example, believes that the repetition denies the rape "the status of an 'event'" and establishes it as "a colonial fantasy on Magda's part" (*J. M. Coetzee*, 67).

[9] In the film *Dust*, the few short fantasy sequences — the arrival of the father's bride, the double murder, the reappearance of the father at the end — are clearly distinguished as such. There is only one version of the disposal of the corpse, the shooting at Hendrik, and the rape, and no Spanish voices or passing aircraft.

[10] This is not to say that modernist disruptive practices are, and will be, effective in this way in all circumstances and for all time: inventive literature is a response to the cultural givens of its time, and these undergo constant change. Coetzee has noted that "anti-illusionism" may only be "a marking of time, a phase of recuperation, in the history of the novel" (*DP*, 27) — although we might also note that his character Elizabeth Costello, in a text that plays self-consciously with the tenets of realism, argues that what she calls the "word-mirror" of realist representation is broken, "irreparably, it seems" (*EC*, 19), and elsewhere in *Doubling the Point*, Coetzee talks of a "massive and virtually determining effect on consciousness" that has undermined our faith in access to an unmediated reality (*DP*, 63).

5: *Waiting for the Barbarians* (1980)

Mike Marais

IF THE HUMAN SUBJECT is not a rational and free agent, but located in society and therefore located by society's values, attitudes, and ways of knowing and seeing, it follows that it is not fully in control of itself and must therefore endlessly question its intentions and actions. The problem with such self-scrutiny is clearly not that it results in a form of solipsism, but rather that the self cannot even claim to know herself and, in the absence of such certitude, is forced to doubt her motives and hence her agency. Even the idea that the rational subject is a free agent is the product of a particular cultural moment — that is, the European Enlightenment — and therefore yet more evidence of its embeddedness in society.

Understandably, the kind of skepticism attendant on the subject's cultural implication is particularly acute and debilitating in oppressive societies where it is ethically imperative to resist tyranny actively. So, for instance, Albert Memmi argues that the leftist colonizer, who aspires to resist colonialism, is, in fact, implicated in the colonial system. The crucial point here is that colonial relations derive not from individual intention and action but preexist the arrival or birth of the individual:

> The leftist colonizer is part of the oppressing group and will be forced to share its destiny, as he shared its good fortune. . . . Colonial relations do not stem from individual good will or actions; they exist before his arrival or birth, and whether he accepts or rejects them matters little. . . . No matter how he may reassure himself, "I have always been this way or that with the colonised," he suspects, even if he is in no way guilty as an individual, that he shares a collective responsibility by the fact of membership in a national oppressor group.[1]

Since the individual is deeply enmeshed in the oppressive society that she attempts to resist, she cannot *not* question the integrity of her actions.

The question of the implicated self who seeks to resist the oppressive social structures that, ironically, have structured her consciousness is omnipresent in J. M. Coetzee's fiction of the apartheid period. In *Age of Iron*, for example, Mrs. Curren eventually arrives at the realization that she is an inextricable part of the "crime" against which she protests:

> A crime was committed long ago. . . . So long ago that I was born
> into it. It is part of my inheritance. It is part of me, I am part of
> it. . . . Though it was not a crime I asked to be committed, it was
> committed in my name. I raged at times against the men who did
> the dirty work . . . but I accepted too that, in a sense, they lived
> inside me. So that when in my rages I wished them dead, I wished
> death on myself too. (149–50)

Since there can be no end to the skepticism and doubt attendant on the
recognition that consciousness is contextual and historical rather than
autonomous, the individual who resists political oppression must ceaselessly question this resistance. In "Confession and Double Thoughts:
Tolstoy, Rousseau, Dostoevsky," Coetzee engages, albeit implicitly,
with this incapacitating problem in his argument that the move of
skepticism — the self's constant examination of his every action and
thought — is infinite.[2] Only grace, Coetzee maintains, can conclude
such trials of doubt. The tacit question posed by this essay is whether,
in an ineluctably secular and political context, there is anything that can
put an end to the self's debilitating interrogation of his every intention.
In an interview with David Attwell that prefaces the section of *Doubling
the Point* that contains his essay on skepticism, Coetzee seems to provide an answer of sorts to this question:

> Whatever else, the body is not "that which is not," and the proof
> that it *is* is the pain it feels. The body with its pain becomes a coun-
> ter to the endless trials of doubt. . . . Not grace, then, but at least
> the body. Let me put it baldly: in South Africa it is not possible to
> deny the authority of suffering and therefore of the body. . . . And
> let me again be unambiguous: it is not that one grants the authority
> of the suffering body: the suffering body takes this authority: that is
> its power. (*DP*, 248)

In this chapter, I examine Coetzee's earliest sustained fictional articulation of this profoundly anti-Cartesian thesis in *Waiting for the Barbarians*
in his depiction of the Magistrate's response to what Theodor Adorno
would call "damaged life."[3] While this character is aware of his location
in the society he resists, and *must* therefore doubt the motives behind
his actions, he is nonetheless obliged to act by his encounters with the
indubitable suffering of the body. My contention is that, in this novel,
the authority of the body is staged in its ability to affect the Magistrate
despite himself. As we will see, when this character protests against the
actions of Empire, he does so involuntarily, almost against his will. By
extension, what the novel presents is a form of ethics that breaks with
Western ethical theory's preoccupation with the rational subject as center
of ethical action.

My argument, in this regard, intersects with that of those relatively few critics who have commented on the Magistrate's loss of rational control in his encounter with the suffering body. For example, after noting that "nearly all of his reactions are visceral ones that he is unable to explain," Josephine Donovan refers to the Magistrate's "unmediated and otherwise inexplicable empathy" for the barbarian girl.[4] In developing this comment, I have found particularly insightful James Phelan and Anne Waldron Neumann's narratological analyses of Coetzee's use of first-person, present-tense narration to foreground the Magistrate's confusion: while Phelan observes that teleology is beyond this character's control,[5] Neumann contends that this technique "records present uncertainty without always drawing retrospective connections, certainly without drawing them simultaneously with the event."[6]

In arguing for an ethic grounded in bewilderment rather than rational control, I part company with critics such as Jennifer Wenzel who, after stating that torture has "transformed" the barbarian girl's body into "a text to be read," ascribes the Magistrate's failure to read and understand this body — that is, his confrontation with its otherness — to some kind of moral flaw. "It is this sense of otherness," she maintains, "that allows torturers to ignore the pain of their victims."[7] Laura Wright tends toward a similar conclusion when she remarks that the Magistrate's "inability to see what motivates his actions is a kind of blindness that results in a failure of the sympathetic imagination."[8] In my argument, it is exactly the Magistrate's perplexed sense of her otherness or strangeness that renders him responsible for the barbarian girl.

Waiting for the Barbarians focuses on the tension between Colonel Joll, who journeys from the unnamed empire's capital to the frontier in order to crush a rumored barbarian rebellion, and the Magistrate of a fortress town. The latter's cultural embeddedness is, of course, evident from the first in his anonymity: the fact that he is known only by the office he bears indicates that he is a functionary of Empire. Importantly, though, he is conscious of his cultural implication and therefore constantly questions his actions and motives. He even becomes aware that his relationship with the barbarian girl is not readily distinguishable from that of Joll, her torturer:

> What depravity is it that is creeping upon me? I search for secrets and answers, no matter how bizarre, like an old woman reading tea-leaves. There is nothing to link me with torturers, people who sit waiting like beetles in dark cellars. How can I believe that a bed is anything but a bed, a woman's body anything but a site of joy? I must assert my distance from Colonel Joll! I will not suffer for his crimes! (*WB*, 44)
>
> For I was not, as I liked to think, the indulgent pleasure-loving opposite of the cold rigid Colonel. I was the lie that Empire tells

itself when times are easy, he the truth that Empire tells when harsh winds blow. Two sides of imperial rule, no more, no less. (*WB*, 135)

What we have here is an articulation of structural complicity: despite his deep and active desire to dissociate himself from the history of Empire, the Magistrate is situated in it.

This character's skepticism is thus produced by his recognition that he is not an autonomous subject and therefore unable to comment authoritatively on the crisis in which he is not only involved but also for which he is partly responsible. In the absence of certitude, he must ceaselessly speculate and doubt. Indeed, Coetzee's use of present-tense narration, which obviates the possibility of sustained retrospection on the part of the Magistrate, emphasizes the fumbling, ineffectual nature of his attempt to grasp the history in which he finds himself. What we have in the novel is not the presentation of knowledge that has been arrived at, but the *attempt* to gain knowledge. What is presented is not understanding, but the process of trying to understand. It follows that the Magistrate never arrives at a final, complete explanation of anything. To be sure, the novel's closing sentence suggests that this, ultimately, is no longer that important to him, that the one thing that he has come to understand is that understanding is only ever provisional: "Like much else nowadays I leave it [the square in which the children are making a snowman] feeling stupid, like a man who lost his way long ago but presses on along a road that may lead nowhere" (*WB*, 155–56).

One of the reasons for the Magistrate's sense of "stupidity" — in itself an epiphenomenon of his skepticism — is his knowledge that Empire's structures of knowledge and ways of seeing, which inform his understanding and perception, are local rather than universal in nature. He knows, for instance, that the barbarians do not exist, that the words "barbarian" and "enemy" with which Empire identifies them do not fit the native inhabitants of the region. While the purpose of Colonel Joll's visit to the frontier may be to crush a barbarian rebellion, the Magistrate tells one of Joll's men that "We are at peace here . . . we have no enemies" (*WB*, 77). There is no rebellion and there are no barbarians. The Magistrate's skepticism in this regard is again evident in his following reflection on Joll's prisoners: "The circuit is made, everyone has a chance to see the twelve miserable captives, to prove to his children that the barbarians are real" (*WB*, 103). As Laura Wright points out, the outcome of such sustained skepticism concerning the reality of the "barbarians" is that the word "'barbarian' . . . becomes a floating signifier devoid of specific meaning" in Coetzee's narrative.[9]

Importantly, the specious difference that it posits between itself and the people it calls "barbarians" by constructing for them an identity in its language enables Empire to respond to them with callous indifference. In the novel, it is only once these people have been identified as barbarians and enemies through language that it becomes possible to violate them physically. By degrading them in language, then, Empire legitimizes torture. And, in torturing them, it seeks actively to deny that which asserts commonality rather than difference — namely, the body of the "barbarian." It seeks to deny that the body of the victim is the same as its own. In a different, yet related, context, John Berger comments as follows on the training of torturers:

> But the first conditioning begins . . . with ideological propositions that a certain category of people are fundamentally different and that their difference constitutes a supreme threat. The tearing apart of the third person, *them*, from *us* and *you*. The next lesson . . . is that *their* bodies are lies because, as bodies, they claim *not* to be so different: torture is a punishment for this lie.[10]

What Coetzee is saying, though, is that the suffering body is indubitable, and hence cannot be denied. Quite perversely and ironically, the suffering the torturers inflict asserts that which they labor to negate. Through its pain, the body, as this writer puts it in *Doubling the Point*, gains an authority that serves as "a counter to the endless trials of doubt" (*DP*, 248). The body in pain transgresses the linguistically and discursively inscribed difference between people by asserting an incontrovertible reality that lies beyond the cultural enclosure and its local forms of knowledge.

In the novel, the authority of the suffering body is apparent in its curious effect on the Magistrate's actions. On a rational level, he decides against intervening in the torture of the barbarians. Indeed, he stops his ears "to the noises coming from the hut by the granary," which has been turned into a torture chamber (*WB*, 9). Nevertheless, irrespective of the fact that he "did not mean to get embroiled" (*WB*, 8), that he is able to formulate self-servingly sensible reasons for not having done so, he does eventually intervene in the tortures, and later still takes in the barbarian girl. The corollary of the dissonance here between intention and action is that the Magistrate does not really have any choice in assuming responsibility for these victims of Empire. What explains this disjunction between intention and action, particularly in the case of the barbarian girl, is simply that, in offering her shelter and succor, he is heeding the authority of the suffering body.

Crucially, in this regard, he is quite unaware why it should be that he offers the barbarian girl his hospitality. In the first of the scenes in which he washes her feet, the Magistrate's confusion is very apparent. As Derek Attridge points out, the scene is developed in a way that enables us to sense this character's "awareness that he is playing out the standard rituals of seduction — the fire, the drawn curtains, the lamp" and so on.[11] The Magistrate's words to the girl, "This is not what you think it is" (*WB*,

27), are, of course, the stock disclaimer of the seducer. At the same time, though, it should be added that this disclaimer reveals to us that *he* thinks he knows what it is that he has in mind for the girl. Clearly, he assumes that he desires her sexually. He assumes that he is acted upon by his desire for her. Thus, for instance, he hears himself speak in a "new thick voice" that he hardly recognizes (*WB*, 28). He knows that he is not himself, that he has been mastered by something he believes to be sexual desire. It is therefore all the more striking that what he anticipates will be his seduction of the girl should culminate in his washing of her feet. While he is acted upon, and suspects that this is so, it is by nothing that he can recognize.

Throughout their time together, the Magistrate fails to understand his attraction to and treatment of the girl. He repeatedly dismisses sexual desire as an explanation — "I have no desire to enter this stocky little body glistening by now in the firelight. It is a week since words have passed between us. I feed her, use her body, if that is what I'm doing, in this foreign way" (*WB*, 30) — and constantly dwells on his inability to account for his actions in *rational* terms:

> What this woman beside me is doing in my life I cannot compre-
> hend. (*WB*, 47)
> I am with her not for whatever raptures she may promise or yield
> but for other reasons, which remain as obscure to me as ever. (*WB*,
> 64)

In fact, the Magistrate is quite obviously surprised, perplexed, and bewildered by his behavior. A few pages after the foot-washing scene, we encounter the following description of his interaction with the girl: "I lie beside her, speaking softly. This is where my hand, caressing her belly, seems as awkward as a lobster. The erotic impulse, if that is what it has been, withers; with surprise I see myself clutched to this stolid girl, unable to remember what I ever desired in her, angry with myself for wanting and not wanting her" (*WB*, 33).

Evidently, the Magistrate no longer knows himself. Since they bear little relation to his assumptions, intentions, and ostensible desires, he finds his actions totally unpredictable.

In his relationship with the barbarian girl, the Magistrate is therefore certainly not in control of himself. Although he acts, he does so under inspiration by the suffering body, which ceaselessly asserts a commonality that overrides the Empire's inscription of difference. It follows that this character's actions are informed by an unconscious desire to see the body before it was named and therefore "known" by Empire. He wants to see the barbarian girl as she would be in the absence of Empire: that is, without knowledge, from outside his linguistic and cultural enclosure. Herein, of course, lies the significance of the hooded girl of the Magistrate's recurring dream: in his sleep — that is, in a state devoid of expectation and intentional assumption — he responds to her without knowledge, as a stranger. Unlike the barbarian girl, the girl of his dreams is outside history. The juxtaposition of the dream-child and the barbarian girl suggests that he, in his relationship with the latter, must *see* the former. He must see beyond the visible marks that Empire has inscribed on the girl's body in its attempt to render it invisible. In fact, his desire to see the barbarian girl in the absence of the history in which he is embedded *is* his assumption of responsibility for her.

Under the burden of a form of responsibility that obliges him to act against his conscious intentions, the Magistrate becomes a stranger to himself, notwithstanding his protestations to the contrary:

> If a change in my moral being were occurring I would feel it. . . . I am the same man I always was; but time has broken, something has fallen in upon me from the sky, at random, from nowhere: this body in my bed, for which I am responsible, or so it seems, otherwise why do I keep it? For the time being, perhaps forever, I am simply bewildered. (*WB*, 43)

The unintentional, involuntary nature of this form of responsibility, the fact that it is accompanied by a dispossession of self, accounts for the Magistrate's "fits of resentment" against what he refers to as his "bondage" to the foot-oiling ritual.[12] He even feels that he has been mastered by the girl: "I light a candle and bend over the form to which, it seems, I am in a measure enslaved" (*WB*, 42). The Magistrate, it would appear, is a servant not of sexual desire, but of responsibility.

Significantly, this responsibility extends well beyond this character's relationship to the girl. In the scene in which Joll first inscribes the word "*ENEMY*" on the backs of the prisoners and then has it erased through flogging (*WB*, 105), we again see the Magistrate acting against his conscious intentions. Upon observing Joll's arrival with the prisoners, the Magistrate consciously decides on a course of action. At least, we infer as much from his actions: he returns to the prison yard where he collects an empty bucket that he then fills. Even so, we certainly do not know what he intends doing. When he reflects that "As a gesture it will have no effect, it will not even be noticed" (*WB*, 104), we do not know the nature of the "gesture" he has in mind. Neither do we know the antecedent of the impersonal pronoun "it." All we know is that when he finally does intervene by speaking out against the brutalization of the prisoners, the Magistrate utterly disregards whatever action it is that he had decided on when he quite deliberately and very purposefully collected the bucket. Tellingly, too, he again hears himself when he speaks. In an ecstasy of responsibility — that is, beside himself, outside himself — he hears what he says and sees what he does: "'*No!*' I hear the first word from my throat, rusty, not loud enough. Then again: '*No!*' This time the word rings like a bell from my chest. The soldier who blocks my way stumbles aside. I am in the arena holding up my hands to still the crowd: '*No! No! No!*'" (*WB*, 106). His actions are involuntary. He acts in being acted upon.

Apart from shouting "*No!*," the Magistrate also shouts "*Men!*" (*WB*, 107), in an attempt to remind the torturers, and their spectators, of the humanity they share with the prisoners. By implication, the Magistrate is responsible for not just the barbarian girl, but all human beings. The form of responsibility that Coetzee thematizes in this novel is even more hyperbolic than this would suggest, though. As the Magistrate shouts "*Men!*," he reflects that "beetles, worms, cockroaches, ants, in their various ways" are also "miracles of creation" (*WB*, 107). Responsibility, if it is to deserve this appellation, must encompass all.

The notion of infinite responsibility here staged is already apparent earlier in the novel when this character goes hunting. In many respects, this is a pivotal scene: the Magistrate obviously goes hunting with the intention of killing animals. On a conscious and rational level, he subscribes to the anthropocentric notion that human animals have dominion over other animals. To be sure, we learn on the very first page of the novel that hunting is one of his favorite pastimes (one, it should be noted, that he shares with Colonel Joll).[13] It is all the more surprising therefore that, once he has a waterbuck ram in his sights, he does not shoot it. "Never before," he later explains to the girl, "have I had the feeling of not living my own life on my own terms." Her response foregrounds the breakdown in intentionality that is here at stake, the fact that the Magistrate is not in control of his actions. "Didn't you want to shoot this buck?" she asks, and then adds: "If you want to do something, you do it" (*WB*, 40).

What is adumbrated in *Waiting for the Barbarians*, then, is a form of ethical action that is *not* grounded in the perceptions, experiences, and understanding of a rational, autonomous individual. Very clearly, this novel treats knowledge and reason with the utmost suspicion. Knowledge, that which invests the rational subject with a sense of control of both world and self, is always local and therefore generates rather than grasps otherness. It can only ever attempt to comprehend others by integrating them into the knowing subject's priorly formed conceptual system. It follows that knowledge, and this has been a prominent concern in my reading of Coetzee's novel, is one of the mechanisms through which community differentiates itself from its others and, in the process, requires its members to respond to them with indifference. In the novel, it is only after the "barbarians" have been identified as barbarians and enemies that it becomes possible to violate them physically. The Magistrate's inability to know either the world or himself must be read in the context of such epistemological violence. For that matter, so must his description of his parting with the barbarian girl, which suggests that he does not know her, that he, at some or other prereflective level, has responded to this stranger as a stranger: "I see only too clearly what I see: a stocky girl with a broad mouth and hair cut in a fringe across her forehead staring over my shoulder into the sky; a stranger; a visitor from strange parts now on her way home after a less than happy visit" (*WB*, 73). It is worth noting that the barbarian girl, due to her impaired vision, does not confront the Magistrate in this scene. He cannot define himself in opposition to her. In other words, he cannot know her from within the subject positions inscribed by his culture.

In conclusion, I should point out that Michael Valdez Moses is quite right in maintaining that this novel, given its deep suspicion of the forms of knowledge that enable the exclusionary movement through which community shapes itself, offers no solution to the problem of constructing difference: "How will the State that follows establish its claim to justice except by discriminating itself, its form, from the Other which lies outside it? . . . For [the Magistrate's] repudiation of the Empire implicitly rejects all political regimes, none of which may lay claim to a philosophically defensible conception of right."[14] I would suggest, though, that it is for exactly this reason that Coetzee stages a kind of nonrational ethical action that cuts across both cultural difference among humans and difference between animal species. In this regard, it is noteworthy that this ethic of bewilderment becomes increasingly evident in Coetzee's writing after *Waiting for the Barbarians*. David Lurie, in *Disgrace*, undergoes an involuntary change: like the Magistrate, he is unable to explain the responsibility that he comes to feel for other beings. One reads that "He does not understand what is happening to him" (*DG*, 143), and that he finds it "curious that a man as selfish as he should be offering himself to the service of dead dogs" (*DG*, 146). He is equally bemused, even surprised, by his inexplicable, irrational concern for the sheep that Petrus intends to slaughter: "A bond seems to have come into existence between himself and the two Persians, he does not know how. . . . Nevertheless, suddenly and without reason, their lot has become important to him" (*DG*, 126). The simple grammatical fact that "A bond," rather than Lurie or the Persians, is the agent in the first of these sentences indicates that Lurie's sense of responsibility for the sheep is not a willed action.[15] His concern arises from an ecstatic surrender of self and therefore of the ability to choose. To the extent that he does, he changes despite himself.

It is in Elizabeth Costello's following words in *The Lives of Animals*, though, that one finds Coetzee's clearest articulation of an epistemological responsiveness to other creatures that is grounded in the fullness of corporeal being, and from which notions of power are conspicuously absent:

"Cogito ergo sum," he [René Descartes] also famously said. It is a formula I have always been uncomfortable with. It implies that a living being that does not do what we call thinking is somehow second-class. To thinking, cogitation, I oppose fullness, embodiedness, the sensation of being — not a consciousness of yourself as a kind of ghostly reasoning machine thinking thoughts, but on the contrary the sensation — a heavily affective sensation — of being a body with limbs that have extension in space, of being alive to the world. This fullness contrasts starkly with Descartes' key state, which has an empty feel to it: the feel of a pea rattling around in a shell. (*LA*, 33)

From Coetzee's argument against the extermination of nonhuman animals in a brief piece read on his behalf at the opening of an exhibition entitled *Voiceless: I Feel Therefore I Am*,[16] we can safely say that he shares Costello's sentiments. Like his character, he locates respect for the other being in a sentient, affective knowledge that offers an alternative to rational knowledge. The corollary of an embodied knowledge of the individual other being is, of course, a corporeal obligation to it. If one relates sensibly to another existent, one becomes obliged to it — that is, one loses the control, power, and freedom to be indifferent that comes with rational autonomy.

What one finds in these two novels, then, is a rearticulation and rendering explicit, rather than development, of concerns first broached in *Waiting for the Barbarians* in the Magistrate's inspiration by the suffering body — an inspiration that precipitates a form of ethical action that is not centered in rational subjectivity.

Notes

[1] Albert Memmi, *The Coloniser and the Colonised* (London: Souvenir, 1974), 38–39.

[2] J. M. Coetzee, "Confession and Double Thoughts: Tolstoy, Rousseau, Dostoevsky" (*DP*, 251–93).

[3] See Theodor Adorno, *Minima Moralia: Reflections from Damaged Life*, trans. E. F. N. Jephcott (London: Verso, 1978).

[4] Josephine Donovan, "'Miracles of Creation': Animals in J. M. Coetzee's Work," *Michigan Quarterly Review* 43, no. 1 (2004): 78–93, http://name.umdl.umich.edu/act2080.0043.112 (accessed 8 June 2008).

[5] James Phelan, "Present Tense Narration, Mimesis, the Narrative Norm, and the Positioning of the Reader in *Waiting for the Barbarians*," in *Understanding Narrative*, ed. James Phelan and Peter J. Rabinowitz (Columbus: Ohio UP, 1994), 234.

[6] Anne Waldron Neumann, "Escaping the 'Time of History'? Present Tense and the Occasion of Narration in J. M. Coetzee's *Waiting for the Barbarians*," *Journal*

of Narrative Technique 20, no. 1 (1990): 67; see also Ene-Reet Soovik, "Prisoners of the Present: Tense and Agency in J. M. Coetzee's *Waiting for the Barbarians* and M. Atwood's *The Handmaid's Tale*," *Interlitteraria* 8 (2003): 259–75.

[7] Jennifer Wenzel, "Keys to the Labyrinth: Writing, Torture, and Coetzee's Barbarian Girl," *Tulsa Studies in Women's Literature* 15, no. 1 (1996): 65.

[8] Laura Wright, *Writing "Out of All the Camps": J. M. Coetzee's Narratives of Displacement* (New York: Routledge, 2006), 80.

[9] Wright, *Writing "Out of All the Camps,"* 82.

[10] John Berger, "The Hour of Poetry," in *Selected Essays: John Berger*, ed. Geoff Dyer (New York: Vintage, 2001), 446–47.

[11] Derek Attridge, *J. M. Coetzee and the Ethics of Reading: Literature in the Event* (Chicago: U of Chicago P, 2005), 44.

[12] See Sam Durrant, *Postcolonial Narrative and the Work of Mourning: J. M. Coetzee, Wilson Harris, and Toni Morrison* (Albany: State U of New York P, 2004), 44.

[13] See Soovik, "Prisoners of the Present," 263.

[14] Michael Valdez Moses, "The Mark of Empire: Writing, History, and Torture in Coetzee's *Waiting for the Barbarians*," *Kenyon Review* 15, no. 1 (1993): 123.

[15] See J. M. Coetzee's discussion of such syntactical constructions in "The Agentless Sentence as Rhetorical Device" (*DP*, 170–80).

[16] J. M. Coetzee, "A Word from J. M. Coetzee" (opening address for *Voiceless: I Feel Therefore I Am*, an exhibition by *Voiceless: The Animal Protection Institute*, 22 Feb. 2007, Sherman Galleries, Sydney, Australia), 26 April 2010 http://www.voiceless.org.au/About_Us/Misc/A_word_from_J._M._Coetzee__Voiceless_I_feel_therefore_I_am.html.

6: *Life & Times of Michael K* (1983)

Engelhard Weigl

J. M. Coetzee's fourth novel, *Life & Times of Michael* K, is in many ways a distinctive work in his early fiction. Not only is it set in an exact geographical location in South Africa, but it also represents a specific reaction to dramatically escalating political developments in that country in the 1970s and 1980s, developments that signaled an approaching apocalypse to many white intellectuals. Apart from approximating fairly closely the political situation in South Africa at the time, Coetzee's novel also engages directly with the work of Franz Kafka. The name of the hero of this fictional biography makes this clear by gesturing toward the protagonists of two of Kafka's novels, Josef K. in *The Trial* and K. in *The Castle*. Coetzee's familiarity with Kafka's work is evident from his essays. "Translating Kafka" (*SS*, 88–103), for instance, presents a detailed examination of a translation of *The Castle*; his 1981 essay "Time, Tense, and Aspect in Kafka's 'The Burrow'" (*DP*, 210–32) is focused on Kafka's use of language. Coetzee has not denied the close relationship of his novel with Kafka's work, but he has never been very specific about it, either. In one interview he said:

> You ask about the impact of Kafka on my own fiction. I acknowledge it, and acknowledge it with what I hope is proper humility. As a writer I am not worthy to loose the latchet of Kafka's shoe. But I have no regrets about the use of the letter K in Michael K, hubris though it may seem. There is no monopoly on the letter K; or, to put it in another way, it is as much possible to center the universe on the town of Prince Albert in the Cape Province as on Prague. (*DP*, 199)

There is no doubting Coetzee's deep respect for Kafka. Writing as a linguist, he demonstrates this in his analysis of time in the short story "The Burrow," and in his introduction to the German translation of Kafka's essays he comments: "Franz Kafka is a writer of enigmatic power, whose texts I read with reverent admiration but also with an attentive ear for his language. The more carefully I read the short story 'The Burrow,' first in the English translation, then in the original, the more captivated I became by its use of time."[1]

In the essay itself, he states that he is "concerned to explore the relations between the verb-system of German (which . . . is very close to the verb-system of English), the narrative (and narratorial) structure of 'The Burrow,' and the conception of time we can postulate Kafka held in 1923" (*DP*, 211). These concerns are manifest in *Life & Times of Michael K*.

There are other notable connections between Coetzee's novel and the novels and stories of Franz Kafka. Like Josef K. and most of Kafka's heroes, Michael K is a loner. Coetzee's novel begins at a critical moment in Michael K's thirty-one-year old life when his sick mother turns to him for help; in *The Trial* Josef K. is executed on the eve of his thirty-first birthday. Michael K's journey into inner South Africa echoes the dialectic of home country (*Heimat*) and the foreign (*die Fremde*) that first found expression in the classical *Bildungsroman* (or novel of education) in the German literary tradition of the early nineteenth-century and is also taken up as a theme in Kafka's three novels. The theme of foreignness, indeed, is prevalent throughout Kafka's works, just as it is prominent in Coetzee's novel. In *The Trial*, Josef K. not only feels alien in his own country; the law — whatever that comes to mean for him — has also cast him out into foreignness. In *The Castle* it is precisely the other way round: K., a surveyor and foreigner in another country, seeks to domesticate the foreign through his surveying of foreign soil. In *Life & Times of Michael K*, the foreign, one could say, has already been surveyed, yet it remains deeply alien for Michael K and is certainly utterly resistant to domestication.

I will begin my discussion of the *Life & Times of Michael K* by sketching briefly the socio-political background of the novel, especially the political developments in South Africa in the late 1970s and first half of the 1980s. Reconstructing the key events of the story, I then analyze the novel's references to the work of Kafka, in particular his short stories "The Burrow" and "A Hunger-Artist." These stories serve as background to *Life & Times of Michael K* and provide key signposts for understanding the novel. Finally, I attempt to show how intertextual references to the work of Kafka indicate the influence of Gnostic and other dimensions of religious thought on Coetzee's thinking. Coetzee's novel, indeed, is directly suggestive of the Gnostic worldview according to which life is lived in isolation in an enclosed world.[2]

"In the middle of the 80s," Coetzee observes retrospectively, "South Africans lived through a time of despair: the government of P. W. Botha seemed to have subscribed to a politics of repression within and a militaristic politics of 'adventurism' without. The spirit of that epoch is mirrored in my speech."[3] Coetzee is referring here to his 1987 Jerusalem Prize Acceptance Speech, in which he attempted to describe the conditions for writing in South Africa under apartheid.

The deformed and stunted relations between human beings that were created under colonialism and exacerbated under what is loosely called apartheid have their psychic representation in a deformed and stunted inner life. All expressions of that inner life, no matter how intense, no matter how pierced with exultation or despair, suffer from the same stuntedness and deformity. I make this observation with due deliberation, and in the fullest awareness that it applies to myself and my own writing as much as to anyone else. South African literature is a literature in bondage, as it reveals in even its highest moments, shot through as they are with feelings of homelessness and yearnings for a nameless liberation. It is a less than fully human literature, unnaturally preoccupied with power and the torsions of power, unable to move from elementary relations of contestation, domination, and subjugation to the vast and complex human world that lies beyond them. It is exactly the kind of literature you would expect people to write from prison. And I am talking here not only about the South African *gulag*. As you would expect in so physically vast a country, there is a South African literature of vastness. Yet even that literature of vastness, examined closely, reflects feelings of entrapment, entrapment in infinitudes. . . . How we long to quit a world of pathological attachment and abstract forces, of anger and violence, and take up residence in a world where a living play of feelings and ideas is possible, a world where we truly have an occupation. . . . We have art, said Nietzsche, so that we shall not die of the truth. In South Africa there is now too much truth for art to hold, truth by the bucketful, truth that overwhelms and swamps every act of imagination. (*DP*, 98–99)

Susan VanZanten Gallagher provides further information about the socio-historical changes to which Coetzee so vividly responds in *Life & Times of Michael K*.[4] At the end of the 1970s, she notes, violence between the government and the oppressed majority continued to increase. Following the brutal suppression of the Soweto uprising by police, violence escalated still further. Many blacks were radicalized as a result of this, and perhaps also because of the brutal treatment of those in detention (see SSA, 137). Those young insurgents who were forced to flee gathered in guerrilla training camps in neighboring countries, and guerrilla warfare became the greatest threat to the South African government.[5] Neighboring states were accused of harboring guerrilla fighters. South African society consequently became militarized, and compulsory military service for the white population was introduced in 1978.[6] A feeling that the end was near spread among the white population who began to leave South Africa in large numbers, abandoning vast farms in the north in the process.

The novel begins by narrating the circumstances of Michael K's entry into the world. The novel's first words tell of Michael K's physical imperfection, the stigma he will bear throughout his life. His class, social status, and even the color of his skin play a role in the sufferings he will endure, but these are minor compared with the physical deformity that will bring about his isolation from others. The midwife attempts to lighten the mother's shock at her child's appearance: "You should be happy," she tells her about children with harelips, "they bring luck to the household" (MK, 3). But these soothing words fall on deaf ears; the mother feels only shame on account of her disfigured child and her first instinct is to reject him. As the child grows older, her mother restricts his interactions with other children, deepening his stigmatization still further. "Year after year Michael K sat on a blanket watching his mother polish other people's floors, learning to be quiet" (MK, 3–4). Social isolation hinders the development of speech and intellect in a child who has learnt to be silent from the first moments of his life.

Erving Goffman's study of stigma provides useful points of reference in this context. Michael K is marked by all three categories of stigma identified by Goffman: in addition to physical deformity and a speech impediment, he is also bears "the tribal stigma of race."[7] He thus conforms to a certain stereotype: "an individual who might have been received easily in ordinary social intercourse possesses a trait that can obtrude itself upon attention and turn those of us whom he meets away from him, breaking the claim that his other attributes have on us. He possesses a stigma, an undesired differentness from what we had anticipated" (NM, 15). Goffman goes on to note that *stigma* means both "brand" and "wound" in Greek:

> The Greeks, who were apparently strong on visual aids, originated the term *stigma* to refer to bodily signs designed to expose something unusual and bad about the moral status of the signifier. The signs were cut or burnt into the body and advertised that the bearer was a slave, a criminal, or a traitor — a blemished person, ritually polluted, to be avoided, especially in public places. Later, in Christian times, two layers of metaphor were added to the term — the first referred to bodily signs of holy grace that took the form of eruptive blossoms on the skin; the second, a medical allusion to this religious allusion, referred to bodily signs of physical disorder. (NM, 11)

I will follow up the question of religious allusions in *Life & Times of Michael K* later in this chapter.

Because of the stigmata, Michael K is put in a special school for handicapped children where he is to be prepared for a future of manual labor and, inevitably, silence. This first and most deeply traumatizing of the "total institutions" (a term coined by Goffman) experienced by Michael K not only employs humiliating teaching methods but also takes away its students' privacy. In such an institution, the only way to grow a measure of self-esteem and autonomy is to escape to a secret hiding place. This Michael K does in order to be able to think for himself: "The problem that had exercised him years ago behind the bicycle shed at Huis Norenius, namely why he had been brought into the world, had received its answer: he had been brought into the world to look after his mother" (*MK*, 7).

This is a key moment in the story, for it provides insight into Michael K's character and motivation. From early on, Michael K knows he will commit his life to the care of his mother; he will do so as soon as she declares a need for him.

After leaving school at fifteen, Michael K finds work as a gardener and later, after a break, becomes a night attendant at the public lavatories on Greenmarket Square. After a mugging, he returns to his previous job. Without women friends "because of his face," Michael K develops singular habits: he prefers his own company and the trees in the park to the blinding fluorescent lights of the public toilets. The uneventful routine he follows until his thirty-first year is eventually disrupted when his aging mother expresses a desire to return to the farm where she spent her childhood.[8] Unable to obtain the necessary documentation, Michael K leaves the Cape Peninsula police area without identity papers, pushing his mother in a wheelbarrow he has carefully modified for her comfort. On the journey out of the city, he then experiences the full force of the state's control. For Dominic Head, these experiences even constitute the main focus of the story: "[We may] read the story of Michael K as a story about the control of social space, and . . . note that this was another key facet of apartheid's systematic rule."[9]

After the death of his mother, Michael K continues his journey away from civilization; each mile he traverses gives him a growing sense of freedom and independence. Police controls, roadblocks, troop movements, and curfews punctuate his journey. For the first time in his life, he has to think for himself and, by instinct as much as accident, finds a way through. In this time of civil unrest, he is nevertheless robbed by a soldier and later summarily interned in a labor camp. Yet, as Susan Gallagher notes, "rather than focusing on the [detail of the] political or military struggle, Coetzee concentrates on the institutional violence of South Africa. One of the great strengths of *Life & Times of Michael K* is its ability to depict this kind of war, the war of the bureaucracy against the individual" (SSA, 146).

Roads, like arteries of power, make visible the control of the state. By abandoning the roads, Michael K gradually slips away from state control and slowly loses his fear. Jumping fences and thus overcoming metaphorical borders brings him closer to his destination. For the first time in his life he senses the prospect — dim though it may be — of happiness:

Having once crossed the fence into the veld, he found it more restful to walk across the country. . . . From horizon to horizon the landscape was empty. He climbed a hill and lay on his back listening to the silence, feeling the warmth of the sun soak into his bones. . . . I could live here forever, he thought, or till I die. Nothing would happen, every day would be the same as the day before, there would be nothing to say. The anxiety that belonged to the time on the road began to leave him. Sometimes, as he walked, he did not know whether he was awake or asleep. He could understand that people should have retreated here and fenced themselves in with miles and miles of silence; he could understand that they should have wanted to bequeath the privilege of so much silence to their children and grandchildren in perpetuity (though by what right he was not sure); he wondered whether there were not forgotten corners and angles and corridors between the fences, land that belonged to no one yet. Perhaps if one flew high enough, he thought, one would be able to see. (*MK*, 46–47)

With his mother's ashes tucked under his arm, Michael K finds the farm he believes to be that of his mother's childhood in the vicinity of Prince Albert. The abandoned farm of the Visagies gives him the prospect of reclaiming land, yet he embarks on this land reclamation not with political or even economic reasons in mind. Rather, it is a mythical project that he follows — a project he shares with many others in the new South Africa that is soon to emerge from civil war. With its connotations of home and earth, this is a project, moreover, that is associated with the mother rather than the father (it is instructive to note for the purposes of comparison that the world of the father for Kafka is identified with bureaucratic institutions):[10]

My mother was the one whose ashes I brought back, he thought, and my father was the list of rules on the door of the dormitory, the twenty-one rules of which the first was 'There will be silence in dormitories at all times,' and the woodwork teacher with the missing fingers who twisted my ear when the line was not straight. . . . They were my father, and my mother is buried and not yet risen. That is why it is a good thing that I, who have nothing to pass on, should be spending my time here where I am out of the way. (*MK*, 104)

Michael K's mother also plays an important role in his dietary conversion. Two nights before she dies, he has a dream: "his mother came visiting him in Huis Norenius, bringing a parcel of food. 'The cart is too slow,' she said in the dream — 'Prince Albert is coming to fetch me.' The parcel was curiously light" (*MK*, 28–29). At this moment, eating begins to take on a spiritual significance for Michael K; at any rate it is now associated with his mother's ashes and with the new life he must now create for himself. As the spiritual dimension grows in him, everyday reality, including normal eating, becomes increasingly alien to him: "It seemed strange to him that children should be riding their bicycles home from school in the afternoons, ringing their bells, racing one another; it seemed strange that people should be eating and drinking as usual" (*MK*, 33). For the first time on his journey he realizes that he has a capacity to endure hunger for long periods. "He had not eaten for two days; however, there seemed no limit to his endurance" (*MK*, 35).

The stay on the farm instills a kind of learning regime into Michael K, but it is only immediate experience that can tutor him. His hunger forces him to hunt a wild goat: "He had sat down and was idly tying his shoe-laces before it came home to him that these snorting long-haired beasts, or creatures like them, would have to be caught, killed, cut up and eaten if he hoped to live" (*MK*, 52). Yet the hunting, killing, and slaughtering of the goat terrifies him so much that he soon forgets about his hunger: "The urgency of the hunger that had possessed him yesterday was gone" (*MK*, 55). The quick decay of the meat teaches him his first lesson: "The lesson, if there was a lesson, if there were lessons embedded in events, seemed to be not to kill such large animals" (*MK*, 57). Michael K uses abandoned objects on the farm to build his new life outside civilization. He makes a slingshot with which to shoot birds. After bathing and washing his clothes he suddenly remembers why he had come to the farm in the first place. It overcomes him like a religious awakening: "The time came to return his mother to the earth" (*MK*, 58). He clears a small patch of field, sprinkles his mother's ashes on the dirt, and ploughs the earth "spadeful by spadeful. This was the beginning of his life as a cultivator. . . . Then he planted a small patch of pumpkins and a small patch of mealies" (*MK*, 59). Michael K not only fulfills the wish of his mother, but he also finds a vocation and a home:

> In a matter of weeks, he found his waking life bound tightly to the patch of earth he had begun to cultivate and the seeds he had planted there. There were times, particularly in the morning, when a fit of exultation would pass through him at the thought that he, alone and unknown, was making this deserted farm bloom. (*MK*, 59)

Joy and newfound happiness — yet a happiness tinged with unreality — periodically flood in on him. He learns to use his resources carefully and regulates his consumption of water, for he "knew it was bad to be prodigal" (*MK*, 60). He lives according to an archaic rhythm and believes himself at a remove from the war that is tearing the country apart. The periphery nevertheless does intervene: the war breaks in silently and suddenly, in the form of a deserter, a figure from the colonial past. It is Visagie's grandson. A reference to eating — the habits of eating of the civilized life that Michael K has rejected — is a reminder of a now forgotten colonial existence: "'Our family used to spend every Christmas here,' [the grandson] said. 'Family would keep coming till the house was bursting at the seams. I've never seen such eating as we used to do'" (*MK*, 61).

Michael K escapes into the mountains to avoid becoming Visagie's grandson's "body-servant" (*MK*, 65). It is another critical moment in his life. He invents a new identity for himself, becoming, in imitation of Kafka's short story of the same title, a veritable "hunger-artist."[11] The mourning for his plants, which through his flight he sentences to death, becomes a longing to melt into his mother's land, to be part of the earth:

> He thought of the pumpkin leaves pushing through the earth. Tomorrow will be their last day, he thought: the day after that they will wilt, and the day after that they will die, while I am out here in the mountains. . . . There was a cord of tenderness that stretched from him to the patch of earth beside the dam and must be cut. It seems to him that one could cut a cord like that only so many times before it would not grow again. . . . He felt hungry but did nothing about it. Instead of listening to the crying of his body he tried to listen to the great silence about him. (*MK*, 65–66)

His love is focused not on the possibility of lush growth, but on the dry yellow-and-red soil. At this moment he experiences a kind of rebirth: "I am becoming a different kind of man, he thought, if there are two kinds of man. . . . I am becoming smaller and harder and drier every day" (*MK*, 67). Having lived one lifetime within the order imposed by the father — the order of the law — Michael K now becomes a child of the earth. Whereas Kafka's protagonist experiences hunger periodically as an intoxication, a lightening deliverance of the body from itself, Michael K experiences it as a rapture of the self-devouring body, as a new way of eating. This form of eating does not depend on the family or on colonial rules of eating. Michael K echoes here an insight of Kafka's hunger-artist: "He alone knew — and none of the cognoscenti knew this — how easy it was to starve. It was the easiest thing in the world" (HA, 254). To Michael K, hunger is a kind of emptying. The beast that ruled him at Huis Norenius "was starved into stillness. . . . Now, in front of his cave, he sometimes locked his fingers behind his head, closed his eyes, and emptied his mind, wanting nothing, looking forward to nothing" (*MK*, 68–69).

Nevertheless, as with Kafka's hunger-artist, it is pressure from state institutions that enjoins Michael K to resume eating. In the beginning his resistance is weak. After his retreat into the mountains, he is picked up by the police and, "almost extinguished with debility" (HA, 258), admitted to hospital. Michael K there yields to the threatening behavior of men and the caring attention of the women just as the hunger-artist yielded to the butchers and the impresario/manager. The ritual of forcing the artist to end his hunger is celebrated:

So then on the fortieth day the door of the flower-garlanded cage was thrown open, an excited audience filled the amphitheatre, a brass band played, two doctors entered the cage to perform the necessary tests on the hunger-artist, the results were relayed to the hall by means of a megaphone, and finally two young ladies, thrilled to have been chosen for the task, came to lead the hunger-artist down a couple of steps to where a small table had been laid with a carefully assembled invalid meal. (HA, 255)

Michael K experiences it in the following way:

Once when he awoke there were a nurse and a policeman in the doorway looking in his direction, murmuring together. . . . It was the first hunger he had known for a long time. He was not sure that he wanted to become a servant to hunger again; but a hospital, it seemed, was a place for bodies, where bodies asserted their rights. (*MK*, 71)

In the "resettlement camp" of Jakkalsdrif where he revisits the traumatic experiences of his childhood, children provide the stimulus for the resumption of Michael K's eating: he eats the children's leftovers given to him by the "Vrouevereniging ladies" (*MK*, 84), the charitable women's association. He plays with the children and so discovers a new connection with the earth: "They clambered over him and fell upon him as if he were part of the earth" (*MK*, 84).

The main difference between Kafka's "A Hunger-Artist" and Michael K is that, at short intervals in his life, Michael K was able to find the food he was longing for. Kafka's hunger-artist, by contrast, starves to death because, as he says, "I couldn't find any food I liked. If I had found any, believe me, I wouldn't have made any fuss, and I would have eaten to my heart's content, just like you or anyone else" (HA, 262). After his escape from the resettlement camp, Michael K gets a second chance as a gardener on the Visagie farm. He returns to the farm, but with the distinct purpose of living there in his own way; he does not want to found his own line in order to claim the land in perpetuity, viewing the land as a mere object: "Because whatever I have returned for, it is not to live as the Visagies lived, sleep where they slept, sit on their stoep looking out over their land" (*MK*, 98).

The description of Michael K's second stay on the farm, the climax of the novel, appears to draw on another short story by Kafka, "The Burrow," which Coetzee had studied closely and written about in 1981. Michael K thinks that he can survive on the farm only as an animal, invisible, hidden underground:

I want to live here, he thought: I want to live here forever, where my mother and my grandmother lived. It is as simple as that. What a pity that to live in times like these a man must be ready to live like a beast. A man who wants to live cannot live in a house with lights in the windows. He must live in a hole and hide by day. A man must live so that he leaves no trace of his living. That is what it has come to. (*MK*, 99)

Between "two low hills, like plump breasts," Michael K digs his "cave or burrow five feet deep" (*MK*, 100). Like Kafka's animal, he is besieged by a fear of being discovered and takes further precautions. At the same time, he is forced to protect his plants against wild animals, which proves to be an almost hopeless struggle. He treats his pumpkins and melons as his own children, for whose life and care he turns the night into his day. "Yet there were times when his fears seemed absurd, spells of clarity in which he would recognize that, cut off from human society, he was in danger of becoming more timorous than a mouse" (*MK*, 105).

The experience of time on the farm as an island outside the war echoes the time references in "The Burrow." Coetzee's analysis of the aspect of time in Kafka's short story is clearly suggestive of Michael K's experience of time:

> The state in which Kafka's creature lives is one of acute anxiety (one would call it irrational anxiety if there were any reliable opposition between rational and irrational in his universe). His whole life is organized around the burrow, his refuge against an attack that may come at any moment and without warning. The key notion here is *without warning*. A warning is the sign of a transition from peace to its opposite. . . . In "The Burrow," however, time does not move through transition phases. There is one moment and then there is another moment; between them is simply a break. No amount of watchfulness will reveal how one moment becomes another; all we know is that the next moment happens. (*DP*, 227)

Experiencing time in this way, Michael K has no reliable capacity to recognize his enemies. While he sees the guerrilla fighters and is able to hide from them, Visagie's grandson, the police, and the soldiers are suddenly upon him. While he appreciates a threat to his person once that threat has arrived, he is unable to defend himself in any way: "He heard the drone of the vehicles when they were far off but thought it was distant thunder" (*MK*, 120). Coetzee notes of Kafka's descriptions of time in the burrow:

> Time is thus at every moment a time of *crisis* (from Greek *krino*, "to separate, to divide"). Life consists in an attempt to anticipate a danger that cannot be anticipated because it comes without transition, without warning. The experience of a time of crisis is colored by anxiety. The task of building the burrow itself represents a life

devoted to trying to still anxiety, naturally without success; for without warning "the enemy" is in the burrow. (*DP*, 228)

Coetzee identifies two distinct concepts of time:

> The first, which we can call historical awareness, imputes reality to a past that it sees as continuous with the present. The second, which we can call eschatological, recognizes no such continuity: there is only the present, which is always present, separated from Ingarden's "dead past" by a moment of rupture, the *entscheidende Augenblick*. Hence the paradox that history is over in "a second," while the present moment is "everlasting." (*DP*, 231)

Coetzee's literary project in *Life & Times of Michael K* is distinctive precisely on account of these references to, and this deployment of, Kafka's metaphysics of time. However, there are also differences. Kafka's protagonists are denied the ecstatic moments of intense happiness that Michael K experiences. Michael K's "incredible bliss" while eating his pumpkin sooner calls to mind Proust's *plaisir délicieux* in his famous madeleine passage in *À la recherche du temps perdu*. As with Proust's protagonist, the entry into the past that these moments make possible is deeply significant, reanimating the past life of his ancestors for whom idleness and labor could happily coexist and idleness was not a sin.[12] It is at this moment that he feels most himself:

> But most of all, as summer slanted to an end, he was learning to love idleness, idleness no longer as stretches of freedom reclaimed by stealth here and there from involuntary labour, surreptitious thefts to be enjoyed sitting on his heels before a flowerbed with the fork dangling from his fingers, but as a yielding up of himself to time, to a time flowing slowly like oil from horizon to horizon over the face of the world, washing over his body. . . . He was neither pleased nor displeased when there was work to do; it was all the same. He could lie all afternoon with his eyes open, staring at the corrugations in the roof-iron and the tracings of rust; his mind would not wander, . . . he was himself, lying in his own house, the rust was merely rust, all that was moving was time, bearing him onward in its flow. Once or twice the other time in which the war had its existence reminded itself to him as the jet fighters whistled high overhead. (*MK*, 115–16)

In the second part of the novel, the narrative changes and the story is told from the perspective of the medical officer who takes care of Michael K in the rehabilitation camp. The medical officer's deep preoccupation with questions about Michael K's identity gives the novel a new direction. The answers he finds to these questions, however, remain limited to the purview of the character; they do not — unlike the first part of the novel — allow (an albeit limited) access to Michael K's direct experiences. The difficulties are further magnified because Michael K is not able to give a proper account of himself.[13] While able to express wishes and ask questions, he is unable to give his life-story narrative coherence, he is unable to tell his own story: "Always, when he tried to explain himself to himself, there remained a gap, a hole, a darkness before which his understanding baulked, into which it was useless to pour words. The words were eaten up, the gap remained" (*MK*, 110).

The medical officer tries again and again to fill in the gaps and holes surrounding Michael K, to provide a narrative where Michael K himself is unable to do so. Obsessed with Michael's silence, the medical officer invents explanations and stories, hoping for a simple confirmation, but none is forthcoming.

Do these attempts at interpretation mirror those of the reader, who might equally fail to guess at Michael K's real identity? Gallagher offers the following observation: "our dissatisfaction with the officer's interpretation of Michael demonstrates the inadequacy of turning human flesh and blood into abstract intellectual meaning. The medical officer's philosophizing overinscribes Michael and robs him of his human mystery" (SSA, 165). Coetzee, then, overtaxes the realism of the novel but, in doing so, allows a new purpose to come into view. This is the attempt in the second part of the novel to construct a kind of metanarrative — a metanarrative whose interweaving with Kafka's texts deepens the novel's contact with Gnostic and other mystical traditions of thought, traditions in which Kafka's writing was clearly embedded. These parallels appear to have the aim of conferring on the suffering of the main character a pronounced spiritual dimension.

The hunger-artist, for example, with his public appearances at fairs or in the circus, appears in a religious tradition of ritualistic starving. Fasting was exhibited as a form of God's miracle and was closely connected with the Eucharist: bread transformed into the body of God, the host, floating down from heaven was the performer's sole sustenance. Acts of this kind were thus performed in *imitatio Christi*, who fasted forty days in the desert.[14] Kafka's hunger-artist also fasts forty days. Other works of Kafka indicate his interest in this mystical and religious tradition: K. in *The Castle* states his occupation as "surveyor," which in Hebrew sounds close to the word for "messiah." That a messianic dimension can also be found in Coetzee's novel becomes apparent when the medical officer imagines his conversation with Michael K after Michael K's escape from the camp:

> Michaels, forgive me for the way I treated you, I did not appreciate who you were till the last days. . . . Yet I am convinced there are areas that lie between the camps and belong to no camp, not even to the catchment areas of the camps. . . . I am looking for such a place

in order to settle there, perhaps only till things improve, perhaps
forever. I am not so foolish, however, as to imagine that I can rely on
maps and roads to guide me. Therefore I have chosen you to show
me the way. (*MK*, 162–63)

In the face of the impending apocalypse, there is a growing hope that the
grain of sand Michael K has moved is able to change the country:

Let me tell you the meaning of the sacred and alluring garden that
blooms in the heart of the desert and produces the food of life. The
garden for which you are presently heading is nowhere and everywhere except in the camps. It is another name for the only place
where you belong, Michaels, where you do not feel homeless. It is
off every map, no road leads to it that is merely a road, and only you
know the way. (*MK*, 166)

We are near a conclusion. In his long essay on Kafka, Walter Benjamin
compares Kafka's figures — figures who are burdened with some unspecified guilt — with that epitome of disfigurement, the "little hunchback" of
the old folk song. "This little man is at home in his distorted life; he will
disappear with the coming of the Messiah, who (a great rabbi once said)
will not wish to change the world by force but will merely make a slight
adjustment to it."[15] In the closing lines of the *Life & Times of Michael K*,
Coetzee searches for an image to suggest how the messiah might appear,
since as Benjamin points out, no direct messianic happening can be countenanced. Michael dreams of returning to the country accompanied by
an older father figure, sowing new crops and then sharing with him the
fruits of his labor. In such an atmosphere of spiritual awareness about
the ends of human life — an awareness that arises from the conscious
dialogue with the fiction of Franz Kafka we have been examining — the
novel concludes by conjuring a vision of community and hope. The old
man looks at the pump that the soldiers have blown up and asks: "What
are we going to do about water?" Michael K, in an image that calls to
mind his being fed as a baby at the novel's beginning, gives this answer:
"He would clear the rubble from the mouth of the shaft, he would bend
the handle of the teaspoon in a loop and tie the string to it, he would
lower it down the shaft deep into the earth, and when he brought it up
there would be water in the bowl of the spoon; and in that way, he would
say, one can live" (*MK*, 184).

Notes

[1] J. M. Coetzee, "Vorwort," in *Was ist ein Klassiker? Essays*, trans. Reinhild
Böhnke (Frankfurt on Main: S. Fischer, 2006), 8.

² According to the Gnostic worldview, both the cosmos and the human body are viewed as a kind of entrapment. Not only does the immeasurability of space make the journey home from foreign parts (specifically, the return of the Jews of the Old Testament who suffered under foreign domination) seem endless, but all exits from the cosmos are cut off because the cosmos has the shape of a sphere. That shape, seen by the Greeks as a representation of the perfection of the world, is now a barrier against the realm of light; the world turns into a frightening dungeon (see Hans Jonas, *Gnosis und spätantiker Geist* [Göttingen: Vandenhoeck, 1934], 163).

³ J. M. Coetzee, "Vorwort," in *Was ist ein Klassiker? Essays*, 7 (author's translation).

⁴ Susan VanZanten Gallagher, *A Story of South Africa: J. M. Coetzee's Fiction in Context* (Cambridge, MA: Harvard UP, 1991). Subsequent references appear as SSA with the accompanying page number.

⁵ Gallagher notes of these events: "More frequent guerrilla attacks and sabotage conducted by black nationalist groups set the entire country on edge. From 1977 to 1982, bombings by underground liberation movements caused damage estimated at \$635 million" (SSA, 137).

⁶ Gallagher notes how political discourse in South Africa at the time "became increasingly concerned with war, revolution, and apocalypse. The end of modern South African society as the whites knew it seemed close at hand. Military planning and budgeting, a steady increase in the length of required military duty, and the reports of the nightly news all suggested that South Africa had reached a breaking point. The prediction of terrorist war made by the *Rand Daily Mail* echoed almost every Afrikaners' deepest fear. During the time he spent living in South Africa, the anthropologist Vincent Crapanzano noted "the constant talk of change, of imminent bloodbath, of takeover and revolution." The South African people, he concludes, are "caught in a deadened time of waiting," most whites in fear, most blacks in hope" (SSA, 140).

⁷ See Erving Goffman, *Stigma: Notes of the Management of Spoiled Identity* (Great Britain: Penguin, 1981), 14. Subsequent references appear as *NM* with the accompanying page number. Michael K is listed by the police as: "Michael Visagie-CM-40-NFM-Unemployed"; CM stands for colored male (*MK*, 70).

⁸ As Gallagher observes: "Against the backdrop of civil war, Michael embarks upon a quixotic mission to bring his mother back to the Karoo farm where she spent an idyllically remembered childhood" (SSA, 140).

⁹ Dominic Head: *The Cambridge Introduction to J. M. Coetzee* (New York: Cambridge UP, 2009), 58.

¹⁰ See, for example, Walter Benjamin, *Selected Writings, vol. 2 1927–1934*, ed. Michael W. Jennings et al., trans. Rodney Livingstone (Cambridge, MA: The Belknap Press, Harvard UP, 1990): "There is much to indicate that the world of officials and the world of fathers are the same to Kafka" (796).

¹¹ Franz Kafka, "The Hunger-Artist," in *Metamorphosis and Other Stories*. Translated by Michael Hofmann (London: Penguin, 2007), 252–63. Subsequent references appear as HA with the accompanying page number.

¹² J. M. Coetzee, "Idleness in South Africa," in *WW*, 12–35.

[13] As Gallagher notes: "One of the most striking and revealing aspects of Michael's character, however, is his silence" (SSA, 161).

[14] Gerhard Neumann, "Hungerkünstler und Menschenfresser. Zum Verhältnis von Kunst und kulturellem Ritual im Werk Franz Kafkas," in Franz Kafka, *Schriftverkehr*, ed. Wolf Kittler and Gerhard Neumann (Freiburg: Rombach, 1990), 406.

[15] Benjamin, *Selected Writings*, 2:811.

7: *Foe* (1986)

Chris Prentice

WHEN J. M. COETZEE WAS AWARDED the Nobel Prize for Literature in 2003, his acceptance speech, entitled "He and His Man,"[1] should have come as no surprise to those familiar with his oeuvre. He had cast his autobiographical works *Boyhood: Scenes from Provincial Life*, *Youth*, and *Summertime: Scenes from Provincial Life* in the third-person voice, and had long engaged in what we may refer to as ficto-criticism.[2] *Elizabeth Costello* contains substantial sections of critical and philosophical discourse (lectures, essays), and *Diary of a Bad Year* includes a narrative "thread" of critical and philosophical commentary, while characters in such earlier novels as *Dusklands*, *Waiting for the Barbarians*, *Life & Times of Michael K*, and *The Master of Petersburg* offer sustained passages of reflection on writing, and on the politics and aesthetics of authority and authorship as these pertain to historical and literary worlds. However, "He and His Man" bears the closest relation to his 1986 novel *Foe*, where the similar ficto-critical concerns share an intertextual affiliation with Daniel Defoe's *Robinson Crusoe*.

Coetzee's ficto-critical speech is ultimately a reflection on the hybrid ontogeny of the literary work. It asks: What is a character, what is a story, and what is an author? How do reading and writing together comprise the work? What does (the report of) the world bring to art and what does art bring to the world? And does the author create character and story, or do these create the author? "He and His Man" reveals the work, and literary creativity, as the product not so much of the merging of these vital constituents but as issuing from a "middle" or hybrid "third" space between them, authority ultimately and undecidably dispersed across them in the creative act.[3]

> How are they to be figured, this man and he? As master and slave? As brothers, twin brothers? As comrades in arms? Or as enemies, foes? What name shall he give this nameless fellow with whom he shares his evenings and sometimes his nights, too, who is absent only in the daytime, when he, Robin, walks the quays inspecting the new arrivals and his man gallops about the kingdom making his inspections? (HHM, 18–19)

He and his man are not the same, but if one is master and one is slave, which is which? If they are twins, they are not identical; as comrades they move and work in different parts of the kingdom, but as enemies, they participate in the same work. Despite shared evenings and nights, they never meet "in the flesh" (HHM, 19), and "he fears there will be no meeting, not in this life" (HHM, 19). Perhaps in another, then?

The final image of literary creativity is one of contingent proximity, momentarily passing across one another's view, but each committed in a life-or-death struggle to its own journey:

> If he must settle on a likeness for the pair of them, his man and he, he would write that they are like two ships sailing in contrary directions, one west, the other east. Or better, that they are deckhands toiling in the rigging, the one on a ship sailing west, the other on a ship sailing east. Their ships pass close, close enough to hail. But the seas are rough, the weather is stormy: their eyes lashed by the spray, their hands burned by the cordage, they pass each other by, too busy even to wave. (HHM, 19)

As each grapples with his own rigging, both tossing in the same storm, this passage offers an image of politics and aesthetics, the world and art, both struggling with and propelled by the same concerns, but both pulling away towards their own distinct destinies. Perhaps the work is born at that moment where their paths cross, a moment characterized by focus and preoccupation, presence and absence. Conventionally seen as distinct and even opposed terms, author and character, world and art, substance and spirit, writing and reading, body and text, authority and subjection are among those concepts examined by both "He and His Man" and *Foe*. Each term in the opposition is open to, and opened by, mutual encounter and transformation.

With its "oblique" relation to authorship,[4] its displacement of the conventional acceptance speech into a fictionalized critical allegory, and more generally with its concern to plot and traverse a passage through questions of literary creativity, "He and His Man" reprises aspects of *Foe* that have generated much of the critical debate over that novel. First published in 1986 by Ravan Press in Johannesburg, South Africa, and by Secker & Warburg in London before being taken up by Penguin in 1987,[5] *Foe* is J. M. Coetzee's fifth novel. Broadly an interrogative reworking of Daniel Defoe's *Robinson Crusoe*, and a fictionalized account of the circumstances of that novel's making, Coetzee's slim volume belies its intertextual and metafictional complexity. *Foe*'s relation to *Robinson Crusoe* is of course immediately signaled in the title, which both cites Defoe's original surname and is a noun meaning "enemy." Naming the novel for the authorial figure rather than character, and invoking the very notion of conflict, further indicates a concern with a range of troubling questions concerning authorship and authority. However, Maureen Nicholson's early response to the novel indicates some of the critical disquiet with which *Foe* would be received:

> In his earlier remarkable novels, *Waiting for the Barbarians* (1980) and *Life & Times of Michael K* (1983), J. M. Coetzee subtly examined brutal actions in what appeared to be an allegorized South Africa. His writing in these novels was moving, convincing and frank. Coetzee seemed to understand and could represent for his readers a grasp of the workings of social injustice and its outcomes for marginalized individuals. . . . With his most recent novel, *Foe* (Stoddart, 1986), Coetzee initially appeared to me to have all but abandoned his usual concerns and literary techniques. . . . I was worried about why he had chosen *now* to write this kind of book. . . . Could he no longer sustain the courage he had demonstrated, turning instead to a radically interiorized narrative? For, in *Foe*, Coetzee has written what is for him a self-reflexive, experimental work.[6]

Nicholson goes on to argue that "the literary representation of race and personal relations, *not* intertextual relations" ("If I," 52) remains Coetzee's strength in *Foe*, and her disappointment with this novel, which she proposes is "transitional" ("If I," 58) in his oeuvre, rests with its apparent failure of courage and conviction in this representation.[7] Nevertheless, concerns of the wider critical debate may be located among the parameters of South African versus metropolitan affiliation and address, "courageous" reference versus interiorized experimentation, materialist versus textual politics.

Mike Marais observes that "during the 1980s, a perennial criticism of Coetzee's fiction was that it did not engage with the depredations of apartheid,"[8] and he cites Michael Vaughan's view that it minimizes "material factors of oppression and struggle in contemporary South Africa,"[9] and Michael Chapman's judgment that *Foe* fails to "speak to Africa."[10] Benita Parry also asks whom, in South Africa, Coetzee's novels address (SSF, 61). She acknowledges and carefully examines *Foe*'s (inter)textual politics, but remains concerned that its literary affiliations owe nothing to Coetzee's South African location, or to non-European knowledges more generally (SSF, 39). Further, she argues, his subversive textual strategies, while appealing to international readers as radical, ironically sustain his own textual power, while effectively participating in the very silencing of oppressed voices that these strategies ostensibly critique: "Coetzee's narrative strategies both enact a critique of dominant discourses and preempt dialogue with noncanonical knowledges through representing these as ineffable" (SSF, 52). However, critics who defend Coetzee's work tend to question the very foundations of many of these concerns. Attwell acknowledges that Coetzee's literary affiliations are predominantly European,[11] but maintains that his intertextual and metafictional strategies do not amount to ahistoricism (PH, 602). Rather, "metafictional and formally reflexive" discourses are "projected into the colonial narrative . . . as loci of critical objectification and reflection" (PH, 591). Thus, he argues elsewhere, the polarization of textuality and politics assumed by Coetzee's materialist critics is a false premise and — agreeing with Dovey's view that they constitute "*different* forms of historical engagement"[12] — Attwell maintains that Coetzee's novels "explore the *tension* between these polarities" (PW, 3). Nevertheless, he argues that the relationship to politics in Coetzee's work is not one of association or affirmation of its terms, but is, rather, "a refusal of association, affiliation, consensus" (PH, 587).[13]

Just as Marais finds a self-conscious problematization of "interpretative authoritarianism" in *Foe*,[14] Attwell defends Coetzee's stance against instrumentalist and particularist views of art that his detractors appear to demand. He points out that "the recognition that meaning in a novel resides in a configuration of elements that are not the same as the elements of real life . . . has cost Coetzee a great deal in terms of his relationship with other writers in South Africa and with readers whose form of politicization demands a realist documentation of life lived under oppression" (PH, 582).[15] He refers to Coetzee's belief that in times of ideological pressure, the writer is faced with a choice between "supplementarity" to history — writing as illustrative of historical discourse — and "rivalry" to history — writing that insists on the principled autonomy of art. He cites Coetzee's choice of "rivalry" that, rather than casting the novel "in a secondary relation to historical discourse," allows that it "operates in terms of its own procedures . . . perhaps going so far as . . . demythologizing history" (PH, 586).[16] Similarly, Durrant (BW; PN) and Marais (FSR) argue, by way of Adorno, that art must be wrested from the domain of politics in order to contest the brutalities of an order such as apartheid. As Durrant puts it, "Coetzee's commitment to the autonomy of his art is precisely that which ensures the political force of his novels, that his novels are only able to engage with the history of apartheid precisely by keeping their distance" (BW, 432).[17] He further argues that the novel's "silence" in regard to naming South Africa, or apartheid, marks it as a work of "inconsolable mourning" (BW, 437); unable to relate or narrate apartheid, its silence is a way of relating to history, remaining inconsolable before history (BW, 459–60). A fuller account of *Foe* itself will help contextualize these debates and their implications.

Foe comprises four sections, the first of which is set on an island and bears the closest relation to Defoe's novel, while the second and third sections are set in houses and lodgings back in England. The fourth section, in two uncanny scenes, is set in an indeterminate spatio-temporal realm that reprises not so much settings as transformative and generative spaces in the previous three sections — house, ship, and ocean. In plot terms,

Foe is the story of Susan Barton who, returning to England after two years' unsuccessful searching for her missing, possibly abducted, daughter in Bahia, has been cast off a ship by its mutinous crew. Set adrift in a rowboat along with the body of the captain, she finally gives up rowing and swims, washing ashore on an island. The only apparent inhabitants of the island are Cruso and the slave Friday, who also came ashore from a shipwreck some fifteen years earlier. Having been found and conveyed to Cruso's habitation by Friday, Susan tells Cruso her story, and the rest of the first section recounts the year Susan spends on the island waiting for rescue. A passing ship eventually brings them back to England, and Cruso dies on the return journey.

Section II begins with Susan's having found an author, Mr. Foe, to set her island story down in a book whose sales will support her and enable her to return Friday to Africa. She quickly prepares a memoir of her experience for Mr. Foe to work with — we now understand Section I as that memoir — and continues writing letters to him, reflecting on her story and her circumstances as she waits with Friday for the book to be finished. Although at a certain point a letter is returned unopened and she learns that Mr. Foe has disappeared, in hiding from debtors, she continues writing and even moves into his plundered and locked-up house where she now refers to herself as writing at Mr. Foe's bureau, with his pen and ink, on his paper. She tries various means of communicating with Friday to elicit more of his story, without success, and in the meantime is faced with the appearance of a girl who says her name is Susan Barton and who claims to be her lost daughter. Susan protests that her daughter's name is not the same as her own, and that the girl bears no physical similarity to her daughter or herself. When this "daughter" tries to substantiate her claims by revealing she knows of the island and Bahia, Susan becomes convinced Mr. Foe has sent her. Eventually she leads the girl into the forest and leaves her there, departing soon after with Friday for Bristol, where she intends to find a ship that will take him back to Africa. Section II concludes with her failure to find a trustworthy captain, and their return to London.

In Section III, Susan has found Mr. Foe in lodgings, and they debate the proper shape of her story for the book. The girl arrives at Mr. Foe's house with her childhood nurse Amy, and although Susan still refuses any maternal connection to her, they pass a pleasant enough evening before young "Susan" and Amy leave for their own lodgings nearby. Between debates with Mr. Foe over writing, authority, and the problem of Friday's silence for the completion of her story, Susan attempts to teach Friday to write, but again cannot be certain of her success. She and Mr. Foe now turn the matter of Friday's story — and silence — to questions of subjection and freedom, while unobserved, Friday slips into Mr. Foe's wig and robe and starts to write on his papers. Although his writing does not give up its meaning to them, the section concludes with an optimistic image of a beginning, the possibility of Friday's self-representation in a world at that point yet to be written.

The final short section, in two parts, begins with an unidentified narrator entering a house whose plaque above the door indicates it is the house of the author Daniel Defoe. The narrator proceeds upstairs and finds the body of a woman or girl curled up on the landing, and in a bedroom, a couple, their dead, dried bodies lying side by side in bed. In a corner alcove lies Friday stretched out on his back, and the narrator finds his skin warm, a faint pulse in his throat. He presses his ear to Friday's mouth and hears the faraway roar of the ocean, the sounds of the island. In the second part, the narrator enters the house, and finds the same bodies, but this time the man and woman in bed are lying face to face, and there is a scar around Friday's neck. He finds a crumbling manuscript whose salutation, "Dear Mr. Foe" is followed by the words with which the novel has opened: "At last I could row no further" (155). It continues to repeat the words with which Susan begins her memoir — Section I of *Foe* — now cited not as Susan's narrative but as the actions of the narrator: "With a sigh, making barely a splash, I slip overboard" (155).[18] The narrator descends to an undersea realm where a shipwreck holds the bloated bodies of Susan Barton, her dead captain, and, in another corner, Friday.[19] As Friday turns in the water, he lies face to face with the narrator and from his open mouth emerges a slow stream, and "Soft and cold, dark and unending, it beats against my eyelids, against the skin of my face" (157).

It is primarily in Section I that *Foe* invokes Defoe's *Robinson Crusoe*, but even in its echoes, Coetzee's novel marks its difference, with clear departures from the island world of Defoe's novel. While it is a "castaway" story in which a Crusoe-figure and his man Friday eke out a basic existence on an island off the coast of Bahia, Coetzee's "Cruso" is not Defoe's "Crusoe," as suggested by the different spelling. Coetzee's Cruso has little of the vigor or determined resourcefulness of Defoe's protagonist. His daily labors comprise the apparently pointless construction of massive "terraces" of cleared and banked-up earth, leveled and walled around by stones, yet barren and destined to remain so, as he has nothing to plant in them. He tells Susan, who finds it "a foolish kind of agriculture" (34), "a stupid labour" (35), that the planting "is reserved for those who come after us and have the foresight to bring seed. I only clear the ground for them. Clearing the ground and piling stones is little enough, but it is better than sitting in idleness. . . . I ask you to remember, not every man who bears the mark of the castaway is a castaway at heart" (33).[20] He shows neither inclination to leave the island, nor any interest in the world before or beyond the island; Susan remarks, "It was as though he wished his story to begin with his arrival on the island, and mine to begin with my arrival, and the story of us together to end on the island too" (34).

Foe's Friday is of African rather than Amerindian origin, and unlike the loquacious and even witty character in Defoe's novel, is mutilated and silent. Susan, who has "given Friday's life as little attention as I would have a dog's or any other dumb beast's" (32), becomes increasingly pre-occupied by his mutilation, the loss of his tongue arousing both fascina-tion and horror. The mystery of his missing tongue, his strange ritual of paddling out from the beach on a log to sprinkle petals and buds over the water, and even his flute-playing, suggest to Susan "that a spirit or soul — call it what you will — stirred beneath that dull and unpleasing exterior" (32); for her, there are depths, secrets, stories to be revealed.

However, while Cruso and Friday are "rewritten," it is the pres-ence and narrative perspective of Susan Barton that constitutes the most obvious departure from Defoe's novel. Here, Coetzee's *Foe* extends its immediate intertext to encompass Defoe's *Roxana*, whose protago-nist is named Susan Barton, as well as other works by Defoe.[21] As she questions Cruso about his experiences and memories, Susan reveals her keen awareness of the qualities of a good story — that it is "a thousand touches which today may seem of no importance" that "makes your story yours alone, that sets you apart from the old mariner by the fire-side spinning yarns of sea-monsters and mermaids" (18). A story's sin-gularity lies in detail that risks being lost with distance and the passage of time if not set down in writing.

During a serious bout of Cruso's increasingly frequent fevers, the passing merchantman ship *John* ᴴ*obart* drops anchor off the island and sends a party ashore to rescue and take them back to England. Cruso is forcibly borne aboard, having "fought so hard to be free that it took strong men to master him and convey him below" (39), while Friday is also retrieved from the island and brought reluctantly on to the ship. Virtually immediately, Susan engages in a discussion with the captain about stories and books — he suggesting she should write her story and offer it to booksellers, she confessing that she has none of the art essen-tial to a successful book. When the captain points out that booksellers will hire an author to "set your story to rights, and put in a dash of colour, too, here and there," Susan insists that she will "not have any lies told," that it must remain the truth, to which the captain replies, "There I cannot vouch for them . . . Their trade is in books, not in truth" (40). This apparent impasse between art and truth will become a motif for the rest of the novel.

If "He and His Man" is a twenty-first-century "sequel" to *Robin-son Crusoe*, set in the eighteenth century, *Foe* is a twentieth-century "prequel" to that novel that might be regarded as a fiction of literary "drafting," foregrounding questions — the politics and aesthetics — of inclusion and exclusion, shaping and framing, and of authority.[22] Susan's insistence, during their island sojourn, on telling her story and eliciting the stories of Cruso and Friday suggests — along with her concern to find an author to put their story into a book — that *Foe* is primarily concerned with questions of story, art, and writing. Indeed, the novel opens with a quotation mark, and the entire first and second sections are presented as citation. It is therefore impossible to discuss the novel in any depth without emphasizing its status as metafiction. The plot events are insepa-rable from literary concerns and broader questions of representation, while narrative dialogue and imagery point increasingly to the fundamen-tally textual world the novel presents. In Section II, Susan speculates that Foe would consider her story "Better without the woman" (72), and as against "two dull fellows on a rock in the sea who filled their time by dig-ging up stones," she observes to Friday that, "We begin to understand why Mr Foe pricked up his ears when he heard the word *Cannibal*, why he longed for Cruso to have a musket and a carpenter's chest. No doubt he would have preferred Cruso to be younger too, and his sentiments towards me more passionate" (82–83). Apart from the reference to his sentiments towards her, she thus foreshadows something closer to *Robin-son Crusoe* as it will appear from the pen of Defoe.

Although the entire novel consists of discussion, meditation, and debate about writing, the two central plot elements that present these preoccupations concern the disagreement between Susan and Foe over the proper shape of her story for the book, and the matter of Friday's silence along with Susan's and Foe's responses to it. Soon after Susan has tracked him down in the lodgings where he is hiding from debtors, Foe discloses his vision of her story as beginning with the disappearance of her daughter and Susan's search for her, within which Bahia and the island form particular episodes, followed by Susan's return to England and her daughter taking up the search for her mother: "It is thus that we make up a book: loss, then quest, then recovery; beginning, then middle, then end. As to novelty, this is lent by the island episode — which is properly the second part of the book — and by the reversal in which the daughter takes up the quest abandoned by her mother" (117).

He has begun his proposed outline, "Your daughter is abducted or elopes, I do not know which, it does not matter" (116), clearly reveal-ing his greater interest in the larger narrative pattern than in any matter of detail or referential truth. However, Susan strongly disagrees both with the reversal that has the daughter take up the quest, and with Foe's view that the island constitutes only an episode within a larger mother-daughter plot. For her, the island is the substance of the story, with the search for her daughter only the circumstance that brings it about. Against Foe's view that "The island lacks light and shade. It is too much the same throughout," she insists on the island as a story in itself, telling him that "The shadow whose lack you feel . . . is the loss of Friday's tongue" (117). Foe concedes that, in this regard, "The true story will not be heard till by art we have found a means of giving voice to Friday" (118).

Friday's silence, the *question* of his missing tongue,[23] is the motif that most clearly signals the postcolonial politics of Coetzee's novel. *Foe*'s relation to *Robinson Crusoe* may be understood as one of postcolonial canonical counter-discourse. Helen Tiffin defines this as a form of intertextual engagement in which "a post-colonial writer takes up a character or characters, or the basic assumptions of a British canonical text, and unveils these assumptions, subverting the text for postcolonial purposes . . . to investigate the European textual capture and containment of colonial and post-colonial space and to intervene in that originary and continuing containment."[24]

Such subversive intertextual revisions are often presented from the point of view of a marginal character in the canonical pre-text; however, this is not the case in *Foe*, both because Susan is not a character in *Robinson Crusoe*, and even more significantly because Friday — who would be expected to be the focalizing character of a postcolonial revision — remains silent, his point of view largely inaccessible. Yet the extension of *Foe*'s intertextuality strengthens its counter-discursivity beyond a reworking of *Robinson Crusoe* specifically towards a speculative interrogation of the conditions of that novel's production, reflecting on how story becomes writing, shaped by exclusion, redistribution, and invention. As a number of critics have remarked, *Foe* pursues larger questions of canonicity and the institutionalization of textual authority.[25] Nevertheless, Coetzee's revision of Friday focuses the more directly postcolonial concerns of the novel, and again it is the production of his silence that drives the novel's interrogation of authority.

Coetzee's silent Friday, as a postcolonial revision of the articulate Friday of *Robinson Crusoe*, constitutes a critique of the politics of literary ventriloquism whereby the European or metropolitan author throws his or her voice through the colonized or racially marked character. In other words, the speech of such a character would serve as an alibi for the silenced voice of the Other. Further, to the extent that such speech would propose a textual subjectivity for the Other, or "give the Other a voice," such an authorial alibi-figure would risk obscuring its own status as the fictional invention of the metropolitan author. Gayatri Chakravorty Spivak has commented on the problem that, "driven by a nostalgia for lost origins," postcolonial intellectuals "run the risk of stepping forward as 'the real Caliban,'" of forgetting that he is a name in a play, an inaccessible blankness circumscribed by an interpretable text."[26] Similarly, a postcolonial Friday who offers up his story to Susan's/ Foe's book within Coetzee's novel risks substantiating their/Coetzee's authority, their/his powers of representation. Rather than obscuring the question of power by representing Friday's speech, or indeed consolidating it by *simply* leaving Friday silent, Coetzee thematizes Friday's "inaccessible blankness," his circumscribed status as a character in a fictional work drawn not from the world but from another fictional work, the invention of a British author. Susan refers to "the story of Friday, which is properly not a story but a puzzle or hole in the narrative (I picture it as a buttonhole, carefully cross-stitched around, but empty, waiting for the button)" (121). However Friday's silence marks a refusal of that circumscription, enabling him to signify a remainder that Coetzee's authority does not pretend to encompass.

Benita Parry is concerned that Coetzee's silencing of subjugated and dispossessed characters such as Friday goes beyond a representation of the silencing effects of colonialism or apartheid to effect its own occlusion of active and activist anticolonial or antiapartheid voices. While Friday is Coetzee's reinvention of Defoe's Friday, not unproblematically a representation of historical subjects of oppression, Parry's argument that his silence is an artifact of Coetzee's narrative must be acknowledged, as must the corollary that it "situates its inarticulate protagonists . . . as the objects of another's narrative" (SSF, 52). Yet this problem is foregrounded in the novel. Foe tells Susan, "We must make Friday's silence speak, as well as the silence surrounding Friday" (142). While Parry interprets Foe's will to "make Friday's silence speak" as pointing to the desire to ventriloquize Friday's story for the purposes of completing his book — and this reading is certainly valid — there is another that haunts it, one to be activated by the reader of Coetzee's novel: we are not offered Coetzee's representation of Friday's speech but compelled to interrogate the violent *production* of his silence, and the systems that perpetuate it. Thus, while it is true that Coetzee's refusal to represent Friday's speech is a different matter than representing Friday as silent, one may also argue that *Foe* enacts the very strategy that Parry endorses when she refers to the possibility of fiction that "inscribes alterity not as a dumb presence but as an interlocutor" (SSF, 43). Because Coetzee's Friday's speech would risk occluding the countervoices more effectively than his silence, though, Friday's interlocutory role is effected through those signs of subjectivity and manifestations of agency that withhold their meaning from Susan and Foe, exerting a pressure on them, forcing them to interrogate their own responses and desires. Coetzee does not recoil from representing the violence of colonialism — it seems that Friday's tongue has been violently removed — but he examines the epistemic violence that subtends and perpetuates such acts. Further, Friday is not wholly contained by the dominant discourse shared by Susan and Foe, and nor is the novel a "sealed linguistic code" (SSF, 43) that renders him unable to disturb that discourse.

Foe's radically provisional, self-reflexive, and ultimately unreliable narrative is a gesture against the arrogation of authority to the dominant

self as a means either to silence or to represent the other. It is this authority that is thrown into question through Friday's interlocutory presence.
At the same time, such narrative provisionality problematizes the trium-
phalist accession to authority by the subjugated in a manner that mirrors
colonial power and that seeks simply to invert it. While presenting Friday
as wholly silent and without agency would be problematic, Coetzee argu-
ably leaves open the question of his capacity for speech as the report of his
missing tongue is unconfirmed, and as Parry herself notes, Friday is given
two alternative endings, another index of the open-ended narrative of his
silence. Within the main body of the narrative, he is shown taking up the
robes, wig, and pen of the author, a move that looks toward the possibility of future self-inscription, without guaranteeing the amenability of his
writing to Susan's story or Foe's book; in the final section, it is Friday
who remains warm, who has a pulse, and who breathes out "to the ends
of the earth" (157).

In short, Coetzee's Friday becomes a principal occasion for the novel's investigation of the politics of representation itself. This concern with
representation, the inaccessibility — and unassimilability — of Friday's
story to Susan's, and ultimately the point that behind his image stands
only a prior image, are all aspects of *Foe*'s metafictional status. However, although metafiction is conventionally identified with postmodern
writing, the political concerns that impel and sustain it are clearly postcolonial.[27] Marais refers to *Foe* as postcolonial metafiction, whose metafictional concerns are produced by colonialism rather than the postmodern
emphasis on the system of writing itself.[28] Yet consistent with the novel's
refusal of closure, Coetzee does not invite a clear distinction between
these critical and political orientations. The postcolonial politics cannot
be extricated from the system of writing, or the history of prior writings.
Similarly, while Attwell argues that "Coetzee positions *Foe* in the discursive field of postcoloniality, but he does so in peculiarly South African
terms" (PW, 103), Attridge maintains that "the South African struggle is
part of a wider, and entirely concrete, struggle" (OS, 185).

Friday's silence enables the novel to focus on the problems of power
and authority represented initially by Cruso, who assumes the right to
determine the limits and tenor of Friday's exposure to language, but
more centrally by Susan and Foe. Susan associates authority and representation with substance and truth, but is increasingly confronted by the
elusiveness of both. As she waits for Foe to write her story, she senses her
own substance, her substantial being, fading; her plea to Foe, "Return
to me the substance I have lost" (51) gains metafictional resonance in
light of her later appeal: "Will you not bear it in mind . . . that my life is
drearily suspended till your writing is done?" (63). The realist implication
of the biographical subject captive to the author's project extends to a
metafictional comment on the status of the fictional character as realized

only within the acts of writing and reading themselves. Susan's sense of suspension in a state of unreality is further evoked in references to herself and Friday as "ghosts"; she feels like "a being without substance, a ghost beside the true body of Cruso" (51), and assures Foe that in her lodgings, she and Friday should be "as quiet as ghosts" (59); when she occupies Foe's house, that she and Friday will "vanish like ghosts, without complaint," when he returns (64). These images point to the condition of absent presence, or present absence, that characterize the production of the literary work. However, their metafictional implications go further as she struggles for her truth against the insistences of the girl who claims to be her daughter.

Susan attempts to expel the girl by leading her into the forest to leave her there, explaining "You are father-born. You have no mother. . . . What you hope to regain in my person you have in truth never had" (91). The girl's response to the term "father-born" — "It is a word I have never heard before" — is followed almost immediately by Susan's words, "I wake in the grey of a London dawn" (91), presenting the possibility that the journey to the forest was a dream, and perhaps the girl herself has been a dream. When the girl and her childhood nurse Amy appear at Foe's lodgings, Susan observes that when the girl kisses her upon their arrival, "a coldness went through me and I thought I would fall to the floor" (129), suggesting the loss of consciousness that might attend an uncanny, even ghostly encounter. She surmises that they are either actors in her story as Foe is inventing it (130), or ghosts he has summoned from another world (132–33). Even the possibility that "these women are creatures of yours, visiting me at your instruction, speaking words you have prepared for them" (133) does not so much confirm their (and Foe's) truth as cause her to doubt her own reality: "But if these women are creatures of yours, visiting me at your instruction, speaking words you have prepared for them, then who am I and who indeed are you? . . . Nothing is left to me but doubt. I am doubt itself. Who is speaking me? Am I a phantom too? To what order do I belong? And you: who are you?" (133).

Susan's sense of insubstantiality is inseparable from the fact that her story is ultimately without substantiation. She acknowledges that she has "brought back not a feather, not a thimbleful of sand, from Cruso's island. All I have is my sandals" (51). Cruso himself is gone, and Friday's silence means he is unable to substantiate her account. Her awareness that her story — and thus her authority — is incomplete, lacking, impels her to seek Friday's own story as its missing part. Susan attempts to elicit from Friday some indication as to the truth of his lost tongue by presenting him with sketches of possible scenes of the mutilation. She looks to Friday for recognition and thus confirmation of the truth of one of these sketches, but is already doubting the very assumptions and terms of her inquiry: his failure to recognize himself or the scene in either sketch may relate to her own inexpert sketching, or to incorrect detail; alternatively, it may be that he is confused as to her purpose with the sketches and questions, or even that she is unable, herself, to interpret, or "read," his response (68–70). The problems of her pictorial "writing" lead to the uncertainties of her reading. She initially concludes that the failure lies in Friday's obtuseness, but ultimately it further erodes her confidence in her authority. Susan differentiates her own silences as "chosen and purposeful" from Friday's "helpless" silence (122), hers as reflecting her authority over her story in resistance to Foe's narrative impositions, Friday's as leaving him "no defence against being reshaped day by day in conformity with the desires of others" (121). However, Foe's assurance that he "would not rob you of your tongue for anything" (150) aligns her with Friday on the very grounds on which she has distinguished herself from him, while also adumbrating her "exclusion" from *Robinson Crusoe*.

Still feeling the absence of Friday's story as the lack in her own, at Foe's suggestion Susan undertakes to teach Friday writing. However, just as the pictures she drew to elicit his history cast that history within her own unreliable representation, the writing lesson is also predicated on her presumption of representational authority. Susan attempts to teach him the letters making "house," "ship," "mother," and "Africa," unable to know whether Friday associates her sketch of a house and the h-o-u-s she inscribes underneath with the sound of the word "house" and whether any of these attach, for him, to the referent as object in the world. When Friday copies shapes "passably like" h-o-u-s (145), she cannot know whether he has intended to copy the letters, or whether he has written something with no relation to her instruction (145–46). When, possibly for "ship," Friday writes h-s-h-s-h-s (and she wonders whether the "s" is actually an "f"), she is unsure whether Friday is locked into a state of benighted stupidity or whether he is in fact mocking her (146);[29] indeed, his actions reveal the possibility of a much stronger agency than Susan can recognize or admit. Left to his own devices with the slate, Friday covers it in what appear to be "eyes, open eyes, each set upon a human foot: row upon row of eyes upon feet: walking eyes" (147).[30] When Susan demands that he give her the slate, "instead of obeying me, Friday put three fingers into his mouth and wet them with spittle and rubbed the slate clean" (147). Friday too, then, is able to make and withhold his meaning. As he literally withholds the slate from her, he contests her right to appropriate it, turning writing itself into a site and act of contestation. Susan therefore approaches Friday's presumed condition of "helplessness" in the face of representational authority, while Friday increasingly asserts the agency such authority presumes.[31]

Similarly, Foe's status as author, as master of representational authority, is thrown into question throughout the novel. Despite Susan's ostensible dependence upon him, and upon his authority, he is narratively associated with various conditions of "lack": he is a debtor, in hiding, and thus captive to the very lack for which he is being pursued; as a writer — though we never see him writing — he is captive to the task, as Susan notes when she reflects on her complicity with the subjection of Friday, holding him effectively captive to her desire to have her story told (150): "might not Foe be a kind of captive too?" (151), bound to the labor of his writing? In many ways he is passive: he leaves it to Susan to teach Friday writing, and later invites her to "Leave Friday here for the afternoon. Go for a stroll. Take the air. See the sights. I am sadly enclosed. Be my spy. Come back and report to me how the world does" (150), and he apparently dozes. Such dispersal of narrative authority and reflection on authorial freedom and subjection is reprised in Coetzee's "He and His Man."

Against the ontological uncertainty that infects the stability of Susan's or Foe's point of view, Friday — silent, shadowy — exerts increasing pressure on their substantiality and authority. It seems that Friday has no interest in communicating with Susan, or in accepting her "invitations" to the worlds of speech and writing. He thus resists submitting his story to the larger purposes of her own. However, during Susan's occupation of Foe's house, Friday has taken up the habit of dressing in Foe's wig and robes, and dancing. As Susan writes to Foe, "In the grip of dancing he is not himself. He is beyond human reach" (92). This image of him in the borrowed habit of the writer, present but departed to another inaccessible realm, invokes the presence and absence that characterizes the author's relation to the literary work. It also foreshadows his later appearance when, momentarily freed from the dozing Foe's and absent Susan's attention and surveillance, he has slipped into Foe's place — seated at his table, writing.

On her return from her stroll, Susan is horrified to find Friday thus, "his hand, poised over Foe's papers . . . a quill with a drop of black ink glistening at its tip" (151). If Susan has described Foe in terms of failed maternity, she now catches Friday on the brink of inseminating Foe's papers. She springs forward to snatch them away, but Foe responds from his bed, "Let him be, Susan, . . . he is accustoming himself to his tools, it is part of learning to write." And to her protests that Friday will "foul" his papers, he replies: "My papers are foul enough, he can make them no worse" (151). While Susan and Foe debate truth and substance — during which Susan neglects to include Friday in her affirmation of beings "in the same world" — Friday remains "busy at his writing":[32]

The paper before him was heavily smudged, as by a child unused to the pen, but there was writing on it, writing of a kind, rows and rows of the letter *o* tightly packed together. A second page lay at his elbow, fully written over, and it was the same.

"Is Friday learning to write?" asked Foe.

"He is writing, after a fashion," I said. "He is writing the letter *o*."

"It is a beginning," said Foe. "Tomorrow you must teach him *a*." (152)[33]

In wanting to bring forth Friday's story to enable the completion of her own, Susan proffers the writing lesson as a means of educating him out of his benighted state, as a means of making him more "like" her. Yet the sight of him in Foe's wig and robes, no longer dancing but writing with Foe's pen on Foe's papers, disturbs the very difference between them upon which her cultural authority is founded. Susan wants Friday's story, but also to preserve the purity of her own; she wants Friday to write, but to preserve the cleanliness of Foe's papers. She has articulated this ambivalence in her earlier concern over whether she wishes to extend Friday's command of English as a means of liberating him or of more fully subjecting him to her will (60), recognizing the difficulty in disentangling these motives and effects. Further, she is unable to be certain of Friday's attitude. His h-s-h-s-h-s causes Susan to lament and then question his apparent obtuseness:

> Was it possible for anyone, however benighted by a lifetime of dumb servitude, to be as stupid as Friday seemed? Could it be that somewhere within him he was laughing at my efforts to bring him nearer to a state of speech? . . . Somewhere in the deepest recesses of those black pupils was there a spark of mockery? I could not see it. But if it were there, would it not be an African spark, dark to my English eye? (146)[34]

The completeness of story that Susan has sought, and the purity of authority she has moved to defend, are negated by the metafictional strategies of Coetzee's novel, described by Lane as a "palimpsest" of "embroiling narratives" (EN, 110) and by Bishop as articulating "a voice in conflict with itself."[35] Chris Bongie's account of the novel effectively conveys the inextricable thematic and narrative movements, its political aesthetic:

> Coetzee moves forward in a motion of ambivalence that always also takes him back to the (lack of a) ground from which he began, and upon which he has planted the sign of a postcolonial literature that takes an apparent dead end as its repeated point of departure. . . . Opposition is always also apposition. Barton and Foe at once antagonize and complement one another in their desire for a return to or

an arrival at a wholeness that they consistently fail to realize. Such failure, Coetzee would claim, is what language, in its partiality, its *figurality*, is destined to: that we inhabit an essentially figural world, a world of "similitudes" . . . a world of likenesses which are always also unlikenesses, is the brunt of the poetics, and politics, that Coetzee traces out in *Foe*.[36]

Friday's interrogative presence in *Foe* produces a thoroughgoing scrutiny of the postcolonial politics of representation. However, he does not signify a simple inversion of their claims. Just as Friday is not contained by the dominant discourse, *Foe*'s own refusal of definitive (en)closure extends to all authority. As a contrapuntal novel, it enacts a contestation of power. Susan and Foe debate the question of freedom (149–50), reaching only the insight that although it may not be possible to know or say what freedom means, one can and must challenge subjection. However, the novel not only refuses any final definition of freedom, it evokes freedom as precisely the other of certainty, determination, and identity. The ambivalently new beginning signaled in Friday's learning to write "*a*" looks ahead to a future that is unknowable because it will forever be in process; at the same time, his accession to the alphabet of his subjection is shadowed by the insistence on an inevitable excess to any system of representation, an "outside" where "bodies are their own signs" (157).

Notes

[1] J. M. Coetzee, *He and His Man*, Nobel lecture, 2003 (New York: Penguin, 2004). Subsequent references appear as HHM with the accompanying page number.

[2] Teresa Dovey describes Coetzee's works as "criticism-as-fiction, or fiction-as-criticism." Teresa Dovey, *The Novels of J. M. Coetzee: Lacanian Allegories* (Johannesburg: Ad. Donker, 1988), 9.

[3] See Homi Bhabha for an account of the hybrid "third space" of enunciation: *The Location of Culture* (London: Routledge, 1994), 36–39. In "A Note on Writing (1984)," in *Doubling the Point: Essays and Interviews*, ed. David Attwell (Cambridge, MA: Harvard UP, 1992), Coetzee refers to Roland Barthes's discussion of voice in terms of "a threefold opposition active-middle-passive," pointing out that "'To write' is one of these verbs. To write (active) is to carry out the action without reference to the self. . . . To write (middle) is to carry out the action (or better, to do-writing) with reference to the self. Or . . . 'today to write is to make oneself the center of the action of *la parole*; it is to effect writing in being affected oneself; it is to leave the writer (*le scripteur*) inside the writing, not as a psychological subject . . . but as the agent of the action'" (*DP*, 94. See also *DP*, 85 for his account of the passive structure as "writing in stereotyped forms . . . where the machine runs the operator"). The "middle voice" is thematized within both "He and His Man" and *Foe*, given that the relation between such terms as author and character, writer and language, writing and reading, is scrutinized in both works.

Fiona Probyn-Rapsey cites Teresa Dovey and Brian Macaskill as two critics who have addressed the middle voice in Coetzee's own writing, "a writing position between the 'active' (such as in the declaration 'I write') and the passive ('it is written')." See Fiona Probyn-Rapsey, "Reconnaissance: The Role of the Feminine and Feminist Theory in the Novels of J. M. Coetzee," in *J. M. Coetzee: Critical Perspectives*, ed. Kailash C. Baral (New Delhi: Pencraft International, 2008), 247–74; here. 249. Denise Almeida Silva glosses Coetzee's short essay as registering his interest in "the essential reflexivity of the middle voice, in which the agent necessarily occupies a position interior to the process of writing," in which, as she quotes Barthes: "the subject is immediately contemporary with the writing." See Denise Almeida Silva, "On Engendering Fiction: Authority and Authorship in *Foe, Elizabeth Costello* and *Slow Man*," in *J. M. Coetzee: Critical Perspectives*, 221–46; here, 222; Silva cites the same source but a different edition to that referred to by Coetzee above.

[4] The term "oblique" has been applied to Coetzee's perspective and his works' relation to politics and aesthetics, adumbrating an argument about their mutual engagement that could be called an underpinning "ethic." Benita Parry describes Coetzee's works as "obliquely situated to the prevailing intellectual formations of his native land"; see "Speech and Silence in the Fictions of J. M. Coetzee," in *Critical Perspectives on J. M. Coetzee*, ed. Graham Huggan and Stephen Watson (London: Macmillan, 1996), 37–65; here, 57. Subsequent references appear as SSF with the accompanying page number. Coetzee himself has conceded, with reference to the question of censorship, that "my books have been too indirect in their approach, too rarefied, to be considered a threat to the order" (*DP*, 298). David Attwell, discussing "the paradox between the *autonomous* and the *communicative* features of the literary work" cites the Prague School insight that "the literary sign has a special way of pointing to reality that preserves the specificity of the aesthetic function: its reference, quite simply, is oblique and metaphorical": "The Problem of History in the Fiction of J. M. Coetzee," *Poetics Today* 11, no. 3 (1990): 590. Subsequent references appear as PH with the accompanying page number. See also Stephen Watson, "Colonialism and the Novels of J. M. Coetzee," in *Critical Perspectives on J. M. Coetzee*, 13–36; here, 22.

[5] Jarad Zimbler examines the different ideological framings offered by *Foe*'s South African publication context and those of metropolitan publishers, in "Under Local Eyes: The South African Publishing Context of J. M. Coetzee's *Foe*," *English Studies in Africa* 47, no. 1 (2004): 47–59.

[6] Maureen Nicholson, "'If I Make the Air Around Him Thick with Words': J. M. Coetzee's *Foe*," *West Coast Review* 21, no. 4 (1987): 52. Subsequent references appear as "If I" with the accompanying page number.

[7] Derek Attridge also acknowledges that "*Foe* came as something of a disappointment to many readers and reviewers." See "Oppressive Silence: J. M. Coetzee's *Foe* and the Politics of Canonisation," in *Critical Perspectives on J. M. Coetzee*, 168–90; here, 171. Subsequent references appear as OS with the accompanying page number.

[8] Mike Marais, "From the Standpoint of Redemption: Aesthetic Autonomy and Social Engagement in J. M. Coetzee's Fiction of the Late Apartheid Period,"

Journal of Narrative Theory 38, no. 2 (2008): 229. Subsequent references appear as FSR with the accompanying page number.

[9] Michael Vaughan, "Literature and Politics: Currents in South African Writing in the Seventies," *Journal of Southern African Studies* 9, no. 1 (October 1982): 126.

[10] Attwell also reviews Marxist readings of Coetzee's work, including Vaughan's argument in "Literature and Politics" that "it [*Dusklands*] privileges an agonized consciousness over material forces," and Paul Rich's view that "the agents of historical consciousness" are "never brought to light" (PH, 593; summarizing "Apartheid and the Decline of the Civilization Idea: An Essay on Nadine Gordimer's *July's People* and J. M. Coetzee's *Waiting for the Barbarians*," *Research in African Literatures* 15, no. 3 [1984]), by way of Teresa Dovey's defense of a "reflexivity that encompasses both 'fiction and criticism of the fiction'" (PH, 594–95; citing Dovey, *The Novels of J. M. Coetzee*, 9).

[11] Watson also notes the specificity of Coetzee's intertextuality as pointing to the English and European sources of his literary training (Watson, "Colonialism").

[12] David Attwell, *J. M. Coetzee: South Africa and the Politics of Writing* (Berkeley: U of California Press, 1993): 5. Subsequent references appear as PW with the accompanying page number.

[13] Attwell concedes that "For Coetzee to be the novelist that he is, he must pursue the path of fictionality; he is a specialist of the story and has declared his allegiance to this vocation without apology. Against this position — I trust, in ways that respect his version of fictionality — I assert again and again the historicity of the act of storytelling, continually reading the novels back into their context. In this sense, I read Coetzee 'against the grain'" (PW, 7). See also Patrick Hayes for a discussion of the relationship between art and politics in Coetzee's work: *J. M. Coetzee and the Novel: Writing and Politics after Beckett* (Oxford: Oxford UP, 2010; available at: Oxford Scholarship Online. Oxford UP. http://dx.doi.org/10.1093/acprof:oso/9780199587957.001.0001 (accessed 16 January 2011). Subsequent references appear as CN with the accompanying page number. In his account of Coetzee's "concern with the origins, history and on-going cultural legacy of the form of the novel" (1–2), Hayes argues that the question of "literariness" is not "depoliticizing" but, rather, consistent with Coetzee's effort to "move beyond a long discursive tradition . . . which attempts to position literary value, or literary truth, or most generally 'culture,' as superior to, or even transcendent of, politics" (CN, 1–3).

[14] Mike Marais, "Interpretative Authoritarianism: Reading/Colonizing Coetzee's *Foe*," *English in Africa* 16, no. 1 (1989): 13. In his later essay, "The Novel as Ethical Command: J. M. Coetzee's *Foe*" (2000), Marais offers a Levinasian reading that concludes that "*Foe*'s rejection of history as an *a priori* structure and insistence on its autonomy . . . is motivated by the desire to effect the justification of the political by the ethical. Quite simply, for Coetzee, politics *begins* as ethics. *Foe* does 'engage' with history but in a way that is very different to that used by most politically committed writers" (81).

[15] See also Derek Attridge, OS, 183–85; Sam Durrant, "Bearing Witness to Apartheid: J. M. Coetzee's Inconsolable Works of Mourning," *Contemporary Literature* 40, no. 3 (1999): 430–63 (subsequent references appear as BW with the

accompanying page number); and Durrant, *Postcolonial Narrative and the Work of Mourning: J. M. Coetzee, Wilson Harris, and Toni Morrison* (Albany, NY: State U of New York P, 2004) (subsequent references appear as PN with the accompanying page number).

[16] Attwell is citing Coetzee, "The Novel Today," *Upstream* 6, no. 1 (1988): 2–5; here, 3.

[17] Durrant refers to Theodor Adorno's 1962 essay, "Commitment," which — in Durrant's words — calls for art to provide a "negative image" of society, "one which stands in dialectical contradiction to society . . . as its critique" (BW, 433). He posits Coetzee's work as similarly insisting on "the autonomy of art in order to retain the possibility of bearing witness to a history of suffering without betraying it" (BW, 434), either by what Adorno refers to as "the untruth of [committed art's] politics" (BW, 434; quoting Adorno, "Commitment," in *Aesthetics and Politics*, ed. Ronald Taylor [London: NLB, 1977], 187), or the problem of aestheticization that haunts art in the face of "the abundance of real suffering" in the world (Theodor Adorno, *Minima Moralia: Reflections from Damaged Life*. Trans. E. F. N. Jephcott [London: Verso, 1978]; 188). Coetzee avoids the latter problem, Durrant maintains, "by refusing to translate such a history, by representing it as untranslatable" (BW, 434). Marais, in turn, positions Coetzee's stance in relation to autonomy by way of Adorno's dialectical view of artistic autonomy, in that it must be "wrested from what is" (FSR, 232, citing *Minima Moralia*, 247), but that despite its "struggle against the repressive identification compulsion that rules the outside world," art has "a two-fold essence" — both in the world and divorced from the world, "'an autonomous entity and a social fact' estranged from history yet unable to take up a position outside it" (FSR, 232, citing Adorno, *Aesthetic Theory* [1984], 6, 8). Marais argues that Coetzee "shares Adorno's dialectical understanding of aesthetic autonomy" (FSR, 234) as "*relationally* constituted" and exemplified in *Foe*'s "attempt to secure an enactment of [the potential beyond its 'givenness'] in the reading process" (FSR, 240). See, however, Hayes's account of *Foe* as keeping politics and aesthetics in productive tension (CN, 106–29).

[18] In Section III, Susan has asked Mr. Foe, "who will dive into the wreck?" (142), a metaphor for plumbing the depths of Friday's silence; the allusion to Adrienne Rich's "Diving into the Wreck" has been noted by Barbara Eckstein, "Iconicity, Immersion and Otherness: The Hegelian 'Dive' of J. M. Coetzee and Adrienne Rich," *Mosaic: A Journal for the Interdisciplinary Study of Literature* 29, no. 1 (1996): 57–77; Manuel Almagro Jiménez, "'Father to My Story': Writing *Foe*, De-Authorizing (De)Foe," *Revista Alicantina de Estudios Ingleses* 18 (2005): 7–24; Judie Newman, "Desperately Seeking Susan: J. M. Coetzee, *Robinson Crusoe* and *Roxana*," *Current Writing: Text and Reception in Southern Africa* 6, no. 1 (1994): 1–12; and Laura Wright, "Displacing the Voice: South African Feminism and J. M. Coetzee's Female Narrators," *African Studies* 67, no. 1 (2008): 11–31. However, the question of who has made this descent, who narrates Section IV, is not clearly resolved.

[19] This scene supports the arguments of Paula Burnett and Richard Lane that Susan has died at the outset of the narrative, Lane suggesting that *Foe* invokes Golding's *Pincher Martin*: Paula Burnett, "The Ulyssean Crusoe and the Quest

for Redemption in J. M. Coetzee's *Foe* and Derek Walcott's *Omeros*," in *Robinson Crusoe: Myths and Metamorphoses*, ed. Lieve Spaas and Brian Stimpson (New York: St. Martin's, 1996), 239–55; Richard Lane, "Embroiling Narratives: Appropriating the Signifier in J. M. Coetzee's *Foe*," *Commonwealth Essays and Studies* 13, no. 1 (1990): 106–11. Subsequent references appear as EN with the accompanying page number.

[20] See Watson's discussion of the economic motive forces, the material factors inherent in colonialism, and Coetzee's critique of colonialism as "unusual" in its greater emphasis on the "dissenting colonising mind" (Watson, "Colonialism," 36).

[21] The intertextuality of *Foe* is extensive. Apart from *Robinson Crusoe*, *Roxana*, *Moll Flanders*, and other works by Defoe, and Rich's "Diving into the Wreck," critics have noted allusions to the works of Dante, Pirandello, Schreiner, Golding, and Beckett; to works such as Shakespeare's *The Tempest* and Dostoevsky's *Crime and Punishment*; and to such figures as Philomela, Frankenstein, Mr. Kurtz, Hansel and Gretel, and the madwoman-in-the-attic.

[22] Attwell refers to the "radically *provisional* and *methodological* character of Coetzee's novels" (PH, 599), and to Coetzee as shedding "a 'preliterary' light on his protagonists in order to place the transformations of the 'literary' in question" (PW, 107). Marais ("The Hermeneutics of Empire: Coetzee's Post-colonial Metafiction," in *Critical Perspectives on J. M. Coetzee*, 66–81), and Ankhi Mukherjee ("The Death of the Novel and Two Postcolonial Writers," *Modern Language Quarterly* 69, no. 4 [2008]: 533–56), also note the temporal ambivalence of *Foe*.

[23] Susan is told his tongue has been removed but when Cruso invites her to look into Friday's mouth, she recounts, "I saw nothing. . . . 'It is too dark'" (22). Later, she admits to Friday, "I have not looked into your mouth. When your master asked me to look, I would not. An aversion came over me that we feel for all the mutilated. Why is that so, do you think? Because they put us in mind of what we would rather forget: how easily . . . wholeness and beauty are forever undone?" (85).

[24] Helen Tiffin, "Post-Colonial Literatures and Counter-Discourse," *Kunapipi* 9, no. 3 (1987): 22.

[25] Derek Attridge outlines the ways in which Coetzee's novels, including *Foe*, "could be said to presuppose and reproduce the canonic status of their predecessors while claiming to join them" (OS, 169), citing style, thematic focus, and both Coetzee's privileged access to most canons and his own South African "mystique" of marginality as contributing to this effect (OS, 170). However, he maintains that this overlooks the significance of "a mode of fiction which expose[s] the ideological basis of canonisation" (OS, 171).

[26] Gayatri Chakravorty Spivak, "Three Women's Texts and a Critique of Imperialism," *Critical Inquiry* 12, no. 1 (1985): 243–61; here, 245.

[27] The distinction as well as overlap between these terms has been a matter of considerable debate. Steven Connor, while discussing the novel in terms that invoke postcolonial counter-discourse, does not use this term, and focuses instead on the novel's postmodern characteristics: "Rewriting Wrong: On the Ethics of Literary Reversion," in *Liminal Postmodernisms: The Postmodern, the (Post-)*

colonial, and the (Post-)Feminist, ed. Theo D'Haen and Johannes Willem Bertens (Amsterdam: Rodopi, 1994), 79–97. In "Silence and Mut(e)ilation: White Writing in J. M. Coetzee's *Foe*," *South Atlantic Quarterly* 93, no. 1 (1994): 111–29, Richard Begam refers to the novel's use of postmodern strategies for postcolonial purposes. Christoph Reinfandt examines the relation between the postcolonial (power) and postmodern (story) concerns in "The Pitfalls of a Postcolonial Poetics: J. M. Coetzee's *Foe* and the New Literatures in English," *Symbolism: An International Annual of Critical Aesthetics* 7 (2007): 299–315. Despite the reference to its postmodern play in Michael Titlestad and Mike Kissack, "The Persistent Castaway in South African Writing," *Postcolonial Studies* 10, no. 2 (2007): 191–218, the novel does not engage in a ludic, but in a politically motivated, fictional self-reflexivity. However, the poststructuralist, deconstructive quality of the novel locates its postcolonialism as a manifestation of postmodernity, a critical challenge to European humanist assumptions that were intrinsic to imperialism and complicit in colonialism.

[28] Marais, "The Hermeneutics of Empire."

[29] David Marshall suggests that the h-s-h-s-h-s represents Friday's attempt to silence — to hush — Susan: "Friday's Writing Lesson: Reading *Foe*," in *Historical Boundaries, Narrative Forms: Essays on British Literature in the Long Eighteenth Century in Honor of Everett Zimmerman,* ed. Lorna Clymer and Robert Mayer (Newark, DE: U of Delaware P, 2007), 225–51.

[30] While Susan makes no attempt to "read" these signs, they have been variously interpreted by critics as referring to the eighteenth-century literary topos of the reader as the traveling eye/I (Marais "The Hermeneutics"); as inscribing Friday's trademark footprint from *Robinson Crusoe* (Ayo Kehinde, "Post-Colonial Literatures as Counter-Discourse: J. M. Coetzee's *Foe* and the Reworking of the Canon," *Journal of African Literature and Culture [JALC]* 4 [2007]: 33–57); as representing the eyes of slaves who see the feet of sailors from inside the hold of a ship (Eckstein, "Iconicity"); and more generally as contesting the very notion of Friday as empty, as nullified (Claudia Egerer, "Hybridizing the Zero: Exploring Alternative Strategies of Empowerment in J. M. Coetzee's *Foe*," in *Postcolonialism and Cultural Resistance*, ed. Jopi Nyman and John A. Stotesbury, 96–101 [Joensuu, Finland: Faculty of Humanities, U of Joensuu, 1999]), a suggestion that is consistent with Marshall's that the pattern does indeed represent the leaves and flowers of his ritual over the water as Susan initially thought.

[31] Patrick Hayes gives important attention to the problem of the novel's ending, where the processes that have given life to Friday are those that entail the death of Susan (CN, 117). Hayes points out that the ending is troubling with regard to the fate of Susan, the feminine subject for whom so much is at stake in the political and ethical legacy of the Enlightenment; yet the realist novel, whose storytelling aesthetics and politics Susan affirms (CN, 121–22) cannot, without the naked "exercise of power — a falsifying transcendence of material inequalities that require political redress" (CN, 127), encompass Friday, the colonial "other." He argues that Coetzee addresses the problem in a metafictional epilogue that is both an echo and a departure from Dostoevsky's solution of the "wisdom tale": he "split[s] the heroes of the novel and the wisdom tale into the occluded female subject and the occluded racial subject respectively, thereby restricting the power

of political imperatives to decide where literary value lies, and leading readers into the problem the novel itself poses" (CN, 128).

[32] As Attridge points out, "For us, of course, that world is the world — substantial or insubstantial — of Coetzee's novel" (OS, 178). The omission of Friday may offer yet another opening to a world beyond that of fictional containment.

[33] Friday's *o*'s have been variously interpreted as his inscription of "omega," as marking the end of an order that "tomorrow" must be followed by a new "alpha"; as representing either an expression of despair (O!), or an affirmation of spiritual life invoking Defoe's Friday's account of the divinity of his god, such that "all men do say "o" to him"; see "Silence and Mut(e)ilation: White Writing in J. M. Coetzee's *Foe*." *South Atlantic Quarterly* 93, no. 1 (1994): 111–29. Other readings posit that "o" is actually "0" — zero — an inscription of Friday's absence into Susan's story (Begam), or the absence in Western culture that takes the mimetic form of space (Egerer, "Hybridizing"). Probyn-Rapsey ("Reconnaissance") reads it as a symbol of the body in disrupting representation while insisting on its own status as sign.

[34] For an analysis that bears on the implications of this passage and the preceding discussion, see Homi Bhabha, "Of Mimicry and Man: the Ambivalence of Colonial Discourse," in *The Location of Culture*, 85–92.

[35] G. Scott Bishop, "J. M. Coetzee's *Foe*: A Culmination and a Solution to a Problem of White Identity," *World Literature Today* 64, no. 1 (1990): 54–57.

[36] Chris Bongie, "'Lost in the Maze of Doubting': J. M. Coetzee's *Foe* and the Politics of (Un)Likeness," *MFS: Modern Fiction Studies* 39, no. 2 (1993): 263, 268.

8: *Age of Iron* (1990)

Kim L. Worthington

IN "THE NOVEL TODAY," J. M. Coetzee famously writes of the distinction between novels that "rival" history and those that "supplement" them.[1] In arguing strongly against the "powerful tendency, perhaps even dominant tendency, to subsume the novel under history," he suggests that readers accord superior moral integrity and "greater truth" to "supplementary" novels not least because they engage with the "facts" of history (NT, 2). The "today" of the essay title marks a very specific period in South Africa, a time in which the moral and political purpose of literature was strongly debated. It refers to the tumultuous years of the second State of Emergency (1985–89) prior to the release of Nelson Mandela in 1990 and the final abolition of the Nationalist Government, and apartheid regime, in 1994. At this time, the political demands made of South African writers who did not support the racist regime were substantial: their role was to bear witness to *real* events and, in doing so, expose and oppose the *truth* of the apartheid state.[2]

Not surprisingly, given his tendency to shun straightforward realism in his own fiction, Coetzee forcefully advocates in the essay not simply fiction's difference from historical narratives but the novel's ability to rival them. He thus overtly challenges the negative assessment of critics who suggested that in his characteristic stress on consciousness and interiority, he "betray[s] an idealist rather than materialist stance," one in which, as Teresa Dovey puts it, he gets "his history *all wrong.*"[3] Against such reasoning, Coetzee argues that the novel "occup[ies] an autonomous place" outside the discourse of history; "it operates in terms of its own procedures and issues in its own conclusions that are not checkable by history" and, as a result, it is able to "show up the mythic status of history" (NT, 2–3). Similarly, the novel's reader is called upon to do more than perform what Peter McDonald calls an "instrumentalized reading" of narrative "facts" (PI, 53). Certainly, metafictional "play" that alerts readers not just to the fabricated untruths of realist writing but also to their own roles in the creation of meaning — in fiction and history — is a hallmark of Coetzee's writing (and one of the bugbears of his detractors). A central question remains, however — one that will inform the discussion that follows: in the face of history's "mythic status," is the novel's rival mode of writing able to articulate (nonmythical) *truth*? Relatedly, what *kind* of truth might this be and how can one express it? I will consider these questions further in relation to Coetzee's sixth novel, *Age of Iron* (1990).

As suggested, "The Novel Today" clearly represents a response to criticism leveled at Coetzee, particularly through the 1980s, which castigated him for his failure to write realist representations of apartheid South Africa, ones that offered a liberal (or even decidedly Marxist) critique of the state.[4] Prior to the publication of *Age of Iron*, only three of Coetzee's fictions were set in a recognizable South African landscape: "The Narrative of Jacobus Coetzee" and *In the Heart of the Country*, both deeply metaphysical; and the futuristic, apocalyptic *Life & Times of Michael K*. The others, despite an insistent engagement with questions about relations of power and racial or gender inequality, were frequently read as revealing a preference for literary gamesmanship at the expense of political commitment. It is somewhat paradoxical, then, that despite Coetzee's assertions in "The Novel Today," the novel on which he was working at the time, *Age of Iron*, appeared at first glance to respond to assessments of his fiction as "insufficiently 'relevant'" (TM, 117) and historically disengaged. In the words of Dominic Head, *Age of Iron* "seemed to represent a clear departure for Coetzee, his most 'realistic' novel evoking the Cape Town unrest of 1986. There is certainly a brooding anger and immediacy in this novel, written between 1986 and 1989, during which period South Africa was governed under a state of emergency."[5]

Age of Iron differs markedly from the earlier novels not only in its clearly evoked and "checkable" setting and factual details[6] but also in its overt — and certainly angry — denunciation of the apartheid state. The allegorical distancing of, say, *Waiting for the Barbarians* (1980), or the revisionary "rewriting" of *Foe*, is apparently renounced in favor of realism.[7] Throughout, Coetzee's scathing assessment of the South African state — its leaders, its rhetoric, its agents (whether the police or the military) and its sheer brutality — is voiced with a directness not seen in the earlier fiction. The words of his epistolary protagonist, Mrs. Curren,[8] for example, are openly condemnatory of the "soul-stunted" South African whites, quite literally separated from nonwhites by barricades, "the great divide." She describes them as:

> spinning themselves tighter and tighter into their sleepy cocoons. Swimming lessons, riding lessons, ballet lessons; cricket on the lawn; lives passed within walled gardens guarded by bulldogs; children of paradise, blond, innocent, shining with angelic light, soft as *putti*. Their residence the limbo of the unborn, their innocence the innocence of bee-grubs, plump and white, drenched in honey, absorbing sweetness through their soft skins. Slumberous their souls, bliss-filled, abstracted. (6–7)

On the "parade of politicians" on evening television, Mrs. Curren's rage and disgust is expressed in scathing terms that surely satisfies the demand for an overtly "engaged" political response to apartheid:

> The bullies in the last row of school-desks, raw-boned, lumpish boys, grown up now and promoted to rule the land. They with their mothers and fathers, their aunts and uncles, their brothers and sisters: a locust horde, a plague of black locusts infesting the country, munching without cease, devouring lives. . . . Legitimacy they no longer trouble to claim. Reason they have shrugged off. What absorbs them is power and the stupor of power. Eating and talking, munching lives, belching. Slow, heavy-bellied talk. Sitting in a circle, debating ponderously, issuing decrees like hammer-blows: death, death, death. Untroubled by the stench. Heavy eyelids, piggish eyes. Plotting against each other too: slow peasant plots that take decades to mature. . . . Pressing downwards: their power in their weight. Huge bull-testicles pressing down on their wives, their children, pressing the spark out of them. In their own hearts no spark of fire left. Sluggish hearts, heavy as blood-pudding.
>
> And their message stupidly unchanging, stupidly forever the same. Their feat, after years of etymological meditation on the word, to have raised stupidity to a virtue. . . . *Viva la muerte!* Their cry, their threat. Death to the young. Death to life. Boars that devour their offspring. The Boar War. (25–26)[9]

There is certainly nothing equivocal in passages such as these, nor is there in the several scenes that detail police brutality (and "stupidity"). Here, writ large, is the political "truth" demanded of Coetzee by his critics. Perhaps too large. For to focus on these passages, with all their forceful directness, is to overlook the far more subtle — and to my mind far more significant — scrutiny of (the possibility of) ethical and personal truth and truthfulness, and its relation to politics.

As in the second part of *Foe* (1986), *Age of Iron* is narrated in the epistolary mode and similarly exploits this to pose questions about truthfulness and authority.[10] The novel ostensibly comprises a long letter from Mrs. Curren, a (white) South African former classics professor who is dying of cancer, to her daughter, who lives in self-imposed exile in the United States. The daughter refuses to return under the reign of apartheid and will not come back, Mrs. Curren believes, even if she knew her mother was terminally ill (which she doesn't). Jane Poyner suggests, perhaps too simply, that "the letter gives [Mrs. Curren] the opportunity to expiate and find absolution for her sense of guilt and shame for 'staying on [in South Africa]'"; it is "a confession of sorts by which Mrs Curren bares her soul: hers is the confessant's desire for endings."[11] In a common slippage from narrator to author, seemingly sanctioned by Coetzee's comment in *Doubling the Point* that "all autobiography is storytelling, all writing is autobiography" (*DP*, 391),[12] the novel, like many of his other works, has been read as a confession on the part of the "white liberal" Coetzee as well.[13] The desired "endings" towards which the narrative tends are personal and political. Both Mrs. Curren and the "old" South Africa she so patently loved — despite her disgust at its "ravishers" (23) and her claim that "I do not love this land any more" (111) — are dying. Indeed, it is the many metaphoric linkages between her own impending death and that of the white regime that are often seen as elevating the novel from what could be a self-absorbed, if intensely lyrical, account of personal grief to the higher ground of political truthfulness and integrity. It is not just her body she must relinquish but also her love for a land haunted by murder and bloodshed. In a perverse imagistic inversion, Mrs. Curren images her cancer as a pregnancy; the "monstrous growths" (59) inside her are also the soon-to-be-birthed new nation and new age:[14] the "age of iron" that will replace the "age of granite" and "regime of death" that was the period of Nationalist rule (47).

If Mrs. Curren's letter is a confession, to whom is she confessing? Within the bounds of the weeks or months she relates, her unlikely confessor is Vercueil, a vagrant alcoholic (of unspecified race) who moves onto her property on the day she learns of her terminal illness, and who eventually moves into her home — and finally her bed. Although a patently sexless union, she does refer to herself, ironically, as "Mrs. V" (174) towards the end and dies in his arms, or perhaps at his hand.[15] Vercueil's name remains uncertain to Mrs. Curren: "His name is Mr Vercueil. . . . Vercueil, Verkuil, Verskuil. That's what he says" (34). A number of critics have noted that his name is suggestive of the Afrikaans words *verkul* (to cheat) and *verskuil* (to conceal),[16] words that seem apposite with respect to his characterization: he is unreliable, shifty, irresponsible, and apparently disinterested in Mrs. Curren and the several lengthy soul- and self-searching lectures she gives to him during their time together (after one of these he responds by asking to borrow money).

For all his unreliability, it is nonetheless Vercueil to whom Mrs. Curren entrusts the posting of her letter to her daughter after her death: "Because I cannot trust Vercueil I must trust him [to post it]" (119). For some, in this paradoxical formulation (repeated later in the idea that "because I cannot love him [the boy John], I must") lies the ethical core of the text.[17] Significantly, moreover, she recognizes that Vercueil cannot grant that which she desires — that which Coetzee has argued, in his essay "Confession and Double Thoughts" (1985), is the desired end of all confession: absolution or forgiveness.[18] Mrs. Curren writes,

> Easy to give alms to the orphaned, the destitute, the hungry. Harder to give alms to the bitter-hearted. . . . But the alms I give Vercueil

are the hardest of all. What I give he does not forgive me for giving. (*Charity?* says Vercueil. *Forgiveness?*) Without his forgiveness I
give without charity, serve without love. Rain falling on barren soil.
(119–20; emphasis in original)

The passage seems to suggest she seeks forgiveness for her "giving," or
rather the power and privilege on which it is predicated. Charity (of/
as privilege) is insufficient in these "new" times, as Mrs. Curren realizes;
it is as redundant as the outmoded vocabulary of "honor" to which she
reverts when attempting to assert her clear liberal conscience:

> I strove always for honor, for a private honor, using shame as my
> guide. As long as I was ashamed I knew I had not wandered into dis-
> honor. . . . Shame never became a shameful pleasure; it never ceased
> to gnaw me. I was not proud of it, I was ashamed of it. My shame,
> my own.
>   It is a confession I am making here, this morning, Mr Vercueil, . . .
> as full a confession as I know how. I withhold no secrets. I have been
> a good person. I freely confess it. I am a good person still. What
> times these are when to be a good person is not enough! (150)[19]

Here, as elsewhere, Vercueil does not respond; he is asleep, or pretend-
ing to be, when Mrs. Curren speaks. And rightly so, perhaps. Hers is
the lament of the "good" white South African: not unkind, charitable
even, but lacking in "the true root" of charity: *care*, that which (for all its
false etymology) comes from the heart.[20] Of this lack — in relation to the
boy John — she writes to her daughter: "I cannot find it in my heart to
love, to want to love, to want to want to love. . . . The more I love you,
the more I ought to love him. The less I love him, the less, perhaps, I
love you," and soon after describes her letter as "the issue of a shrunken
heart" (125).

Of course, beyond the recounted "present" of the letter and her
relationship with Vercueil is another anticipated or intended confessor,
Mrs. Curren's daughter, to whom the letter is ostensibly addressed (to
be read after her death). Mrs. Curren specifically uses the phrase "I confess" at several points of direct address to her child: "My dearest child,"
she writes, "As far as I can confess, to you I confess" (124). Shortly after
the long passage quoted in the previous paragraph, she writes, "Is a true
confession still true if it is not heard? Do you hear me, or have I put you
to sleep too?" (151). The repeated references to her shame and disgrace
as a white South African might imply, then, that this is a confession of
her complicity in the "regime of death" in which she still occupies a
privileged place by virtue of her skin color. If Vercueil is unresponsive
or uncaring (in its several senses), the daughter, having left the country
in political protest, surely will not be indifferent to such a confession

and yet her role as confessor, outside the bounds of dialogic exchange, remains "theoretical" rather than literal.[21] Near the start, Mrs. Curren writes of "the disgrace of the life one lives under them [the Nationalist politicians]: to open a newspaper, to switch on the television, like kneeling and being urinated on" (9), but, with what could be seen as self-pitying absorption in her own suffering, for much of the letter's length she wavers between refusing and acknowledging her role in the nation's oppressive politics: "the country smolders, yet with the best will in the world, I can only half-attend. My true attention is all inward" (36). She asks, "Is it my doing that my times have been so shameful? Why should it be left to me, old and sick and full of pain, to lift myself unaided out of this pit of disgrace?" (107) Only a few pages later she again writes of her shame: "In order not to be paralyzed with shame I have had to live a life of getting over the worse. What I cannot get over anymore is that *getting over*. . . . For the sake of my own resurrection I cannot get over it this time" (115).

Mrs. Curren's apparently selfish motive for confessing her disgrace (the desire for absolution or "resurrection")[22] is pointedly shown up by John, the friend of Bheki, her servant's (Florence's) son. When she says to him, in another act of ostensible confession, "I have cancer from the accumulation of shame I have endured in my life," he replies (or she imagines him replying): "What is the point of consuming yourself in shame and loathing? I don't want to listen to the story of how you feel, it is *just another story*. Why don't you *do* something?" (132; my emphasis)

The "doing" implied is active protest, rather than passive liberal breast-beating, notably figured as "just another story" about how one feels. But, as active protest, "doing" appears inherently linked to violence and Mrs. Curren abhors violence, whether that of the police or the retaliatory violence she sees enacted in the townships and squatter camps. She repeatedly voices disgust not only at the rules and agents of the state but also at the rising generation of (largely nonwhite) South Africans birthed by the desperate conditions of apartheid inequality, "the new guardians of the people" (42), "the new puritans" (75) who are "*careless* of their own lives . . . [and] of everyone else's" (45; my emphasis). Their counter-violence and "steely" resolve is the subject of several angry liberal meditations. Again and again she returns to what she refers to as the new generation, the brutalized children who have been "taught that the time of parents is over" (46), who "have left childhood behind and turned brutal, knowing" (71), the children who are "like iron" (46) and will take up the reins in the wake of the apartheid. She speaks bitterly to Mr. Thabane, Florence's cousin, about the comradeship these children share in the liberation struggle:

as for this killing, this bloodletting in the name of *comradeship*, I detest it with all my soul. I think it is barbarous. . . . Comradeship is nothing but a mystique of death, of killing and dying, masquerading as what you call a bond (a bond of what? Love? I doubt it.). I have no sympathy with this comradeship. You are wrong . . . to be taken in by it and, worse, to encourage it in children. (136–37; emphasis in original)

For all her desperate desire to return to the sanctuary of childhood (the "long[ing] to creep into her own mother's lap and be comforted": *AI*, 17) and the innocence of a bygone era,[23] in the course of her letter Mrs. Curren is forced to recognize the impossibility of such a return to the "days of innocence" (21). She literally confronts or is confronted by those outside apartheid's "walled gardens" — those on *die buiterkant* (the out — or outer — side).[24] Initially engagement with these others comes in the form of Bheki, whom she has known since he was a small child. Now fifteen and boycotting school, he takes up residence in his mother's servant's quarters on Mrs. Curren's property. Both he and his friend John are committed to the violent struggle for liberation and are deliberately injured by the police in the course of the narrative before both meet violent deaths at the hands of the same.

It is often argued that as the narrative/letter progresses, Mrs. Curren comes to understand just how unimportant she is in the wider scheme of national emergency and learns to forgo the priority of her individual "I" (ironically, the grounding principle of the liberalism she espouses). This might be seen to invite a reading of the novel in terms of the ethical philosophy of Emmanuel Levinas insofar as Mrs. Curren must learn to relinquish the egoistic "I" in recognition of her responsibility to the singular "other" (be it John or Vercueil).[25] But this is complicated when the relations under scrutiny are not simply those between two individuals; indeed, as the text invites, we might also understand the "other" as (or symbolic of) a larger collective (*all* those on the "other" or "outer" side), so ushering in what Levinas designates as the "third" — the order of politics and judgment where choices between the claims of *specific* individual others become relative and problematic in the face of numerous potentially competing claims. Of course, apartheid, as a regime based on (racial) categorization, was premised on the disavowal of the other's uniqueness. But revolutionary protest against the state, such as in this time of "war" (the word used by Mrs. Cullen to describe the nation's civil unrest), similarly reduces individuals to members of classified categories.[26] In this respect, the notion that the ethical relation between individuals (Mrs. Curren and John, say) should precede and inform the political relations of competing collectivities ("blacks" against "whites," for example) can be inferred as a central assertion in the text.

Dominic Head suggests that Mrs. Curren's "emerging sense of personal insignificance is made manifest through an exploration of the confessional mode, a distinctly literary project that comes to dominate the book."[27] As her illness rages through her body, Mrs. Curren witnesses — and bears witness to — the horrors raging through her homeland: this is "a country prodigal of blood," "a land that drinks rivers of blood and is never sated" (57, 59). On the simplest level, to utilize a dominant trope from the novel, as she awakens to the "disease" infecting the social "body"[28] and she comes to recognize (and eventually confesses) her complicity with the overt agents of terror that maintain the state — despite (and even because of) her liberal aversion to any form of violence as a means to effect political change:[29] "Though [the assertion of white dominance] was not a crime I asked to be committed, it was committed in my name" (149), she finally acknowledges. Likewise, she revises her earlier liberal assertions about revolutionary comradeship: "But now I ask myself: What right have I to opinions about comradeship or anything else? . . . Opinions must be heard by others, heard and weighed, not merely listened to out of politeness" (148). In such terms, what this confession offers, then, is an account of Mrs. Curren's growing awareness of those on the margins, the mass of the ignored and silenced nonwhites that exist, "unseen" and "unheard" beyond the "walled" enclosures, the modern *kraals*, of the infanticidal "Boar"/Boer state or, in a resonant image from the novel, outside the frame of the white photographer's lens. Mrs. Curren remembers a family photograph of herself and her brother in their childhood garden:

> Year after year fruit and flowers and vegetables burgeoned in that garden, pouring forth their seed, dying, resurrecting themselves, blessing us with their profuse presence. . . . But by whose love tended? . . . Whose was the garden rightfully? . . . Who laid the melon-seeds in their warm, moist bed? . . . Who are the ghosts and who the presences? Who, outside the picture, leaning on their rakes, leaning on their spades, waiting to get back to work, lean against the edge of the rectangle, bending it, bursting it in? . . . [Now] we begin to see what used to lie outside the frame, occulted. (102–3)

The allusion to the titular gardener of Coetzee's *Life & Times of Michael K* (1983) seems evident, as does the nod to the image of the resurfacing black corpse in Nadine Gordimer's *The Conservationist*. Following the death of Bheki, Mrs. Curren says: "Now that child is buried and we walk upon him. Let me tell you, when I walk upon this land, this South Africa, I have a gathering feeling of walking upon black faces" (115). Both images suggest the presence — and pressure — of the murdered (black) others that white South Africa has tried, but failed, to "occult."

At Florence's request following an emergency late-night call about her son, Mrs. Curren takes her servant on an early morning visit to Gugu-letu township and surrounding squatter camps where she witnesses first-hand the violence and suffering that is occurring just beyond the bounds of Cape Town, unreported in the censored media: the clash between residents and vigilante *witdoeke* whose arms have probably been supplied by the police (83). Cold, in pain and exhausted, she asks to return home, a request to which Mr. Thabane replies "But what of the people who live here? When they want to go home this is where they must go" (90). Soon after, they are shown the body of Bheki, laid out (ironically) in an abandoned "hall or school" (92). Of the sight of the child's body and its open eyes, Mrs. Curren writes later to her daughter, "Now my eyes are open and I can never close them again" (95). The episode is thus figured as "eye-opening," a climactic turning point in Mrs. Curren's perceptions. Many have commented on the ethical significance of this moment in the novel/letter. As a result of the events of the morning, Sam Durrant argues, for example, that Mrs. Curren becomes "receptive to the call of the other," she can "no longer [be] insulated from the world of the other."[30]

After Bheki's death, things change for Mrs. Curren. She contemplates suicide by immolation in front of the Cape Parliament Building, not to end her own suffering — "What set me off was not my own condition, my sickness, but something quite different" (113) — but as a means of protest against the state. (She later realizes that such a grand political gesture would be misunderstood.) Bheki's death is followed soon after by the shooting of his friend John, who has taken refuge in Florence's vacated room on Mrs. Curren's property. Before the police open fire on the cornered boy, they try to remove Mrs. Curren from her house. She refuses them in her first overt announcement of the boundary she has crossed as a result of her visit to the township: "'*Ek staan nie aan jou kant nie* [I don't stand on your side]. . . . *Ek staan aan die teenkant.*' I stand on the other side" (140; translation in square brackets mine; unbracketed translation appears in the text).[31]

Mrs. Curren's distance from the police is linguistically marked (throughout the novel their speech is given in Afrikaans that remains untranslated apart from the one line given in the passage above). This serves to accentuate her difference from them (presumably as an English-speaking liberal) and, when the single translation is given, to stress the significance of her assertion that she stands on the "other side." But the emphasis on the limits of language, and the gulfs between people it cannot bridge, are not only evident in the engagement of Mrs. Curren and the police. Declaring herself on the "other side" to that of the police, she is still not truly on the side of the others existing beyond the bounds of white Cape Town: she can recross the boundary and return "home" to the white enclave that is not smoldering or corpse-strewn — unlike the truly "other" inhabitants of Guguletu, those *outside*. The barriers of language are emphasized throughout: she not only struggles to communicate with the unresponsive Vercueil but also with Florence in anything other than the familiar discourse of mistress and servant. It is Mr. Thabane who most overtly challenges the efficacy of her outmoded liberal language and, perhaps, by means of whom Coetzee also asks pointed questions about the demand for politically truthful writing as well. When Mr. Thabane asks, "What sort of crime is it that you see [in Guguletu]? What is its name?" Mrs. Curren responds, in a passage noteworthy for its emphasis on the desire to speak *truth* and the difficulty of doing so:

> There are many things I am sure I could say, Mr Thabane. . . . But then they must truly come from me. When one speaks under duress — you should know this — one rarely speaks the truth. . . . There are terrible things going on here. But what I think of them I must say in my own way. . . . These are terrible sights. . . . They are to be condemned. But I cannot denounce them in other people's words. I must find my own words, from myself. Otherwise it is not the truth. . . . To speak of this . . . you would need the tongue of a god. (91)

Here, perhaps, Coetzee is answering those critics who sought from him the truth of apartheid, in realist terms. Unable to "condemn" or "denounce" in "other people's words" he, like his protagonist, must find his *own words* to speak a truth that is larger than, or other than, historical fact or the simple binary of us and them: neither the rhetoric of revolution nor the platitudes of liberalism will suffice to articulate this (perhaps unspeakable) truth with authority. With respect to the issue of authority, Coetzee's comments, made in an interview with David Attwell about the novel, are particularly pertinent:

> Elizabeth Curren brings to bear against the voices of history and historical judgment that reside around her two kinds of authority: the authority of the dying and the authority of the classics. Both these authorities are denied and even derided in her world: the first because hers is a private death, the second because it speaks from long ago and far away.
>   So a contest is staged . . . a contest about having a say. . . . What matters is that the contest is staged, that the dead have their say, even those who speak from a totally untenable historical position. So: even in an age of iron, pity is not silenced. (*DP*, 250)

That said, in this interview Coetzee immediately distances himself from his character and stresses his phrasing in the foregoing passage: "*is staged, is heard;* not *should be staged, should be heard.* There is no ethical imperative that

I claim access to. Elizabeth [Curren] is the one who believes in *should*, who believes in *believes in*" (*DP*, 250). Yet we must ask — as the text demands of us — what "authority" does Coetzee bring to bear "against the voices of history"? Is his (also a white, liberal academic) position as "totally untenable" as Mrs. Curren's? How effective is his "stag[ing]" of "a contest" between competing *political* discourses in the novel? Carrol Clarkson suggests that in the novel, "what matters is that a countervoice is heard" (CV, 160). But, as I have intimated, the contest staged by Coetzee is surely more than that between two categories, between the oppressor and the oppressed. For *within* this contest — a fundamentally political one — the voice that counters the self's authority is a personal one as Mrs. Curren struggles to articulate her *own* truths, "in [her] own way" and in her "own words, from [her]self."[32] Despite the sincerity of the attempt, there seems here also an awareness of the impossibility of the task — for only "the tongue of a god" can succeed.

In response to a question about autobiography, Coetzee responds, in *Doubling the Point*, "that we should distinguish between two kinds of truth, the first truth to fact, the second something beyond that," which he calls a "'higher' truth." Truth to fact is something of a given, he contends, albeit with the rider that any (autobiographical) writing is selective and omits things, and so is inevitably partial: "as long as it does not lie [autobiography] invokes a fairly vacuous idea of truth." But the "higher" truth "beyond" this is the truth about the self. He then asks whether "among the fictions of the self . . . there [are] any that are truer than others," and suggests "truth [about the self] is something that comes in the process of writing, or comes from the process of writing" (*DP*, 17–18). Coetzee articulates similar ideas in "Truth in Autobiography," his inaugural professorial lecture at the University of Cape Town: "we can equally see the confessional enterprise as one of *finding* the truth as of *telling* the truth"; "there is a certain sense in which . . . an autobiographer can be said to be *making* the truth of his life" (*TA*, 3–4; emphasis in original).

If not overtly autobiographical, Mrs. Curren nonetheless characterizes her letter as "my life, these words" (120) and, as suggested, conceives of the letter as confessional: she refers to "this letter, this confession" (178). In this respect she can be seen to *make* rather than *tell* the truth about her self via the act of confessional (autobiographical) writing. Her emphasis on truth becomes more and more insistent as the letter progresses. She tells Vercueil that she chooses not to tell her daughter about her illness because: "on the telephone, love but not truth. In this letter . . . truth and love together at last" (118). And, she suggests, should Vercueil not post the letter, should the daughter not read it, "a certain body of truth will never take on flesh: my truth: how I lived in these times, in this place" (119). "Forgive me," she says to her daughter after writing that she knows Vercueil better than she does her child: "Time is short, I must trust my heart and tell the truth. Sightless, ignorant, I follow where the truth takes me" (148; see also 174); hers is a truth to be found by "follow[ing] the pen, going where it takes me" (99).

The "truth" posited here is "my truth," a truth about the self found, or made, in (confessional) writing. It is truth of another order to that of historical "fact," a "'higher' truth" in the words of Coetzee quoted above. In his extended essay on confession, "Confession and Double Thoughts," Coetzee writes that

> Confession is one component in a sequence of transgression, confession, penitence and absolution. Absolution means the end of the episode, the closing of the chapter, *liberation from the oppression of memory*. Absolution in this sense is therefore the indispensable goal of all confession, sacramental or secular. In contrast, transgression is not a fundamental component. (*DP*, 251–52; my emphasis)

Toward the end of this essay, Coetzee shifts from the assertion that confession is motivated by the desire to articulate truth to a confessor who is able to able to absolve, to the suggestion that the desired "end" of confession is "to tell the truth *to and for oneself*" (*DP*, 291; my emphasis). This end, however, is unachievable; the self "cannot tell the truth of itself to itself and come to rest without the possibility of self-deception" (*DP*, 291). Coetzee suggests that the writing of Rousseau, Tolstoy, and Dostoevsky, considered in the essay, reveals a particularly modern ontological problem insofar as they "confront or evade the problem of how to know the truth about the self without being self-deceived, and how to bring the confession to an end in the spirit of whatever they take to be the secular equivalent of absolution" (*DP*, 252). On such an account, absolution is equivalent to knowing a/the essential truth about one's self; so too, perhaps, for Mrs. Curren who seeks truth she can call *her own*.

But, as Coetzee asks in "Confession and Double Thoughts," how can one know such a truth when the confessing self is plagued by the "double thoughts" of self-deception? The problem is particularly acute for an agnostic confessant, as Mrs. Curren decidedly is. Comparing her letter to a maze and herself to a bitch in heat lost within it, she says that "God is another dog in another maze" (126), who can smell but not reach her. How, then, does one attain "liberation from the oppression of memory" without the intercession of one premised as being above/beyond the self and so able to grant definitive absolution: God, or his interlocutor, the priest? The question raised, Coetzee asserts, is "whether secular confession, for which there is an auditor or audience, real or fictional, but no confessor empowered to absolve, can ever lead to that *end of the chapter* whose attainment is the goal of confession" (*DP*, 253; emphasis in original). Mrs. Curren, a (self-narrating) secular self, for all her appeals to the "real or fictional" auditor (Vercueil) or her intended audience (her daughter), is, in the final analysis, both confessor and confessant in this letter that may never be read by another: "To whom this writing then?" she asks. "The answer: to you but not to you; to me; to you in me" (5).

The problem posed, then, is one of truthfulness, certainly, but not one of truth to fact; in this novel Coetzee has carefully ensured his history is *not* "all wrong." The truth Coetzee interrogates is of another order entirely: "Because the basic movement of self-reflexiveness is a doubting and questioning movement," Coetzee writes, "it is in the nature of the truth told to itself by the reflecting self not to be final" (*DP*, 263). For the (modern) writers he considers, "the project of confession . . . raises intricate and, on the face of it, intractable problems regarding truthfulness, problems whose common factor seems to be a regression to infinity of self-awareness and self-doubt" (*DP*, 274). Put another way, how does one confess to oneself "*with authority*" (*DP*, 264; my emphasis)? Towards the end of the essay, following analysis of confessional episodes in three of Dostoevsky's novels, Coetzee again asserts what he sees as the writer's (and the modern self's) insoluble dilemma:

> The endless chain manifests itself as soon as self-consciousness enters; how to enter into the possession of the truth of oneself, how to attain self-forgiveness and transcend self-doubt, would seem, for structural reasons, to have to remain in the field of mystery; and even the demarcation in this field, even the specification of the structural reasons, would similarly have to remain unarticulated; and the reasons for this silence as well. (*DP*, 291)

Again, it is worth noting Coetzee's claim that (self)forgiveness, which is equated with the possession of "the truth of oneself," is impossible. He moves on to voice his central question: "what potential for the attainment of truth [and so of forgiveness] can there be in the self-interrogation of a confessing consciousness?" (*DP*, 293). Head argues that this is the question that animates *Age of Iron*:

> *Age of Iron* seems to have been constructed in such a way as to confront the problem of double thought and tainted confession. . . . There is a clear sense that the narrative functions primarily as a confession by and for the self — or, at least, that Coetzee is trying to construct a narrative situation that comes as close as possible to this confessional ideal, and to the revelation of truth. (CI, 68).

In such terms, Mrs. Curren can be seen to confess, and seek forgiveness, for truths that are personal, ones found via confessional writing and directed, ultimately, to herself, alone. Paradoxically, however, her confession confesses her failure to attain or articulate such a truth. It is a failure, I contend, attributable to the need for another, an "other" who can hear/read her truth and — perhaps — extend the desired absolution in the face of the self's inability to do so. In this respect she relinquishes, at last, the sovereignty of the monologic "I" that dominates the text; she overcomes her will to live and gives her life, literally, into Vercueil's hands — just as Coetzee, figuratively, relinquishes authority over his text in giving it to his reader. Set within a novel that, of all his fictions to this point, most overtly appears to treat the *facts* of apartheid history, the *truths* Coetzee asserts (or has his protagonist attempt to assert) are those of the most personal, intimate, subjective kind. These are ethical truths, perhaps — those of self-abnegation and the acceptance of personal irrelevance — which are most forcefully articulated in Mrs. Curren's claim that "death is the only truth left" (23): death for Coetzee's protagonist, yes, but also (in what we might call Barthesian terms) the "death of the author" too.[33]

On the difficulty of killing oneself, Mrs. Curren writes of a giving over to thoughtlessness, a loss of the self-conscious self: "One clings so tight to life! It seems to me that something other than the will must come into play at the last instant, something foreign, something thoughtless, to sweep you over the brink. *You have to become someone other than yourself*" (109; my emphasis).

It is with precisely such a giving over to otherness that the novel ends. We need to be wary, however, and not just reverse the prioritization of historical fact over subjective ethics.[34] For while the ethical truth towards which Mrs. Curren's writing finally tends is a "thoughtless" (nonegoistic) one, the need to "become someone other than yourself,"[35] this, it is also implied, is the impulse that should inform politics, the pressing subject of the novel's realism. It is not only a necessary recognition of another "I" that subsumes the importance of the subjective self, but also of an "other" that is needed because s/he can forgive where the self cannot and so bring confession to an end.

In *Age of Iron* a contest is certainly staged. It is not a contest between competing (political) factions or competing (historical) facts, nor even one between fact and fiction. Moreover, the uncontestable lyricism of the novel, the sheer poetry of Coetzee's prose, cuts against any reductive claims regarding its political realism. If the novel *seems* to respond to the demand for realism from Coetzee, at the same time it undermines the naive notion that politics is somehow divorced from metaphysics or (personal) ethics — and, for that matter, from aesthetics. Indeed, how questions about aesthetics intersect with questions of ethics is fundamental to the novel's concerns, as it is to all of Coetzee's writing. How *does* one speak the truth if to do so requires "the tongue of a god"? The contest staged in this novel, then, is one in which the political, the ethical, and the aesthetic "are heard," and resonate in ways that render problematic any simple requirement of the writer to bear factual witness to politics and history, and the desire of any self to (self)-confess with authority.

Notes

[1] While I refer to this as an essay and quote from the published version ("The Novel Today," *Upstream* 6, no. 1 [1988]: 2–5), the paper was originally given as an address in 1987. Subsequent references appear as NT with the accompanying page number. Of the essay, David Attwell notes, "Paradoxically, his address at the *Weekly Mail*'s book festival of 1987, published obscurely in a Cape Town poetry magazine as 'The Novel Today' and never subsequently collected, is probably [Coetzee's] most widely cited statement [about the right to public recognition of fiction] outside his fiction": "The Life and Times of Elizabeth Costello: J. M. Coetzee and the Public Sphere," in *J. M. Coetzee and the Idea of the Public Intellectual*, ed. Jane Poyner (Athens: Ohio UP, 2006), 25–41; here, 28. Subsequent references appear as PI with the accompanying page number.

[2] This notion of the political function of (resisting) writing, of course, provided perverse support for the regime's censorship of (realist) literature and may explain in part why, in Peter McDonald's words, "Coetzee escaped the censor" ("'Not Undesirable': How J. M. Coetzee Escaped the Censor," *TLS* 19 [May 2000]: 14–15.). Patently, Coetzee is not suggesting that literature operates in a realm distinct from the political — far from it; nonetheless, as McDonald argues in "The Writer, the Critic, and the Censor" (PI, 42–62), the polarity between art and politics apparently set up in Coetzee's essay may well have reinforced the simple binary terms employed by the censors themselves.

[3] Quoted in Mike Marais, "Interpretative Authoritarianism: Reading/Colonizing Coetzee's Foe," *English in Africa* 16, no. 1 (May 1989): 9–16; here, 10; my emphasis.

[4] See Ménan du Plessis for a discussion of the left-wing rejection of Coetzee's fiction in these terms and a counter to this stance in relation to *Waiting for the Barbarians*: "Towards a True Materialism," *Contrast* 13, no. 4 (1981): 77–78. Subsequent references appear as TM with the accompanying page number. Best known, perhaps, is Nadine Gordimer's critique, published under the guise of a review of *The Life & Times of Michael K* in "The Idea of Gardening," *New York Review of Books* (2 February 1984): Available at: www.nybooks.com/articles/archives/1984/feb/02/the-idea-of-gardening. On Coetzee's "involvement with Gordimer's writing — the one-sided polemic," see Karina Szczurek, "Coetzee and Gordimer," In *J. M. Coetzee in Context and Theory*, ed. Elleke Boehmer, Robert Eaglestone, and Katy Iddiols, 36–46 (New York: Continuum, 2009).

[5] Dominic Head, *J. M. Coetzee*, Cambridge: Cambridge UP, 1997, 4–5; subsequent references appear as JMC with the accompanying page number. *Age of Iron* is sometimes read as the prequel to Coetzee's final "South African" novel, *Disgrace*, which also portrays a clearly recognizable (albeit postapartheid) setting. Supporting such a linkage of the two novels are the many references by Mrs. Curren to the disgrace she feels as a white South African, as discussed below.

[6] This includes the names of specific Cape Town streets (Breda Street, Orange Street, Government Avenue) and buildings (Groote Schuur Hospital and the Parliament Buildings), landscape features (Chapman's Peak, Hout Bay, Outeniqua Mountains, Prince Alfred's Pass), references to media censorship and the boycott of schools by nonwhite children at the time of writing, descriptions of Guguletu township and squatter camps on the Cape Flats, and clear reference to the vigilante gangs encouraged by police — the so-called "*witdoeke*" — who roamed the latter, wreaking wanton destruction. On the "precisely evoked" political context, see JMC, 132–33 and 176n5. On the debate regarding realism in Coetzee's fiction and its relationship to the South African political context, see, especially, Susan VanZanten Gallagher's *A Story of South Africa: J. M. Coetzee's Fiction in Context* (Cambridge: Harvard UP, 1991) and David Attwell's essay "The Problem of History in the Fiction of J. M. Coetzee," in *Rendering Things Visible: Essays on South African Literary Culture*, ed. Martin Trump, 94–133 (Athens: Ohio UP, 1990), and his *J. M. Coetzee: South Africa and the Politics of Writing* (Berkeley: U of California P and Cape Town: David Philip, 1993).

[7] Of course, there is an allegorical dimension to the novel, one to which Mrs. Curren herself points (84); in this respect it is sometimes read for its allusions to the *Aeneid* from which Mrs. Curren quotes to Vercueil, her unlikely "ferryman" (192). On this point, see Laura Wright, *Writing "Out of All the Camps": J. M. Coetzee's Narratives of Displacement* (New York, London: Routledge, 2006): 66–72. See also David Attwell, who refers to Vercueil as the "Angel of Death" (*DP*, 250), as well as Attwell's "'Dialogue' and 'Fulfilment' in J. M. Coetzee's *Age of Iron*" in *Writing South Africa: Literature, Apartheid, and Democracy, 1970–1995*, ed. Derek Attridge and Rosemary Jolly, 149–65 (Cambridge: Cambridge UP, 1998) — a reading apparently encouraged by Mrs. Curren's several references to Vercueil in such terms (14, 146), while dismissing the same at other times. According to Attridge: "At the very least, we have to say that an allegorical reading of Vercueil's part in the novel cannot be straightforward" ("Against Allegory: *Waiting for the Barbarians*, *Life & Times of Michael K*, and the Question of Literary Reading," in PI, 64). There are also many references to the ancient Greek Furies and Circe, opening other avenues for allegorical reading: see Mike Marais, "Places of Pigs: The Tension between Implication and Transcendence in J. M. Coetzee's *Age of Iron* and *The Master of Petersburg*," in *Critical Essays on J. M. Coetzee*, ed. Sue Kossew (London: Prentice Hall, 1998), 226–38. The many metaphoric parallels between Mrs. Curren's dying body and that of the South African state are also open to allegorical reading, as discussed below.

[8] Although Coetzee refers to her as Elizabeth Curren in *Doubling the Point* (*DP*, 250), her first name is not given in the novel (and a husband is mentioned), hence my use of the designation "Mrs. Curren" rather than the name "Elizabeth Curren" that is more often used in critical accounts of the text.

[9] The infanticide of the state is not only figured as enacted by boar/Boer "fathers" but also by the "motherland" (111) that incessantly drinks the blood of its offspring/populace and remains unsated.

[10] For a novel reading of Coetzee's use of the epistolary form in *Age of Iron*, see Patrick Hayes, "Literature, History and Folly," in *J. M. Coetzee in Context and Theory*, ed. Elleke Boehmer, Katy Iddiols, and Robert Eaglestone (London: Con-

tinuum, 2009), 112–22. The epistolary form also functions, as it does in the second section of *Foe*, to stress the monologic quality of the writing. Mrs. Curren's letter is inescapably written in her voice and from her perspective, stressing her role as a controlling (albeit limited) narrator with the power to include or omit as she sees fit. On the use of the epistolary form in *Foe* and its relation to questions of power, see Worthington, *Self as Narrative: Subjectivity and Community in Contemporary Fiction* (Oxford: Clarendon, 1996), 258–63.

[11] Jane Poyner, *J. M. Coetzee and the Paradox of Postcolonial Authorship* (Farnham, UK: Ashgate, 2009), 111. Subsequent references appear as PPA with the accompanying page number.

[12] See Carrol Clarkson for an elaboration on Coetzee's statement and his later qualification of it: *J. M. Coetzee: Countervoices* (Basingstoke: Palgrave Macmillan, 2009), 45. Subsequent references appear as CV with the accompanying page number.

[13] On the other hand, Benita Parry argues that in the novel, Coetzee presents Mrs. Curren's letter as "pastiches of naturalist reportage and morally outraged protest writing, modes which Coetzee is known to despise, and which are directed to displaying the banality of a white South African literature which undertakes to write the voice of the oppressed": "Speech and Silence in the Novels of J. M. Coetzee," in *Critical Perspectives on J. M. Coetzee*, ed. Graham Huggan and Stephen Watson (London: Macmillan, 1996), 37–67; here, 49.

[14] She writes: "To have fallen pregnant with these growths, these cold, obscene swellings. . . . My eggs, grown within me. . . . Monstrous growths, misbirths: a sign that one is beyond one's term. This country too: time for fire, time for an end, time for what grows out of ash to grow" (59).

[15] At the very end of the novel, the epistolary conceit is stretched to its limits, its truth value and authority undermined as we are asked to imagine Mrs. Curren writing fully grammatical sentences in the narration of her final "embrace" with Vercueil, one of such force that "the breath went out of [her] in a rush" (181).

[16] See Attwell ("Dialogue," 176), Head (JMC, 140), and Poyner (PPA, 116).

[17] For an excellent discussion in these terms, see Attridge, "Trusting the Other: Ethics and Politics in J. M. Coetzee's *Age of Iron*," in *The Writings of J. M. Coetzee*, ed. Michael Valdez Moses, 59–82 (a special issue of *South Atlantic Quarterly* 93, no. 1 [1994]). Of John, Mrs. Curren writes, "He is part of my salvation. I must love him. But I do not love him. Nor do I want to love him enough to love him despite myself" (125). Not long after, however, she writes of a significant change: "Yet something went out from me to him. I ached to embrace him, to protect him" (139). Hania A. M. Nashef suggests that part of Mrs. Curren's realization is that she has "failed to love *the unlovable*" (*The Politics of Humiliation in the Novels of J. M. Coetzee* [New York: Routledge, 2009], 124; emphasis in original), something she corrects, perhaps, in the growing attachment she forms with Vercueil and in her "ache" to embrace and protect John. Mike Marais similarly argues that the novel urges the love of the unlovable, "and in subverting the boundary between subject and object, self and other, it holds out the hope of constructing an ethical system which is grounded not in subject-centred consciousness, but in intersubjectivity" ("Places of Pigs," 233).

[18] "Absolution is . . . the indispensable goal of all confession," writes Coetzee in his essay "Confession and Double Thoughts" (*DP*, 151).

[19] See also her claimed desire for the "shamelessness" of the "shamefulness" of her childhood (119).

[20] Mrs. Curren says to Vercueil, in defence of her refusal to give him money unless he works for it: "The spirit of charity has perished in this country. Because those who accept charity despise it, while those who give give with a despairing heart. What is the point of charity if it does not go from heart to heart? . . . Charity: from the Latin word for heart" (19–20). But of this "false etymolog[y]" she writes to her daughter, "A lie: charity, *caritas*, has nothing to do with the heart. . . . Care: the true root of charity" (20).

[21] See Head on the "theoretical" function fulfilled by the daughter and the suggestion that there is "no auditor or confessor to engage Mrs Curren in dialogue" enabling her to "progress towards the purity of a confession untainted by self-justification": Dominic Head, *The Cambridge Introduction to J. M. Coetzee* (Cambridge: Cambridge UP, 2009), 68.

[22] Elsewhere she writes, "I want to sell myself, redeem myself" (107), and "that is my first word, my first confession . . . I want to be saved" (124–25; ellipses in original).

[23] She writes, "*In my day*: a phrase one came across in this day only in Letters to the Editor. . . . In my day, now over; in my life, now past" (48; emphasis in original).

[24] It is no coincidence that Mrs. Curren lives on "Buitenkant Street." On the significance of this, see Hayes, "Literature, History and Folly," 120.

[25] Eduard Jordaan suggests that novel is, in part, "a narration of how the other ruptures a specific subject's self-regarding egoism" ("A White South African Liberal as Hostage to the Other: Reading J. M. Coetzee's *Age of Iron* through Levinas," *South African Journal of Philosophy* 24, no. 1 (2005): 22–32). He reads Mrs. Curren as "a subject whose self-regard is displaced and hollowed out by the appearance of the other, Mr Vercueil" (23–24).

[26] Mrs. Curren speaks to John (a generic "*nom de guerre*" [*AI*, 134] rather than individuating name) of Thucydides and the lessons one can learn from his work about "what can happen to our humanity in time of war. . . . Thucydides wrote of people who made rules and followed them. Going by rule they killed whole classes of enemies without exception. Most of those who died felt, I am sure, that a terrible mistake was being made, that, whatever the rule was, it could not be meant for them, 'I! —': that was their last word as their throats were cut. A word of protest, the exception" (73). For a thought-provoking discussion of the significance of this passage, particularly in support of a Levinasian reading of the novel, see Eduard Jordaan ("A White South African Liberal"). Jordaan is, of course, not the first to read Coetzee in light of Levinas's ideas regarding the responsibility of the subject to the other, and although his essay significantly postdates major interventions in this respect (by Mike Marais in particular), he makes no mention of such accounts of Coetzee's work.

[27] Dominic Head, "A Belief in Frogs: J. M. Coetzee's Enduring Faith in Fiction," in PI, 100–117; here, 102. Head argues that in this novel, as in *The Master of Petersburg*, Coetzee "engages in an extended investigation of the potential of the confessional mode, seeking to extract from it a secular equivalent of absolution" (103).

[28] For a reading that explores the allegorical equivalence between Mrs. Curren's dying body and that of the apartheid state, see Fiona Probyn, "Cancerous Bodies and Apartheid in J. M. Coetzee's *Age of Iron*," in *Critical Essays on J. M. Coetzee*, ed. Sue Kossew, 214–25. Probyn writes "because cancer poses a threat to binary oppositions such as inside/outside and self/other, it provides a paradoxically enabling tool for understanding the (complicit) nature of binary oppositions, and therefore, the nature of complicity itself" (214).

[29] Compare Coetzee who, in *Doubling the Point*, says that he is "unable to, or refuse[s] to, conceive of a liberating violence" (*DP*, 337).

[30] Sam Durrant, "J. M. Coetzee, Elizabeth Costello, and the Limits of the Sympathetic Imagination," in PI, 118–34; here, 125.

[31] Interestingly, the Afrikaans word *teenkant* is more often used to designate the "opposing side," not simply the "other side." Coetzee's choice of the word "other" in his given translation should, then, not be overlooked.

[32] It is not so much that Coetzee sets the private against the political but, rather, as I have argued elsewhere with James Meffan, that he understands the ethical relationship between an individual self and other as that which must inform — indeed, come before — politics; see James Meffan and Kim L. Worthington: "Ethics before Politics: J. M. Coetzee's *Disgrace*," in *Mapping the Ethical Turn: A Reader in Ethics, Culture and Literary Theory*, ed. Todd F. Davis and Kenneth Womack (Charlottesville: UP of Virginia, 2001). See, also, Attridge, "Trusting the Other," on the significance of the ethical in relation to the political in *Age of Iron*.

[33] Mrs. Curren characterizes "writing . . . [as] the foe of death" (106) but at the novel's end, of course, her writing comes to an end as surely as her life does.

[34] See Coetzee on the ethical and political in *Doubling the Point*: while acknowledging the tendency in his work to focus on the ethical he says, "the last thing I want to do is *definitely* embrace the ethical as against the political. I don't want to contribute, in that way, toward marking the ethical pole with lack" (*DP*, 200; emphasis in original).

[35] Here we might recall Coetzee's claim that "if all of us imagine violence as violence against ourselves, perhaps we would have peace" (*DP*, 337).

9: *The Master of Petersburg* (1994)

Michelle Kelly

IN AN INTERVIEW WITH DAVID ATTWELL in the early nineties, J. M. Coetzee lamented not having the "badge of honor" of having had a book banned under the repressive apartheid censorship regime, which at that point was nearing the end of a forty-year reign. In the same interview, he suggests that "the intensity, the pointedness, the *seriousness* of Russian writing from the time of Nicholas I is in part a reflection of the fact that every word published represented a risk taken" (*DP*, 299). Playing down the power of South African censorship to thwart the circulation of texts that had been published abroad, he nonetheless notes its "uglier, deforming side effects": "The very fact that certain topics are forbidden creates an unnatural concentration upon them" (*DP*, 300). Indeed, while rejecting the "stupidity" of censorship and advocating its abolition, he speculates about what the absence of boundaries might mean: "in an abstract way I think there ought to be bounds to what is licit, if only as a way of making it possible to be transgressive" (*DP*, 298–99). These comments were made as the settlement that would lead to the first democratic elections in South Africa in 1994 was being negotiated. While the new state would clearly bring into being new boundaries of acceptability, Coetzee's comments raise questions about the relationship between transgression and risk in the postapartheid state.

In a series of essays published between 1988 and 1993, and collected in *Giving Offense* (1996), Coetzee focuses on the "uglier, deforming side effects" of censorship. He suggests that censorship affects the writing process as well as the material dissemination of texts, opening the possibility that all writing produced under censorship may bear traces of the encounter with those most forensic of readers, as the censor may be "repudiated with visceral intensity but never wholly expelled" (*GO*, 10). Here I will take up this idea in Coetzee's first postapartheid novel, *The Master of Petersburg* (1994). Written as the threat of censorship in South Africa dissipated, the novel provides a fictional account of the period in the life of Fyodor Dostoevsky when he was writing *The Possessed*. Famously subject to censorship by Dostoevsky's editor, *The Possessed* is now published with the excised chapter "At Tikhon's" included as an appendix; Coetzee's novel culminates in the writing of what appears to be an early draft of the chapter.

Coetzee's Dostoevsky is very much a public figure, an author recognized by strangers, subject to gossip and rumor, and targeted by the
police and revolutionaries. Writing, however, remains a private activity,
"a private matter," he insists, "till it is given to the world" (*MP*, 40).
Significantly, the writing that is staged within *Petersburg* is not published,
and therefore not subject to official scrutiny. It is premised on the violation of certain limits nonetheless; Dostoevsky's writing in the final pages
of the novel is portrayed as obscene, "an assault on the innocence of a
child," but it is also a self-conscious violation of the private life of his son
and, by extension, of his own private life (*MP*, 249). This is significant,
I will argue, in a novel published as apartheid and its repressive legacy is
finally set aside in favor of a new postapartheid state with an emphasis on
human rights, civil liberties, and freedom of expression. No longer faced
with the boundaries imposed by the censor, Coetzee's novel seeks out
and transgresses new boundaries. These issues are brought into view, I
will suggest, when read alongside the series of essays published in *Giving
Offense*, which range in their focus between the paranoia that results from
the threat posed by repressive censorship regimes, on the one hand, and
the liberal values that underpin opposition to censorship on the other.
While the threat of a paranoid state embodied in the police officer Maximov casts a shadow over Coetzee's novel, the risks taken by his fictionalized Dostoevsky are those of transgressing the limits of decency and
privacy rather than the political.

Set in St. Petersburg in the late 1860s, *Petersburg* begins as Dostoevsky returns to the city from exile in Dresden to tie up loose ends following the death of his twenty-two-year-old stepson, Pavel Isaev. The
grief-stricken writer installs himself in his stepson's former lodgings,
awaiting the return of papers that were seized by the policeman Maximov
as part of the investigation into Pavel's death, while making surprising
discoveries about his stepson's revolutionary politics. Pavel was part of a
nihilist group led by Sergei Nechaev, and Dostoevsky gradually finds himself drawn into his stepson's former circle as the Machiavellian Nechaev
seeks to exploit the reputation of his former follower's stepfather. Indeed,
as the novel develops, Dostoevsky suspects that Pavel was murdered for
precisely this reason.

While the novel frequently portrays its writer-protagonist seated at a
table poised to begin writing, he is in mourning, absorbed in memories
of his stepson and his desire, as father and writer, to bring Pavel back
to life, a desire that finds expression in recurring references to the myth
of Orpheus and Eurydice. Writing, when it is contemplated, becomes
something obscene. "Possessed" by grief, the novelist hesitates to put
pen to paper, afraid that his anguish would find expression only in an
offensive form: "the writing, he fears, would be that of a madman — vile-
ness, obscenity, page after page of it, untameable. . . . What flows onto

the page is neither blood nor ink but an acid, black, with an unpleasing green sheen when the light glances off it" (*MP*, 18). In the attention to the materiality of the writing, the passage suggests that writing itself becomes a thing, as opposed to a representation. This echoes ideas about the pornographic in *Giving Offense*, where Coetzee finds that in "offering to be the thing itself" (*GO*, 33), rather than standing for something else, the pornographic presents its greatest challenge to representation. Later in *Petersburg*, Dostoevsky suspects that his relationship with Anna Sergeyevna, Pavel's landlady, will give rise to a pornographic text: "a book of the kind one cannot publish in Russia. . . . A book of the night, in which every excess would be represented and no bounds respected" (*MP*, 134). But it is only in the closing chapter that Coetzee's Dostoevsky actually puts pen to paper. Named "Stavrogin" after the protagonist of Dostoevsky's *The Possessed*, this final chapter finds the fictional novelist writing stories that seem to form the basis for "Stavrogin's Confession" in the chapter "At Tikhon's," which, as I noted earlier, Dostoevsky was actually forced to omit from the serialized novel by his editor. Significantly, the stories are not presented in the confessional form of "At Tikhon's" — indeed, the confessor Tikhon is omitted — and they are written not under the name of author Fyodor Dostoevsky, but into the pages of his dead stepson's diary, and left for the attention of Matryona, the nine-year-old daughter of Pavel's landlady. Written and positioned to corrupt Matryona, the writing is, once more, "the thing itself." The stories, the circumstances in which they are written, and the audience for which they are intended, lead Dostoevsky to reflect that this writing "is an assault upon the innocence of child. It is an act for which he can expect no forgiveness" (*MP*, 249).

Given the textual history of "At Tikhon's" and the terms in which this creative act is elaborated, it is not difficult to see why critics have suggested that Coetzee's novel is an act of creative restoration, returning the excised chapter to the public record. According to Jane Poyner, "by engaging with a novel that effectively has been censored, Coetzee notionally enacts an evasion of the censor."[1] But Coetzee's novel is not a straightforward work of restoration. Insofar as it deals with historical events, they are subject to substantial reworking. While *The Possessed* is widely believed by scholars of the Russian author to have been inspired by the murder of a student in Moscow in 1869, Coetzee reinvents the episode as the possible murder of Dostoevsky's stepson, who in fact outlived his famous stepfather. Coetzee's reworking of the material therefore shifts the emphasis from the political drama of the Russian novel into a private, domestic tragedy. Nor is it an unambiguous plea for freedom of expression. Pavel's private diary will not be subject to official censorship. Indeed, the most immediate challenge to the story that is taking shape at the end of *Petersburg* comes from Dostoevsky himself, who detects in his own writing a betrayal of his beloved stepson: "Not a matter of fidelity at all. On the contrary, a matter of betrayal — betrayal of love first of all, and then of Pavel and the mother and child and everyone else. *Perversion*: everything and everyone to be turned to another use, to be gripped to him and fall with him" (*MP*, 235). This is not a liberal argument for the uncensored dissemination of offensive material, but acknowledgement that the impulses behind the writing process, behind the creation of literature, might be anything but benign. For Derek Attridge, writing in this novel is presented "as having nothing to do with traditional understandings of ethics, or with human responsibility — only responsibility to and for the new, unanticipatable thing that is coming into being."[2] In addition, the renaming of "At Tikhon's" as "Stavrogin" and the omission of the confessor figure Tikhon suggests an opposition in purpose to Dostoevsky's novel with implications peculiar to the postapartheid context in which Coetzee was writing. Coetzee's treatment of censorship and authorship in *Giving Offense* allows the relevance of *Petersburg* to this context to come to the fore. *Giving Offense* provides a fascinating account of the way in which the supposedly private creative process is vulnerable to and reliant on the public world — of publishing, reading, politics — and this becomes particularly acute in the case of state censorship. The preoccupation with various forms of censorship in *Petersburg* reinforces this, but it is in staging the myth of Orpheus and Eurydice that the force of the ban, and the risk of breaking it, acquires its sharpest focus.

The two most important books on apartheid censorship give some insight into the uneasy proximity of Coetzee and his official readers during the apartheid period. One of these is Coetzee's own *Giving Offense*, in which he compares the experience of writing under censorship to "being intimate with someone who does not love you, with whom you want no intimacy, but who presses himself in upon you" (*GO*, 38). For Coetzee, "creativity of a certain kind involves inhabiting and managing and exploiting quite primitive parts of the self," the "inner menagerie" (*GO*, 38). This is not, he says, a particularly dangerous activity but it is delicate, and profoundly private, "so private that it almost constitutes the definition of privacy: how I am with myself" (*GO*, 38). It is into this private world that the state censor intrudes, "the dark-suited, bald-headed censor, with his pursed lips and his red pen and his irritability and his censoriousness" (*GO*, 38). So, while Coetzee's novels appear to have escaped censorship, according to this account, the censor was nonetheless a vivid presence for the writer.

In *The Literature Police*, Peter McDonald's more recent cultural history of apartheid-era censorship, the censor of Coetzee's imagination is named, and it turns out to be not the "dark-suited" and "bald-headed" character depicted in *Giving Offense*, but minor figures in the South African intelligentsia — writers, Coetzee's fellow academics.[3] Their response to his novels was not to wield the "red pen" but to point out that those aspects of *In the Heart of the Country*, *Waiting for the Barbarians*, and *Life & Times of Michael K* that were, in the terminology of the South African censors, "undesirable," were mitigated by the literariness of the works and consequently posed no great threat to the apartheid state (LP, 309–15). Drawing on correspondence between Coetzee and his publishers and on the reports on those novels submitted by official readers, McDonald portrays a writer aware of what was likely to be judged "undesirable" by the censors — identifying, for example, potentially problematic passages in *In the Heart of the Country* — yet playing at the fringes of the rules nonetheless (LP, 310–12).

There is, of course, ample evidence in McDonald's book and elsewhere of the legitimate threat posed by apartheid censorship or, more destructive still, the power of the security forces to "ban" individuals. But the image of censors as well-meaning guardians of the literary nonetheless contrasts sharply with the intrusive figure conjured in Coetzee's description. In a sense, the gap between the two accounts vindicates Coetzee's analysis of censorship as a paranoid discourse that breeds paranoia. Indeed, he admits to having "felt within myself some of its more secret and shameful effects," and that the essays in *Giving Offense* itself "may be a specimen of the kind of paranoid discourse it seeks to describe" (*GO*, 37). But while censorship is constructed as an external threat or invasion into the private world of writing, Coetzee's description also suggests that it is continuous with the psychic drama of the creative process, which is portrayed as a state of openness, vulnerability, and strategic engagement with others. He describes the modern self, divided against itself, as "a zoo in which a multitude of beasts have residence, over which the anxious, overworked zookeeper of rationality exercises a rather limited control," and creative activity emerges from this (*GO* 37). But, significantly, "writing not only comes out of the zoo but (to be hypermetaphorical) goes back in again. That is to say, insofar as writing is transactional, the figures *for whom* and *to whom* it is done are also figures in the zoo: for instance, the figure-of-the-beloved" (*GO*, 38). The relevance of this for censorship is evident in his essay on Afrikaans poet Breyten Breytenbach, who endured censorship, banning, and imprisonment. Coetzee's reading of Breytenbach negotiates between the defiant public utterances of the writer who views the censor unequivocally as a foe and the private world of his writing that bears the scars of his engagement with this foe. Coetzee describes the public statements as: "an unambiguous struggle between a voice struggling to utter itself and a gag that stifles it" (*GO*, 232). But his account of Breytenbach's "private" encounter with the censor in his work is more typical of the struggle between the private and the public that characterizes *Giving Offense*: "the doctrine to be teased out of his more intimate writings, is that the writer writes against and cannot write without a manifold of internalized resistances that are in essence no different from an internalized censor-twin, both cherished and hated" (*GO*, 232). So, whether imagined as censor-twin or figure-of-the-beloved, what Coetzee describes as the transactional nature of the writing process clearly serves that process.

While *Giving Offense* is notable for the elaborate private life of writing constructed by Coetzee, the above examples suggest that the various intrusions into this private sphere are more significant still. The private world of writing described by Coetzee is situated within a discussion of authorship as an institution constructed by the public demands placed on writers. To this extent he follows Foucault's description of the "author" whose function is "to characterize the existence, circulation, and operation of certain discourses within a society," as well as the role of censorship in defining the institution: "Speeches and books were assigned real authors . . . only when the author became subject to punishment and to the extent that his discourse was considered transgressive."[4] But Coetzee exceeds Foucault's account both in his emphasis on the private experience of writing and his consideration of the emergence of authorship as a profession: "The notion that, by dint of writing, a person could aspire to and attain fame" (*GO*, 41). He traces the "mystique" of the author and the desire for "fame and immortality" to the invention of printing that allows the author to "project his signature — and indeed sometimes his portrait — into the world, in a multiplied form" (*GO*, 41). This is the source of the writer's power but also the origins of the rivalry between writer and state; the "master author" is targeted by the state not just for what he writes, as in Foucault's account, but on account of "a certain disseminative power of which the power to publish and have read is only the most marked manifestation" (*GO*, 43). So authorship, in *Giving Offense*, is not merely "the definition of privacy," an "inner menagerie" subject to invasion by the hostile forces of the state, but the willingness and compulsion to sacrifice this "privacy" in the sphere of publishing. In other words, in spite of Coetzee's assertion that writing is the "definition of privacy," writing's claim to privacy is tenuous indeed. To return to his remarks in the interview with Attwell about boundaries enabling transgression, *Giving Offense* constructs a private sphere of writing in order to dramatize creativity in terms of invasion and sacrifice. Similarly, he constructs a private life for Dostoevsky in *Petersburg* so that the fictional author can be seen to betray it, and can experience writing as a betrayal of the private.

The relevance of this to the postapartheid period in which *Giving Offense* and *Petersburg* were published emerges in debates about the changing place of the literary in South Africa. McDonald's *The Literature Police* situates apartheid censorship in a context in which pressure was exerted on writers, publishers, and commentators by the opposing demands of the apartheid state and the necessity for political resistance to it. *Giving Offense* could be seen as a late installment in this debate, reinforcing Coetzee's commitment to the distinctiveness of writing and storytelling from history and politics as outlined in his earlier essays "Into the Dark Chamber" (1986) and "The Novel Today" (1987). McDonald places "The Novel Today" in this context, emphasizing its echoes of similar critical interventions in the early 1980s. But *Giving Offense* could also be seen to engage directly with a later intervention in this debate by lawyer and ANC-activist Albie Sachs. In "Preparing Ourselves for Freedom," a paper first submitted to an ANC seminar on culture in Lusaka, Zambia, in 1989, Sachs famously proposed a temporary ban on the phrase "culture is a weapon of the struggle."[5] Instead, he sought to shift the emphasis from political struggle to the private and the everyday. "What are we fighting for," he asked, "if not the right to express our humanity in all its forms, including our sense of fun and capacity for love and tenderness and our appreciation of the beauty of the world?" (POF, 21) Sachs posited a model of a future liberal, multilingual, multicultural state that would facilitate freedom of expression: "This is not to give a special status to artists, but to recognise that they have certain special characteristics and traditions. Certainly, it ill behoves us to set ourselves up as the new censors of art and literature" (POF, 28).

Sachs's paper set the agenda for debates on culture in South Africa in the early 1990s, and while his remarks on writing and political commitment proved controversial, his proposals on culture, rights, and freedom of expression would form the basis of the 1993 Interim Constitution. For Sachs, the kind of liberal values that informed the political negotiations provided a solution to the problems that had faced writers and artists under apartheid, removing both the threat of official scrutiny and the need for political resistance. But in spite of their shared concern with a space for culture distinct from politics, Coetzee's essays in *Giving Offense* are to an extent marked by the very logic that Sachs was trying to shake off, suggesting that the pathologies engendered by apartheid cannot easily be set aside.

In their essays on *Petersburg*, both Jane Poyner and Graham Pechey point to the necessity of continuing critique of the state in the post-apartheid period. For Pechey, "the danger of the post-apartheid condition is that writing will appear to be aligned with the beneficent moves of the state, seeming to have nothing to do after the end of oppression."[6] Poyner, on the other hand, reads the novel as a warning against the "pitfalls of national consciousness" identified by Frantz Fanon in *The Wretched of the Earth*, since the preoccupation with censorship and the critique of authority in the novel "endeavours to cultivate a critical and self-reflexive reading community" (PPA, 130). Poyner identifies the demands for political commitment with a loss of privacy. This is the position taken by the revolutionary Nechaev in Coetzee's novel, as he tries to get Dostoevsky to write a political pamphlet. When a printer steps in to defend the integrity of writers — "Writers have their own rules. They can't work with people looking over their shoulders" — Nechaev responds in typically belligerent fashion: "Then they should learn new rules. Privacy is a luxury we can do without. People don't need privacy" (*MP*, 198). In keeping with this, Poyner identifies the critique of revolutionary politics (embodied in Nechaev) in *Petersburg* with "the gaze turned inward of post-apartheid writing" (PPA, 137). This would appear to resonate with Sachs's turn away from the literature of struggle towards literature as an expression of "humanity in all its forms" (POF, 21). But the ideas that I have sketched out above about writing and creativity in *Giving Offense* — and *Petersburg* — suggest that there is no easy separation of private and public, or that their separation is at least produced by the writer. Coetzee's key contribution to the debate initiated by Sachs is to draw attention to the continuities between the private and the public worlds of the author, to the extent that in the case of the writer, especially the "master author," the distinction between the two all but collapses. Coetzee challenges the notion that a change in the political environment can initiate a straightforward withdrawal from the public world of politics to the private, domestic, human sphere, pointing to the danger of identifying "private" with "free." In *Petersburg* we have a turn to the private, but also the gradual erosion of the private, firstly by the public demands of the police officer Maximov and the revolutionary Nechaev, and then by the demands of writing itself — all of which comes at immense cost.

Crucial to understanding Coetzee's position in *Petersburg* is his reluctance to resort to conventional liberal arguments in his rejection of censorship. In his response to Catherine MacKinnon's critique of pornography in *Giving Offense*, he does not seek recourse to the liberal principles that she attacks, suggesting that: "Freedom of expression is desirable; but like all desires . . . the desire for freedom is devious, does not fully know itself, cannot afford to fully know itself" (*GO*, 74). Instead, he posits a challenge to MacKinnon in the form of a representation of desire "that sees (but also does not see), in its own desire to know its desire, that which it can never know about itself," and this representation would mimic the form and content of the pornographic (*GO*, 73). For Coetzee, the "radicalism" of such a critique would come from "its embrace of the pornographic medium as its own," and he compares it with "the twists and turns of erotic abasement in the novels of Dostoevsky" (*GO*, 73). Because of its "seriousness," this project lays claim to the status of high art rather than pornography, but Coetzee insists that regardless of the censures in place, "serious writers" will continue to explore "the darker areas of human experience" (*GO*, 74). The attempts of censors to prevent the circulation of obscene material, or of MacKinnon to "delegitimize" pornography, merely add to the risk undertaken by the writer, so that for

Coetzee the question that remains is: "at what cost to them; and do we want to add to that cost?" (*GO*, 74)

While I have placed *Giving Offense* in the context of debates about culture in South Africa epitomized by Sachs's "Preparing Ourselves for Freedom," Coetzee's emphasis on the cost of writing is not in keeping with the celebratory tone of Sachs's intervention. Indeed, Coetzee's preoccupation with the cost of writing and his construction of the private in terms of risk provides an interesting twist on Sachs's insistence that writing should turn away from the political in favor of the personal; one might even describe it as a *perversion* of Sachs's intentions.

The Dostoevsky's constructed in *Petersburg* is clearly a "master author" as described in *Giving Offense*. Although he is traveling under false documents and not named until page thirty-four of the novel, the reader quickly discovers his identity through his encounters with other characters, all of whom recognize him as the author, Fyodor Dostoevsky. His reputation becomes a key to the developing political drama, as Nechaev attempts to manipulate him into writing a pamphlet, and such is his celebrity that the details of his private life are as well-known as his work: the detective Maximov incautiously hints at rumors about his uneasy relationship with his father, as does Nechaev. Indeed, Coetzee's novel relies on the reader's knowledge of Dostoevsky's work and biography. It becomes clear that Dostoevsky's biography is public property before he ever contemplates selling it in the closing pages of the novel: "it is not so much a life as a price or a currency. It is something I pay with in order to write" (*MP*, 222). But the novel also owes even more to Coetzee's reading of Dostoevsky's oeuvre, the fictional output that constitutes his life's work and a more significant reflection of what we know, or think we know, about Dostoevsky. The reader/confessor figure of Maximov embodies this in his attitude towards Dostoevsky: "knowing you as I do, that is, in the way one knows a writer from his books, that is to say, in an intimate yet limited way" (*MP*, 147). The biographical elements that Coetzee has chosen to emphasize are those that are most frequently read back into Dostoevsky's fiction: his epilepsy, gambling, debts, the suggested assault on a child.

The significance of this is not just the status of Dostoevsky within the literary canon, but Coetzee's construction of a private life for his protagonist that is based on the fiction, and his construction of a protagonist who experiences writing as a violation and sacrifice of this private life. In spite of the writer's attempt to dedicate himself to the supposedly private activity of mourning for his stepson — "there is a measure to all things now, and that measure is Pavel" (*MP*, 167) — the competing demands of authorship consistently violate the private experience of mourning. We might understand Pavel as the "figure-of-the-beloved" described in *Giving Offense*, but the writing is also responding to other imperatives. The conflicting interests of Dostoevsky's different roles, father and author, and the slippage between the private and the public, reach a crisis point in the final chapters of the novel as he appears to answer the Orphic imperative to bring Pavel back to life by writing a version of "At Tikhon's" in the empty pages of his stepson's diary: the beloved son, Pavel, is transformed into Stavrogin. The instability of the boundary between private and public is intensified by our awareness of Coetzee's own biography: his son, Nicolas, died in 1989 at the age of 23. This detail is frequently included in biographical accounts of Coetzee and has been noted by numerous critics of *Petersburg*; in other words, it has become part of the set of things we "know" about J. M. Coetzee, and has consequently come to shape the way this novel in particular is read, in spite of the fact that it is often referred to only in passing.[7] One could say that the novel's careful invention of a private life for Dostoevsky paradoxically constructs the death of Coetzee's son as the private dimension of *Petersburg*. But if the novel's transformation of Pavel into Stavrogin draws attention to the slippage between the private and the public, the biographical and the fictional, it also cautions against a simple mapping of the biographical onto the fictional, and indeed onto the private; what circulates as the "private" may or may not correspond to the biographical.

This is complicated further in the course of the novel as Pavel also emerges as an author; he was a writer, albeit an unpublished one, something Dostoevsky only learns after his death. For this reason, Pavel's private papers, containing some stories, journals and letters — all that remains to his stepfather — acquire an added value. And, crucially, it is on the basis of these papers that the limits of the private and public dimensions of authorship are contested in the novel. In his eager pursuit of Nechaev and his circle, the detective Maximov engages in a thorough investigation of Pavel's papers and insists that his stories be admitted as evidence of his political radicalism. Dostoevsky, on the other hand, refuses Maximov's allegorical reading of Pavel's story, equating his son's stories with his diaries and letters on the basis that they were unpublished. For Dostoevsky, a story is "a private matter, an utterly private matter, private to the writer, till it is given to the world" (*MP*, 40).

However, as the novel shows, this does not protect such papers from being read. As Dostoevsky explores Pavel's personal effects, he finds the marks of previous readers — ticks that he assumes to be the work of the policeman/censor Maximov, and Latin inscriptions in a copy of Cicero's *De Officiis* (a quotation from Locke's *Second Treatise on Government*) that may be in the hand of the revolutionary Nechaev. But it is Dostoevsky's reading of his stepson's papers that is presented as the greatest violation. Just as the examples quoted earlier illustrate his association between writing and the pornographic, Dostoevsky also associates violations of privacy with the pornographic, and in exploring Pavel's papers, reading becomes obscene. Earlier in the novel, as he rifles through Anna Sergeyevna's private possessions, he recalls violations of his childhood: "As a child he used to spy on visitors to the household and trespass surreptitiously on their privacy. It is a weakness that he has associated till now with a refusal to accept limits to what he is permitted to know, with the reading of forbidden books, and thus with his vocation" (*MP*, 71). As he first opens Pavel's diaries, he recalls "long, sweaty afternoons in his friend Albert's bedroom poring over books filched from Albert's uncle's shelves" (*MP*, 148), and the violence and repulsion aroused in them both as they watched two flies copulate (*MP*, 149). Contrary to the political allegory that Maximov finds in Pavel's story, Dostoevsky reads it as a veiled autobiography: "Not untrue, not wholly untrue, yet how subtly twisted all of it!" (*MP*, 151). When for the third time he turns to Pavel's diary, he focuses on the words, once more in an undeniably material and antirepresentational sense: "Dear, every scratch on the paper dear to me, he tells himself" (*MP*, 216). But he acknowledges that his attitude to Pavel's papers is not simply out of love: "There is something ugly in this intrusion on Pavel, and indeed something obscene in the idea of the *Nachlass* of a child" (*MP*, 216).

Yet, if Dostoevsky's reading of Pavel's papers is presented as obscene, what register do we resort to in describing his actions in the closing chapter when he *writes* in his dead stepson's diary? For readers familiar with Dostoevsky, Coetzee's novel culminates in the writing of "At Tikhon's." But within the logic of *Petersburg*, the final chapter represents the moment when the grieving father's efforts to bring his son to life finally succeed. It is the myth of Orpheus and Eurydice, half-forming in the mind of Dostoevsky throughout the novel, that allows us to bring these two parallel narratives into the same frame of reference.

In Maurice Blanchot's "Orpheus' Gaze," it is the question of risk and the writer's willingness or compulsion to embrace it that defines artistic inspiration. For Blanchot, the ban that prevents Orpheus from turning back to look at Eurydice suggests that "a work of art can only be achieved when the artist does not seek the experience of unrestrained intensity as an end in itself."[8] So, while not strictly speaking a form of censorship, the artist must work within certain limitations. At the same time: "the myth simultaneously implies that Orpheus' fate is to refuse to submit to this law. . . . Thus he betrays his purpose, Eurydice and the dark. Yet not to look back would be no less a betrayal" (*OG*, 177–78). Blanchot implies that Orpheus must exercise a certain impatience and recklessness with regard to both Eurydice and art because his inspiration lies in his willingness to risk both; this is the paradoxical necessity of art: "To look at Eurydice without a thought for art, with the impatience and recklessness of a desire oblivious of laws, that is what inspiration is" (*OG*, 179). Part of the necessity of art is that there is no guaranteed gain from Orpheus's gamble: "it does not ensure the success of the work of art any more than it celebrates in art the triumph of Orpheus' ideal or Eurydice's survival. Art is no less threatened than Orpheus by inspiration. The moment of inspiration is, for art, the point of maximum insecurity. That is why art tends so often and so violently to resist what inspires it" (OG, 179–80).

Blanchot's account of the myth of Orpheus can help us to bring together Coetzee's comments about the existence of limits enabling transgression, his preoccupation with censorship in the period of transition between apartheid and democracy, and the elaborate and fiercely protected private worlds constructed and invaded in *Giving Offense* and *Petersburg*. Just as the "seriousness" of writers working under censorship results from the idea that "every word published represented a risk taken," so risk dominates *Petersburg*. This is explicit in the description of Dostoevsky's gambling: "Without the risk, without subjecting oneself to the voice speaking from elsewhere in the fall of the dice, what is left that is divine?" (*MP*, 84) It is also evident in the recovery of the excised chapter of Dostoevsky's *The Possessed*. But it acquires its greatest force in the betrayal of the private that takes place in the final chapter. In these pages Coetzee's Dostoevsky sees himself as gambling with his soul. He describes himself as a voluptuary of the moment before the fall: "For which he will be damned" (*MP*, 242). Writing in the pages of his stepson's diary, he gambles with God: "To corrupt a child is to force God. The device he has made arches and springs shut like a trap, a trap to catch God" (*MP*, 249). In return for whatever material gains attach to writing, "he had to give up his soul" (*MP*, 250).

Among papers donated by Coetzee to the National English Literary Museum in Grahamstown are unpublished preparation notes for a seminar on Olive Schreiner at UCT in 1993.[9] In a series of notes on Schreiner's career, Coetzee speculates about the source of her inspiration or, to be precise, her anxiety about the source of her inspiration following the success of *Story of an African Farm*. He attributes this to her unwillingness "to absorb herself deeply enough in the project [a late novel] to transform it and allow it to transform her." At this point in the notes, Coetzee breaks with the discussion of Schreiner to write: "Of course I am talking about myself. Whenever we talk about something else we are talking about ourselves." But he closes off this autobiographical moment just as quickly, claiming that it is not in his interest to pursue this line of thought: "But I choose not to reflect on it, turn myself back to look upon it (like Orpheus). Life is too short. (The meaning of the Orpheus story: you kill your inspiration by turning back to look at it.)" The wariness expressed here is consistent with comments Coetzee has made in interviews about the risk to the creative enterprise of the kind of self-scrutiny demanded by forms such as the literary interview. But the comments on Schreiner are particularly interesting given his invocation of the myth of

Orpheus. What Coetzee chooses to omit in this account of the myth as a story of inspiration is the aspect of the myth emphasized in Blanchot's reading: that it is precisely the risks implicit in how one treats one's inspiration that gives inspiration its power.

In *Petersburg*, in contrast, the myth of Orpheus and Eurydice comes to embody the risks of the creative enterprise, risks that involve slippage between the public and the private worlds of master author Dostoevsky. The myth is invoked consistently throughout the novel to describe the nature of Dostoevsky's duty towards his stepson. The earliest example sees Dostoevsky trying to conjure Pavel's presence in his own room by repeatedly invoking his name: "He thinks of Orpheus walking backwards step by step, whispering the dead woman's name, coaxing her out of the entrails of hell; of the wife in graveclothes with the blind, dead eyes following him, holding out limp hands before her like a sleepwalker. No flute, no lyre, just the word, the one word, over and over" (*MP*, 5).

In this early reference to the myth, the focus is on the power of Orpheus to bring the dead back to life and, by implication, the power available to the writer to do likewise. But subsequent examples focus more on the risks implicit in such an activity. Some pages later, seated at the desk in Pavel's room, Dostoevsky is flooded with what he calls memories, among them a scene of farewell that is articulated in the terms of the myth of Orpheus:

> All that I am left to grasp for: the moment of that gaze, salutation and farewell in one, past all arguing, past all pleading. . . .
>   I hold your head between my hands. I kiss your brow. I kiss your lips.
>   The rule: one look, one only; no glancing back. But I look back. . . .
>   Forever I look back. Forever I am absorbed in your gaze. A field of crystal points, dancing, winking, and I one of them. Stars in the sky, and fires on the plain answering them. Two realms signalling to each other. (*MP*, 54)

The shift from free indirect discourse to direct speech or thought (from "he" to "I") seems to be a symptom of a more profound loss of consciousness or self-consciousness when, in full knowledge of the consequences, he dares to look back on the forbidden image. Yet in keeping with Blanchot's discussion of the myth, there is no option but to look back. In other words, there is no real calculation of interests at work in this episode; Dostoevsky cannot choose not to look back, as Coetzee does in his piece about Schreiner.

Later examples show a slight shift in the way the myth is used:

> On the streets of Petersburg, in the turn of a head here, the gesture of a hand there, I see you, and each time my heart lifts as a wave

does. Nowhere and everywhere, torn and scattered like Orpheus. Young in days, chryseos, golden, blessed.

The task left to me: to gather the hoard, put together the scattered parts. Poet, lyre-player, enchanter, lord of resurrection, that is what I am called to be. (*MP*, 152)

Once more we have Dostoevsky in the role of Orpheus assuming the obligation to resurrect Pavel ("you"), but crucially, Pavel is also figured as Orpheus, albeit the dead Orpheus, the poet who has gambled and lost. These images acquire a more forceful, material form in the final chapter, however:

An image comes to him that for the past month he has flinched from: Pavel, naked and broken and bloody, in the morgue; the seed in his body dead too, or dying.

Nothing is private anymore. As unblinkingly as he can he gazes upon the body parts without which there can be no fatherhood. And his mind goes again to the museum in Berlin, to the goddess-fiend drawing out the seed from the corpse, saving it.

Thus at last the time arrives and the hand that holds the pen begins to move. But the words it forms are not words of salvation. (*MP*, 241)

Dostoevsky's efforts throughout the novel have been directed to bringing Pavel back to life, conjuring him up in words or breathing life into Pavel's own words. But in this final section of the novel he accepts that this will not happen, at least not in the form he expected: "Ultimately it will not be given to him to bring the dead boy back to life. Ultimately, if he wants to meet him, he will have to meet him in death" (*MP*, 237–38). One way of meeting him in death is to gaze on his corpse, as he does in the above scene, and this is explicitly described as a violation of the private. Couched in the terms of Orpheus's betrayal of Eurydice, Dostoevsky's gaze leaves him exposed to all kinds of risk; his intention is "not to emerge from the fall unscathed, but to . . . wrestle with the whistling darkness" (*MP*, 235). While he has consistently and self-consciously engaged with the world as material for his art, it seems more and more that he is willing to look on his stepson as a source of inspiration while simultaneously betraying him.

In addition, the doubling of the figure of Orpheus that I mentioned earlier occurs again in the final chapter: "Letters from the whirlwind. Scattered leaves, which he gathers up; a scattered body, which he reassembles" (*MP*, 246). In this way we can see that in the process of attempting to resurrect his stepson, Dostoevsky is also resurrecting Orpheus: that is to say, bringing the figure of the poet/writer back to life. Beside his stepfather, the master author, Pavel represented a more private dimension of authorship: unpublished, but read nonetheless. In other words, it is the private sphere of writing, constructed by Coetzee in both *Giving Offense* and *Petersburg*, that Coetzee's Dostoevsky resurrects. He compares his exploitation of Pavel's memory to the goddess saving the seed from the corpse, a seed that is undoubtedly writing. But just as Pavel cannot be imagined as himself, this is not quite the dimension of authorship that we get. In these pages the beloved stepson becomes Stavrogin, but so too does the author — a cold, amoral figure willing to risk everything. That this occurs in the absence of Tikhon, the confessor figure from Dostoevsky's novel that represents the availability of self-forgiveness, grace, and absolution for Coetzee, intensifies the risk and the cost.[10]

In Georges Bataille's critique of the principles of utility, gambling is an example of "unproductive expenditure," a type of activity where "in each case the accent is placed on a loss that must be as great as possible in order for that activity to take on its true meaning."[11] This is echoed in the fictional Dostoevsky's comments about his recklessness in *Petersburg*: "Money is there to be spent, and what form of spending is purer than gambling?" (*MP*, 159). Artistic production is similar to gambling in Bataille's account, in that it too is an example of "unproductive expenditure." He goes so far as to say that artistic production "can be considered synonymous with expenditure; it in fact signifies, in the most precise way, creation by means of loss. Its meaning is therefore close to that of sacrifice." In vivid economic terms, Bataille comments that while artistic production is a form of symbolic expenditure, "poetic expenditure ceases to be symbolic in its consequences."[12] While creativity in this view is a form of symbolic expenditure, as an aspect of lived experience it has real consequences.

These consequences take an unforgiving, official form for writers working under state censorship and, as *Giving Offense* suggests, this is felt not just by those writers whose work is suppressed but by all who experience the unwanted attentions of the censor. But censorship can also make a writer unusually and acutely aware of the boundaries within which he or she works. In a context such as early 1990s South Africa, in the period of transition between the repressive apartheid regime and the new liberal postapartheid state, the "turn inward," as Poyner describes it, is presented as a liberation from the multiple tyrannies of the political. For Coetzee, ever contrary, the turn inward represents a new boundary to transgress and the embrace of the private, a new desire to test. In "The Novel Today," a precursor to the concerns of *Giving Offense*, Coetzee suggests that for centuries censors had been ineffective in laying down rules to control writers because "in laying down rules that stories may not transgress, and enforcing these rules, they fail to recognize that the offensiveness of stories lies not in their transgressing particular rules but in their faculty of making and changing their own rules."[13] This is evident in Coetzee's contribution to the debate about the literary in postapartheid South Africa and in the perversions of the private staged in *Petersburg*. It is also evident in Coetzee's next piece of fiction, *Disgrace*, a novel that would scandalize South Africa in ways not yet conceived in *Giving Offense*.

Notes

[1] Jane Poyner, *J. M. Coetzee and the Paradox of Postcolonial Authorship* (Farnham, UK: Ashgate, 2009), 133. Subsequent references appear as PPA with the accompanying page number.

[2] Derek Attridge, *J. M. Coetzee and the Ethics of Reading: Literature in the Event* (Chicago: U of Chicago P, 2004), 132–33.

[3] Peter D. McDonald, *The Literature Police: Apartheid Censorship and its Cultural Consequences* (Oxford: Oxford UP, 2009), 38–82. Subsequent references appear as LP with the accompanying page number.

[4] Michel Foucault, "What Is an Author?" Trans. Donald F. Bouchard and Sherry Simon, in *Language, Counter-Memory, Practice: Selected Essays and Interviews*, ed. Donald F. Bouchard (Ithaca: Cornell UP, 1977), 124.

[5] Albie Sachs, "Preparing Ourselves for Freedom," in *Spring is Rebellious: Arguments about Cultural Freedom*, ed. Ingrid de Kok and Karen Press (Cape Town: Buchu Books, 1990), 19. Subsequent references are cited using "POF" and the page number.

[6] Graham Pechey, "The Post-Apartheid Sublime: Rediscovering the Extraordinary," in *Writing South Africa: Literature, Apartheid, and Democracy, 1970–1995*, ed. Derek Attridge and Rosemary Jolly (Cambridge: Cambridge UP, 1998), 62–63.

[7] The exception to this is Derek Attridge's essay on the novel in *J. M. Coetzee and the Ethics of Reading*, 136–37.

[8] Maurice Blanchot, "Orpheus' Gaze," trans. Sacha Rabinovitch, in *The Sirens' Song: Selected Essays*, ed. Gabriel Josipovici (Brighton: Harvester Press, 1982), 177. Subsequent references appear as OG with the accompanying page number.

[9] J. M. Coetzee, Seminar Notes from University of Cape Town, Master's in Literary Studies, 1993, NELM 2002.13.2.3.4 (Coetzee Collection), (National English Literary Museum, Grahamstown, South Africa), n.p.

[10] For the significance of Tikhon for Coetzee, see "Confession and Double Thoughts: Tolstoy, Rousseau, Dostoevsky" in *Doubling the Point*, 251–93.

[11] Georges Bataille, "The Notion of Expenditure," trans. Allan Stoekl, with Carl R. Lovitt and Donald M. Leslie, Jr., in *Visions of Excess: Selected Writings, 1927–1939*, ed. Allan Stoekl (Minneapolis: U of Minnesota P, 1985), 118.

[12] Bataille, "The Notion of Expenditure," 120.

[13] J. M. Coetzee, "The Novel Today," *Upstream* 6, no. 1 (1988), 3.

10: *Disgrace* (1999)

Simone Drichel

> *In a society of masters and slaves, no one is free. The slave is not free, because he is not his own master; the master is not free, because he cannot do without the slave. . . . At the heart of the unfreedom of the hereditary masters of South Africa is a failure to love.*
>
> — J. M. Coetzee, Jerusalem Prize Acceptance Speech

D ISGRACE IS NOT JUST THE MOST-DISCUSSED NOVEL in Coetzee's oeuvre; it is also one of the most widely discussed novels of the late twentieth century.[1] As well as two special issues of journals in 2002, recent years have seen the publication of both a collection of essays dedicated exclusively to the novel[2] and a short introductory monograph.[3] Besides these book-length studies, there are a number of recent books on Coetzee that contain large sections or chapters on *Disgrace*.[4] In addition, there is a profusion of scholarly articles that foreground a range of critical concerns and discuss these concerns from feminist,[5] intertextual,[6] contextual,[7] postcolonial,[8] and, most insistently, ethical[9] points of view. The ethical frameworks focus, in turn, on the novel's engagement with the Truth and Reconciliation Commission,[10] the politics of rape,[11] as well as an intricately interwoven network of ideas around the role played by dogs (or animals more generally), the body, and the sympathetic imagination.[12]

Before negotiating my own path through this abundance of material, let me give a quick reminder of the main events of the novel. *Disgrace* tells the story of middle-aged David Lurie, a one-time professor of modern languages with expertise in Romantic poetry (notably Wordsworth and Byron), now reduced to teaching Communications 101 to students with whom he, rather tellingly, fails to communicate. Believing himself to have "solved the problem of sex rather well" through regular "ninety-minute session[s]" with Soraya from "Discreet Escorts" (*DG*, 1–2), Lurie sinks "into a state of disgrace" (*DG*, 172) when he engages in sexual misconduct with a student, Melanie Isaacs, after losing access to Soraya.[13] Subsequently subjected to a "hearing" (47), Lurie refuses to perform the necessary "spirit of repentance" (58) that would get him off the hook.

Because he does not oblige in delivering the "spectacle" that he, somewhat melodramatically, suggests is required of him — "breast-beating, remorse, tears if possible. A TV show, in fact" (66) — he loses his teaching job. Like the Biblical scapegoat — an analogy he himself refutes (see 91) — Lurie leaves the city to "wande[r] in the wilderness" (91), taking up temporary residence on his lesbian daughter Lucy's smallholding in the country. In an inverted mirror image of the first sexual violation, the smallholding soon after becomes the setting for a second major violation in the novel: Lurie and Lucy become victims of an attack in which Lurie is beaten and burnt, and Lucy is raped and impregnated by their three (implicitly black) attackers. The aftermath of that attack drives a wedge between father and daughter. Lurie urges his daughter to report the crime so that the attackers can be "brought before the law and punished" (119), and to leave the smallholding so as not to expose herself to the risk of future attacks. Lucy, on the other hand, insists not only on staying but on carrying the child to term and accepting the "deal" (203) offered to her by her (also implicitly black) neighbor Petrus, formerly Lucy's "assistant" and now a "co-proprietor" (62): in exchange for her land, Petrus will make Lucy his third wife, thus allowing her "to creep under his wing" (203). This arrangement, by which Lucy will effectively "become a tenant on his [Petrus's] land" (204), Lurie deems deeply "humiliating." Lucy, by contrast, albeit agreeing with Lurie's verdict, willingly embraces it as a suitable point for a new beginning:

> "Yes, I agree, it's humiliating. But perhaps that is a good point to start from again. Perhaps that is what I must learn to accept. To start at ground level. With nothing. Not with nothing but. With nothing. No cards, no weapons, no property, no rights, no dignity."
> "Like a dog."
> "Yes, like a dog." (*DG*, 205)

The parallel that is drawn here between human and animal existence alerts us to the second important narrative strand in *Disgrace*. If the first strand focuses on the interhuman drama that unfolds mainly between Lurie and Lucy, and sees Lurie emerge from his initial state of obstinate nonrepentance to being able to apologize to Melanie's father, the second strand revolves around what we may call an interspecies drama: the human attempt to "lighten the load of Africa's suffering beasts" (*DG*, 84). This interspecies drama, which is only apparently secondary to the interhuman plot, revolves around the love, care, and attention that Bev Shaw — a "dumpy, bustling little woman with black freckles, close-cropped, wiry hair, and no neck," in Lurie's ungenerous estimation (72) — offers to the countless sick or unwanted animals she euthanizes at the Animal Welfare League clinic. Getting drawn into the work of the clinic, to the extent that it ultimately "becomes his home" (211), Lurie increasingly becomes affected by the disgrace of the animals' deaths. The novel ends on a note of painful sacrifice: Lurie gives up the young crippled dog to whom he has grown particularly attached.

Given the relentless bleakness, which even such a cursory account of the novel cannot quite gloss over, it is perhaps hardly a surprise that, as Attridge puts it, "this incendiary material provoked a strong reaction from many quarters."[14] What is interesting, however, for the work by a writer who has regularly been in the firing lines over his purported political quietism, his failure or unwillingness to make his work politically relevant by offering recognizable fictional portraits of South Africa under apartheid, is that *Disgrace* should come under attack for exactly that quality that his previous novels were said to lack: its politics. Published to international acclaim, *Disgrace* seems to deliver exactly the kind of critical engagement with an identifiable South African reality that a number of South African critics — among them, most notably and perhaps notoriously, Nadine Gordimer — have long wished Coetzee's fiction would deliver. However, with apartheid now consigned to the realm of historical memory, the mood of the country had shifted, and Coetzee was once again perceived to be out of step: his challenging portrayal of, in the words of Derek Attridge, "a society in which crime is rampant, the police service is inadequate, and the middle classes are barricaded in their fortress-homes" (DI, 315), seemed not just belated but, more problematically, inappropriate and ultimately damaging to the "new" South Africa: a country anxiously nurturing the small seed of hope for a better future that the abolition of apartheid had implanted in the collective psyche. Published in the wake of the historic 1994 democratic elections in South Africa, which saw the ANC take a landslide victory, Nelson Mandela emerge from prisoner to president of his country, and the Truth and Reconciliation Commission established as the body that, as the official website puts it, would "help deal with what happened under apartheid,"[15] *Disgrace* did not join the general spirit of hopefulness. As Attridge notes, the novel contains not even "a tinge of celebration and optimism" (ER, 164).

Instead of celebration and optimism, *Disgrace* offers the portrayal of a country in crisis, or better, in disgrace. Small wonder, then, that the novel's political agenda should come under scrutiny. What emerged as a particularly painful bone of contention was the novel's presentation of the rape of Lucy by three black men and her enigmatic response to this violation, which Lurie (mis)reads as an acceptance of a form of historical payback. Where the rape itself gave rise to charges of racism,[16] Lucy's response was (mis)read as white South Africans' resigned acceptance of retributive violence for historical injustice — a reading most prominently advanced by Athol Fugard in a widely noted response to the novel (Fugard, notoriously, had not read the novel at the time):

I haven't read it, and I'm sure the writing is excellent, . . . but I could not think of anything that would depress me more than this book by Coetzee — *Disgrace* — where we've got to accept the rape of a white woman as a gesture to all the evil we did in the past. That's a load of bullshit. That white women are going to accept being raped as penance for what was done in the past? Jesus! It's an expression of a very morbid phenomenon, very morbid. (Cited in M, 32)

While the diagnosis of what has subsequently been termed a "Lucy-syndrome"[17] seems equally as misplaced as the designation of *Disgrace* as racist, there were serious concerns from many quarters that the novel, with its "nihilistic view with no prospects of a real bright future" (GRR, 43), as one South African reader puts it, would reinscribe rather than challenge racial violence in South Africa. As Attridge observes:

It's hardly surprising, then, that mixed in with the huge acclaim that greeted Coetzee's far from affirmative novel there were expressions of annoyance and anger, especially from South African commentators. The overriding question for many readers is: does this novel, as one of the most widely disseminated and forceful representations of post-apartheid South Africa, impede the difficult enterprise of rebuilding the country? Does the largely negative picture it paints of relations between communities hinder the steps being made towards reconciliation? (ER, 164)

Given the charged responses the novel has provoked, it is clear that a good many readers of *Disgrace* would offer a resounding "yes" in response to Attridge's questions. What I want to do in this chapter, by contrast, is to resist such an easy "yes" and instead reflect more insistently on the question of Coetzee's politics in this novel: rather than calling Coetzee's politics questionable, I want to ask what the novel might take politics to mean.

These criticisms about the novel's assumed complicity with what can only be described as a dead-end racial politics are highly instructive for a discussion of *Disgrace*. A source, no doubt, of intense irritation for Coetzee, the criticisms reveal precisely that which Coetzee *himself* would consider to be the problem in postapartheid South African politics: a certain imaginative failure, or what he in his 1987 Jerusalem Prize Acceptance Speech calls, with reference to Don Quixote, a certain "capitulation of the imagination to reality"; "We have art, said Nietzsche, so that we shall not die of the truth. In South Africa there is now too much truth for art to hold, truth by the bucketful, truth that overwhelms and swamps every act of the imagination" (*DP*, 99).

More specifically, he suggests that this overpowering of the imagination by reality finds expression in what is an imaginative failure to transcend the limitations imposed by racialized thought and to allow for a new kind of politics — based on what Coetzee calls "love" — to emerge in the country. As he maintains in this speech, in a statement cited as an epigraph to this chapter: "In a society of masters and slaves, no one is free. The slave is not free, because he is not his own master; the master is not free, because he cannot do without the slave. . . . At the heart of the unfreedom of the hereditary masters of South Africa is a failure to love" (*DP*, 96–97).

Although this speech was delivered a few years before the abolition of apartheid, the sentiments expressed in it reverberate powerfully through the pages of Coetzee's postapartheid novel *Disgrace*, suggesting that the end of apartheid has not ended the "unfreedom" of a racialized politics based on the abstract collectives of "masters and slaves." Given that he associates the cause of this "unfreedom" with a "failure to love," it is not difficult to discern what task Coetzee sets himself and his white characters in *Disgrace*, with whom he is aligned through their shared subject position as "hereditary masters of South Africa": the task to love the other. Importantly, approaching the other with love rather than with violence necessitates encountering the other in their irreducible singularity rather than as part of an abstract category such as race, gender, class, or even species. The task the novel sets its white South African protagonist is to suspend the violent dynamics that inhere in political socialities in order to allow for a different form of sociality to emerge, a sociality one would not be mistaken to call ethical. In my reading of the novel, such an *ethical* sociality constitutes the condition of possibility for justice in postapartheid South Africa.

In this movement from the political to the ethical, from the ideal category to the singular existent, Coetzee's novel follows a trajectory familiar to us from the ethical philosophies of Emmanuel Levinas and Jacques Derrida, and advances, in Coetzee's words, "an idea of justice . . . that transcends laws and lawmaking" (*DP*, 340). What this distinction implies, most fundamentally, is that, as Derrida states with uncharacteristic bluntness: "Law is not justice." He elaborates:

> Law is the element of calculation, and it is just that there be law, but justice is incalculable, it demands that one calculate with the incalculable; and aporetic experiences are the experiences, as improbable as they are necessary, of justice, that is to say of moments in which the *decision* between just and unjust is never insured by a rule.[18]

Where "law" refers to the abstract juridical and political structures and processes that institute and protect a politics of exchange and calculation — a politics that abstracts from the unique so as to make the incomparable comparable — "justice," Derrida insists, "always addresses itself to singularity, to the singularity of the other."[19]

Disgrace is premised on Derrida's contention that "law is not justice," or rather, and more specifically, that the law, or politics, cannot bring about justice in postapartheid South Africa. The novel presents us with an inquiry into the conditions of possibility for justice to happen in a society where such justice cannot be imagined, a society where "truth" — the reality of a violent history of racialization — "overwhelms and swamps every act of the imagination." *Disgrace* stages this inquiry through a trajectory that begins with "the law and lawmaking" and ends with justice. Because justice, as Levinas argues, "comes from love,"[20] this trajectory is fundamentally dependent on a redefinition of sociality and, by implication, subjectivity: it consists of transforming a violent sociality (where a masterful ego reduces the other to the structures of its own consciousness) into an ethical sociality (where the self is affected by the other's irreducible singularity). The two events that frame this trajectory in the novel and represent the two poles of law and justice are the hearing Lurie undergoes after his sexual violation of Melanie and the sacrifice of the young crippled dog, Driepoot, for whom Lurie "has come to feel a particular fondness" (*DG*, 214–15).

Lurie's hearing "before an officially constituted tribunal, before a branch of the law" (*DG*, 58), is a thinly veiled allegory of the many hearings conducted by the Truth and Reconciliation Commission and bears all the hallmarks of the inherent contradictions that characterized the TRC. Chaired by Archbishop Desmond Tutu, the TRC was a secular institution aimed at airing painful truths about apartheid atrocities so as to be able to produce racial reconciliation. Key to such reconciliation was the idea of forgiveness — as in the title of Tutu's memoir of his time as a chairperson of the Commission: *No Future Without Forgiveness.*[21] However, forgiveness, as Derrida reminds us, is a concept that belongs to a "religious heritage,"[22] and it is this heritage that Lurie renounces:

> "Manas, we went through the repentance business yesterday. I told you what I thought. I won't do it. I appeared before an officially constituted tribunal, before a branch of the law. Before that secular tribunal I pleaded guilty, a secular plea. That plea should suffice. Repentance is neither here nor there. Repentance belongs to another world, another universe of discourse." (*DG*, 58)

Rejecting the idea that repentance has a place in secular discourse, Lurie here misguidedly invests the law, or what Derrida calls the "element of calculation," with the power to bring about the "incalculable": justice.

At the point at which he begins his "wanderings in the wilderness," Lurie, the "commentator upon, and disgraced disciple of, William Wordsworth" (*DG*, 46), to whom, as he admits elsewhere, "he has not listened well" (179), is thus firmly established as the novel's true representative of such core Enlightenment principles as secularism, reason, autonomy, and "freedom of speech" (*DG*, 188). Following Jane Taylor, Mike Marais has argued that there is "a relation between [the novel's] treatment of violence in contemporary South Africa and the European Enlightenment's legacy of the autonomy of the individual," where each individual is "a living consciousness separated totally from every other consciousness."[23] These are valuable insights. Even more important, however, than the problem of the autonomous *individual* — Leibniz's monad cut off from others — is the Enlightenment legacy of the *autonomous* individual, the rational subject with its investment in freedom from heteronomy. To explain this point more fully, a brief diversion via Levinas's account of Western philosophy as a philosophy of freedom and autonomy may be helpful.

For Levinas, Western philosophy is a philosophy of narcissistic reflection that cannot tolerate any otherness outside of its own projections. This type of reflection uses abstract concepts to translate the specificity of alterity — absolute otherness — into known and knowable categories. In a subsection of his important early essay "Philosophy and the Idea of Infinity" (1957), entitled "Narcissism, or the Primacy of the Same," Levinas argues that Western philosophy's investment in freedom and autonomy (especially the freedom and autonomy of the rational subject) has no room for "a term foreign to the philosophical life, other." Traditional Western philosophy, he argues, cannot tolerate any otherness that escapes the categories of the self-same subject. It is therefore a philosophy "engaged in reducing to the same all that is opposed to it as *other*."[24] "The same," a term Levinas borrows from Plato, refers to both the self-identity of the narcissistic subject and the abstract concepts that this subject utilizes to reduce the singularity of the actual existent to a universal structure: a process that buffers the impact of any true foreignness of the other. The concept, in other words, overcomes the irreducible difference between knowledge and being by violently reducing one to the other. Building on the etymological link between knowledge (*Begreifen*) and grasping (*greifen*), Levinas describes knowledge as a way "of seizing something and making it one's own, of reducing to presence and representing the difference of being, an activity that *appropriates* and *grasps* the otherness of the known."[25] Levinas associates this "ontological imperialism" with the Socratic idea of freedom, where to be free means "to receive nothing of the Other but what is in me."[26] Freedom thus means, first and foremost, autonomy: freedom from otherness or exteriority. The "shock" of exteriority can be buffered only by translating alterity into the categories of the same that receives it — the third term of the concept. Jeffrey Dudiak notes that for the "neutral third to do its job, for mediation to be effective, the other must surrender, must cease to be genuinely other."[27] This surrender, in Levinas's eyes, occurs on the basis of violence. Western philosophy thus emerges as a philosophy of violence denying the alterity — the singularity — of the other. Through what Levinas calls a process of "adequation," the knowing ego reduces the exteriority of the world to the structures of the self, thus "consuming" exteriority and abolishing alterity.

As the novel's principal upholder of the Enlightenment principles of reason, freedom, and autonomy, David Lurie is set up as such a knowing ego who, "adequating" singular otherness, reduces it to the structures of his own perceiving mind. It is not primarily Lurie's individuality, then, but his investment in abstract concepts and principles, the mechanisms of reason, that is ultimately responsible for the violent sociality he engenders. This investment in abstractions is emphasized throughout the novel. Lurie insists, for example, on "playing it by the book" (*DG*, 55), and later defends himself in front of his ex-wife Rosalind by suggesting that he was "standing up for a principle," the principle being freedom of speech, which also means the "freedom to remain silent" (*DG*, 188). Rosalind's retort to this defence is revealing; she suggests: "That sounds very grand. But you were always a great self-deceiver, David. A great deceiver and a great self-deceiver" (188). It is this deceit, by which Lurie reduces the other to the structures of his own consciousness, that engenders Lurie's violent encounters with others: "initially depicted as being wholly self-absorbed in his dealings with others," Lurie, as Marais observes, "self-indulgently deludes himself into believing that [Soraya] reciprocates his feelings for her," just as he "evinces a singular lack of concern for Melanie's views and feelings: she is simply an adjunct to his ego" (SI, 163–64).

The most marked example of what Marais aptly calls Lurie's "pathological disregard for others" (SI, 164), a solipsism founded on freedom from exteriority, is found in Lurie's encounters with Lucy. Persistently misunderstood by her father, Lucy explicitly rebukes her father, just after revealing that she is pregnant as a result of the rape, for projecting his own ideas of how she should run her life onto her:

> "David, I can't run my life according to whether or not you like what I do. Not any more. You behave as if everything I do is part of the story of your life. You are the main character, I am a minor character who doesn't make an appearance until halfway through. Well, contrary to what you think, people are not divided into major and minor. I am not minor. I have a life of my own, just as important to me as yours is to you, and in my life I am the one who makes the decisions." (*DG*, 198)

The irony of this passage is of course that Lucy *is* a minor character in the novel who only makes an appearance halfway through. However, rather than discredit Lucy's complaint, this irony compounds it, for it directs us to the problem of focalization in the novel. In other words, focalization of the novel through Lurie replicates and *performs* the problem of narcissistic projection played out on the level of the plot: the reader is caught in the limitations of Lurie's view of the world, in the structures of his "adequating" consciousness. Further, as Lucy reminds Lurie, it is the limitations of abstract thought that lead to misreadings:

> "Stop it, David! I don't want to hear this talk of plagues and fires. I am not just trying to save my skin. If that is what you think, you miss the point entirely."
> "Then help me. Is it some form of private salvation you are trying to work out? Do you hope you can expiate the crimes of the past by suffering in the present?"
> "No. You keep misreading me. Guilt and salvation are abstractions. I don't act in terms of abstractions. Until you make an effort to see that, I can't help you." (*DG*, 112)

Given Lucy's express rejection of her father's assumption that her apparent acceptance of the rape constitutes an attempt to "expiate the crimes of the past," it is particularly poignant that this is exactly how the novel itself has been (mis)read. Readings that diagnose a "Lucy-syndrome" or charge the novel with racism replicate the violence of Lurie's solipsistic consciousness because they fail to attend to what this consciousness forecloses: in this case, Lucy's enigmatic reasons for doing what she does. As Marais reminds us, "the passivity of Lucy's response to her rape is pivotal: it is *meant* to be perplexing and to invest her with a degree of alterity that renders her resistant to interpretation" (RaR, 280). The reader who pathologizes her translates the alterity of her enigmatic response into abstract concepts — be they guilt, salvation, expiation, or worse — and thereby involuntarily becomes complicit with Lurie's violating consciousness.

The ethical task Coetzee sets his reader, as much as his protagonist, is thus to "make an effort to see" an alterity outside Lurie's projections. In other words, it is an invitation into what Gayatri Spivak has called "counterfocalization." Inasmuch as, she says, "This provocation into counterfocalization is the 'political' in political fiction" (EP, 22), Coetzee's politics must be sought precisely in this counterfocalization rather than in the focalization. She insists: "If we, like Lurie, ignore the enigma of Lucy, the novel, being fully focalized precisely by Lurie, can be made to say every racist thing" (EP, 24). The task for the reader (and for Lurie himself) is to transcend the limitations of the governing solipsistic point of view so as to engender an encounter with a singular alterity that is not already reduced to the generality of the concept.

Much scholarly criticism on *Disgrace* has framed this particular task as "the ethical task of developing a sympathetic imagination" (SI, 163). The sympathetic imagination, as Margot Beard reminds us, concerns "the major proposition of Romanticism," whereby the imagination "is our only means to enter the experience of another, of overcoming our atomistic isolation from the rest of creation" (LDM, 74). In *Disgrace*, Beard suggests, "Coetzee's concern [is] with the power of the empathetic imagination to awaken us to the needs of others, both human and animal" (LDM, 60). The sympathetic imagination aims to create the empathetic bond or connection with the other that Lurie's solipsistic consciousness forecloses. In *The Lives of Animals*, published in the same year as *Disgrace*, Coetzee advances this discussion more overtly. Here, novelist Elizabeth Costello associates the Nazi horror of the "death camps" with the killers' refusal "to think themselves into the place of their victims" (*LA*, 34). She elaborates: "they closed their hearts. The heart is the seat of a faculty, *sympathy*, that allows us to share at times the being of another" (*LA*, 34). According to Costello, "there is no limit to the extent to which we can think ourselves into the being of another. There are no bounds to the sympathetic imagination" (*LA*, 35).

Seductive though this claim may be, "*Disgrace*," as Laura Wright observes, "is Coetzee's critique of the vanity of such an assertion."[28] The primary testing ground for Costello's assertion lies in Lucy's claim, later repeated by Bev Shaw, that Lurie was not there during her rape and cannot "*know what happened*" (*DG*, 134). "Outraged at being treated like an outsider" (*DG*, 141), Lurie asks himself:

> Where, according to Bev Shaw, according to Lucy, was he not? In the room where the intruders were committing their outrages? Do they think he does not know what rape is? Do they think he has not suffered with his daughter? What more could he have witnessed than he is capable of imagining? Or do they think that, where rape is concerned, no man can be where the woman is? (*DG*, 140–41)

Lucy insinuates that, if anything, Lurie may be able to imagine himself into the place of the raping man: "You're a man, you ought to know" (*DG*, 158), and Lurie indeed reluctantly confirms this: "Lucy's intuition is right after all: he does understand; he can, if he concentrates, if he loses himself, be there, be the men, inhabit them, fill them with the ghost of himself. The question is, does he have it in him to be the woman?" (*DG*, 160).

These reflections expose precisely what the imagination is — and is not — capable of achieving. According to Marais, it is "in assaulting Pollux [that] Lurie shows a failure of imagination" (SI, 178). However, as I have indicated, Lurie is capable of thinking himself into the position of Lucy's attackers. In fact, the parallel between the rape of Lucy and Lurie's sexual violation of Melanie (that Lurie never quite acknowledges to be rape) is all-too-obvious in the novel: it does not seem that Lurie needs to "lose himself" to create that connection, for it is not such a stretch of the imagination, after all. Further, it is not just Lurie who, in misreading Lucy's passivity as guilt or expiation, "is grounded in the discourse of race in South Africa" (SI, 181). The attackers, as Marais acknowledges, also "know her through the generic categories of race in South African society" (*DG*, 182). However, for Marais, even though "history speaks through both Lurie and the rapists when they presume to know Lucy," the difference between the respective "positions they occupy in history's economy of exchange" means that Lurie has no imaginative access to the attackers. Thus, even though "Lurie and the rapists are guilty of a similar failure of imagination in their respective interactions with Lucy," they are also imaginatively barred from each other (*DG*, 182).

While I believe Marais is right in diagnosing a similarity between Lurie and the attackers vis-à-vis Lucy, I do not think that their different positioning in history overrides the more fundamental fact *of* their positioning in history. Thus, as Lucy reflects on the "shock of being hated" (156), it is Lurie who is able to explain this hatred to her:

> "It was so personal," she says. "It was done with such personal hatred. That was what stunned me more than anything. The rest was . . . expected. But why did they hate me so? I had never set eyes on them."
>
> He waits for more, but there is no more, for the moment. "It was history speaking through them," he offers at last. "A history of wrong. Think of it that way, if it helps. It may have seemed personal but it wasn't. It came down from the ancestors." (*DG*, 156; ellipsis in original)

Contrary to Marais's suggestion that both Pollux and Lucy reveal Lurie's failure of imagination, I believe it is only Lucy, but not Pollux, who constitutes the limit of the sympathetic imagination for Lurie. With Pollux, Lurie shares a historical narrative: a narrative based on abstract idealities of race. That they are positioned antagonistically vis-à-vis that narrative, that one is (former) "master" and the other (former) "slave," does not mean they cannot think themselves into the other's position. What does constitute a limit of the sympathetic imagination, however, is a position that refutes that narrative altogether. The imagination, as a faculty of the mind, cannot but trade in generalities and abstractions. As such, it has no room for a position such as Lucy's that refuses to engage in those abstractions. Lurie thus cannot but continue to misread his daughter, for Lucy makes claims to a singularity, an alterity, that cannot be accounted for and that therefore escapes the accounting mind.

This claim to singularity becomes particularly obvious when Lucy explains why she does not lay rape charges, insisting, as she does, that it is "a purely private matter":

> "You want to know why I have not laid a particular charge with the police. I will tell you, as long as you agree not to raise the subject

again. The reason is that, as far as I'm concerned, what happened to me is a purely private matter. In another time, in another place it might be held to be a public matter. But in this place, at this time, it is not. It is my business, mine alone."

"This place being what?"

"This place being South Africa." (*DG*, 112)

Lucy's insistence on the private nature of a rape that is so obviously historically motivated, and therefore anything but private, constitutes a refusal to participate in the discourse of race in South Africa. Yet it is not through imagination that she achieves this. As Marais explains, the imagination is ultimately limited because it "must achieve what appears to be impossible: it must enable the self to abandon its point of view in culture and, in so doing, construct for it a position that is precisely not a position, which would therefore allow the self to be within the world while viewing it from nowhere within it." Lucy's shock at being the object of racial hatred, her insistence on the private nature of the rape, as well as her renunciation of Lurie's abstractions, all point to her refusal to engage with others through "predetermined relations" and highlight her investment in singularity: that is, in "locating an interstitial nonposition within culture" (SI, 178–79). Such an interstitial nonposition — in-between and beyond the violent exchange between "masters and slaves" — constitutes the condition of possibility for "an idea of justice . . . that transcends laws and lawmaking" (*DP*, 340) in postapartheid South Africa. It is a position that refuses abstraction, for it is aware that, as Levinas insists, "it is in the knowledge of the other (*autrui*) as a simple individual — individual of a genus, a class, or a race — that peace with the other (*autrui*) turns into hatred; it is the approach of the other as 'such and such a type.'"[29]

Instead of encountering the other as an instantiation of a type, Lucy's position demands that the other be encountered as what Levinas calls a "face," a face that is "denuded of its own image" and that is "without any cultural ornament" (BPW, 53). In a rare moment of extreme lucidity, Levinas suggests that the face is "signification without context"; "I mean that the Other, in the rectitude of his face, is not a character within a context. Ordinarily one is a 'character': a professor at the Sorbonne, a Supreme Court justice, son of so-and-so, everything that is in one's passport, the manner of dressing, of presenting oneself."[30]

Insisting on the face as a form of pure signification, "meaning all by itself,"[31] Levinas even goes to the extent of saying that the "best way of encountering the Other is not even to notice the color of his eyes!"[32] for even such a small gesture as noticing the color of somebody's eyes already indicates that one has reclaimed the other conceptually and positioned her within culture and history. As Derrida puts it: "Categories must be missing for the Other not to be overlooked; . . . the face is not 'of this world.' It is the origin of the world."[33]

That Lurie keeps misreading Lucy thus indeed points to the failure of the sympathetic imagination: the failure to grasp singularity through concepts. This failure, however, is a productive failure, because it opens up new ethical possibilities. As James Meffan and Kim Worthington suggest, "it is precisely this failure, the necessary failure of the imaginative attempt, that may be ethically productive," and the "best that can be hoped for is an ongoing recognition of the limits of one's own ego, the boundaries of one's knowing, a recognition that ensures respect for, albeit not complete understanding of, alterity."[34] How, then, does Lurie respond to this failure of the sympathetic imagination? How does he make it ethically productive in coming to recognize the limitations of his own ego and becoming attentive to the alterity of the other? How does he arrive at an interstitial position, such as Lucy's, that is liberated from the strictures of history and as such is "not 'of this world'"? Or, more carefully, *does* he arrive at such a position at all?

In addressing these questions, it is important to revisit the scene in the novel that perhaps best encapsulates Lucy's "nudity as a face" — that is, the scene of what Paul Patton terms "Lucy's becoming-dog":[35]

> "Yes, I agree, it's humiliating. But perhaps that is a good point to start from again. Perhaps that is what I must learn to accept. To start at ground level. With nothing. Not with nothing but. With nothing. No cards, no weapons, no property, no rights, no dignity."
> "Like a dog."
> "Yes, like a dog." (*DG*, 205)

The simile, with its unmistakable echo of the closing passage of Kafka's *The Trial*, is significant inasmuch as it signals the stripping away of "cultural ornaments," thus suggesting that a rebuilding of the country has to begin from an encounter of singularities, where singular human beings face each other "with nothing," where they stand in their absolute nudity and vulnerability. Coetzee compares this vulnerability with that of an animal, a dog, a comparison that points to the ethical trajectory of the novel. The ethical task the novel sets its protagonist is therefore that of "becoming-animal," by which I mean becoming a face, a singularity "without cultural ornament." With the exception of Lucy — enigmatic, singular Lucy — Lurie's becoming-animal is facilitated by his encounters with animals, rather than with humans, because, unlike humans, animals are not grounded in the discourse of race in South Africa: animals, in *Disgrace*, have a "face."[36]

What, then, does Lurie's becoming-animal look like? Given that it is consciousness, the mind, that supplies the categories for understanding the other within history, any attempt to encounter the other *outside* history must necessarily begin from a place outside consciousness. This place lies in the body. Through and with the body, the other is touched, rather than grasped: "Consciousness is . . . always the grasping of a being through an ideality. . . . In starting with *touching*, interpreted not as palpation but as caress, and *language*, interpreted not as the traffic of information but as contact, we have tried to describe *proximity* as irreducible to consciousness and thematization" (BPW, 80). For Levinas, proximity means "a relationship with a singularity, without the mediation of any principle or ideality" (BPW, 81). Similarly, the ethical trajectory that Coetzee establishes for Lurie is not to *imagine* the life of another but to enter into proximity with it — and it is the body that ultimately enables such proximity.

It is significant that Lurie who, for the best part of the novel, insists that he "wants to go on being himself" (*DG*, 77) and is "too old to change" (209), does indeed change. He changes in ways that are incomprehensible to him, in ways that lie beyond the grasp of his reason. The changes he experiences occur in the body, in an affective bond he develops with the vulnerable animal-other. Thus he "mak[es] friends" (78) with the abandoned dog Katy, for example, by lying down beside her, and, a little later, finds that he is affected by the fate of two young sheep that Petrus has designated as slaughter animals for his party: "A bond seems to have come into existence between himself and the two Persians, he does not know how. The bond is not one of affection. It is not even a bond with these two in particular, whom he could not pick out from a mob in a field. Nevertheless, suddenly and without reason, their lot has become important to him" (126).

As Laura Wright rightly emphasizes, "the connection [with the two sheep] is not imagined, is not Costello's arrogant claim that she 'can think [her] way into the existence of a bat or a chimpanzee or an oyster.'" Instead, she continues, the connection "is visceral, felt, quite literally, in the gut. It is a physical reaction to suffering, not an intellectualized exercise in mimesis; it is the bodily realization that one cannot 'be' the other, but that empathy is possible regardless" (PD, 97). Lurie increasingly experiences such a "physical reaction to suffering" in relation to the vulnerable animal-other; becoming affected by the fate of the animals he helps euthanize, he in fact struggles to "recover himself":

> He had thought he would get used to it. But that is not what happens. The more killings he assists in, the more jittery he gets. One Sunday evening, driving home in Lucy's kombi, he actually has to stop at the roadside to recover himself. Tears flow down his face that he cannot stop; his hands shake.
>
> He does not understand what is happening to him. . . .
>
> His whole being is gripped by what happens in the theatre. (*DG*, 142)

Entering into proximity with the vulnerable animal-other, Lurie becomes affected by their fate and begins to "lose himself," trading his rational, autonomous ego for an *altered* — ethical — subjectivity. The end result is that Lurie becomes able to take ethical action: when the workmen who load the incinerator with the bags containing dead dogs begin "to beat the bags with the backs of their shovels before loading them, to break the rigid limbs" (*DG*, 144–45), Lurie "intervened and took over the job himself" (145), surprising himself at the ultimately irrational concern he takes for the dead dogs: "Curious that a man as selfish as he should be offering himself to the service of dead dogs" (146).

The failure of imagination Lurie encounters in relation to Lucy thus ultimately challenges him to enter into proximity with those to whom he has no imaginative access, those singular "others" who stand outside South Africa's racialized history of "masters and slaves." Such proximity sets in motion a process of ethical change in Lurie that sees him transform from someone who approaches the world through abstractions — and who hence "disapproves of cruelty" only in an "abstract way" (*DG*, 143) — to "dog-man" (146): a man who is physically and emotionally *affected* by such cruelty and who takes it upon himself to honor the dignity of dead dogs "because there is no one else stupid enough to do it" (*DG*). Ultimately, this transformation signals Lurie's emergence as an ethical subject. By taking responsibility for the dogs, Lurie effectively responds with what Levinas describes as the ethical gesture par excellence: a simple "here I am" (*me voici*) — that is, an acceptance of his "assignation."

As the accusative case in the French *me voici* indicates, the ethical self is "through and through a hostage"; further, and importantly, it is "through the condition of being hostage that there can be in the world pity, compassion, pardon, proximity."[37] Heteronomous to the core, this alter ego clearly has little in common with the autonomous Enlightenment subject; rather than *animal rationale*, this ego is "an irritability, a susceptibility, or an exposure to wounding and outrage" (BPW, 86). Exposed to, and defenseless before, the other, the ethical subject is pure affectivity; unable to shut itself off against the other, it cannot evade the responsibility it is assigned by (and for) the other. Levinas explains:

> Under assignation, the pronoun "I" [*je*] is in the accusative: it signifies *here I am*. . . . "Here I am" [*me voici*] is the saying of that inspiration that could not to be confused with the gift of fine words or with that of the song. . . . The *here I am* signifies a being bound to giving with hands full, a being bound to corporeity; the body is the very condition of giving, with all that giving costs.[38]

Inasmuch as ethical subjectivity is only possible when it is tied to sensibility, Lurie's emergence as an ethical subject is predicated on a reconnection with his own embodiment — such as it is triggered, rather painfully, by Lurie's "exposure to wounding" in the attack. Painful though it may be, this "exposure to wounding" ultimately enables Lurie's ethical transformation, for it is only once Lurie recognizes that he is "a being bound to corporeity," as Levinas puts it, that he can begin to "lose himself." The *loss* of Lurie's rational, autonomous ego is of course a gain in *Disgrace*, because it constitutes the condition of possibility for the emergence of an ethical existence predicated on the body, on the hands that give.

Given this carefully prepared process of ethical change in the novel, it is perhaps no surprise that Coetzee makes us revisit Lurie's original point of departure: his refusal to show repentance for the sexual violation of Melanie "before a branch of the law" (*DG*, 58). In a scene directly recalling this point of departure, Lurie seeks out Melanie's father, Mr. Isaacs, so as to "say what is on [his] heart" (165). Exchanging the abstract anonymity of the hearing for the face-to-face encounter with those affected by his actions, Lurie moves away from the relative protection afforded by the law to expose himself to judgment outside and beyond the law. However, despite the potential this scene holds for bringing about a singular justice transcending the law, it quickly transpires that Lurie's ethical trajectory is as yet incomplete. Although well-intentioned, the encounter begins awkwardly, with Lurie, after having his desire for Melanie rekindled through coming into contact with Melanie's sister, "Desiree, the desired one" (164), attempting to explain, "in self-defence" (166), his desire for Melanie to her father. Arriving with the promise to "say what is on [his] heart" (165), Lurie in fact offers little in the way of actual apology; however, Isaacs nonetheless takes Lurie up on his promise, and invites him to share a meal with the family, after which Lurie eventually brings himself to apologize: "I am sorry for what I took your daughter through. You have a wonderful family. I apologize for the grief I have caused you and Mrs. Isaacs. I ask for your pardon" (171).

This hard-won apology, however, is immediately undercut in the next line, where Lurie's reflection reveals not just a remorseful heart but also an accounting mind to be at work: "*Wonderful* is not right. Better would have been *exemplary*" (171). That Lurie's apology is at best "half-hearted" is further suggested by Isaac's response:

> "So," says Isaacs, "at last you have apologized. I wondered when it was coming." He ponders. He has not taken his seat; now he begins to pace up and down. "You are sorry. . . . But I say to myself, we are all sorry when we are found out. Then we are very sorry. The question is not, are we sorry. The question is, what lesson have we learned? The question is, what are we going to do now that we are sorry?" (*DG*, 171–72)

Thus invited to demonstrate his remorse, Lurie responds with a carefully calculated performance of repentance: "With careful ceremony he gets to his knees and touches his forehead to the floor. Is that enough? he thinks. Will that do? If not, what more?" (173).

The irony of this response is, of course, that Lurie here belatedly delivers the kind of "spectacle" (66) he refused to deliver at the hearing: the performance of a "spirit of repentance" (58). However, while this direct echo of an earlier scene may superficially invite us to believe that Lurie has indeed evolved as an ethical character and is now capable of delivering that which he previously was unable to, the overriding impression is that he has still learned very little, for he continues to put his trust in mechanisms offered by the law, when the law, with its abstractions and calculations, in fact stands in the way of singular justice. What Lurie's "careful ceremony" of repentance ultimately signals, then, is that, for Lurie, calculus continues to override repentance, suggesting that he has not yet let go of his investment in the law (the "element of calculation") as the appropriate means to bring about justice (the "incalculable") in postapartheid South Africa.

The necessary severance of the law from justice — which allows for the kind of "love" to emerge that can transcend an inheritance of historical violence — does not take place until the very end of the novel, when Lurie is adopted by a young crippled dog who appears to share Lurie's passion for music and who, Lurie knows, "would die for him" (*DG*, 215). That Lurie should decide to give up this dog makes the end deeply disturbing, and makes of Lurie — plain, rational Lurie — an enigmatic figure. In this, Lurie perhaps comes closer to Lucy than he has been throughout the novel, at least to the reader's mind, for if Lurie and the reader have formerly struggled to understand Lucy's passivity, they now struggle to understand Lurie's sacrifice: why does he have to give up the one dog to whom he is tied by an affective bond?

Many critics (and no doubt many readers) have puzzled over this question. Thus, Josephine Donovan, for example, remarks that "Lurie could have adopted the dog he gives up for euthanasia" (MC, 91), implicitly asking why he did not. Similarly, Adriaan van Heerden notes the Christian overtones in the final scene but also suggests that it is "oddly unrecognizable"; "The imagery here (the 'sacrifice' of the 'lamb') is reminiscent of Christianity and yet oddly unrecognizable as anything with which we were previously acquainted. What does this strange ending tell us?"[39]

What does this strange ending tell us indeed? Why does Coetzee make a novel that is already unbearably bleak even bleaker with this final act? There are many possible answers. The most obvious perhaps is that the sacrifice of Driepoot achieves what Lurie's previous encounters with animals did not: it singularizes the animal. The bond that comes into existence between Lurie and the dog is the bond of "a generous affection" (*DG*, 215) that was still lacking, for example, in Lurie's bond with the sheep: it is a bond that can only grow between singular beings: a bond of love. This bond makes of the animal a "face" that communicates not just to Lurie but also to the reader through affect. As Donovan argues: "This moment of pointless animal sacrifice — conceived as a betrayal of a devoted companion — serves to particularize the otherwise abstract mechanized slaughter of millions of animal companions that happens every day in animal shelters worldwide" (MC, 88). Lucy Graham notes a similar sense of singularization when she argues that "at the end of *Disgrace* the sacrifice, 'the gift of death,' is not given in the name of an abstract other, but for the suffering body of another."[40]

Curiously, however, what has insinuated itself into an otherwise persuasive reading here is a significant *mis*reading: namely, that the singular embodied other should be a suffering other. The dog is vulnerable, to be sure, but suffering? Somewhat surprisingly, Mike Marais advances a similar reading when he argues that, "irrespective of his love for it, Lurie must sacrifice the dog. . . . Lurie must give up the dog because it is in the dog's interests that he does so" (SI, 174). Why should it be "in the dog's interests" to die? It seems to me that these are patent misreadings. The dog is not suffering for he is young and, albeit crippled, healthy and fully alive: he is capable of bonding with others and of gaining pleasure from Lurie's music. Similarly, to state that it is in the dog's interests to die involuntarily replicates an earlier anthropocentric judgment that Bev Shaw explicitly renounces. As she notes, the reason the animals are euthanized is not always because they are sick but because "there are just too many of them." Significantly, she adds, "Too many by our standards, not theirs. They would just multiply and multiply if they had their way, until they filled the earth. They don't think it's a bad thing to have lots of offspring. The more the jollier" (*DG*, 85).

These misreadings are instructive because, as in Lurie's misreading of Lucy or, for that matter, in the earlier misreadings of the novel as either racist or the symptom of a "Lucy-syndrome," they point to a failure of the imagination at the site of enigmatic singularity, suggesting that at this point in the novel Lurie himself has become a "face." Now "without cultural ornament," and therefore outside the historical narrative, Lurie is irreducibly singular, and hence no longer easily readable. According to Levinas, what singularizes the subject and makes it an ethical subject is precisely the act of taking responsibility for the singular other: "Responsibility is an individuation, a principle of individuation. Concerning the famous problem, 'Is man individuated by matter, or individuated by form?' I maintain individuation by responsibility for the other" (RB, 169–70).

What singularizes Lurie in the novel — what makes him a "face" — is his "gift of death" to the singular dog. In attending to the dog as he is about to be killed, Lurie faces up to what Levinas calls the ethical "obligation not to let the other man [*sic*] face death alone."[41] Paradoxical as this may seem, the "gift of death" is thus ultimately a gift of love, as Lurie recognises at the end: "He and Bev do not speak. He has learned by now, from her, to concentrate all his attention on the animal they are killing, giving it what he no longer has difficulty in calling by its proper name: love" (*DG*, 219).

This love is what is crucial in reimagining sociality in postapartheid South Africa. If "at the heart of the unfreedom of the hereditary masters of South Africa is a failure to love," as Coetzee contends, love emerges as the condition of possibility for freedom from violence. In loving the *singular* dog that is removed from the historical narratives of "masters and slaves" and, more generally, from the abstract designations of identity (race, gender, species, etc.) engendering violence in the political realm, Lurie recognizes the nudity and vulnerability of the dog's "face." And in taking responsibility for this face, Lurie shows the "new" South Africa the way toward freedom: the freedom of a society where people encounter each other as "faces" rather than through the violent abstractions of racialized subject positions, and where "an idea of justice . . . that transcends laws and lawmaking" (*DP*, 340) becomes possible.

The very mysteriousness of Lurie's final sacrifice, the very fact that readers and critics alike have puzzled over (and misread) this ending, is thus vital, for it points to the novel's refusal to submit to an economic calculus where loose ends are tied up and everything is made to add up. As Rita Barnard argues:

> [I]t is perhaps in the very disconcerting and morally ambiguous nature of this "giving . . . up" that we may begin to detect an ethos that relies on something other than a settling of accounts and the paying of a price. . . . The final scene, in short, is not one that is readily processed; and it is essential that we do not, as it were, try to beat it into convenient shape with a critical shovel.[42]

Deliberately enigmatic, the ending realizes the novel's ultimate investment in a secret that refuses to be grasped. Just as Lucy's passivity "is *meant* to be perplexing and to invest her with a degree of alterity that renders her resistant to interpretation" (RaR, 280), Lurie's sacrifice is *meant* to be enigmatic so as to evade the reader's interpretative grasp. In facing this enigma, the reader is brought face to face with his or her own failure of imagination — a failure designed to launch the reader's ethical trajectory. Accordingly, an appropriate ethical response to the novel would be to resist the meaning-making impulse with which we habitually approach a text and instead uphold the enigma the novel seeks to protect. The ultimate mark of our ethical subjectivity would thus be whether we are capable of taking responsibility for the alterity of the text: whether we have it in us to face the text as a "face" — a "face" that affects and unsettles us, that perhaps even traumatizes us, and that is forever in danger of being covered over and reclaimed, full of meaning, for the world.

Notes

[1] A comprehensive overview of the ever-expanding list of publications on *Disgrace* is beyond the scope of this chapter; the titles cited here are intended only to indicate the sheer breadth of scholarship the novel has attracted to date.

[2] Bill McDonald, ed., *Encountering "Disgrace": Reading and Teaching Coetzee's Novel* (Rochester, NY: Camden House, 2009).

[3] Andrew van der Vlies, *J. M. Coetzee's "Disgrace"* (London: Continuum, 2010).

[4] See, for example, Derek Attridge, *J. M. Coetzee and the Ethics of Reading: Literature in the Event* (Chicago: U of Chicago P, 2004) (subsequent references appear as ER with the accompanying page number); Katherine Stanton, *Cosmopolitan Fictions: Ethics, Politics, and Global Change in the Works of Kazuo Ishiguro, Michael Ondaatje, Jamaica Kincaid, and J. M. Coetzee* (London: Routledge, 2006); Jane Poyner, ed., *J. M. Coetzee and the Idea of the Public Intellectual* (Athens: Ohio UP, 2006); Kailash Baral, ed., *J. M. Coetzee: Critical Perspectives* (New Delhi: Pencraft International, 2008); Elleke Boehmer, Katy Iddiols, and Robert Eaglestone, eds., *J. M. Coetzee in Context and Theory* (London: Continuum, 2009); Mike Marais, *Secretary of the Invisible: The Idea of Hospitality in the Fiction of J. M. Coetzee* (Amsterdam: Rodopi, 2009) (subsequent references appear as SI with the accompanying page number); and Anton Leist and Peter Singer, eds., *J. M. Coetzee and Ethics: Philosophical Perspectives on Literature* (New York: Columbia UP, 2010).

[5] See, for example, Elleke Boehmer, "Not Saying Sorry, Not Speaking Pain: Gender Implications in *Disgrace*," *Interventions* 4, no. 3 (2002); and Elleke Boehmer, "Sorry, Sorrier, Sorriest: The Gendering of Contrition in J. M. Coetzee's *Disgrace*," *J. M. Coetzee and the Idea of the Public Intellectual*, ed. Jane Poyner (Athens: Ohio UP, 2006).

[6] Coetzee's intertextual references to Wordsworth and Byron have been of particular interest to scholars. See, for example, Margot Beard, "Lessons from the Dead Masters: Wordsworth and Byron in J. M. Coetzee's *Disgrace*," *English in Africa* 34, no. 1 (2007) (subsequent references appear as LDM with the accompanying page number); and Colleen M. Sheils, "Opera, Byron, and a South African Psyche in J M Coetzee's *Disgrace*," *Current Writing* 15, no. 1 (2003).

[7] Many discussions here focus on the novel's engagement with South Africa's pastoral tradition, specifically the Afrikaans *plaasroman*. See, for example, H. P. van Coller, "A Contextual Interpretation of J. M. Coetzee's Novel *Disgrace*," *A Universe of (Hi)Stories*, ed. Liana Sikorska (Frankfurt am Main: Peter Lang, 2006); Rita Barnard, "Coetzee's Country Ways," *Interventions* 4, no. 3 (2002); and Rita Barnard, "J. M. Coetzee's *Disgrace* and the South African Pastoral," *Contemporary Literature* 44, no. 2 (2003).

[8] While a general postcolonial sensitivity is part of most critical responses to the novel, there are surprisingly few that explicitly invoke a postcolonial framework. Most noteworthy are Gayatri Chakravorty Spivak, "Ethics and Politics in Tagore, Coetzee, and Certain Scenes of Teaching," *diacritics* 32, nos. 3–4 (2002) (subsequent references appear as EP with the accompanying page number); Ranjana Khanna, "Indignity," *Ethnic and Racial Studies* 30, no. 2 (2007); Ranjana Khanna, "Indignity," *positions* 16, no. 1 (2008); Georgina Horrell, "Postcolonial

Disgrace: (White) Women and (White) Guilt in the 'New' South Africa," in *Bodies and Voices: The Force-Field of Representation and Discourse in Colonial and Post-colonial Studies*, ed. Merete Falck Borch, Eva Rask Knudsen, Martin Leer, and Bruce Clunies Ross (Amsterdam: Rodopi, 2008); and, although his focus is more generally on race rather than the postcolonial per se, David Attwell, "Race in Disgrace," *Interventions* 4, no. 3 (2002): 331–41.

[9] The ethical is undoubtedly the single most significant theoretical framework critics invoke in relation to *Disgrace*, and within this overall framework there are a couple of different strands. Where most critics draw, to a greater or lesser extent, on the ethical philosophy of Emmanuel Levinas (and Jacques Derrida), the recently released book on *J. M. Coetzee and Ethics: Philosophical Perspectives on Literature*, ed. Anton Leist and Peter Singer (New York: Columbia UP, 2010), by contrast, contains not a single mention of Levinas in its index, but instead draws on the work of a wide range of other philosophers. Writing from within a distinctly Levinasian framework are two of Coetzee's most established and sophisticated critics, Derek Attridge and Mike Marais. For discussion of *Disgrace* from a Levinasian/Derridean perspective, see, in particular, Derek Attridge, "Age of Bronze, State of Grace: *Disgrace*," in ER; and the following works by Mike Marais: "'Little Enough, Less Than Little: Nothing': Ethics, Engagement, and Change in the Fiction of J. M. Coetzee," *Modern Fiction Studies* 46, no. 1 (2000); "The Possibility of Ethical Action: J. M. Coetzee's *Disgrace*," *scrutiny2: Issues in English Studies in South Africa* 5, no. 1 (2000); "Very Morbid Phenomena: 'Liberal Funk,' the 'Lucy-Syndrome' and J. M. Coetzee's *Disgrace*," *scrutiny2: Issues in English Studies in South Africa* 6, no. 1 (2001) (subsequent references appear as M with the accompanying page number); "Impossible Possibilities: Ethics and Choice in J. M. Coetzee's *The Lives of Animals* and *Disgrace*," *English Academy Review* 18, no. 1 (2001); "Reading against Race: J. M. Coetzee's *Disgrace*, Justin Cartwright's *White Lightning* and Ivan Vladislavić's *The Restless Supermarket*," *Journal of Literary Studies* 19, no. 3 (2003) (subsequent references appear as RaR with the accompanying page number); "The Task of the Imagination: *Disgrace*," in *Secretary of the Invisible: The Idea of Hospitality in the Fiction of J. M. Coetzee* (Amsterdam: Rodopi, 2009). A further important discussion of *Disgrace* from the point of view of Levinasian ethics is found in James Meffan and Kim L. Worthington, "Ethics before Politics: J. M. Coetzee's *Disgrace*," in *Mapping the Ethical Turn: A Reader in Ethics, Culture, and Literary Theory*, ed. Todd F. Davis and Kenneth Womack (Charlottesville: UP of Virginia, 2001).

[10] See, for example, Jane Poyner, "Truth and Reconciliation in J. M. Coetzee's *Disgrace*," *scrutiny2: Issues in English Studies in South Africa* 5, no. 2 (2000); Rebecca Saunders, "*Disgrace* in the Time of a Truth Commission," *parallax* 11, no. 3 (2005); Rosemary Jolly, "Going to the Dogs: Humanity in J. M. Coetzee's *Disgrace*, *The Lives of Animals*, and South Africa's Truth and Reconciliation Commission," in *J. M. Coetzee and the Idea of the Public Intellectual*, ed. Jane Poyner (Athens: Ohio UP, 2006); Jacques van der Elst, "Guilt, Reconciliation and Redemption: *Disgrace* and Its South African Context," in *A Universe of (Hi) Stories: Essays on J. M. Coetzee*, ed. Liana Sikorska (Frankfurt am Main: Peter Lang, 2006) (subsequent references appear as GRR with the accompanying page number); and Elizabeth S. Anker, "Human Rights, Social Justice, and J. M. Coetzee's

Disgrace," *Modern Fiction Studies* 54, no. 2 (2008). Linking a reflection on the TRC with an analysis of the verbal aspect of the novel, Mark Sanders, in his contribution to a special issue of *Interventions* on *Disgrace*, offers one of the most original and persuasive discussions of Coetzee's engagement with the TRC: Mark Sanders, "Disgrace," *Interventions* 4, no. 3 (2002).

[11] See, for example, Lucy Valerie Graham, "'A Hidden Side to the Story': Reading Rape in Recent South African Literature," *Kunapipi* 24, nos. 1–2 (2002); Gareth Cornwell, "Realism, Rape, and J. M. Coetzee's *Disgrace*," *Critique* 43, no. 4 (2002).

[12] See, for example, Louis Tremaine, "The Embodied Soul: Animal Being in the Work of J. M. Coetzee," *Contemporary Literature* 44, no. 4 (2003); Josephine Donovan, "'Miracles of Creation': Animals in J. M. Coetzee's Work," *Michigan Quarterly Review* 43, no. 1 (2004) (subsequent references appear as MC with the accompanying page number); Tom Herron, "The Dog Man: Becoming Animal in Coetzee's Disgrace," *Twentieth-Century Literature* 51, no. 4 (2005); Geoffrey Baker, "The Limits of Sympathy: J. M. Coetzee's Evolving Ethics of Engagement," *Ariel* 36, nos. 1–2 (2005); Sam Durrant, "J. M. Coetzee, Elizabeth Costello, and the Limits of the Sympathetic Imagination," *J. M. Coetzee and the Idea of the Public Intellectual*, ed. Jane Poyner (Athens: Ohio UP, 2006); Rosemary Jolly, "Going to the Dogs"; Paul Patton, "Becoming-Animal and Pure Life in Coetzee's *Disgrace*," *Ariel* 35, nos. 1–2 (2006); Travis Mason, "Dog Gambit: Shifting the Species Boundary in J. M. Coetzee's Recent Fiction," *Mosaic* 39, no. 4 (2006); Denise Almeida Silva, "Cartesianism Reviewed: The Logic of the Body in J. M. Coetzee's Fiction," *Stirrings Still: The International Journal of Existentialist Literature* 3, no. 1 (2006); Don Randall, "The Community of Sentient Beings: J. M. Coetzee's Ecology in *Disgrace* and *Elizabeth Costello*," *English Studies in Canada* 33, nos. 1–2 (2007); and Noam Gal, "A Note on the Use of Animals for Remapping Victimhood in J. M. Coetzee's *Disgrace*," *African Identities* 6, no. 3 (2008).

[13] Coetzee is careful to avoid explicit racialization in this novel. However, from a range of subtle markers — Soraya has a "honey-brown body" and is "tall and slim, with long black hair and dark, liquid eyes" (*DG*, 1) and Melanie is described as "the dark one" (*DG*, 18) — we are led to deduce that both Soraya and Melanie are black, whereas Lurie himself is white.

[14] Derek Attridge, "J. M. Coetzee's *Disgrace*: Introduction," *Interventions* 4, no. 3 (2002): 315–20; here, 315. Subsequent references appear as DI with the accompanying page number.

[15] Truth and Reconciliation Commission, available at: www.justice.gov.za/trc/ (accessed 30 June 2011).

[16] The charge that *Disgrace* is racist was laid in the African National Congress (ANC) submission to the Human Rights Commission's investigation into racism in the media.

[17] The term was coined by Dan Roodt. See M, 32.

[18] Jacques Derrida, *Acts of Religion*, ed. Gil Anidjar (London: Routledge, 2002), 244.

[19] Derrida, *Acts of Religion*, 248.

[20] Emmanuel Levinas, *Is It Righteous to Be? Interviews with Emmanuel Levinas*, ed. Jill Robbins (Stanford: Stanford UP, 2001), 169. Subsequent references appear as RB with the accompanying page number.

[21] See Desmond Tutu, *No Future without Forgiveness* (London: Doubleday, 2000).

[22] Jacques Derrida, "On Forgiveness," trans. Mark Dooley and Michael Hughes, in *On Cosmopolitanism and Forgiveness* (London: Routledge, 2001), 28.

[23] Marais, "Possibility," 57. Marais is drawing on Jane Taylor, "The Impossibility of Ethical Action. Review of *Disgrace*, by J. M. Coetzee," *Mail & Guardian* 23–29 July 1999.

[24] Emmanuel Levinas, *Collected Philosophical Papers*, trans. Alphonso Lingis (Dordrecht: Martinus Nijhoff Publishers, 1987), 48–49.

[25] Emmanuel Levinas, *The Levinas Reader*, ed. Seán Hand (Oxford: Blackwell, 1989), 76.

[26] Emmanuel Levinas, *Totality and Infinity: An Essay on Exteriority*, trans. Alphonso Lingis (Pittsburgh: Duquesne UP, 1969), 43.

[27] Jeffrey M. Dudiak, "Structures of Violence, Structures of Peace: Levinasian Reflections on Just War and Pacifism," in *Knowing Other-Wise: Philosophy at the Threshold of Spirituality*, ed. James H. Olthuis (New York: Fordham UP, 1997), 161.

[28] Laura Wright, "'Does He Have It in Him to Be the Woman?' The Performance of Displacement in J. M. Coetzee's *Disgrace*," *Ariel* 37, no. 4 (2006): 92. Subsequent references appear as PD with the accompanying page number.

[29] Emmanuel Levinas, *Basic Philosophical Writings*, ed. Adriaan Peperzak, Simon Critchley and Robert Bernasconi (Bloomington: Indiana UP, 1996), 166. Subsequent references appear as BPW with the accompanying page number.

[30] Emmanuel Levinas, *Ethics and Infinity: Conversations with Phillipe Nemo*, trans. Richard A. Cohen (Pittsburgh: Duquesne UP, 1985), 86.

[31] Levinas, *Ethics and Infinity*, 86.

[32] Levinas, *Ethics and Infinity*, 85. What should be noted here, however, is that Levinas, while insisting on encountering the other in their singularity, nonetheless invokes the category of gender ("the colour of *his* eyes") without any apparent self-reflexivity.

[33] Jacques Derrida, *Writing and Difference*, trans. Alan Bass (London: Routledge and Kegan Paul, 1978), 103.

[34] Meffan and Worthington, "Ethics before Politics," 145.

[35] Patton, "Becoming-Animal," 112.

[36] I am fully aware that the suggestion that animals have a "face" conflicts with Levinas's own insistence that the face of the other is always the face of the *human* other. However, it seems to me that *Disgrace* indeed challenges Levinas on this point, suggesting that in such a violently racialized society as South Africa, humans appear inevitably "in a context," whereas animals are without context,

they are racially nude. In thus implicitly proposing that the animal has a "face," and that it is in response to, and responsibility for, the animal's "face" that ethical subjectivity can emerge in South Africa, Coetzee calls into question one of the core assumptions of Levinasian ethics.

[37] Emmanuel Levinas, *Otherwise Than Being, or, Beyond Essence*, trans. Alphonso Lingis (Pittsburgh: Duquesne UP, 1998), 117.

[38] Emmanuel Levinas, *God, Death, and Time*, trans. Bettina Bergo (Stanford: Stanford UP, 2000), 188 (Bergo's interpolations).

[39] Adriaan van Heerden, "Disgrace, Desire, and the Dark Side of the New South Africa," in *J. M. Coetzee and Ethics: Philosophical Perspectives on Literature*, ed. Anton Leist and Peter Singer (New York: Columbia UP, 2010), 55.

[40] Graham, "Reading Rape in Recent South African Literature," 9.

[41] Emmanuel Levinas, "Bad Conscience and the Inexorable," *Face to Face with Levinas*, ed. Richard A. Cohen (New York: State U of New York P, 1986), 38.

[42] Barnard, "J. M. Coetzee's *Disgrace* and the South African Pastoral," 222–23.

11: *Elizabeth Costello* (2003)

James Meffan

E LIZABETH COSTELLO CANVASSES the interrelated problems of self-
knowledge, self-expression and other-knowledge: phenomenological problems. How can we truly represent ourselves when language — a
social institution that preexists and constitutes every individual's entry
into subject-hood — requires a deviation from our direct, bodily experience in and of the world? How can we know what life is like for others
when they too must constitute themselves in secondhand language in
order to represent themselves to us? And does the removal of language
from the relationship help matters? How successfully can we imagine
ourselves into the lives of beings not like us, whether we conceive of
them as below us (animals) or above (gods)? As linguistic beings, can we
even imagine an extralinguistic utopia? What would it look like? How
would we behave in it?

To present these relational questions as a problem is to express a
desire for a solution — in this case, a desire for true self- and other-knowledge and reliable, authentic self-expression undiluted and undiverted by
language. This desire (and its frustration) is evident throughout J. M.
Coetzee's work. The extraordinary closing section of *Foe* seems to offer
exactly this ideal of a transcendent realm beyond language, "a place where
bodies are their own signs" even as it undercuts that possibility: the claim
that "this is not a place of words" is a performative self-contradiction, a
phrase that undoes itself simply by being written down. If there is a place
beyond language, where expression is simply embodied, we are not going
to find it in a novel, a "place" that exists only in words. While Friday, the
only character in *Foe* who does not use language, might seem a more vivid
presence precisely because of his silence, it is only through his contextu-
alization in language (Susan's, Foe's, Coetzee's) that we can interpret his
silence in this way. In the end, then, the representation of "the home of
Friday" (157) expresses a desire rather than an actuality. While it may be
insatiable, this desire for transparent access to consciousness nevertheless
animates the constant reapplication of readers and writers to the language
games that constitute much of serious contemporary literature.

Like *Foe*, *Elizabeth Costello* also concludes with a gesture towards
the idealization of silence. The postscript, "Letter of Elizabeth, Lady

Chandos, to Francis Bacon," establishes a direct intertextual relationship to what is seen by some as one of the founding documents of modernism: Hugo von Hofmannsthal's *Letter of Lord Chandos to Lord Bacon*. Hofmannsthal's fictional letter articulates a young man's crisis as he realizes the inadequacy of language to the task of relating to a world teeming with consciousness and the consequent exponential generation of meaning that this implies. The letter represents the confession by Philip, Lord Chandos, to Francis Bacon, a founding figure of Enlightenment rationalism, of the younger man's renunciation of language. The fiction may dramatize a young man's retreat from language as an individual response to a phenomenological crisis, but the relationship that the fiction as a whole rehearses is rather more complex. Had Hofmannsthal shared his young protagonist's views he would, presumably, likewise have given up on language and left the fiction unwritten. Instead, its existence testifies to a third alternative, neither accepting rationalism's unreflective optimism towards language as an adequately transparent medium with which to represent the world as it is, nor being so despairing of language as to relinquish it altogether, but choosing to represent both positions in a fiction that combines historical and fictional elements.

With this intertextual reference, Coetzee acknowledges a debt to Hofmannsthal, but also to a whole tradition of thought dealing with the "crisis of language" or *Sprachkrise* that came to prominence around the beginning of the twentieth century.[1] This debate was an important antecedent to the more radical interrogations of the referential capacity of language widely referred to under the umbrella term poststructuralism, theories that also exert a significant influence on Coetzee's writing.[2] Like Hofmannsthal, Coetzee may represent language as more adversary than ally, yet he nevertheless continues to engage with these linguistic challenges through writing. I want to suggest, though, that Coetzee is doing rather more than simply offering an updated representation of this particularly intractable linguistic crisis. What he adds is a consideration of the role of the author (the real author), and the reader (the real reader, you and me) to these phenomenological debates.

To talk about the relationship of the author to the text is often seen in contemporary literary criticism as something of a false step. Ever since "The Intentional Fallacy"[3] there has been a widely held view that claims about what authors intend by their literary fictions, or about how those fictions evidence what kind of person the author really is, demonstrate a naive misunderstanding of the creative enterprise. But at the same time it seems equally misguided to deny that some relationship is established when we attend to words that have been offered by an author for us to read. Aren't most of our relationships generated out of linguistic transactions, whether oral or written? Why should not literary transactions be said to generate relationships between people?

It seems reasonable, then, to think that in order to make sense of our own relationship with the author J. M. Coetzee, we must first know something of Coetzee himself. Yet the notoriously reclusive Coetzee does not readily encourage such investigation. Even when working in that genre of self-disclosure, the memoir, he places strict limits on our access to what we might think of as his inner self. Despite offering the kind of excoriating detail that, since Rousseau at least, has been taken as the hallmark of candid self-revelation, he also deploys an array of devices that prevent simple identification of the author with the protagonist "John Coetzee." We do not finish Coetzee's memoirs with any comfortable sense that we know the man himself.

It is one of the operating principles of this volume that Coetzee's fictions can be usefully read in the light of his critical essays. Behind this principle lies the assumption that we might find in Coetzee's nonfiction explanatory statements that will tell us something about the motivations and techniques behind his fiction. We can see the same assumption at work in the Derek Attridge's introduction to *Inner Workings: Literary Essays 2000–2005*, an anthology of Coetzee's critical writing. "Why might one be drawn to read a collection of the book reviews and literary introductions of a writer known above all for his fiction?" asks Attridge. His answer asserts a clear distinction between the artfully fabricated voice(s) of fiction and the direct, authentic and sincere voice of nonfiction:

> There are two obvious incentives for turning from the fiction to the critical prose: in the hope that these more direct compositions will throw light on the often oblique novels, and in the belief that a writer who in his imaginative works can penetrate to the heart of so many pressing concerns is bound to have much to offer when writing, so to speak, with the left hand.[4]

There is something paradoxical and slightly apologetic in this formulation. Attridge recognizes in his initial question that Coetzee's popularity is due to his fiction, and that readers might therefore need to be persuaded to turn their attention to his critical output. So the argument is couched in terms of the greater directness and clarity of Coetzee's critical "compositions"; the criticism, it is hoped, "will throw light" on the "often oblique novels." Yet Coetzee has repeatedly resisted the call to provide commentary on his own fictions.[5] And the anthology to which Attridge's words form an introduction is a collection of essays by Coetzee but on writers other than himself. Seeking for clues to unlock Coetzee's own novels in his thoughts on other writers seems a path no more direct, no less oblique, than reading Coetzee's novels themselves.

Attridge's second reason for reading these critical essays seems equally questionable, and in contradiction with his first: given the penetration of his fiction, Attridge suggests, Coetzee's critical work "is bound to have much to offer." The phrase Attridge uses for Coetzee's nonfictional work, "writing . . . with the left hand" is telling. It suggests something less accomplished, or at least a mode that is less obviously Coetzee's forte. Here, the critical writing is offered as possibly less immediately appealing, yet we may nevertheless expect some of the perspicacity evident in the fiction to rub off on it. If Coetzee's fiction and nonfiction are such different beasts, which should we prefer and why, and what is the relationship between the two? Attridge is not clear on the matter.

Rather than an essay, I take as my starting point a lecture delivered by Coetzee. The lecture I have chosen is perhaps most notable for the way it *fails* to live up to the sorts of expectations voiced by Attridge. Indeed, while the presentation in question was advertised and continues to be classified as a lecture, it does not, by most measures, fit that category at all. The lecture I have chosen is Coetzee's 2003 Nobel Prize lecture.[6]

Called upon to give a lecture at his investiture as Nobel laureate for 2003, J. M. Coetzee's response was characteristically obtuse. As is stated in the Nobel Foundation Statutes, "it shall be incumbent on a prize-winner, whenever this is possible, to give a lecture on a subject relevant to the work for which the prize has been awarded."[7] To the surprise of some, given his well-known reticence towards public ceremony, Coetzee attended the event and delivered a lecture in accordance with statute and protocol. More surprising still, perhaps, was the manner of this "lecture."

Colloquial usage suggests that the proper form of a lecture is something direct and nonfictional — instructional, expository, or essayistic — using fictions to illustrate a point, perhaps, but in a wider framework of "straight-talking." In the case of the Nobel lecture, precedent suggests that the laureate for literature will deal with questions of the value of literature and the origins of a specific individual's literary impulses. Coetzee instead read out a fiction called "He and His Man," featuring an aging Robinson Crusoe, recipient of "reports" from "his man" Daniel Defoe. These reports, of decoy ducks or "duckoys," of "execution engines" with impossible escape clauses, and of London during the plague, are clearly inventions even though they draw upon some of Defoe's supposedly nonfictional publications, and the most outrageous claims are very near to their source material in the matters they recount. Their recipient, Robinson Crusoe, is one of literary history's most famous fictional "authors," *Robinson Crusoe* the novel one of the most well known "autobiographical charades."[8]

Coetzee's prefatory remarks to his lecture offer a kind of frame connecting the rhetorical situation with the lecture's fictional content, but they could not be called explanatory. In this introduction Coetzee recalls a time in his childhood when, eight or nine years old and having read *Robinson Crusoe*, Crusoe having become "a figure in [his] imagination," he discovers another, hitherto unknown name associated with the island story:

A man with a wig named Daniel Defoe. What was not clear from *The Children's Encyclopedia* was exactly how this man fitted into the story. The encyclopedia referred to the man as the author of *Robinson Crusoe*, but this made no sense since it said on the very first page of *Robinson Crusoe* that Robinson Crusoe told the story himself. Who was Daniel Defoe? What had he done to get into *The Children's Encyclopedia* along with Robinson Crusoe? Was Daniel Defoe perhaps another name for Robinson Crusoe, an alias that he used when he returned to England from his island and put on a wig?[9]

There is an obvious parallel to be drawn here between the doubtful status of Daniel Defoe (doubtful, that is, to young John Coetzee despite the authoritative assertions of *The Children's Encyclopedia*) and Coetzee himself. This anecdote is offered by Coetzee at the moment that he and his works are being given the strongest possible endorsement for posterity. The Nobel Prize may not be a guarantee of inclusion in the literary canon, but there is no higher recommendation available to living writers. At a podium, white and gilt, in a fine suit and tie, he presents the kind of respectability seldom seen among the characters of his novels, just as bewigged Daniel Defoe couldn't be at a further social remove from Robinson Crusoe with his improvised clothes and wild hair.

We might well wonder: what light does Coetzee's account of his early confusion over the relationship between the author and his work shed on the lecture he is about to give? Coetzee's youthful uncertainty expresses what we might call an ontological confusion. When he wonders "exactly how [Defoe fits] into the story," he is making a category error, ignoring a distinction that as experienced readers of fiction we are very careful to preserve. In an important sense, the author of fiction does not *fit into* his creation at all, but belongs to another realm: the real rather than the fictional world. By convention, when we are dealing with fiction, we treat all fictional utterances as distanced from the author, using the concept of the narrator to operate as both intermediary and barrier between author and fictional world. The narrator may him or herself be conceived of as internal to the fiction (a homodiegetic narrator) or external to it (heterodiegetic) but it is a matter of critical orthodoxy not to confuse the "speaker" of the narrative — even an external one — with the author. To assume that Defoe is part of the story of *Robinson Crusoe* is to ignore this crucial separation.

"He and His Man" takes this confusion a step further. Whereas our historical knowledge tells us that Robinson Crusoe was actually an invention of Defoe, in Coetzee's lecture Defoe is revealed on the contrary to be Crusoe's invention; Defoe is not simply included on Crusoe's level, he is subordinated to it. Initially, it seems that Defoe coexists with Crusoe, sending in "reports" from his travels. However, we soon learn that the possessive of the title indicates an even greater level of "ownership" and control: Crusoe is writing Defoe into existence as a narrational device to lend an air of verisimilitude to Crusoe's inventions.

Crusoe's concerns in creating the mediating figure of Defoe are revealed to be fundamentally realist, supplying the details of a plausible fictional world:

> what species of man can it be who will dash so busily hither and thither across the kingdom, from one spectacle of death to another (clubbings, beheadings), sending in report after report? A man of business, he thinks to himself. Let him be a man of business, a grain merchant or a leather merchant, let us say; or a manufacturer and purveyor of roof tiles somewhere where clay is plentiful, Wapping let us say, who must travel much in the interest of his trade.[10]

But if Crusoe aims to convince the reader of the truth of what he presents, what are Coetzee's aims? Why, in a forum where direct self-expression is expected, does he offer instead a plainly fictional figure struggling to make his inventions credible?

One possible explanation was offered, rather surprisingly, before Coetzee even stood to speak. Horace Engdahl, the Permanent Secretary of the Swedish Academy who gave the Nobel lecture presentation (that is, who introduced Coetzee to his lecture audience), clearly anticipated Coetzee's departure from custom, prefiguring Coetzee's lecture by noting the paradox facing the private writer called upon to produce a public performance. Having introduced Coetzee to the assembled luminaries, Engdahl qualified his welcome thus:

> The Academy is delighted to receive Mr. John Coetzee today. Yet we can't fail to perceive a certain irony in the situation given the laureate's reputation for reclusion. An occasion like the Nobel Lecture inevitably puts the author in the centre as a public figure and a celebrity, which is not what literary writing is about as we understand it through the works of J. M. Coetzee. To direct the attention away from oneself on this stage may seem a hopeless undertaking, and yet there are perhaps ways, literature being after all the third alternative to speaking and remaining silent. It is with great expectation and curiosity that we now ask Mr. Coetzee to read his lecture.[11]

There is something stagey, something *knowing* about this, hinting that the text of the lecture has been made available in advance to the academy. The intuition that Coetzee's apparently resistant gesture has already been accommodated by the academy is soon confirmed as a panning shot takes in members of the audience, some of whom are clearly following the line of his delivery through their printed copies. What Coetzee goes on to perform is plainly what Engdahl meant when he identified "the third alternative to speaking and remaining silent," which is using a distinctively *literary* mode of address: telling a story.

Engdahl's is an odd formulation, though, suggesting as it does that telling a story is neither "speaking" nor "remaining silent." How are we to understand this assertion that fictional narrative is somehow *not speaking*, not simply one among many kinds of communicative utterance? The simplest explanation is that Engdahl is not really distinguishing speech and silence from some intermediate category but the directness of nonfiction from the indirection of fiction. Framed together with the mention of Coetzee's "reputation for reclusion," Engdahl's comments seem to suggest that Coetzee's decision to read out a fictional narrative is a kind of evasion, a protection of the writer's privacy despite the performance taking place in a very public forum. Following this line of thought, what fiction offers Coetzee above all is the freedom to resist talking about himself, or put into formal terms, the opportunity to avoid the equivalence of the narrative "I" and himself. Fiction allows him to speak in other voices, voices we might say, that are *not his own*.

The implication that Coetzee's fiction is evasive is not new. His early fiction was generally read against its context: apartheid-era South Africa. The role of the writer living under such an oppressive regime was a topic of heated debate, and Nadine Gordimer, South Africa's most well-recognized and -regarded novelist at the time, clearly spelt out an argument for an undeniable political demand operating on the serious writer in her essay "The Essential Gesture" (originally delivered as the 1984 Tanner Lectures on Human Values at Princeton University). More than simply demanding political engagement, Gordimer joined others in specifying the appropriate mode of engagement. From her Marxist position, Gordimer followed the arguments of Georg Lukács in identifying historical realism as the manner most appropriate for the writer to speak truth to power and demand the end to the injustices and illegitimacy of the totalitarian state. It was from this position that she made her now notorious criticism of Coetzee's earlier fiction in her review of *Life & Times of Michael K*:

> J. M. Coetzee . . . chose allegory for his first few novels. It seems he did so out of a kind of opposing desire to hold himself clear of events and their daily, grubby, tragic consequences in which, like everyone else living in South Africa, he is up to the neck, and about which he had an inner compulsion to write. So here was an allegory as a stately fastidiousness; or a state of shock. He seemed able to deal with the horror he saw written on the sun only — if brilliantly — if this were to be projected into another time and plane.[12]

Here Gordimer identifies Coetzee's fictional mode as allegorical, a means of displacing his "inner compulsion" to write about the oppression of apartheid while assuaging that compulsion through indirect allegory.

At the heart of the criticism is the harsh assessment that while Coetzee recognizes the demand that his situation makes on him as a committed writer, he has ultimately experienced a failure of nerve.

Over a decade after Gordimer used the Tanner Lectures on Human Values at Princeton University to outline her views on the responsibility of writers, Coetzee had the opportunity to set the record straight on his literary-ethical commitments when he was invited to give the 1997–98 Tanner Lectures. However, as in the case of the Nobel lecture, Coetzee eschewed the opportunity to speak directly, instead inventing the protagonist who would endure into a number of subsequent literary-critical works: Elizabeth Costello. When Coetzee took the stage, he spoke in the third person of Elizabeth Costello, a writer who, like himself, had been invited to give a lecture on the strength of her literary reputation. Coetzee's lectures give an account of the events surrounding Costello's lectures as well as reporting the content of the lectures themselves, which become, technically, lectures within lectures. The fictional frame to Costello's lectures also includes responses from fictional academics. Coetzee's lectures were subsequently published in *The Lives of Animals*, a volume that included "reflections" by four prominent academics.

What is most striking about these academic reflections on Coetzee's lecture-fictions is the confusion that Coetzee's disruption of genre expectations induces. Apart from Marjorie Garber, the sole literary critic in the group, none of the responding academics seems to know quite what to make of the frame narrative. Wendy Doniger apologetically sidesteps the matter of the metafictional frame and responds directly to the arguments made by Elizabeth Costello and the counterarguments of her fictional respondents. Barbara Smuts likewise directs her response to the content of Costello's lectures, although she cautiously allows that Costello's views may equate with Coetzee's.[13] Peter Singer expresses consternation at the use of this metafictional device. Despite his misgivings, however, he responds in kind, adopting the register of narrative fiction (or Socratic dialogue) but has his character, "Peter," insist that he "prefer[s] to keep truth and fiction clearly separate" (*LA*, 86). Rather disingenuously, he concludes that "It's a marvelous device" that allows Coetzee to have Costello "blithely criticize the use of reason . . . without . . . really committing himself to any of these claims" (*LA*, 91). The common assumption among these respondents, and indeed in a number of critical reviews, is that despite all of the metafictional dressing up, Costello's lectures express what Coetzee really wanted to say in *his* lectures. The indirect nature of fiction is seen by such critics as rhetorical cleverness at best, evasion and sophistry at worst.

If Coetzee was at all stung by these criticisms, it did not deter him from producing further lecture-fictions. Indeed, the two lectures from *The Lives of Animals* have been gathered with another six Elizabeth

Costello episodes, which, along with the postscript discussed at the beginning of this chapter, make up the novel *Elizabeth Costello: Eight Lessons*. In her various lectures, arguments, ruminations, and petitions, Elizabeth Costello meditates on topics as diverse as realism in the novel and the erotic interactions of gods and men. Gathered together in this way, the diversity of topic along with the persistence of the protagonist makes it less sensible to read the lessons in terms of their central arguments than it does to treat the novel as being *about*, as the title suggests, Elizabeth Costello. Nevertheless, as the final acknowledgments page reminds us, each of the novel's chapters has had a life elsewhere, usually in the form of an academic essay or lecture. The varied history of the elements of *Elizabeth Costello* reminds us of the importance of context in the production of meaning. While we may think that words have limited ranges of semantic value that will hold regardless of the context of the utterance, we cannot help but note that the experience of reading about Elizabeth Costello has quite different hermeneutic potential if the performance is accounted a lecture, or alternatively a novel.

In *Elizabeth Costello*, we see various rehearsals of the same desire: to get at the truth of things through language. Many of the positions canvased so far associate truth with "directness" — that is, an unimpeded relationship between the being of the speaker and the utterance performed by that speaker. Many critics see the invention of Elizabeth Costello as a device to allow Coetzee to remain coy in the face of this demand for truth by frustrating the desire for direct utterance. There is something rather odd about this accusation. After all, if the writer wishes to hide, why use a device in which the relationship between author and character is so strongly suggested, and in which the expectations of direct communication from author to auditor have been raised by the genre of the performance? Very obviously, Elizabeth Costello's surname is graphically similar to Coetzee's; less superficially, she shares his métier, and some of his principles (his ethical vegetarianism, for instance). Surely, if Coetzee wished to discourage attribution of Costello's ideas to himself, he could have chosen a more dissimilar character? In order to think about what Coetzee is playing at with these lecture-fictions, I will look at the way the various critical positions already examined are dealt with in *Elizabeth Costello*. It is my contention that this novel is as much concerned with the performative aspects of language use as it is with the claims that are made within those performances.

Our knowledge of genre influences our reading strategies. Certain nonfiction genres represent a commitment to speak or write honestly, whereas fiction allows that the writer will be making things up. It is appropriate to concern ourselves as readers with the verifiability of nonfictional utterances, but not fictional ones. Obviously, a nonfictional utterance, offered in all honesty and sincerity, may still be false however, knowing that it is offered as nonfiction alerts us to a particular type of relationship between speaker and utterance: what is said, whether true or false, represents something that the speaker believes. This special relationship between the sayer and what is said is sometimes spoken of as *embodiment*, a metaphor that aims to capture the ideal of self and utterance being one, that what is said is in some sense integral to the speaker, a true representation of an essential part of them. *Elizabeth Costello* thematizes the idea of embodiment in order to challenge the intractable binaries — direct/indirect; fact/fiction; sincere/insincere — that it presents.

The critical approach that suspects Coetzee of evasion instead valorizes directness, which it assumes betokens a unity of material being and belief. In this view, the unified self precedes each utterance that a person makes; thus, the sincerity of an utterance is the measure of the extent to which that utterance directly represents the self. For such a critic, it is assumed that there is an author (in this case, J. M. Coetzee) with views, opinions, and beliefs of his own. From time to time Coetzee presents these views to the reading public *directly* in various nonfictional forms (the academic essay, the literary introduction or review, the lecture, the interview). There are also, without doubt, views held by Coetzee that he does not air. As readers we get a sense of a decision to remain silent on some matters in some rather prickly interviews, or we may infer it from the use of fiction in situations that precedent suggests call for nonfiction. Yet it is also generally assumed that fiction also, even if in a more indirect form, does represent the author's views, although these are seldom taken to be immediately or simply identifiable with opinions or beliefs expressed or demonstrated by a single character. The idea of the "implied author" is a notion developed to account for a single unifying sensibility that accounts for both the array of views represented in a work of fiction and the manner of their representation.

In Nadine Gordimer's criticism of Coetzee's use of allegory and her preference for historical realism, we see a valorization of a mode of writing that, while fictional, is nevertheless best equipped to represent conditions as they actually are. Realism is a mode that distrusts the "dressing up" of thought in rhetorical devices but instead seems to guarantee through its focus on material detail a directness that allegory — "saying one thing always for another" (*EC*, 228) — works against.

In the postscript to *Elizabeth Costello*, Elizabeth Chandos writes of allegory as the "contagion" of which her husband's language crisis is a symptom. Her attempts to get to the heart of this crisis, to explain it to Bacon the great rationalist, are repeatedly derailed by a reversion into figurative language. Even the notion of the crisis as a "contagion" is, she recognizes, figurative. The problem with figures, her argument suggests, is that they readily lead to confusion between the figure and its referent. Even if contagion is the figure rather than the thing to which she wishes to refer, she fears that the mere transmission of ideas in this way may infect their reader: "who is to say that through the agency of his letter or if not his letter then of mine you may not be touched by a contagion that is not that, a contagion but is something else, always something else?" (*EC*, 228–29). While there is something comical in the circularity of this logic, there is also pathos, since what she has come up against is the impossibility of finding a metalanguage with which to describe linguistic experience that does not itself rely on the very techniques it seeks to describe. Robinson Crusoe, in "He and His Man," seems to be likewise afflicted with the contagion of "saying one thing always for another," finding in the "reports" he invents for his character Defoe figures for his own experiences. Again, there is both comedy and pathos in the logical circularity with which Crusoe tries to chase down the original belief that gave rise to the story that he assumes must be allegory:

> Thus in the narrative of his island adventures he tells of how he awoke in terror one night convinced the devil lay upon him in his bed in the shape of a huge dog. . . . Only many days later did he understand that neither dog nor devil had lain upon him, but rather that he had suffered a palsy of a passing kind, and being unable to move his leg had concluded there was some creature stretched out upon it. Of which event the lesson would seem to be that all afflictions, including the palsy, come from the devil and are the very devil; that a visitation by illness may be figured as a visitation by the devil, or by a dog figuring the devil, and vice versa, the visitation figured as an illness, as in the saddler's history of the plague; and therefore that no one who writes stories of either, the devil or the plague, should forthwith be dismissed as a forger or a thief. (HHM, 17)

Crusoe's search for the referent behind all of these figures merely compounds the confusion.

There may be no position outside of language from which to objectively comment on the operations of language but, Gordimer's demand suggests, there are modes of writing that are less prone to figurative or rhetorical diversion. Her preference for realism as a mode less dressed in rhetoric is challenged in *Elizabeth Costello*'s first lesson: "Realism," a chapter in which Costello delivers an embedded lecture titled "What is Realism?" Both the third-person narrator and Elizabeth Costello comment on the procedures of realist narrative, challenging in different ways the assumption that realism promises a more direct, more accurate fictional mode than other manners of writing. The narrator fires the first salvo. Having introduced Elizabeth Costello, we are offered a metacommentary on the narrative technique employed: "The blue costume, the greasy hair, are details, signs of a moderate realism. Supply the particulars, allow the significations to emerge of themselves. A procedure pioneered by Daniel Defoe" (*EC*, 4). The irony here is, of course, that by commenting on the procedures of realism, the fiction we are reading ceases to be realist. In its focus on empirical detail, realism seeks to give the impression of presenting scenes objectively rendered so that the reader may sustain the illusion of unmediated access. Attention to form is precisely attention to the manner of mediation of the content. Against the representation of empirical detail, of *things*, the narrator poses "ideas":

> Realism has never been comfortable with ideas. It could not be otherwise: realism is premised on the idea that ideas have no autonomous existence, can exist only in things. So when it needs to debate ideas, as here, realism is driven to invent situations — walks in the countryside, conversations — in which characters give voice to contending ideas and thereby in a certain sense embody them. The notion of *embodying* turns out to be pivotal. In such debates ideas do not and indeed cannot float free: they are tied to the speakers by whom they are enounced, and generated from the matrix of individual interests out of which their speakers act in the world. (*EC*, 9)

The suggestion that realist narratives must "invent situations" for the discussion of ideas "*as here*" refers to the scene narrated immediately prior. This "necessity" of that scene's invention is immediately undercut by the intrusive commentary on narrative necessity quoted above which must itself be seen as *disembodied* narrative unless the narrator is somehow to be treated as an embodied source of enunciation.

And here's the rub: the narrator is considered third person by dint of his being external to the action represented in the novel, that externality being assumed from the lack of self-reference that the first-person pronoun would confer. This "externality" has at times encouraged the equation of the third-person narrator with the author of the work, perhaps partly on the grounds that the author represents the body external to the narrative to which it makes the most sense to link the text. Studies in narrative point of view and voice, however, have demonstrated the dubiety of asserting such equivalence. In this sense, the third-person narrator becomes the disembodied origin of thoughts and opinions that are not otherwise embodied by the text. The development of realism from Defoe onwards that represents a rejection of intrusive narration is not simply a refinement, but a positive development in another direction: the development of the *unobtrusive* narrator, the acme of which is the modernists' refinement "out of existence" of any figure overtly claiming authority over textual pronouncements.

The postmodern return to the intrusive narrator represents a challenge to the suggestion that this technical refinement actually offers what it seems to: a text without directive authorial control. Yet poststructuralist theories also foreground the fact that control over the hermeneutic capacity of the text — the capacity, that is, for the text to produce meaning — ultimately rests with the reader. This transfer of power from author to reader lies behind Roland Barthes's announcement of "the death of the author." Costello acknowledges this transfer of power when she asserts to her lecture audience that "the word-mirror is broken, irreparably, it seems. About what is really going on in the lecture hall your guess is as good as mine" (*EC*, 19). This leads to a pessimistic view of our capacity to represent our (true) selves:

> There used to be a time, we believe, when we could say who we were. Now we are just performers speaking our parts. The bottom has dropped out. We could think of this as a tragic turn of events, were it not that it is hard to have respect for whatever was the bottom that dropped out — it looks to us like an illusion now, one of those illusions sustained only by the concentrated gaze of everyone in the room. Remove your gaze for but an instant, and the mirror falls to the floor and shatters. (*EC*, 19–20)

So much for the ideal that realism offers a more truly mimetic reflection of the world.

This line of argument works in particular to undo the notion of the author as *origin* of the meaning-making capacity of the text. Indeed, it seems to challenge the very idea of an integral self that precedes textual production at all. If the meaning-making capacity of the text is circumscribed by linguistic conventions that precede authors and their utterances, it makes more sense to see the author as a conduit for pre-established linguistic possibilities. Against the notion of the originary, Romantic genius, theorists such as Louis Althusser argue that subjecthood is generated in the interstices of social interaction. In this model, the individual becomes a functioning subject through the taking on board of ideology, social rules, and conventions. The process by which the individual becomes socialized in this way is termed "interpellation" by Althusser, who uses the distinction between "individual" and "subject" to differentiate between human consciousness before and after its entry into language. While this may seem to preserve the Romantic category of the authentic, extrasocial individual, the individual in this account is not really agential in the manner conceived by the Romantics, for prior to ideological interpellation the individual is in no position to express itself and thus function socially as a person. And after interpellation, the subject-consciousness is so structured by ideology that it cannot see that identity as constructed, instead reading its ideologically driven conclusions as "natural" and "obvious." The interpellative process is on-going, subjects being constantly "hailed" or called upon by social institutions. Insofar as the individual responds to this hail, they are effectively acceding, at some level, to their social *situation* (in the active sense of *being* situated).

Earlier, I claimed that Coetzee was "called upon to give a lecture" by the Nobel committee that had just awarded him the Nobel Prize for Literature. On the face of it, this "call" is simply a polite invitation by a philanthropic organization that seeks to honor an individual for his contribution in one valued sphere of human endeavor (a "hail" very few of us would mind receiving). Alternatively, this hail can be seen as an institutional mechanism for the maintenance of certain values, the invitation to lecture a demand that Coetzee answer the hail and in doing so accede to the way the institution uses his name and constructs his social meaning. Stripped of individuality, we might think of the process simply as the operations of an institution designed to respond to certain *instances* of expression as in some way exemplary of their time and place *within ideology.* Rather than a celebration of the peculiar and individual (the Romantic genius), it can be seen as a mechanism for ideological reproduction: its reward standing as a special incentive to others to follow Coetzee's example in some fashion.

Lest this view of the recognition of a writer seem a mean-spirited dishonoring of a special individual, it is worth noting that it is precisely this view that is put to Elizabeth Costello by her son John on the eve of her reception for "the Stowe Award." In response to Costello's anxiety that her review panel is "rather lightweight" (*EC*, 7), John suggests that the "heavyweights" are brought out only for those writers whose works have "been demonstrated to be a problem":

> "Once you offer yourself as a problem, you might be shifted over into their court. But for the present you're not a problem, just an example."
>
> "An example of what?"
>
> "An example of writing. An example of how someone of your station and your generation and your origins writes. An instance."
>
> "An instance? Am I allowed a word of protest? After all the effort I put into not writing like anyone else?"
>
> "Mother, there's no point in picking on me to fight with. I am not responsible for the way the academy sees you. But you must surely concede that at a certain level we speak, and therefore write, like everyone else. Otherwise we would all be speaking and writing private languages. It is not absurd — is it? — to concern oneself with what people have in common rather than with what sets them apart." (*EC*, 8)

The poles of individuality and ideologically constructed subject-hood are laid out here as the topology of a pressing but irresolvable problem for the writer. As a counter to the constructivism of theorists such as Althusser, the ideal of Romantic individuality is rendered impossible because its search for self-expression founders on the rock of intersubjective legibility. Insofar as language allows for communication, it disallows true singularity.[14] It is language, shared language, that ensures that "at a certain level" any linguistic expression is "an *instance* of writing" rather than an expression of individuality. A linguistic system may allow in the permutative and combinative possibilities of its elements an effectively infinite set of possibilities for expression; however, the possibilities for meaningfulness, and for an utterance to be recognized as well formed by a given audience, are significantly limited by local, historical conditions. Whatever its semantic content, an utterance will also always bear the trace of the conditions under which it was produced, marked not so much by the individuality of the producer but by that person's social and historical situation. Put in Elizabeth Costello's terms, no matter how much "effort [one] put[s] into not writing like anyone else," writing is only recognizable *as* writing if it has more similarities to than differences from other instances. This is what Derrida means by *iterability*.

The ideal of embodied expression is rendered impossible following such logic, and indeed we see a critique of this ideal in the chapter "The Novel in Africa." In this chapter, Elizabeth Costello takes up a position lecturing on the subject of the novel to wealthy passengers on a cruise liner and finds herself sharing the program with fellow novelist Emmanuel Egudu, with whom she is not only acquainted but has had a brief sexual liaison many years previously. Now, however, she finds herself irritated by Egudu, particularly his argument in favor of "the oral novel" as the "true African novel" (*EC*, 45). His argument denies that for Africans there is a clear distinction between "the way that people live in their bodies" and their self-expression in language. Egudu's litany of the "intangibles of culture" that are apparently embodied by all true Africans works very carefully to place language-use on a continuum of bodily expression:

> "The way they move their hands. The way they walk. The way they smile or frown. The lilt of their speech. The way they sing. The timbre of their voices. . . . The way they make love. The way they lie after they have made love. The way they think. The way they sleep.
>
> "We African novelists can embody these qualities in our writings."
> (*EC*, 44)

While Egudu assures his listeners that "There is nothing mystical . . . nothing metaphysical, nothing racist" (*EC*, 44) in such an argument, there are plainly problems with its level of generalization. Costello expresses her own misgivings at these arguments, but it is her performance as a lecturer that most successfully counters Egudu's argument. Both Costello and Egudu are engaged in a program of oral delivery, the lecture circuit, so widespread that it hardly makes sense to see it as peculiar to any one culture. In their respective performances and receptions, we see the flaws in the assumption that oral delivery offers any greater guarantee of "embodiment." Costello speaks but "is not sure, as she listens to her own voice, whether she believes any longer in what she is saying": "after so many repetitions [ideas like these] have taken on a worn, unconvincing air" (*EC*, 39). The repetition that orality demands may actually lead away from embodiment. In contrast, Emmanuel Egudu seems to have no trouble convincing his audience of his sincerity. With his "effortlessly booming voice" (40), he makes his presence felt from the outset, "The applause when Egudu ends his talk is loud and spirited. He has spoken with force, perhaps even with passion" (45). By delivering a convincingly committed performance, Egudu has been rewarded by an audience that seems to recognize sincerity. Yet Egudu's speech is full of sly, ironic digs at colonialism and its Western successors. In response to one of Egudu's self-deprecating jokes, we learn of Costello's private doubts about his sincerity: "Egudu smiles his big smile, engaging, to all appearances spontaneous. But she cannot believe it is a true smile, cannot believe it comes from the heart, if that is where smiles come from" (48). Passion, spontaneity, even sincerity may simply be aspects of performance. Being in the presence of "the living voice" (50) is no guarantee of true coincidence of sayer and said.

The desire for true speech is a desire for transcendence, some realm, order, or genre in which language allows for true expression. Logically, we might expect this transcendent realm to be figured as the afterlife, a place where bodily and social concerns are left behind. Yet in the final lesson, "At the Gate," Elizabeth Costello finds herself no less constrained by linguistic demands than she was in life. It seems that the truly transcendent realm, apparently on the other side of "the gate," can only be accessed by submitting to a panel of judges a statement of belief. We have, by now, been thoroughly alerted to the kinds of problems that "a statement of belief" might raise for someone such as Elizabeth Costello. The judges, on the other hand, seem oblivious to the subtleties of Costello's position, insisting that, "Without beliefs we are not human" (*EC*, 200). To the judges, Costello's denial of belief amounts to a refusal of ethical commitment, a failure of responsibility (all criticisms that have been leveled at Coetzee). Belief is, for the judges, the sign of the stable self, the only kind of self over which it is meaningful to pass judgment.

If Costello has learned anything from her first hearing, she fails to demonstrate it in her second appearance. Challenged for changing tack in her statement, she replies in a way that she must know will frustrate her panel's demands:

> You ask if I have changed my plea. But who am I, who is this *I*, this *you*? We change from day to day, and we also stay the same. No *I*, no *you* is more fundamental than any other. You might as well ask which is the true Elizabeth Costello: the one who made the first statement or the one who made the second. My answer is, both are true. Both.

And neither. *I am an other*. Pardon for resorting to words that are not my own, but I cannot improve on them. You have the wrong person before you. If you think you have the right person you have the wrong person. The wrong Elizabeth Costello. (*EC*, 221)

It is no surprise that her panel refuses to take her statement seriously: "They cannot contain themselves. . . . First they titter like children, then abandon all dignity and howl with laughter" (221). Costello's statement breaks the laws of logic, in particular the law of noncontradiction. However, the application of the law of noncontradiction to selves must assume the existence of selves in the first place. When Costello asks, "who is this *I*, this *you*?" she is asking about the nature of the things to which these pronouns apparently refer. The peculiar nature of mutable being-in-time that is human experience points to the problems for a logical system that deals with differentiated *things* (such as bodies, for instance) when it tries to account for human *being*, a process rather than a fixed state. Because humans, in the process of being, "change from day to day [but] also stay the same" it makes no sense to assert the absolute identity, or absolute difference, of a person from one moment to the next.

In seeking a statement of belief, Costello recognizes, the judges seek "the true Elizabeth Costello," whereas she asserts they have "the wrong Elizabeth Costello." How are we to square this with her argument that there is no "true Elizabeth Costello," that "No *I*, no *you* is more fundamental than any other?" The denial of a fundamentally true self derives from both the idea of individual change over time, but also the contingency of self-hood that is only accessible through language. If, as has been argued, language is not simply in control of the author but also requires an interpreting reader to function as language, then the author is reliant on the reader for the image of the self constructed out of language. Costello's panel, with their simple reliance on questionable notions of integral self-hood, cannot adequately "hear" Costello's arguments as long as they refuse to challenge their own expectations as readers. Rather than simply failing to see the person before them, they are attempting to perform the wrong task with the wrong tools. Her judges are, effectively, intentionalist readers of a writer who sees herself not as linguistic originator but as conduit. This peculiar afterlife is not a place where the presence of the body guarantees understanding of the self it holds. It is plainly a "place of words," a literary place, as Costello frequently notes with considerable dismay. Her judges are not of another order, they are not adequate confessors able to test the accuracy of her claims even if she cannot say for certain what her own beliefs are.[15]

In a way that Elizabeth Costello has already considered, the afterlife for the writer is, of course, achieved by the endurance of their works.[16] As much as the writer might desire the perfect reader to achieve unimpeded understanding, the reality of language use means that endurance requires a leap of faith from the writer, making his or her work available to generation after generation of readers, leaving the work open to the interpretations those readers will construct, and the evaluations they will make. With no means to reliably test the truth of what is said or written, the appropriateness and adequacy of the discourse, or even the transparency of the self, the writer can only try to view his or her own words with a cold eye, or as Costello figures it, listen for the soundness of his or her own words: "to send out a word into the darkness and listen for what kind of sound comes back. Like a foundryman tapping a bell: is it cracked or healthy?" (*EC*, 219). This too is a leap of faith, an exercise of instinct rather than reason.

Writing that desires to solve the phenomenological problems of self- and other-knowledge must reach out beyond the speaking self. Yet intelligibility, iterability, demands the subordination of the desire for access to the different, the unknown, to what Emmanuel Levinas has called "the order of the same." To some extent, all writing is a submission to a secondhand logical system, a system ill-equipped to deal with experience that does not simply reflect the world constructed by logic. Nevertheless, writers submit themselves to their readers knowing that at some level the transaction is governed by inimical linguistic logic, hoping for the life, the preservation, that only a reader can bring. Thus Elizabeth Chandos concludes her appeal to Francis Bacon:

> Not Latin, says my Philip — I copied the words — *not Latin nor English nor Spanish nor Italian will bear the words of my revelation.* . . . Yet he writes to you, as I write to you, who are known above all men to select your words and set them in place and build your judgements as a mason builds a wall with bricks. Drowning, we write to you out of our separate fates. Save us. (*EC*, 230)

Without the intervention of a being from another order — a perfect confessor or reader; a god — writers must submit themselves to these "fidelities": "*Fidelities.* Now that she has brought it out, she recognizes it as the word on which all hinges" (*EC*, 224).

If writers must submit themselves to their readers, there is also an implicit plea that the reader will attend fully to writers as they offer themselves through their writing. Earlier in this chapter, following the line of criticism that sees in Coetzee's use of fiction and allegory an evasion of self-disclosure, I suggested that his lecture-fictions allow him "to speak in . . . voices . . . that are *not his own.*" Elizabeth Costello, you will recall, also begged pardon "for resorting to words are not my own." Yet in an important sense already discussed, words do not belong to, do not originate with, any user of language. At the same time, we can say that all of the words presented by J. M. Coetzee, whether fictional or nonfictional, or apparently straddling both genres, are in his own voice. They may not aim to simply deliver embodied beliefs by focusing on verifiable detail, but they nevertheless represent what someone we identify as J. M. Coetzee has offered to readers. Writing so conceived is not a game of hide-and-seek but an example of the same process by which each of us prosecutes his or her own existence, by which we continue to *be* through language. The reminder that this process is not peculiar to writers is made by the keeper of the gate when he tells Costello, "We see people like you all the time" (*EC*, 225). Because all knowledge involves interpretation, we are all engaged in the process of making each other up, each utterance we make bespeaks our attempt to control part of the process and is thus in some way self-revelatory. The assessment that Costello offers of her own writing might also be applied to Coetzee: "Her books teach nothing, preach nothing; they merely spell out, as clearly as they can, how people lived in a certain time and place. More modestly put, they spell out how one person lived, one among billions: the person whom she, to herself, calls *she*, and whom others call *Elizabeth Costello*" (*EC*, 207–8).

Notes

[1] Lucy Graham, "Textual Transvestism: The Female Voices of J. M. Coetzee," in *J. M. Coetzee and the Idea of the Public Intellectual*, ed. Jane Poyner, 226 (Athens: Ohio UP, 2006). Many of the essays collected in this volume are relevant to the topics canvassed in this chapter, and specifically to *Elizabeth Costello*.

[2] It is beyond the scope of this essay to elaborate the relevant aspects of poststructuralist theory, yet some understanding of the challenges to linguistic reference is essential in order to understand, for instance, Elizabeth Costello's claim that "The word-mirror is broken" (*EC*, 19). There are numerous introductions to these matters; the reader will no doubt find one that serves. For my part, I recommend Mark Currie's *Postmodern Narrative Theory*, especially the chapter "Terminologisation" which achieves a rare balance between the demands of economy, lucidity, and respect for the complexity of ideas. Mark Currie, *Postmodern Narrative Theory* (London: Palgrave, 1998).

[3] W. K. Wimsatt, Jr., and Monroe C. Beardsley, "The Intentional Fallacy," in *The Verbal Icon: Studies in the Meaning of Poetry*, 3–20 (Lexington: U of Kentucky P, 1954).

[4] Derek Attridge, introduction to *IW*, ix.

[5] For example: "I am uncomfortable with questions . . . that call upon me to answer for (in two senses) my novels, and my responses are often taken as evasive" (*DP*, 205).

[6] In focusing on such an idiosyncratic performance, I do not dismiss out of hand the aims of this volume; I, too, see Coetzee's nonfiction as essential reading for any serious Coetzee scholar. I do, however challenge the adequacy of the fiction/nonfiction distinction as a guide to the appropriate uses we can make of

his work, and as a basis for assessing the transparency, integrity, and directness of these utterances.

7 *Statutes of the Nobel Foundation*, Statute 9, available at http://nobelprize.org/nobelfoundation/statutes.html.

8 J. M. Coetzee, "Daniel Defoe, *Robinson Crusoe*" (*SS*, 20).

9 These remarks are not included in the textual publication of "He and His Man." They can however be heard on the video of Coetzee's lecture: "Nobel Prize Lecture: He and His Man" (video), The Nobel Prize Website, http://nobelprize.org/mediaplayer/index.php?id=555 (accessed 28 February 2010).

10 J. M. Coetzee, *He and His Man*, Nobel lecture, 2003 (New York: Penguin, 2004). Subsequent references appear as HHM with the accompanying page number. The textual version of Coetzee's Nobel Prize lecture is also available at: http://nobelprize.org/nobel_prizes/literature/laureates/2003/coetzee-lecture-e.html (accessed 28 February 2010).

11 Horace Engdahl, Nobel lecture presentation (video), available on The Nobel Prize Website, http://nobelprize.org/mediaplayer/index.php?id=716 (accessed 28 February 2010). Quotations have been transcribed directly from the video.

12 Nadine Gordimer, "The Idea of Gardening," in *Critical Essays on J. M. Coetzee*, ed. Sue Kossew (London: Prentice Hall and New York: G. K. Hall, 1998), 139.

13 In an equivocal parenthesis she identifies a blind spot in the argument "where, perhaps, Costello (and maybe even Coetzee) feared to tread" (*LA*, 108).

14 In *Disgrace*, David Lurie counters the subordination of literature to the discipline of "communication" with a view — "which he does not air" — that "the origins of speech lie in song, and the origins of song in the need to fill out with sound the overlarge and rather empty human soul" (*DG*, 4).

15 For Coetzee's discussion of the problems of secular confession and, in particular, the impossibility of guaranteeing the "adequacy" of a confessor, see his essay "Confession and Double Thoughts: Tolstoy, Rousseau, Dostoevsky" in *Doubling the Point*.

16 See, for example, chapter 1 of *EC*, "Realism," 16–18.

12: *Slow Man* (2005)

Tim Mehigan

Two EVENTS OF SIGNIFICANCE preceded the appearance of Coetzee's novel *Slow Man* (2005). One was the awarding of the Nobel Prize for Literature to Coetzee at the end of 2003; the other Coetzee's move from South Africa to Australia in 2002. Both events resonate at different levels of a novel whose setting is Coetzee's adopted country of Australia. On the one hand, the novel can be read as a set of reflections on a problem that emerges in later life where one's main accomplishments now lie in the past. For a writer who holds the conviction that, in the final analysis, all writing is autobiography (*DP*, 391), the question of how to redirect one's striving, reorient the head and the heart under the insistent pressure of time's passing without reference to past accomplishments or projects is as urgent for the sixty-year-old protagonist Paul Rayment as it undoubtedly is for the sixty-five-year old Coetzee, who has already reached the zenith of literary achievement.[1] This question becomes even more pointed for a writer who has chosen to leave his homeland late in life — a homeland whose society and landscape have been central to his literary concerns. Coetzee was reported to have said at the time that he did not consider he was moving *away* from the country of his birth so much as *toward* his new adopted country. Yet, despite this statement, Coetzee's thematic concerns in the first novel published after his relocation to Australia bear no South African imprint, nor even a faint afterimage of South Africa. Nor do they display an abiding concern with the new country. Coetzee's fictional protagonist instead seeks to make common cause with foreigners, with those who have left their home country and experience the manifold levels of displacement wrought by migration. Not even the Australian woman Elizabeth Costello, Rayment's sometime companion in the novel, offers significant points of alignment with the Australian experience in a way that might temper the focus on the concerns of the migrant: Costello is more alter ego than companion, more a dweller in the mind of the central character than an emissary from the new society of which Rayment is now a part. The character of Elizabeth Costello, in other words, does not deepen the sense of attachment to the new country. If anything, her interactions with the protagonist underscore the isolation that Paul Rayment still feels in a country decades after the migration of his family from Europe to Australia.[2]

Slow Man, for these reasons, offers both an extended reflection on the situation of the immigrant who inhabits the cultural terrain of the in-between — the peculiar métier of those who have migrated to a new place but not yet in all senses truly arrived — just as it also offers insight into the postmaturity of its author Coetzee who, now in a new cultural setting, begins to grapple with encroaching senescence and other end-of-life questions.

These questions emerge from the actual life experience of the novel's author, even as they cannot be equated with this same life experience. Coetzee heightens awareness of these questions in the novel in several ways. For one thing, a rupture between the past and the future can be assumed from the beginning. The protagonist Paul Rayment does not look back to the achievement of a successful career, but instead laments a "frivolous"[3] life of squandered achievement, an unsuccessful marriage, and the absence of children. For another thing, Rayment is not described as having freely chosen the moment to relocate to a new country in the manner of the novel's author. This is rather revealed as the choice of Rayment's forebears, in particular of a father who is referred to with palpable distance in the novel as "the Dutchman." Although this migration occurred long ago, Rayment in his own eyes remains a foreigner in the new country. Moreover, and most importantly, the protagonist's need to reorient his striving late in life does not result from an active choice, but is dictated by the intrusion of outward circumstance: the novel begins by recounting the experience of the main character as he is knocked from his bicycle by a motorist and thereby suffers an incapacitating injury (the young motorist who is responsible for the accident bears the name of the functional impairment, the "blight" he brings about[4]). Rayment's right leg is amputated above the knee as a result of the accident. By these means, then, Coetzee assembles the components that make up the dilemma of an unaccommodated man, of a man variously bereft of that which might sustain him in later life: the memory, perhaps, of past accomplishments, the palliating comforts of wife, family and a few good friends, even the functionality of an intact body where normal movement can still be taken for granted. Paul Rayment therefore faces later life at a moment of acute physical and existential dislocation. The novel is not given over to relating the circumstances occasioning this dislocation. Rather, the novel begins at the point where these circumstances come into view and engender the psychological problem situation of its protagonist.

Although autobiographical concerns inform *Slow Man* — as they hold, Coetzee believes, for all creative writing, and certainly, we can assume, for Coetzee's own literary production — the novel nevertheless goes far beyond the confines of autobiography in detailing its account of a man, as the title reminds us, rendered "slow" by the incapacitating nature of a major injury, but a man dogged as well by a pronounced temperamental reserve, a "tortoise character" (*SM*, 228),[5] and a head that is slow to follow the promptings of a deeply sensitive heart. From an initial position where the attributes of the slow man — the compassionate heart on one side, the predilection for rumination and "second thoughts"[6] on the other — are precisely those attributes that will bring least advantage in his new circumstances, the novel opens upon the rich interiority of a protagonist whose name speaks to the core of his predicament: Rayment rhymes with "vraiment" (really, truly), if the French pronunciation of the proper name is followed, and thus connotes a certain search for truth; yet, as Elizabeth Costello points out, it also rhymes with "payment" (as pronounced in English) and thus alludes to the mundane imperatives that increasingly govern Rayment's situation — his need to secure the practical assistance from others that will make his reduced state of life bearable. Rayment's predicament is that his new immobility provides the least prospect for the attainment of the truths about his own person that he now urgently seeks and that now seem to cloud upon him. These truths about self, as the novel richly conveys, can only be accessed in the name of a love that would speak their name: "Truth is spoken, if it ever comes to be spoken, in love" (*SM*, 161). Following this assumption about the importance of love, it is the main character's uncompromising desire for truth that brings about the "unsuitable passion" (*SM*, 89) that in turn drives most of the novel forward, a passion that quickly comes to be centered on the Croatian nurse who is assigned to help him and whose ministrations in daily visits to Rayment's home initially provide relief from pain, but increasingly also bring about the desire for love. This is no ordinary passion, no desire confined to the stirrings of a still-ardent body. The passion the novel tells about instead connects with Rayment's need to drive into his inner self in order to release a feeling that lies close to the general lack of fulfillment he senses about his life. This passion, "unsuitable" though it may be, arises from Rayment's need to disclose the truth of his inner being while there is still time to do so.

The witness to this project of profound self-disclosure is not the Croatian immigrant nurse Marijana; it is Elizabeth Costello, a character introduced by the author in the thirteenth chapter of the novel, immediately following Rayment's confession of love for his nurse. Costello, as has been variously explained in Coetzee scholarship,[7] is hardly to be considered a character at all: her interactions with other characters are heavily circumscribed and indeed entail no real consequences for these characters. Even the main character himself is affected by Costello only insofar as she is attuned to his hopes and longings, improbably commanding the ability to peer into his thoughts and feelings. For this same reason, despite her being a famous writer ostensibly gathering material for a new novel, she clearly lacks the ontological status of other characters in the novel. While this difference in status invites questions about Coetzee's deployment of postmodern conceits such as competing levels of metafictional narration as well as of pastiche and intertextuality[8] — Elizabeth Costello is herself the protagonist of Coetzee's directly preceding novel — it is also the case that Coetzee's purpose is not to destabilize the narration so much as render a narrative intention more clearly — namely, to subject the interiority of the central character to ever greater scrutiny and thereby to acquaint the reader with ever more deeply embedded levels of that character's conscious and unconscious awareness. Coetzee's project might be likened to that of the vivisector, of the surgeon who, with scalpel in hand, probes ever more deeply through layers of tissue in search of the affliction that has brought about the subject's suffering — a suffering hinted at in the novel's title though not explained by it, and a suffering that acquires a visual correlate in the form of the missing leg.

In considering the way forward for this physically and emotionally unaccommodated central character, the novel discusses the nature and function of replacements, of how that which impairs a subject's functionality might be restored and a proper mobility thereby reintroduced. In the concrete case of Rayment's missing leg, this discussion initially takes the form of imagining a replacement leg — which is to say, a prosthetic limb molded onto the stump of the leg that is left after the operation and that, after a period of therapy and adjustment, might give him back some semblance of normal locomotion. That Coetzee means to elevate this discussion of replacements beyond a mundane level is revealed in a variety of ways. Coetzee first calls attention to the word "prosthesis" itself, to its singular pronunciation, and then, as object, to its singular appearance. For the main character Rayment, "prosthesis" is a "difficult word" (*SM*, 7), a word that brings to mind "a wooden shaft with a barb at its head like a harpoon and rubber suckers on its three little feet. It is out of Surrealism. It is out of Dali" (*SM*, 9). Later in the novel Marijana pronounces it "like a German word": "*Prosthese*. . . . Thesis, antithesis, then prosthesis" (*SM*, 62) — a word, considered in these terms, that lies outside the realm of everyday experience and calls to the mind the elevated transpositions of Hegelian logic according to which the prosthesis as synthesis sublates the first two positions (thesis, antithesis) and provides a new forward movement of the dialectic; a device, in short, that would provide Paul Rayment, metaphysically and practically, with a thoroughly artificial transition to a new state of existence and, by implication, perhaps also of consciousness.[9]

In contemplating the question of artificial prosthetic replacements, the novel thus considers whether a technical contrivance from the realm of human calculation and ingenuity can provide a way forward that might reconcile the main character to his reduced state and perhaps enhance it. At a further remove from this concrete question, a more general question is put as to whether the technical contrivances of modernity have traction on the emotional plane of human consciousness, whether they can enhance our emotional lives as well as our physical lives, whether our investment in a technical modernity can provide us with an emotional-spiritual return alongside the undoubted material return. From the reverse perspective — the perspective Rayment encounters when he attends a rehabilitation class — a related question is raised in regard to the progress of this technical modernity, whether, referring again to Hegel, humanity is indeed traversing ever higher movements of a historical dialectic and whether, as individuals in a wider historical process, we are obliged to move with it. Madeleine Martin, the class teacher, touches on this question in reference to the memory systems that are bound to our old limbs but that appear to become obsolete when these limbs are removed: "we must not hold on to them [these memory systems] when they hinder our progress" (*SM*, 60), she tells the class. From this perspective, our locomotion and our progress, with all the allusiveness that the latter word brings with it, demands that we leave behind a part of ourselves, that we reprogram our memory systems, even reconfigure the aesthetic standards that have conditioned us over time to past standards of beauty and proportion that we have come to regard as "natural."

In this debate about the way forward — a debate made urgent by the progress of technical modernity and its capacity not only to redirect life but, of late, also to clone and thereby to engender new life — Rayment, at least initially, takes up (in Madeleine Martin's terms) a critically "obsolete" position: he rejects the suggestion of a prosthetic limb, he removes himself quickly from Martin's classes, he commits himself to the path of nature: "'I do not want to look natural,' he says," spurning the possible advantages conferred by a prosthetic limb, "'I prefer to feel natural'" (*SM*, 59). This preference for nature over contrivance and artifice returns at the end of the novel when Rayment, who has established an avuncular relationship with Marijana's son Drago, suspects Drago of having tampered with one of the images in Rayment's prized collection of old Fauchery[10] photographs — a collection he intends to bequeath to the state of South Australia. While certainly irritated by a youth's supposed breach of trust and apparent petty theft, Rayment is actually disturbed by a far greater kind of loss: the threat to notions of art after the advent of the technological reproducibility of the artwork, as lamented also by Walter Benjamin — which is to say, the undermining of the particular authority of the artist to articulate timeless truth in view of technical advances that have corrupted the concept of the original:

> That was why, later on, he began to lose interest in photography: first when colour took over, then when it became plain that the old magic of light-sensitive emulsions was waning, that to the rising generation the enchantment lay in a techne of images without

substance, images that could flash through the ether without resid-
ing anywhere, that could be sucked into a machine and emerge from
it doctored, untrue. (*SM*, 65)

Two concerns come together here, both of which borrow heavily
from Benjamin's 1936 essay "The Work of Art in an Age of Mechanical
Reproduction." One is that images lose contact with their initiators, that
techniques of mechanical reproduction are applied to the original artwork
in such a way that a circulation of "images without substance" is introduced. New images emerge from "a machine," i.e., from the process of
mechanical reproduction, which are not any more aspects of the original
but become in essence "doctored" images, images that are "untrue" with
respect to the original and lack palpable contact with that original. The
other concern, also alluded to in Benjamin's essay, turns on a view of how
the artwork communicates its "aura," its peculiar claim to articulate truth.
Benjamin's view is that the aura of the artwork is communicated through
an act of bearing witness to the original work of art. The artwork, in
this view, possesses an "auratic" power precisely on the grounds that it
is an original that is directly witnessed and received. It is this quality as
an original that brings about the special, "live," and embodied effects in
those who witness it, and that are then disseminated through a process
of critical reception among living communities. Moreover, the aura of
the artwork would depend on its original integrity, on the fact that its
originality is not compromised or tampered with in any way. Rayment's
critically "obsolete" view, which accords with Benjamin's culturally pessimistic standpoint, is that the loss of the original entails ipso facto a loss
of the truth-quality of the artwork. (Benjamin's further point is that the
susceptibility of the artwork to technical reproduction in the new age of
mechanical reproduction also makes it usable for purposes of the manip-
ulation and control of large numbers of people — purposes seemingly
quite opposed to the original design of the artwork's creators.)

Paul Rayment's unwillingness to consider a prosthetic replacement
for his amputated leg is thus linked to a culturally skeptical view about all
technical enhancements. Rayment, the photograph collector, is as resistant to the idea of a new self-image ("I do not want to look natural") that
would tamper with his original sense of self ("I want to feel natural"), as
he is to the replacement of one of his original photographs with a doctored, and therefore untrue, new image. The sixty-year-old Rayment, who
has already foresworn the technical reproduction of images of the "rising
generation" as soon as the "old magic of light-sensitive emulsions" began
to wane, fears the loss of originality as a loss of quality, a loss of substance.
And yet, in this same view, he must face that loss as a real possibility for
himself since he now, in one sense, patently lacks his own originality. Does
this lack essentially and finally reduce him? Or is the aura of his person

located elsewhere — not in the obvious circumstances of an intact body moving in harmony with an intact mind, nor in the carefully maintained habits of mind of a previously intact "integrity," but in the special quality of his feelings, his striving, and his longing that do not inhere in his physicality? If so, how does such a person signal this special quality, this nonmaterial essence of himself to an outsider, someone whose job is to observe and treat this reduced outside of himself, to provide only superficial ministrations? How, in other words, is such a man to communicate his love?

These questions lie at the core of the novel. They open up a deep meditation on the nature of love, of how love becomes utterable between two people, of how, as already mentioned, love and truth are intertwined such that our truth discourses are bound up with our capacity to speak about love. For Paul Rayment they bring about a passion that is only "unsuitable" because it initially appears fundamentally self-motivated. Since Rayment requires the assistance of an efficient nurse, it is only natural, perhaps, that he should fall in love with her. Passion would thus be a willing agent of self-interest and follow it. Moreover, the nurse Marijana herself has a husband, and an arduous life that consists, apart from duties to her large family, of the long working hours of the migrant to make ends meet. Marijana clearly has no time for the all-too-predictable passion of a physically impaired sexagenarian patient.

Elizabeth Costello enters the novel partly in order to make this skepticism about the motivation of Rayment's passion plain to Rayment: "Do you seriously mean to seduce your employee into abandoning her family and coming to live with you?" (*SM*, 82), she asks him. Costello, to this extent, is an echo of Rayment's conscience, a client-figure in the novel whose function is to prick her host's conscience and help him assemble a picture of reality. Yet in doing so, Costello is no crusader in the cause of morality and good behavior. Instead, she has a Mephistophelean quality, the quality of an "evil" spirit whose role is to question, negate, and oppose: "I am rather a doubting Thomas" (*SM*, 81) she says, immediately after her first appearance in the novel.[11] And just as Mephistopheles moves in and out of Goethe's drama *Faust*, not only jabbing Faust with thought-barbs but also delivering him Gretchen, a woman on whom Faust's lustful passion can be brought to bear, so Elizabeth Costello seeks to intercede in her host's rising passion for Marijana in order to redirect him not toward love, but to the possibly more suitable, and certainly more mundane and predictable, pleasures of the blind invalid Marianna. Although Rayment goes through with the transaction arranged by Costello in order to secure relief for his sexual urges, he finds that it transacts nothing of consequence for his spirit and the true cause of love. Profane Marianna-Gretchen is not his longed-for, sacred Marijana-Gretchen. Moreover, he has been obliged to pay Marianna for her services and, through a charade orchestrated by Mephistopheles-Costello that obliged him to wear an elaborate blindfold made of lemon leaves pasted with flour and water and a stocking pulled over his head, perhaps also made himself the butt of a joke. As Rayment tells himself later in the absence of Costello, the purportedly blind woman Marianna was perhaps no more than an all-too-knowing prostitute paid to provide sex to an eccentric customer. For one thing, the label on her underwear was worn on the outside. For another, the tremblings that Rayment took as the stirrings of passion of the equally sexually frustrated Marianna during the encounter might have been nothing more than the barely suppressed convulsions of laughter of the prostitute.

Elizabeth Costello, who appears in the novel as a well-known author, thus also has a palpable function in the novel: namely, to provide an outlet for the clamor of doubting voices in Rayment's head and to direct him toward action, on occasion quite unsuitably. Although Costello is fully acquainted with Rayment and his motivations — how she has acquired such knowledge is never disclosed in the novel, unless we take her, metatextually, to be the author of the reflections published under the title *Slow Man* — her role is not to support his ethical projects, nor to direct him toward true feeling in his search for a deeper fulfilment of being. Costello was notably absent from Rayment's bedside immediately after his bicycle accident, just as she was absent during his early convalescence. She enters Rayment's life at the moment when his feelings reach out toward the nurse Marijana; her goal, at the very least, is to temper such feelings. From this moment on in the novel, she moves in and out of Rayment's life, holding skeptical positions where Rayment searches for idealism, prompting action where Rayment would appear to prefer reflection. Her only clear motivation comes into view at the end of the novel when she attempts to interest her host in a life of cohabitation in her home in the Melbourne suburb of Carlton — an offer Rayment is at pains to refuse, even if his refusal, on purely functional grounds, would have no lasting capacity to end her intrusions on his mind.

Despite such intrusions, Costello, like her literary counterpart Mephistopheles, is unable to direct her host completely away from countervailing endeavors. Although she introduces the seductions of Marianna, Rayment does not give up his passion for Marijana, even as it appears increasingly unlikely that Marijana will ever return his affection. As the prospect of unrequited passion looms larger, Rayment does not seek another rendezvous with Marianna, but strives to align his feelings with the opposite of self-interest, viewing his passion for Marijana as the attempt to love her as a god would do so: selflessly, for her own sake, or for the sake of love itself. Again we recall Faust, who is a willing agent in the seduction of Gretchen, but feels profound remorse that he has loved her on account of profane desire. Marijana, of course, is no virginal Gretchen, but a mature woman well acquainted with the erotic effect her ministrations have on her male clients. She tolerates Rayment's confession of love, even as it begins to constitute a burden for her and leads her to reduce the frequency of her visits. She equally does not stand in the way of Rayment's affection for her son Drago, even though this can only have the effect of increasing the likelihood of further contact with Rayment — a contact that might ultimately prove unwelcome. For her own part, she comes to see Rayment ultimately as a good man with an honest, though certainly misplaced, desire, a desire she assumes is linked with the emotional privation arising from Rayment's impaired physical circumstances.

Although Rayment can be pleased about this view of the soundness of his character, he finds no joy in Marijana's pity, and certainly seeks no advantage from it. In a dilemma that coats every act of affection for Marijana with the appearance of self-interest, Rayment chooses to communicate his love through an action that speaks to the prosaic associations of his name — that is, he undertakes to make a payment. This is to be a payment not directed at Marijana, but her son Drago, in the form of an interest-free loan that would enable Drago to attend a feeder school for an elite military academy. By paying Drago's school fees for two years, Drago would be given a chance to qualify for entry to the academy and later embark on a successful career. Rayment, the propertied immigrant without a family, thus seeks to restore to an immigrant family without property, at least in part, the loss of status that has resulted from migration to the new country — a status it could otherwise not hope to attain by unassisted means as migrants of the first generation. In doing so, Rayment seeks to involve himself in a business of restoration and thereby to become an ally of Marijana — Marijana the physical restorer of amputees, but also Marijana the graduate in restoration (*SM*, 148) who held a position before her emigration at the Art Institute in Dubrovnik (*SM*, 86). Rayment's restorative payment, then, is to be considered as an act of *caritas*, of care for another human being or beings: it aims at a restoration that does not seek to exact a return favor, sexual or otherwise. It depends only on Drago's future capacity to make good the potential that Rayment finds in him. Rayment asks only that he be allowed to maintain contact with Marijana's family and occasionally to visit.

By means of such a proposal Rayment finally takes up a position on the question of the way forward. Characteristically for Coetzee, whose fiction is steeped in European traditions and who makes liberal reference to these traditions throughout his writings, this is to be a way forward that speaks to the more noble aspects of a European sensibility that holds artistic traditions in high regard — traditions that have not been translated with the migrating Europeans to the new country as a matter of course (note that Marijana is described as smoking in "an unreconstructed old-European way" [*SM*, 31].) Evidence for Rayment's cleaving toward a peculiarly European instinct to elevate the spirit through acts of (cultural and spiritual) restoration — an instinct perhaps shared by the former art restorer Marijana — can be found in Rayment's intention to bequeath his collection of antique photographs to the archives of South Australia. The images Rayment has collected — images he avowedly trusts more than words *(SM,* 64) — are described as being "last survivors," a "unique" testimony to a now-lapsed age of early modernity, survivors, too, of a process of reproduction where an image was "immutable" as soon as it left the darkroom (*SM*, 64–5). The age that Rayment is acutely aware he now inhabits upholds no insight into the unique quality of such images. Rather, in this age, all images are placed on the same metaphysical footing; all can be tampered with, nothing is privileged, there is no longer any strict criterion separating the original from its descendants.

In positioning his protagonist as an advocate of a world that is spiritually and geographically removed from the present, of a world, moreover, that in many ways remains frozen in time for the European migrants who have left it, Coetzee invites comparison with the concerns of a literary tradition that never seems far from his writing. These are the concerns of Pound, Beckett, Faulkner, and Ford Madox Ford in the English-speaking tradition, of Rilke and Robert Musil in the German tradition.[12] By and large, they are the concerns of authors writing at a moment where the transition to a new cultural world of technical modernity was already beckoning, where the loss of the cultural traditions of the thought-world predating this modernity was already obvious — where, in short, literary discussions were shaped by the need to confront "the shock of the new"[13] and to explore its potential repercussions for human awareness. Notwithstanding the usual view about Coetzee's use of postmodern conceits in his fiction, Coetzee's literary forebears to my mind are not to be found among the postmodernists so much as the (predominantly European) modernists — those literary fictionalizers who saw the way forward in terms of the problem of the new, of how to connect the new with past traditions, or, failing this, how to reinvigorate the human being and, as Nietzsche, one of the philosophical guides for the modernists, advocated, organize nothing less than the invention of "die freien Geister,"[14] those "free spirits" of the new generation of human beings who, on the most optimistic view about the way forward, would realize the spiritual benefits that a dawning new age would bring with it.

Among these benefits, the prospect of a radically new psychological understanding of the human being was perhaps the most significant. At the turn of the twentieth century, Freud had already published *Die Traumdeutung* (The Interpretation of Dreams), the first in a series of major forays into human psychology that posited the existence of a common psychology of the human being below the level of conscious awareness. In a programmatic statement about the implications of this new psychology for literature, Hugo von Hofmannsthal in his *Brief des Lord Chandos* (Letter of Lord Chandos, 1902)[15] announced the bankruptcy of old views of the human being even as the advantages of new approaches to understanding human concerns that ushered in a scientific perspective on humanity could not yet be specified (note that Hofmannsthal's "letter" is addressed to the early seventeenth-century philosopher of science Francis Bacon). While the movement of literary modernism that reached its high point in the first decades of the twentieth century reached no consensus about the way forward, about whether the gains for human awareness might outweigh the losses, much of the important literature of this period did not portray the question of the new as a choice at all so much as the new reality. However the new age of modern sensibility came about, what is dramatized in much of modernist literature is the question of how the scientifically dispassionate, technologically progressive new age of the human being would be reconciled with the spiritual and emotional disposition of ordinary humanity. In this literature, new experience and old emotionality meet on common ground, but this is a ground where the old certainty that a successful project of education and spiritual formation, such as was encountered a century before in the *Bildungsroman* (novel of education), a popular literary genre of early modernity, has been lost.

Typical of this literature are the three stories Robert Musil published in 1923 under the title of *Drei Frauen* (Three Women). As Coetzee himself has pointed out, Musil's fiction, particularly the earlier fiction predating the major novel *Der Mann ohne Eigenschaften* (The Man without Qualities), has served him as an important stimulus and point of literary orientation (EI).[16] In each of these stories, a bourgeois male protagonist, typically a dominant male with a rational outlook on the world and a predilection for new challenges, encounters a woman who unsettles, even unhinges him. These protagonists pursue love as they pursue truth: in order to become acquainted with the true nature of themselves. In each of the three stories of *Drei Frauen*, different outcomes for the main character are envisaged that are linked to both the difficulty of the inner struggle each character faces and the general uncertainty entailed in all such struggles. In only one of the stories does the attainment of love conclude the project to renew the self successfully, and, by implication, result in a higher level of self-awareness. In this story, *Die Portugiesin* (The Portuguese Woman), the second in order of its occurrence in the collection, the main character, a proud and successful aristocrat and warrior, overcomes a debilitating illness and the wavering affections of his new wife through an act of death-defying daring that drives the mortal illness from his body and renews his love and his life. An answer of sorts is thus provided for the modernist's question about the new. The question of whether the challenge of the new might lead to greater disclosure of self, and, in turn, open onto a more profound experience of life in the living of it, is tentatively affirmed. Moreover, Musil's warrior does not fall back on any prosthetic means in order to overcome his condition; rather, what overcomes the paralyzing malaise he suffers from takes root in his inner being: it is the path of unaided nature back (and forward) to its own inner nature. This same path of nature back to nature is the way forward that Rayment also instinctively advocates. The path that Rayment abjures is Dali's way (see *SM*, 9), if Salvador Dali's images of propped-up body parts, of prosthesis, are taken to endorse discussion of the advantages of a new technological modernity (it may be noted in passing that the appearance of surrealism in the history of art, in certain views, brings the era of modernism to a close).

The way forward for Paul Rayment, therefore, is not countenanced in Coetzee's novel merely in mundane terms as the question of whether or not to acquire a prosthetic replacement in order to repair the movement of a body part. The prosthesis itself[17] is also part of a broad discussion about the way forward that is also conceived as a discussion about art, about the moment when modern art faced a crisis about the way forward in view of the advent of technological modernity, and about the scenarios that the artists of modernism entertained to ask deeper questions about spiritual renewal in the face of the challenge of technological modernity. A favored vehicle for the modernists, though not the surrealists, in promoting this discussion about the way forward was love, a love arising from the urgent need for profound self-disclosure. In Coetzee's novel *Slow Man*, where a similar discussion is brought into view, love equally becomes the key factor motivating the self-disclosure of the protagonist, even if this love appears under the unusual sign of the love of the cripple for the nurse, the reticent "slow" man for the Croatian immigrant herself rendered slow by a foreign language she imperfectly commands.[18] And just as language has turned into the functional hybrid it must perhaps become for the immigrant, with few subtleties in its dynamic range, so the modernist's dream of a richly textured language of the soul, where, as for Proust, every subtlety in the flavor of the madeleine might be expressible, is now abandoned, at least in its most idealistic form. In place of the dream of a language of the soul there is the occupational therapist Madeleine Martin's injunction to cast aside old (body) memory as obsolete and just get on with things. This, the new pragmatism arising from an affirmative view of technological modernity, is of course a path Paul Rayment, the cultural skeptic, consistently refuses to tread.

The novel, for all this, does not immediately endorse Rayment's skepticism. This is suggested in the novel's final sequences. After much self-questioning aided and abetted by his advisor Elizabeth Costello, Rayment seeks out the family in order to call Drago to account for tampering with his photograph and to demand back the original. The visit goes badly. Rayment is not able to prove anything against Drago directly, and the question of who might have perpetrated the digital doctoring of the photograph remains unanswered. Instead of an answer, Rayment is forced to undergo tuition from Marijana in the protocols of image reception in the new age of digital reproduction: "'No: images is free,' she tells him, '— your image, my image. Is not secret what Drago is doing. These photographs —' she waves towards the three photographs on the wall — 'all on his website. Anyone can see. You want to see the website?'" (*SM*, 249).

This is not merely a straightforward rebuke (although it is that as well); it also constitutes a critical milestone in Rayment's education. Rayment, who hordes timeless images just as he defends the ground of high art against those who would tamper with them, is urged by Marijana to welcome the free circulation of images as a kind of democratic good, as part of the openness that includes callow youths in the enterprise of art, just as it provides for the role of great artists. In the new society of which Rayment has become a part, art, like the artist, is no longer privileged and unique. Art has truly become available to all, even if this reduces the special truth-claims of art overall. Nor is this lesson in artistic reception the only lesson Rayment learns from youth and the immigrant family. Drago, as Rayment now learns for the first time, has painstakingly constructed a recumbent bicycle for Rayment from the remains of Rayment's damaged bicycle in order to express his appreciation of the offer to sponsor his education. Rayment, therefore, has not only misjudged Drago, he has also underestimated him. And while the recumbent bicycle does not delight him on all levels, it represents the most concrete attempt in the novel to provide a truly satisfactory way forward for Rayment — no prosthetic limb, perhaps, but a second-order prosthetic device molded to fit him as he is now, as well as to reconnect him with a form of conveyance he had preferred in a previously unblighted state.

The slow man Rayment, in the end, does not attain any fulfilment in love; no physical expression of his unsuitable passion is countenanced in the novel. Nevertheless, the course of love does acquaint him with a good family, and it does bring about a certain return: a return not from the mother but the son that, in the form of the recumbent bicycle, is both a gift and a technical enhancement. Rayment is thereby shifted, however reluctantly, into a new position with respect to the age of technological modernity, while undoubtedly still remaining attached to the habits of locomotion of the far slower, and certainly less mechanically enhanced, age that has preceded it. Moreover, Rayment has been moved in another sense outside himself. While his anger at Drago was precipitate and misplaced, it brought him to the house of the woman for whom he had earlier declared his love. And this is a love he holds onto, even though the object of his love remains aloof and cannot return his affections on the same grounds. However much these circumstances fall short of what his longing as a man had been directed at, they come ahead of anything that the Mephistophelean Elizabeth Costello herself can promise. As Rayment observes at the end of the novel, the prospect of the cerebral companionship Costello offers should Rayment agree to accompany her back to Carlton is "not love. This is something else. Something less" (*SM*, 263).

Whether the rejection of Costello's offer of companionship might end Coetzee's deployment of her in future novels remains to be seen. What this rejection nevertheless conveys is that the path of truth through love that Rayment treads in sympathy with other heroes of modernist fiction is clearly affirmed. That such a path should not necessarily entail satisfaction for the passionate stirrings of our physical selves is one of Coetzee's points. Instead, the pleasures this path confers appear ultimately to reside in an ethical disposition of renunciation, a disposition brought about through a free act of love for another human being.[19]

Notes

[1] Coetzee (1940–) was sixty-five years of age when the novel was published.

[2] As Rayment explains to Elizabeth Costello: "I had three doses of the immigrant experience, not just one, so it imprinted itself quite deeply. First when I was uprooted as a child and brought to Australia; then when I declared my independence and returned to France; then when I gave up on France and came back to Australia. *Is this where I belong?* I asked with each move. *Is this my true home?*" (*SM*, 192; emphasis in original).

[3] "frivolous is not a bad word to sum him up" (*SM*, 19).

[4] This "speaking" name is Wayne Blight.

[5] These are Elizabeth Costello's words.

[6] This is a motif also linked to the activity of writing, thus providing an indirect link between Rayment and the writer. As Costello assures Rayment, writing is "second thoughts raised to the power of n" (*SM*, 228).

[7] David Attwell, for example, considers Elizabeth Costello's function in the novel in the context of "the relationship between authorship and its creations," such that that the mystery around the roles of "the authorial self and the self written into being" are presented in ordinary ways. See David Attwell: "Coetzee's Estrangements," *Novel* 41, nos. 2–3 (2008): 229–43; here, 235.

[8] Kenneth Pellow has also noted Coetzee's use of intertextual and intratextual reference in *Slow Man*. See his essay "Intertextuality and Other Analogues in J. M. Coetzee's *Slow Man*," *Contemporary Literature* 50, no. 3 (Fall 2009): 528–52.

[9] The German word for prosthesis is *Prothese*, a word meaning both *prothesis* (the addition of a letter or syllable at the beginning of a word) and *prosthesis* (the surgical replacement of deficiencies, as with artificial limbs or teeth). The German term does not carry the additional dimensions of the English word "prothesis," i.e., a credence table on which elements are placed for use in the Eucharistic office. An

interesting discussion that hints at this further meaning is nevertheless put forward by Zoë Wicomb, who maintains that the "linguistic shift from prosthesis to prothesis references transformation, instantiated in the first place in the figure and name of Paul Rayment, the boy from Lourdes where miracles of healing are available to believers": "Slow Man and the Real: A Lesson in Reading and Writing," *Journal of Literary Studies* 25, no. 4 (Dec. 2009): 7–24; here, 17.

[10] Antoine Julien Fauchery (1823–61) was commissioned in 1857 by the French Government to travel to Australia and record his impressions of that country. Separate collections of Fauchery's photographs depicting early colonial life in and around the city of Melbourne are preserved in the State Library of Victoria and the State Library of Queensland.

[11] That Costello is a parasite and a predator, but "still insists on Rayment's taking charge," would be entirely consistent with her role in the novel and resolve the implicit contradiction that David Attwell has pointed to. See his "Coetzee's Estrangements," 235. The idea that Costello assumes the function of an evil spirit gains further support at the end of the novel when Costello claims the motto "*malleus maleficorum*" for herself (*SM*, 263).

[12] See David Attwell's interview with Coetzee in the Swedish newspaper *Dagens Nyheter*, in which Coetzee responds to Attwell's questions about writers who might have influenced him and how they might have influenced him: Attwell, "An Exclusive Interview with J. M. Coetzee," *Dagens Nyheter*, 8 December 2003, 1–4; www.dn.se/kultur-noje/an-exclusive-interview-with-j-m-coetzee-1.227254 (accessed 31 March 2008). Subsequent references appear as EI.

[13] This is a phrase popularized by Robert Hughes in a work of art criticism under the same name: *The Shock of the New* (New York: Knopf 1981).

[14] Discussion of "die freien Geister" can be found, among other works, in book 5 of Nietzsche's *Die fröhliche Wissenschaft* (The Gay Science), which is subtitled "Die Furchtlosen" (the fearless ones). This book was added to the second edition of *Die fröhliche Wissenschaft* in 1887.

[15] See also James Meffan's discussion of Hofmannsthal's *Letter of Lord Chandos to Lord Bacon* in his discussion of *Elizabeth Costello* in chapter 11.

[16] See also Coetzee's discussion of Musil's *Drei Frauen* and the two early stories of *Vereinigungen* (Unions) in *DP*, 233–39. In a passage that seems to cast forward to his own literary intentions in *Slow Man*, Coetzee refers in this discussion to Musil's "constant theme" in these stories, "the unbridgeability of the gap between the rational and the irrational, between the moral, based always on the example of the past and therefore on calculation, and the ethical, calling for a leap into the future" (*DP*, 234).

[17] Rebecca L. Walkowitz has linked the discussion about prosthetic replacements in *Slow Man* to questions relating to the translation of artworks ("a spare leg or a translated edition"). See "Comparison Literature," *Literary History* 40, no. 3 (Summer 2009): 567–82; here, 577.

[18] As Attwell points out, Rayment, too, "speaks English like a foreigner, phlegmatically, with deliberation" ("Coetzee's Estrangements," 234).

[19] Already in the early 1990s, Attwell saw Coetzee's writing as evolving toward a "reconstructed ethics" based on traditional values such as "the need for reciprocity, the integrity of childhood, the possibility of community, and the status of compassion or charity." *Slow Man* certainly continues this defense of values reminiscent "of a kind of historical deprivation suffered by the people as a whole": David Attwell, *J. M. Coetzee: South Africa and the Politics of Writing* (Berkeley: U of California P, 1993), 119.

13: *Diary of a Bad Year* (2007)

Johan Geertsema

> *Among Señor C's latest set of opinions there is one that disturbs me, makes me wonder if I have misjudged him all along. It is about sex with children. He doesn't exactly come out in favour of it, but he doesn't come out against it either. I ask myself, Is this his way of saying his appetites run in that direction? Because why would he write about it otherwise?*
>
> — J. M. Coetzee, Diary of a Bad Year

ONE OF THE MOST CONTENTIOUS of the strong opinions presented in J. M. Coetzee's *Diary of a Bad Year* must be that of "On paedophilia" (*BY*, 53–57). While some, perhaps even many, readers may have considerable sympathy for the elderly writer JC's opinions on torture, the war on terror, and animal rights, Anya — the young woman he has engaged as a secretary (*BY*, 15) and with whom he has grown "obsessed" (*BY*, 89) — probably speaks for the skeptical reader when she says that the opinion "On paedophilia" is disturbing and asks why he is writing about it. So why *is* JC writing about paedophilia, and what *is* this opinion doing among the larger set of opinions in the book? More broadly, what are we to make of the opinions presented in *Diary of a Bad Year*? Should we take them seriously, and — a related question — to what extent can we attribute them to the author of the text, the one who signs the text "JMC" (*BY*, 231)? This complex text raises many questions, but surely that of authority (and "author-ity"), and thereby the status of the various opinions collected in the text, is among the most pressing. Not only is this topic directly addressed, for instance in opinion 30, "On authority in fiction" (*BY*, 149–51), but it is also evident in the text's engagement with other authors, their relation to their work, and the effects of that work. Thus, the text engages in these terms with such authors as Harold Pinter (127), Flaubert (e.g., 146), Tolstoy (149–51, 189–90), Kierkegaard (151), García Márquez (192), Antjie Krog (199), Beckett (201), and Dostoevsky (223–27).

In this chapter I propose to examine the question of what we are to make of JC's opinions. My argument will be that in *Diary of a Bad Year* Coetzee is staging these opinions parodically, and that one of his reasons for doing so may be understood, paradoxically, with reference to his seriousness as an artist. In making this argument I draw on two important essays from *Giving Offense*, Coetzee's 1996 book on censorship: "The Harms of Pornography: Catharine MacKinnon" and "Erasmus: Madness and Rivalry." In the former, Coetzee defines the seriousness of "a certain kind of artist" (*GO*, 73) with reference to the desire to explore "the darker areas of human experience" (*GO*, 74); he defines this project — I would argue — as parodic in character. Understanding this parodic character of the project could, moreover, help account for the peculiar form of *Diary of a Bad Year*: it is an attempt to negotiate politics, which Coetzee, in the second essay, argues is implicitly rivalrous. It is this attempt to engage in politics without being subject to its logic, without being reduced to the position — or rather opposition — of "rivals on the same plane, one of whom has stifled and silenced the other" (*GO*, 85), which in the end marks *Diary of a Bad Year* as an engagement with politics that, impossibly, does not itself want to be political: that is, without taking up a position of power that can in any simple sense be *opposed*.

Before making this argument, it will be useful first of all to consider *Diary of a Bad Year* more closely, specifically with reference to its relation to Coetzee's earlier fiction. While it may at first seem quite different from that earlier work, we need to realize that there are important continuities both on a formal and conceptual level. Now, it is true that Coetzee's more recent fiction — since his migration to Australia in 2002 — in a number of ways would appear to constitute a more-or-less radical departure from his earlier work. This would seem especially to be the case with the focus of this chapter, *Diary of a Bad Year* (2007). This text, like *Elizabeth Costello* (2003) and *Slow Man* (2005), the other two novels that have appeared since Coetzee's move, appears to chart a direction away from his earlier body of writing up to and including *Disgrace* (1999).[1] All of his earlier novels — the work that made his name — either directly concern themselves with South Africa and its political trauma, or lend themselves to being read as concerned with this topic indirectly. On the other hand, the more recent novels, if they can be called that, would seem to depart from this apparent concern, featuring as they do the aged Australian novelist Elizabeth Costello; South Africa does not figure centrally (in the case of *Elizabeth Costello* and *Diary of a Bad Year*) or even at all (*Slow Man*) in these texts.

A second difference that is apparent, as I have already intimated, is that these texts seem less straightforwardly to be *novels* than Coetzee's earlier, decidedly novelistic works: few readers would quibble about the generic status of such texts as *Waiting for the Barbarians* (1980), *Life & Times of Michael K* (1983), *Foe* (1986), *Age of Iron* (1989), *The Master of Petersburg* (1994), or indeed *Disgrace*. But *Elizabeth Costello*, the subtitle of which is "eight lessons," has no central plot; it consists for the most part of revised lectures that Coetzee had delivered before in the guise of Elizabeth Costello, and this figure's appearance in each of the lessons is the main unifying element of the text. If *Slow Man* appears more conventionally novelistic, then it is nevertheless a novel that questions what being a novel might mean. Very little happens in the novel, so little that Elizabeth Costello, its apparent author, enters one-third into the text precisely in order to speed things up and get the protagonist, Paul Rayment, to act. On one level, *Slow Man* is then about its own impossibility, or at least its own dissolution. In short, what Mike Marais calls the "perfunctory treatment of narrative"[2] in this text is very much in evidence in all of Coetzee's recent work, especially when compared to the earlier novels.

This judgment certainly applies to *Diary of a Bad Year*. Formally, as its title suggests, the text is structured episodically: its fifty-five fairly short essays read like entries in a diary. The essays, and thereby the text as such, are divided into two parts, "Strong Opinions" (*BY*, 1–154) and "Second Diary" (*BY*, 155–227); the loose, episodic structure of the text is further in evidence in the split architecture of almost all the pages, the sole exception being the final chapter of the first part of the text, "31. On the afterlife" (*BY*, 153–54). While the diary-like essays appear at the top of each page, it is split into two or, more often, three sections, the second of which is empty at the start of the second part (*BY*, 157–67). Upon turning to the opening of the novel in order to start reading it, the reader is thus faced with the problem of reading a page divided into two parts, at the top an essay concerning the origins of the state, and at the bottom a narrative that is written in a different register altogether and reads much more like a fictional story than the section at the top. Each of these sections, one soon realizes, functions quite independently from the other, and can be read in various sequences. The main, if not only, element of narrative unity in the text is built up slowly in the course of reading the narrative in the bottom section/s, as the reader follows the essayist's or diarist's infatuation with the woman he meets in a laundry (Anya); his employing her to do secretarial work (typing up the essayistic opinions at the top of the page, as it turns out); their discussions and disagreements, especially on the topic of honor; her boyfriend's plan to steal the writer's money electronically; the dinner party to celebrate the completion of the manuscript, during which the boyfriend gets drunk and insults the writer; and the woman's subsequent breakup with her boyfriend.[3]

But, despite its episodic character and rather thin narrative of infatuation and financial intrigue, the text is in fact very tightly structured: a significant function of the form of the text is that the narrative that unfolds below the line, as the writer recounts his infatuation and the woman provides her perspective, acts as a counterpoint, an echo, an interrogation of the opinions being presented at the top of the page. The opinions that

JC is putting together with the help of Anya are his contribution to the book *Strong Opinions*, in which "six eminent writers pronounce on what is wrong with today's world" (*BY*, 21); he confesses to having "jumped to accept" the invitation to contribute and sees it as an "opportunity to grumble in public, an opportunity to take magic revenge on the world for declining to conform to my fantasies" (*BY*, 23).

Indeed, "Strong Opinions," the first part of the text, consists of a series of strong, one might go so far as to say, outraged and certainly in many cases highly contentious opinions on such topics as the totalitarian character of democracy (*BY*, 15); the justification of torture on the basis of necessity (17–18); the "*hysterical*" response to terror attacks by the liberal democracies of the United States, Britain, and Australia (19; emphasis in original); suicide bombings and their tragic potential (21); the role of the hermeneutics of suspicion, as taught in literature classes in the United States in the 1980s and 1990s, in the war on terror (33); the corporatization of universities (35–36); the slaughter of animals (63–65); intelligent design (83–86); the cruelty and inequity of Australian asylum policies (111–13); deteriorating English usage (143–47); and the afterlife (153–54). "Second Diary" is "*a second, gentler set of opinions*" (145; emphasis in original), as JC puts it in his letter to Anya, who calls it his "Soft Opinions" (193) and prefers it to his "Strong Opinions."

An important initial response to the question with which I am concerned in this chapter — what we are to make of the opinions collected in *Diary of a Bad Year* — is provided by JC, who explains the set of opinions that he is writing, and Anya is typing, in ethical terms when he calls them "a response to the present in which I find myself" (*BY*, 67).[4] This is an important pointer concerning the opinions and their function provided by the text itself, to the extent that one can even refer to this text as a unified whole: in other words, as a *coherent* response. The fact is that the text consists of a "miscellany" (*BY*, 54) of opinions and narrative voices, and this is precisely why the question of authority — and what we are to make of the opinions — arises in the first place: as a miscellany of diverse, and perhaps even divergent, responses, it is unclear to what extent the text can constitute a "response to the present" that would make sense on its own terms as an ethical — that is, a *responsible* — response. For, as Brian Macaskill remarks, an unreliability is built into the text that is "guaranteed by hybrid representation: it is not at all clear to what genre or even mix of genres this writing belongs";[5] the text, consisting as it does of "numbered sections" (*CCMV*, 456), comes to resemble, among other things, an "undated diary" and an "exhibition of photographs in massive montage" (*CCMV*, 457). Remarkably, Macaskill is here discussing not *Diary of a Bad Year* but Coetzee's very first novel — if we take *Dusklands* (1974) to be less a novel than a set of novellas — namely, *In the Heart of the Country* (1977). Though the two texts were published exactly thirty years apart,

Macaskill's analysis clearly implies the very real links between *In the Heart of the Country* and *Diary of a Bad Year*, both as far as their generically hybrid form — "numbered sections"; "undated diary" — and its consequence, unreliability, are concerned.[6] Macaskill's discussion, to which I return below, addresses the issue of response in terms of the notion of the middle voice. But for now I merely want to highlight that the connection between these texts serves both to underscore the overall question with which I am concerned here, and — despite appearances — the larger connection between *Diary of a Bad Year*, and thereby Coetzee's recent work since his migration to Australia, and his earlier fiction.

Another important link consists of Coetzee's view of himself as an artist, one who takes both his art and his ethical responsibility seriously. In the remainder of this chapter I would like to consider this point more closely in order to demonstrate how, in *Diary of a Bad Year*, Coetzee strives to attain a position — one he realizes is impossible — that is not political but grounded in the aesthetic, and thereby has the potential to offer an ethically responsible response to the present in which he finds himself. In a passage to which I already referred at the start, from "The Harms of Pornography," the essay that is the most explicit antecedent for JC's opinion "On paedophilia," Coetzee writes that "seriousness is, for a certain kind of artist, an imperative uniting the aesthetic and the ethical" (*GO*, 73). We need to understand the essay with reference to Coetzee's larger examination of censorship in *Giving Offense*.[7] In discussing his views on censorship in an interview in *Doubling the Point*, Coetzee makes an important point concerning the political character of both censorship and discussions of it. While he dislikes censorship, he says that he finds "the general debate [on it] an uninteresting one, failing to rise above the level of the political in the worst sense. It remains stalled at the level of . . . stupidity" (*DP*, 299); for this reason he has, in the essays that are collected in *Giving Offense*, "left the pros and cons of censorship aside and turned my attention to trying to understand the dynamic of that stupidity." The political "in the worst sense" consists of an endless, and pointless, debate in which rival positions remain opposed in an unresolvable argument concerning "pros and cons." But, even more importantly, from Coetzee's perspective, censorship itself is, in fact, the embodiment of the political. For if politics is a power play between opposing camps, and if the censor "has only two words in his lexicon: *Yes* and *No*," then it is evident that censorship is an enactment of this unresolvable argument of pros and cons, of — as he puts it in his essay on Erasmus — "rivals on the same plane, one of whom has stifled and silenced the other" (*GO*, 85), which is one definition by Coetzee of the political to which I have already alluded and will return below. In politics as in censorship, indeed in censorship-as-politics, all complexities are reduced to the simplicity of opposition, to a binary system of "pros and cons," "Yes" and "No."

With regard to censorship in particular, and the political more generally, Coetzee is therefore trapped in a difficult, if not impossible, position. To resist censorship effectively, he needs to refuse the "Yes" and "No" of the censor; but this means that he cannot say "No" to censorship, cannot in any simple way *oppose* it, since then he would precisely be replicating its structure, which is one of saying "No," of refusing; to oppose censorship genuinely, he needs to refuse its refusal, which thus paradoxically means *not* opposing it. He needs to carve out a nonposition between the rival, binary positions of "Yes" and "No." This is why, in another interview (which deals with, and appeared just before, the publication of *Giving Offense*) Coetzee quite strenuously expresses his reluctance to accept the interviewer's "comment that the book expresses a general *opposition* to censorship," and again, "to endorse . . . the statement that the book is written to express an *opposition* to censorship" (my emphasis).[8] Indeed, it is precisely such "structures of opposition, of Either-Or, which I take it as my task to evade" (IwC, 108); significantly, and this returns us to Coetzee's view of the political, he also directly links such structures of opposition, which in an essential way characterize censorship, with the "nature of the vote: Yes or No, Either-Or" (IwC, 108). It is worth noting parenthetically that we find here an important antecedent of, and explanation for, JC's claim that "democracy is totalitarian" (*BY*, 15). This is so since "democracy does not allow for politics outside the democratic system," since it forces the subjects of democracy to choose between "A" and "B" (*BY*, 8–9) *within* that system.[9]

Instead, Coetzee seeks to transcend these simplistic, and indeed oppressive, binary structures in his work, as Macaskill has rightly argued with reference to his interest in the grammatical category of the middle voice.[10] Macaskill invokes the following passage from *In the Heart of the Country*, which he argues articulates not only Magda's but Coetzee's desire for a position between positions, a kind of in-between nonposition: "The medium, the median — that is what I wanted to be! Neither master nor slave, neither parent nor child, but the bridge between, so that in me the contraries should be reconciled!" (*IHC*, 133; CCMV, 465). As Macaskill puts it in his helpful commentary on this passage, "Magda seeks a median place from which to articulate herself, and the numbered entries in which she seeks to record this articulation come in turn to constitute Coetzee's act of 'doing-writing' in the middle voice: a means, no less, of enumerating (for Coetzee) equally complex negotiations facing the writer in that time and place of contemporary South Africa" (CCMV, 465). In other words, Coetzee's work — in the case of the novel he is analyzing and the time and place with which it is concerned (South Africa in the 1970s), but surely also more generally — is oriented towards a future that would "[relocate] from the inside the imminently repressive categories of master-slave, transitive-intransitive, active-passive, and structure-agent.

Coetzee's practice . . . insists that this future, this relocation, must be predicated upon mechanisms more responsible than simple reversal" (CCMV, 467). The point is therefore that, from the beginning, Coetzee has attempted to *deconstruct* binaries rather than merely inverting — and thereby perpetuating — them.

This deconstructive position that is not a position, or at least that cannot be buttonholed in the terms of clearly delineated positions (either this or that; yes or no) perhaps finds its clearest articulation in Coetzee's essay on Erasmus. In the essay, Coetzee considers — with reference to Foucault's work on madness in relation to reason, Derrida's reading of Foucault, Lacan's thinking of this relation, and Girard's analysis of mimetic violence — Erasmus's attempt to attain a practical position beyond the two rival camps of the Pope and Luther. Referring to Foucault's *Madness and Civilization*, he offers a suggestive comment on the nature of politics and its link with rivalry: Foucault's project is to "reveal the opposition of reason to madness as a merely political opposition, that is, an opposition of rivals on the same plane, one of whom has stifled and silenced the other" (*GO*, 85). What interests me here is less the paradoxical character of Foucault's project — to make madness speak he needs the language of reason — than the notion that politics consists of rivalry. If this is the case, then a position outside of politics would appear to be untenable, if not impossible, since such a position would then oppose politics and would therefore stand in a position of rivalry in relation to it, thereby merely replicating the politics from which it seeks to escape. *Not* merely replicating these political positions with which one engages is extremely difficult, which is why, very early in *Diary of a Bad Year*, JC laments: "Why is it so hard to say anything about politics from outside politics? Why can there be no discourse about politics that is not itself political?" (*BY*, 9). Like Erasmus, Coetzee therefore desires an ironic "*non*position" (*GO*, 84) that engages politically without being reduced to its field: the position of folly, of the marginalized, the powerless, the fool free to "criticize all" without being co-opted by either side in a particular conflict, "off the stage of rivalry altogether."[11]

To return, now, to the essay "The Harms of Pornography," which deals with Catharine MacKinnon's work in opposition to pornography: in line with these considerations, though Coetzee is critical of her, we can understand better why he would "hesitate to say that I am opposed to MacKinnon" (IwC, 110). His hesitation to express his opposition to her is of a piece with his position on censorship itself. Because in MacKinnon's work "all arguments are power moves and power is gendered" (*GO*, 72) — which is to say, for her everything is ultimately political; everything can be reduced to the struggles of gender politics — Coetzee is of the view that a *direct* response would be fruitless. In her "arena of disputation," Coetzee thinks there is little room for nuance: his position

would *either* be affirmed *or* — more likely, given his skepticism about censorship — negated by MacKinnon. That is, it would not be taken seriously by her, except "in the stupid way characteristic of the censor, who
has only two words in [her] lexicon: *Yes* and *No*" (*DP*, 299). He therefore
chooses "to skirt the most direct form of response" (*GO*, 72). Rather
than opposing MacKinnon, and in order to be taken seriously (which he
thinks will in fact not be the case should he oppose her) Coetzee, as I will
now try to explain, paradoxically responds by means of parody, if parody
is understood in Bakhtin's terms: namely, as *novelization*.[12]

   "Against" (in inverted commas) MacKinnon, whose "heart" Coetzee
suggests "lies with the censors" (*GO*, 66) and who has (embarrassingly)
"herself been absorbed into the projects of conservative popular religion" (*GO*, 81) in her campaigns against pornography,[13] Coetzee imagines a hypothetical "male writer-pornographer" who claims the right to
offer "an account of power and desire . . . not in the discursive terms of
'theory,' but in the form of a representation, an enactment" (*GO*, 72).
Rather than *either* opposing pornography (like MacKinnon) *or* opposing
its opposition (by MacKinnon), Coetzee here makes a case for a different, perhaps impossible position: that of a pornographer who is critical of
pornography or, better, a critic of pornography who engages in it. Might
it be possible, Coetzee asks, to imagine such a scenario? What would an
opponent of pornography such as MacKinnon make of someone who,
though critical of pornography, nonetheless engages in a critical *enactment* of it? What, moreover, would such an opponent make of this kind of
procedure that, since it could not in any *simple* way be pornographic (after
all, it is critical of pornography), moves beyond the opposition between
pornography and opposition to it — its "pros and cons" — and thereby
would also be a critique of *opposition* to pornography, a "critique of the
account of power, gender, and desire given by [MacKinnon's] 'feminism
unmodified,' a critique whose radicalism would consist not necessarily in
its conceptual power but — if the two could ever be disentangled — *in its
embrace of the pornographic medium as its own*" (*GO*, 73; my emphasis)?
Lest this embrace of pornography against pornography as well as against
opposition to it be seen as an outrageous suggestion, Coetzee notes that
"the kind of project I outline is not fanciful" (*GO*, 73); he gives the example of Dostoevsky as an artist who takes seriously the project of "exploring the darker areas of human experience" (*GO*, 74).

   Coetzee knows full well that such a project would cut no ice with
someone opposed to pornography; as he notes, "it is . . . deconstructible
as a feature of the ideology of so-called high art and the drive to power of
the high artist. It is hard to believe that . . . the project I outlined above
would be saved" (*GO*, 73). Nevertheless, it is Coetzee's wager to pursue precisely this kind of project; despite its risks it is preferable to the
two alternatives (the "either-ors"). This is so for the reason that he sees

himself as a serious artist, as driven by "an imperative uniting the aesthetic and the ethical" (*GO*, 73) since, like Dostoevsky, he precisely wants to explore "the darker areas of human experience" — the Dostoevsky who, as "a follower of Christ" (*BY*, 226), nonetheless allows Ivan, in *The Brothers Karamazov*, "such powerful words" against Christ. Like Dostoevsky, who enacts positions in his writing with which he does not necessarily agree, positions from those darker areas, Coetzee in his fiction stages positions, perhaps most in/famously in *Elizabeth Costello* and, now, in *Diary of a Bad Year*, which we cannot in any simple way attribute to him, as one cannot attribute those in Dostoevsky to *him* in any simple way.

One of the most famous commentators on Dostoevsky is, of course, Bakhtin, and in the essay "Discourse in the Novel" — to cite one example — he pays particular attention to this staging of ideas in the dialogues of characters, arguing that their "world views" must be understood "as unresolved and unresolvable dialogue," with the consequence that "in Dostoevsky's novels, the life experience of the characters and their discourse may be resolved as far as plot is concerned, but internally they remain incomplete and unresolved."[14] Put most basically, no simple "message" can be taken from the complexity that is Dostoevsky's writing, and no simple "Dostoevskyian" position can be inferred from his staging of his characters' ideas and dialogues. Indeed, it is this very dialogism that renders such inferences problematic. And, from the perspective of genre, it is for Bakhtin the *novel* that enables this. For according to him the novel is, as he puts it in the essay "Epic and Novel," inherently a parodic genre: "Parodic stylizations of canonized genres and styles occupy an essential place in the novel" (DI, 6). The novel is constantly reinventing itself as it appropriates and reappropriates other genres in a process Bakhtin terms novelization. That is, the novel, as "the only developing genre" (*DI*, 4), a "genre-in-the-making" (DI, 11), always open-ended, incomplete, and unable to congeal because of its "contact with the spontaneity of the inconclusive present" (DI, 27), develops and grows exactly by renewing and thereby perpetuating older genres within itself. The novel performs other genres, novelizes them; to put it in Coetzee's terms, it embraces those genres as its own.

Might *Diary of a Bad Year*, in part, be understood as putting into practice the project articulated by Coetzee in "The Harms of Pornography" — namely, that of "embrac[ing] the pornographic medium as its own" (*GO*, 73)? It is true that a work quite clearly seeks to take seriously the challenge of exploring "the darker areas of human experience," and to do so on its own terms — that is, those of the aesthetic: from the violence of imperialism and its use of torture in *Waiting for the Barbarians*; to the complexities of the struggle against apartheid in *Age of Iron*; to the complexities of life postapartheid in *Disgrace*; to the incredibly huge scale of human cruelty to nonhuman animals in not only *The Lives of Animals* but also *Diary of a Bad Year* itself. But I believe the case can be made that *Diary of a Bad Year* specifically is a contribution to this project that quite explicitly relates back to the concerns articulated in the essays collected in *Giving Offense*. This is most obviously so for the reason that JC refers to his "collection of essays on censorship" (*BY*, 22) published in the 1990s, which must be *Giving Offense* (and which thereby invites the reader to identify JC with Coetzee).[15] Even more importantly, "On paedophilia" directly harkens back to "The Harms of Pornography," especially in its invocation of Catharine MacKinnon (*BY*, 55). The notion that Coetzee may in *Diary of a Bad Year* be engaging in quite direct terms with the project articulated in "The Harms of Pornography" — namely, a parodic "embrace of the pornographic medium as its own," which is lent further impetus by the striking and, frankly, somewhat surprising prominence of pornography in the text. From the opening page which, even if it is not graphic nonetheless verges on the pornographic in its reference to the "tomato-red shift" that Anya wore, and that was "so startling in its brevity" (*BY*, 3); to the reference to red shift and thongs, quickly qualified as "thongs of the kind that go on the feet" (6); to Anya's saucy confession that, when she passes JC, she makes sure that "I waggle my behind, my delicious behind, sheathed in tight denim" (25); to Anya and Alan's racy pillow-talk (e.g., 37); to JC's alleged stash of pornography (92, 226): *Diary of a Bad Year* is things, quickly qualified as literally replete with not only references to pornography, but passages that are pornographic (or quasi-pornographic) in character. This phenomenon is the more striking given Coetzee's reticence in his other novels; his famously spare style also extends to sexual matters, or their relative absence, in the texts. *Disgrace*, even though it is saturated with sex — the opening sentence of the novel: "For a man of his age, fifty-two, divorced, he has, to his mind, solved the problem of sex rather well" (*DG*, 1) already alerts us to this, while the novel then proceeds to relate, or perhaps rather intimate, various scenes involving sexual intercourse, including violent rape — of course refuses to describe the central events involving the rape of Lucy. Even though there is a fellatio scene in *Life & Times of Michael K*, this is again spare, indeed clinical — the sentence "Against his will the memory returned of the casque of silver hair bent over his sex, and the grunting of the girl as she laboured on him" (*MK*, 181) is perhaps as untitillating a sexual description as is possible to imagine, especially when compared with *Diary of a Bad Year*.

Immediately prior to the opinion "On paedophilia," in JC's narrative section, he has asked Anya whether she and Alan are planning to have children. JC then, on the very same page that Catharine MacKinnon is mentioned, offers Anya "a word of benevolent advice: don't leave it too late" (55). He proceeds to assert that "[children] are a gift from above" (57) on the same page as that on which the opinion "On paedophilia" ends. The juxtaposition on the same pages of this view, that children are a gift of inestimable value, indeed a *divine* gift, with his provocative discussion of the potential paradoxes involved in a ban on child pornography, is at first glance piquant. This is further brought to the fore by the pornographic content of JC's narrative at this point. On the same page as "On paedophilia" commences, he reflects upon his earlier question/ statement to Anya: "So you have no plans for children" (50), to which she has replied: "No. Alan doesn't want children" (51), and he does so in the following way:

> There is an innocent, a purely sociable, an even routine way of raising the question of children. At the moment when I pronounce the first word, the word *So*, my curiosity could not be more innocent. But in between *So* and the second word *you* the devil waylays me, sends me an image of this Anya on a sweaty summer night, convulsed in the arms of ginger-haired, freckle-shouldered Alan, opening her womb in gladness to the gush of his male juices. (*BY*, 53)

JC here clearly conjures up, whether willingly or not (he claims the devil made him do it), an image that is pornographic: of Anya and Alan engaging in sexual intercourse, as testified not only by the adjective "sweaty," the participle "convulsed," but especially the phrase "opening her womb in gladness to the gush of his male juices." The crucial point for my argument is that the opinion "On paedophilia" and the (quasi-) pornographic descriptions in *Diary of a Bad Year* cannot be read in isolation: that is, *as pornographic*. Rather, in terms of the logic outlined above in my discussion of "The Harms of Pornography," and with reference to the peculiar form of *Diary of a Bad Year*, consisting as it does of generically diverse sections on the same page, this text is pornographic *but not only pornographic*. The same of course goes for the various opinions: *Diary of a Bad Year* offers opinions *but not only opinions*. On the contrary, the different voices in the text — JC's essayistic opinions at the top of the page; his narrative below the opinions; and Anya's narrative at the bottom, which includes lengthy sections of opinions very critical of JC by her boyfriend Alan (*BY*, 104: "Every word he says is bullshit, says Alan") — very much interact and relativize one another. *Diary of a Bad Year* performs opinions (for instance, on paedophilia) in the same way that it performs pornography: in such a way that each is subject to commentary and critique. Whether it is a performance of opinions or pornography, it is also — in principle and in practice — a critique of each. Instead of the two alternative responses to, for instance, pornography — namely, *either* reproducing it *or*, on the other hand, banning it — Coetzee wants to *explore* it. This exploration is complex and confusing; it does not lend itself to easy positions, but instead stands in a parodic relation to such positions. As Anya says, with regard to the opinion "On paedophilia," he — or rather, JC — "doesn't exactly come out in favour of it, but he doesn't come out against it either" (*BY*, 88)

We have seen that one way in which to understand JC's opinion "On paedophilia," as well as the pornographic passages in *Diary of a Bad Year*, is that they put into practice the project articulated by Coetzee in "The Harms of Pornography." I trust, therefore, that the usefulness of seeing Coetzee as engaged in a parodic, "jocoserious" (*GO*, 103) project that seeks to avoid the oppositionality and rivalry of politics will be apparent. Referring to Erasmus's *In Praise of Folly*, in particular the pages in this text on the *theatrum mundi* (see *GO*, 98–99), in terms of his preceding analysis of the text with regard to especially Lacan, he argues that "the power of the text lies in its weakness — its jocoserious abnegation of big-phallus status, its evasive (non)position inside/outside the play" (*GO*, 103). From this perspective, *Diary of a Bad Year* — as a performance of positions that refuses their final attribution to a figure of authority — is an Erasmian text. But Coetzee's essay on Erasmus does not end here. Coetzee continues by noting the weakness of *In Praise of Folly*, which paradoxically lies in its (phallic) strength, "lies in its power to grow, to propagate itself, to beget Erasmians" (*GO*, 103), and thereby willy-nilly inserts the text into politics as rivalry (see *GO*, 100–103). It is just this weakness that Coetzee seeks to avoid in *Diary of a Bad Year*. Since the opinions raise the question as to what we are to make of them, Coetzee seems to be hoping that his readers will not turn into "Coetzeans," but that they will instead take the text seriously enough not simply to position themselves *either* for *or* against it, but will ask questions of it: specifically, what we are to make of the opinions presented in *Diary of a Bad Year*.

Notes

[1] For the purposes of the present chapter, I assume that *Youth* (2002) and *Summertime* (2009), the other major recent texts — aside from the collections of essays *Stranger Shores* (2001) and *Inner Workings* (2007), which consist in the main of reviews from the *New York Review of Books* — are memoirs, although they of course are themselves quasi-novelistic, and hence unsettle generic boundaries.

[2] Mike Marais, *Secretary of the Invisible: The Idea of Hospitality in the Fiction of J. M. Coetzee* (Amsterdam: Rodopi, 2009), 193. Subsequent references appear as SI with the accompanying page number.

[3] The text's concern with honor and dishonor — especially with reference to the "war on terror" and the use of torture — forms a very important narrative strand that lends coherence to the text's ethical response to the present (see e.g., 30, 39–45, 92). Indeed, it directly informs the story Anya tells JC of her and her girlfriend's rape by three Americans (96–102), a story she tells him as part of *her* response to his sense that "Dishonor descends upon one's shoulders" (92; see 40) given the shamefulness of the United States and more broadly Anglo-American

response to terror. It thereby also informs the disagreement between them that leads to JC's reconsidering, if not his opinions, then his opinions of his opinions that he realizes have become too settled and rigid (see 125, 136). In the terms of my argument here, what JC realizes is that his opinions have become oppositional in the problematic political sense that Coetzee finds fruitless.

[4] As Derek Attridge (*J. M. Coetzee and the Ethics of Reading: Literature in the Event* [Chicago: U of Chicago P, 2004]) and Mike Marais (SI) have convincingly argued in their different ways, Coetzee's work is preoccupied with, indeed haunted by, its sense of ethical responsibility to the other. See especially Marais (211–12) and, in a discussion that relates it to Derrida's notion of the *arrivant*, Attridge (120–21). An ethical response would be one that is infinite: as Derrida says, "responsibility must be infinite . . . because I'm finite and because there are an infinite number of others to whom or for whom or from whom I should be responsible. I'm always not responsible enough, and responsibility is infinite or it *is* not" (quoted in SI, 48–49). For Derrida, therefore, as Mike Marais comments in an insightful discussion of *The Master of Petersburg*, "it is precisely its infinite nature that makes of responsibility a burden, a persecution" (SI, 138). The other, therefore, as Marais discusses, *haunts* the self. Though I cannot pursue this line of thought here, this would imply that for a response to be ethical, it could *not* be coherent — since it would have to be infinite, it could never be complete, and therefore never be sufficient on its own terms: in other words, coherent. The implication of this would be that the apparently incoherent form of a text such as *Diary of a Bad Year*, evident in its generic diversity, would precisely be an indication of its seriousness in pursuing the infinite project of the ethical.

[5] Brian Macaskill, "Charting J. M. Coetzee's Middle Voice," *Contemporary Literature* 35, no. 3 (Autumn 1994): 441–75; here, 456–57. Subsequent references appear as CCMV with the accompanying page number.

[6] Though the first part of *Diary of a Bad Year* is dated from 12 September 2005 to 31 May 2006 (*BY*, 1) the individual entries — that is, the essayistic opinions — are not.

[7] See Peter McDonald (especially *The Literature Police: Apartheid Censorship and its Cultural Consequences* [Oxford: Oxford UP, 2009], 207–16; also "The Writer, the Critic, and the Censor," *Book History* 7 [2004]: 285–302) for a full and very helpful examination of both Coetzee's views of censorship, and also his place within the history of censorship in apartheid South Africa.

[8] J. M. Coetzee, "An Interview with J. M. Coetzee." *World Literature Today* 70, no. 1 (Winter 1996): 107–10; here, 107. Cited in the text following with the abbreviation "IwC" and the page number.

[9] Elsewhere I argue that Coetzee's alternative to this totalitarian aspect of democracy, or rather, quasi-totalitarian conception of it, may be fruitfully compared to Derrida's notion of the democracy-to-come ("Coetzee's *Diary of a Bad Year*, Politics, and the Problem of Position"; the essay is currently forthcoming in *Twentieth Century Literature*).

[10] For Macaskill's definition of this category, as well as the notion of "doing-writing" as neither active nor passive, especially as this relates to Coetzee, see CCMV, 448–54.

[11] In characterizing the "*non*position" as ironic, we should note Coetzee's hesitancy in characterizing Erasmus's Folly as ironic (*GO*, 84, 97). The reason for this, of course, is that irony might be characterized as implying a hierarchy of knowledge: "To attribute irony to her [Moria], to call her *o eiron*, the dissembler, is to put her back in the position of the subject supposed to know" (*GO*, 97). As Coetzee himself writes in a subsequent endnote that explains this point further (*GO*, 249), "in the notion of the key that will unlock Erasmus's irony or paradox I detect an ambition to freeze it in a single, locked position." That is, only to the extent that it is possible for irony *not* to be hierarchical, to resist the oppositionality of the dialectic, could one call Coetzee's nonposition ironic.

[12] Two especially useful recent readings of Coetzee in terms of parody are of *Disgrace* (Laura Wright: *Writing "Out of All the Camps": J. M. Coetzee's Narratives of Displacement* [New York: Routledge, 2006], 102–5) and of *Slow Man* (Marais, SI, 207–11). However, neither of them draws on Bakhtin.

[13] In his opinion "On paedophilia," JC, somewhat mischievously, says that "on the issue of pornography, feminism, in other respects a progressive movement, chose to go to bed with the religious conservatives" (*BY*, 54). See also Coetzee's own assertion that "MacKinnon has landed herself with some uncomfortable bedfellows from the moral right wing in the United States" (IwC, 110).

[14] M. Bakhtin, *The Dialogic Imagination: Four Essays*, trans. Caryl Emerson and Michael Holquist (Austin: University of Texas Press, 1981), 349. Subsequent references appear as DI with the accompanying page number.

[15] Indeed, it is among other things the reference to *Giving Offense* that brings us back to the question relating to authority that is my point of departure in this essay. It is worth pointing out that this question is brought into focus when one pays attention to the issue of names in the text, since the text never reveals the name of the author of the opinions: while Anya and her boyfriend, Alan, call him Señor C — Anya "declines to call me by my name, instead calling me *Señor* or perhaps *Senior*" (*BY*, 60) — the writer for whom Anya acts as a secretary merely signs himself JC in a letter to her (123). But these initials, among a number of other coincidences, strongly suggest that the identity of the writer is in fact "JMC" (231), to use the initials with which he signs the acknowledgements at the end of the text and thereby the book itself — that is, J. M. Coetzee himself. Some of these other coincidences are that JC, like Coetzee, in the 1990s published a collection of essays on censorship (22) — namely, *Giving Offense*; that JC explicitly refers to "my novel *Waiting for the Barbarians*" (171); and that both figures are white, male expatriate South Africans now resident in Australia. But even as the text suggests this similarity, it also highlights differences between them that would make any identification between JC and Coetzee problematic: JC is said to have been born in South Africa in 1934 (50), while Coetzee was born in 1940; Coetzee resides in Adelaide while JC lives in Sydney; and so on. In other words, JC is a figure like Elizabeth Costello that one is tempted, but ultimately unable, to identify with Coetzee.

14: Coetzee's Criticism

Carrol Clarkson

I N HIS ESSAY, "DIE SKRYWER EN DIE TEORIE" ("The Writer and Theory"),
Coetzee makes a claim that, by his own admission, surely scandalized
his South African literary audience when he first presented this paper at
the SAVAL conference in Bloemfontein in 1980: "I must confess," says
Coetzee,

> dat die beste kritiek vir my meer inhou as die letterkunde. Dit is
> miskien 'n skande, maar ek lees liewer Girard oor Sofokles of Barthes
> oor Balzac as romans.[1]

> [the best criticism holds more for me than literature does. It is
> perhaps scandalous, but I prefer reading Girard on Sophocles, or
> Barthes on Balzac, than novels.]

In the course of his paper, Coetzee identifies two attitudes to literary
criticism that he sets himself against, and this provides the inspiration for
the double entendre in the title of my chapter: the following discussion is
about Coetzee's own critical essays, but it also addresses Coetzee's critique
of assumptions about the relation between fiction and critical writing. To
date, Coetzee's novels have attracted far more scholarly attention than his
critical essays have — and when his essays and interviews are cited, this
is typically done within the context of a discussion primarily concerned
with the fiction. However, Coetzee has produced no fewer than five volumes of nonfiction (*White Writing*, 1988; *Doubling the Point*, 1992; *Giving Offense*, 1996; *Stranger Shores*, 2001; *Inner Workings*, 2007) and has
published several other essays, interviews, and literary reviews besides.
Coetzee's master's thesis on Ford Madox Ford (1963),[2] which he wrote
while working as a mathemetician and computer programmer in England,
and his doctoral dissertation on Samuel Beckett (1969)[3] each play a significant and distinctive role in Coetzee's own development as a writer. At
the time of writing his master's and his doctorate, Coetzee found himself at a busy intersection of literary studies and linguistics, computational
logic, and mathematics (Coetzee holds postgraduate degrees in literature
and linguistics, and also in mathematics). In his MA thesis, Coetzee writes
of Ford Madox Ford's *The Good Soldier* that it is "probably the finest

example of literary pure mathematics in English" (FMF, x), and in his doctorate on Beckett, he developed and experimented with a statistical method of analyzing literary style. Despite Coetzee's final dismissal of the usefulness of numerical analysis in the attempt to come to a finer appreciation of style in literature — "What do the figures tell us? and specifically, What do the measures measure?" Coetzee asks in his dissertation (SA, 159) — the work that he did for his doctorate would prove vital in developing his own craftsmanship as a writer of fiction. As Coetzee explains in conversation with David Attwell:

> The essays I wrote on Beckett's style aren't only academic exercises, in the colloquial sense of that word. They are also attempts to get closer to a secret, a secret of Beckett's that I wanted to make my own. And discard, eventually, as it is with influences. (*DP*, 25)

Coetzee's nonfiction ranges through diverse topics, reflecting on issues such as the relation between fiction and history,[4] the challenges and responsibilities of South African authors writing under apartheid, pornography, censorship, early British colonial travel writing in the Cape Colony, photography, rugby and cricket, translation, and the linguistic constraints of syntax, tense, and voice that confront writers in specific historical and political contexts. Many of these questions are revisited in Coetzee's book reviews, for the most part first published in the *New York Review of Books*, and collected in *Stranger Shores* and *Inner Workings*. Coetzee's critical writing thus constitutes a substantial body of work in its own right, and yet it is not generally considered in this way: the tendency amongst literary scholars is to draw on the essays only insofar as they shed light on themes in the novels.

My engagement with Coetzee's critical writing in this chapter is somewhat different from the current trend, but at the same time it is worth reiterating that the terrain of Coetzee's critical oeuvre is extensive, to say the least, and a brief overview of Coetzee's nonfiction would not even begin to give a clear sense of the nuanced inflections of argument and dialogue in each of Coetzee's texts. Nevertheless, standing back from the body of critical work, I would say that what characterizes Coetzee's nonfiction is an intense and self-questioning engagement with the linguistic, political, and conceptual challenges facing other *writers* — on the understanding that philosophers, scientists, theorists, translators and literary critics are writers too, just as novelists and poets are. In following through with this idea, I take the excerpt cited from Coetzee's talk at the outset of this chapter along two lines of inquiry: the first line is to ask, what does a reading of Coetzee's critical work hold for us? The second line of inquiry pays attention to the ways in which Coetzee explores the relation between creative and critical modes of writing — but in that this exploration ranges through Coetzee's own essays, interviews, novels, and fictional autobiographies, the reader is challenged to ask an unsettling question: where does one draw the line between fiction and criticism in Coetzee's writing? It is in this challenge, and in an appreciation of the risky aesthetic and ethical effects of linguistic choices any writer is bound to make, that Coetzee makes a significant contribution to contemporary literary-critical debates. The discussion to follow does not attempt to summarize or give a detailed account of the extent and range of Coetzee's criticism. Instead, it clusters questions of fiction and criticism, linguistics and ethics in relation to Coetzee's accreted conception of the term "writing," with a special emphasis on the interviews and essays collected in *Doubling the Point*.

If it is for his fiction that Coetzee is best known (quite apart from his winning of the Nobel Prize for Literature in 2003 and the Booker Prize twice), there are several cues in Coetzee's own essays and interviews that seem to cede higher ground to creative, rather than critical, practices of writing. In a much-cited passage from *Doubling the Point*, Coetzee (responding to a question posed by David Attwell) has this to say about the differences between writing fiction and criticism:

> Stories are defined by their irresponsibility: they are, in the judgment of Swift's Houynhnhms, "that which is not." The *feel* of writing fiction is one of freedom, of irresponsibility, or better, of responsibility toward something that has not yet emerged, that lies somewhere at the end of the road. When I write criticism, on the other hand, I am always aware of a responsibility toward a goal that has been set for me not only by the argument, not only by the whole philosophical tradition into which I am implicitly inserting myself, but also by the rather tight discourse of criticism itself. (*DP*, 246)

Fiction offers the writer freedom from the logical constraints of philosophical argument, and Coetzee affirms, "I feel a greater freedom to follow where my thinking takes me when I am writing fiction than when I am writing criticism"; even more specifically, it is a place where Coetzee feels he does "my liberating, my playing with possibilities" — compared with the philosopher who is "unduly handicapped" by the teleological process of academic discourse (*DP*, 246).

And yet the phrase "playing with possibilities" should give us pause, not least within the context of appreciating Coetzee's experience as a mathematician and computer programmer, and his own preoccupation with linguistics as an active part of his practice as a writer of fiction. This is already evident in the thesis on Beckett, which (we learn from the abstract) "treat[s] style as linguistic choice within the economy of the work of art as a formal whole." In his critical essays and interviews, Coetzee stresses the *continuity* between his interest in linguistics and his "activities as a writer": in an interview with Jean Sévry in 1985, for example, Coetzee says, "in many ways I am more interested in the linguistic than the literary side of my academic profession." He adds, "I think there is evidence of an interest in problems of language throughout my novels. I don't see any disruption between my professional interest in language and my activities as a writer."[5]

In his opening address at the Linguistics at the Millennium conference held at the University of Cape Town in January 2000, Coetzee acknowledges his debt to the linguistic sciences: "although I cannot any longer call myself an active linguist, my own approach to language has been shaped more deeply than I know by immersion in ways of thinking encouraged by linguistic science."[6] It is at this juncture that one begins to feel uneasy about making hasty and clear-cut distinctions between writers of fiction and writers in other disciplines; on a linguistic level, novelists are no more free than their fellow-writers of nonfiction.

In a discussion of Kafka, Coetzee speaks of "the kind of writing-in-the-tracks one does in criticism" (*DP*, 199). Again, a distinction is being drawn between fiction and criticism, where the work of the critic at first glance seems to come off second best. But close attention to the passage shows that Coetzee is drawing another distinction, too — between reading and writing — and the activity of critical writing is highly valued *as part of* a creative exercise. Hasty assumptions about the derivative nature of criticism are thus qualified in an important way. Here is the passage from *Doubling the Point*:

> I work on a writer like Kafka because he opens for me, or opens me to, moments of analytic intensity. And such moments are, in their lesser way, also a matter of grace, inspiration. Is this a comment about reading, about the intensities of the reading process? Not really. Rather, it is a comment about writing, the kind of writing-in-the-tracks one does in criticism. For my experience is that it is not reading that takes me into the last twist of the burrow, but writing. (*DP*, 199)

I am continuously reminded of this passage when I read Coetzee writing about Beckett in his doctoral dissertation, or about Lacan and Foucault in his essays on censorship, or about Barthes and Rousseau in his inaugural professorial address, or about nineteenth-century English travel writers in *White Writing* and *Youth*. The implicit message is that Beckett, Lacan, Barthes, Rousseau, and Burchell are all writers themselves, and it is in their capacity *as writers*, with Coetzee writing in their tracks, that his own creativity is sparked.

To think of Coetzee exclusively as a novelist would be to disregard his active participation in contemporary literary-critical debates, where he often engages explicitly with the work of other writers. In several of his essays and interviews, Coetzee casts himself primarily as a *writer*, the novel happens to be one genre in which he writes, and the creative act of making linguistic decisions applies as much to the critic or the philosopher as it does to the novelist. Thus: "As you write — *I am speaking about any kind of writing* — you have a sense of whether you are getting closer to 'it' or not. You have a sensing mechanism, a feedback loop of some kind; without that mechanism you could not write" (*DP*, 18; my emphasis). And, in a little aside from a BBC interview that Patrick Hayes has chosen as the epigraph of the introduction to his book on Coetzee, the author is quoted as saying, "For a novelist [*pause*]; for a writer working in the medium of the novel . . ."[7]

Yet if fiction is sometimes associated with a freedom from logical argument, there is a further important context in which writing (in the broad but special sense that Coetzee accords to the term) can never be "free": "Writing is not free expression," says Coetzee,

> there is a true sense in which writing is dialogic: a matter of awakening the countervoices in oneself and embarking upon speech with them. It is some measure of a writer's seriousness whether he does evoke/invoke those countervoices in himself, that is, step down from the position of what Lacan calls "the subject supposed to know." (*DP*, 65)

In its juxtaposition of Bakhtinian dialogism, and a Lacanian insight regarding the relation of author to text, this passage strikes me as an important one in Coetzee's literary criticism; I shall be returning to this passage several times in the discussions to follow. The use of the word "seriousness" is pivotal in the passage. In an essay in *Giving Offense*, Coetzee writes that "seriousness is, for a certain kind of artist, an imperative uniting the aesthetic and the ethical" (*GO*, 73), and in other essays where he speaks specifically about ethics, Coetzee foregrounds the notion of a responsiveness to other writers, in ways that challenge the certainties of the "I" (that is to say, the posited author of the utterance) as grounding his understanding of ethics. Thus, in the interview with Attwell on the occasion of winning the Nobel Prize, Coetzee has this to offer:

> I would say that what you call "the literary life," or any other way of life that provides means for interrogation of our existence — in the case of the writer of fantasy, symbolization, storytelling — seems to me a good life — good in the sense of being ethically responsible.[8]

And in the essay "Homage," Coetzee writes, "in the process of responding to the writers one intuitively chooses to respond to, one makes oneself into the person whom in the most intractable but also perhaps the most deeply ethical sense one wants to be."[9] If this deep-level engagement with the work of other writers is what Coetzee appreciates as "ethical" — and if one wants to gain a better sense of how a notion of ethics plays out across his work — then it seems to me imperative to pay close attention to Coetzee's responses to other writers. Not only in his book reviews, but in several other texts, Coetzee engages rigorously with theorists and philosophers, gaining much from, but at the same time extending or adapting to a specific context what Barthes, Benveniste, Shklovsky, or Soshana Felman (for example) might have to offer. Coetzee's responsiveness to the work of other novelists is surely appreciated (Beckett, Dostoevsky, Kafka, and Nabokov spring immediately to mind, although Coetzee has written with great insight about countless others), but an extended consideration of Coetzee's active engagement with the work of literary critics, theorists, and philosophers makes for a very different kind of discussion from the more usual literary-critical approach of providing a theoretical or philosophical lense as a way of highlighting thematic concerns in the fiction. What an attentiveness to Coetzee's encounters with theoretical and philosophical texts opens up is the realization that the writer is not simply staging as a set of thematic concerns in his fiction concepts and ideas that have already found expression and resolution in scholarly discourses; instead, Coetzee can be understood to be an active contributor to contemporary literary-theoretical debates.[10] The extent of this contribution leaves much scope for future discussions. In the paragraphs to follow, I pick out just one strand of conversation that runs through a few of the essays, highlighting what I take to be a unique and distinctive pattern that emerges in Coetzee's criticism. I start out by referring again to Bakhtin's notion of dialogism that underwrites the "countervoices" passage just cited. "Imagine a dialogue of two persons," writes Bakhtin,

> in which the statements of the second speaker are omitted, but in such a way that the general sense is not at all violated. The second speaker is present invisibly, his words are not there, but deep traces left by these words have a determining influence on all the present and visible words of the first speaker. We sense that this is a conversation, although only one person is speaking, and it is a conversation of the most intense kind, for each present, uttered word responds and reacts with its every fibre to the invisible speaker, points to something outside itself, beyond its own limits, to the unspoken words of another person.[11]

Coetzee writes about Bakhtin at several important junctures in his own critical writing — in the essay, "Confession and Double Thoughts: Tolstoy, Rousseau, Dostoevsky" (an essay Coetzee would later identify as pivotal in his career in its turn to a more philosophical engagement with his situation in the world); in the essay on Breyten Breytenbach in *Giving Offense*; and in a review of Joseph Frank's five-volume biography of Dostoevsky (in *Stranger Shores*). In the *Stranger Shores* essay, Coetzee engages with Bakhtin's concept of dialogism: in the world of the dialogic novel there is no overriding authorial voice, and hence no central claim to truth since each word is inflected by the potential countervoice of its addressee. But Bakhtin's analysis, useful as it is in formal and structural terms for Coetzee, is lacking in other respects. "What is missing in Bakhtin," says Coetzee, is the failure to recognize that "dialogism as exemplified in the novels of Dostoevsky is not a matter of ideological positioning, still less of novelistic technique" (*SS*, 123). For Coetzee, what matters is a sense of ethical affect in relation to authorial voice: "Dostoevskian dialogism grows out of Dostoevsky's own moral character, out of his ideals, and out of his being as a writer" (*SS*, 145–46). If the emphasis in Bakhtin is on linguistic and novelistic strategies, it is Coetzee who reintroduces a question of authorial consciousness in terms that raise "dialogism" to a question of ethics — "his own moral character," "his ideals" — and in terms that demand a consideration of the relation of the writer to his writing. In the phrase, "his being as a writer," we are led back to the Nobel Prize interview and to the realization that the raising of voice *and* countervoice in one's written word is one way of providing "means for interrogation of our existence," for questioning the authority of the one who writes.

This is the distinctive and unique pattern emerging in Coetzee's criticism that I mentioned earlier: Coetzee's own interest in the linguistic sciences and his engagement with other literary theorists enables us to appreciate how material linguistic criteria ground, as much as they are exceeded by, ethical interpretations of literary works. In several of his essays, Coetzee makes it possible for us to think about the tenuous *link* between the linguistic choices the writer is bound to make on the one hand, and the aesthetic and ethical effects the work may have on the other. In the "countervoices" passage and in other essays, Bakhtin's conception of dialogism is activated by Coetzee in ways that lead to questions of the authority and ethical commitments on the part of the writer through the words that he chooses to write. In other essays a similar pattern emerges. For example, in the essay, "Achterberg's 'Ballade van de Gasfitter': the Mystery of I and You" (reprinted in *Doubling the Point*),[12] Coetzee discusses the difficulty of translating the Dutch poet's sonnet sequence, and focuses on the relation between "I" and "you" in the poem. He begins by considering the grammar of pronouns, referring to linguists Roman Jakobson on deictics and shifters, and Emile Benveniste on subjectivity in language. But what starts out as a rather technical discussion about the grammar of pronouns very quickly becomes, in Coetzee's essay, a consideration of what he terms (in an interview about Kafka) "the deep semantics of person, as carried by the pronoun" (*DP*, 197). In juxtaposing the linguistic insights of Jakobson and Benveniste with the ethical philosophy of Martin Buber's *I and Thou*, Coetzee invites us to think about the ethics of address as it is enabled and limited by linguistic subject positions: differently put, what "field of tension" (IW, 122), what gestures of dominating or ceding ground are set in the taking up of the linguistic positions "I" and "you"?

Again, I think it is important to realize that a careful reading of any of Coetzee's critical essays summons up a wealth of conversation with other writers, and I would add, a conversation across Coetzee's own essays too. Here is a taste of this in relation to the Achterberg essay: In *Inner Workings*, Coetzee writes on Paul Celan, who in turn had conversations with Martin Buber (IW, 121). In his poetry, Celan explores the relation between "I" and "you," and in his speeches and essays, he speaks explicitly about the ethics and aesthetics of literary address. Derrida, Blanchot, Levinas, and Lacoue-Labarthe have written essays on Paul Celan, and in *Inner Workings* Coetzee engages specifically with Lacoue-Labarthe's *The Poetry of Experience*, which in its turn refers to the works by Derrida, Blanchot, and Levinas. Levinas was deeply influenced by the thinking of Martin Buber, whose work is pivotally placed alongside the linguists Jakobson and Benveniste in the Achterberg essay to pitch the discussion from a consideration of the *grammar* of address to an *ethics* of address. What we experience across Coetzee's critical essays, then, is a rich *conversation* about pronouns, rather than a monologic thesis on the topic written by one person.

Not least amongst situations of address is the I-you relation instantiated between writer and reader. Bakhtin is helpful on this: "Every literary discourse more or less sharply senses its own listener, reader, critic, and reflects in itself their anticipated objections, evaluations, points of view. In addition, literary discourse senses alongside itself another literary discourse, another style" (PDP, 196).

Again, though, for Bakhtin "style" may be reducible to a literary feature; for Coetzee it is much more than this, inseparable from one's "being as a writer": "a style, an attitude to the world, as it soaks in, becomes part of a personality, part of the self, indistinguishable from the self" (H, 7). It is in this very context that Coetzee writes about responding to other writers as a way of making "oneself into the person whom in the most intractable but also perhaps the most deeply ethical sense one wants to be" (H, 7). Earlier, I spoke about Coetzee's referring to a way of life that provides the means of interrogating our existence as one that is ethically responsible (EI, 3). If writing is part of Coetzee's way of life, and if the act of writing necessarily instantiates you and I along the linguistic tracks of a certain style, then an exploration of what Coetzee terms "the mystery of I and you" in the Achterberg essay is an exploration, at a fundamental level, of an ethical relation.

Again in an interview with David Attwell — the interview after winning the Nobel Prize in 2003 — Coetzee responds to a question about

Elizabeth Costello: "I tend to resist invitations to interpret my own fiction. If there were a better, clearer, shorter way of saying what the fiction says, then why not scrap the fiction?" (EI, 3).

Taken out of its context of thinking about the relation between criticism and fiction that spans several decades, Coetzee's comment here could lead one to think that fiction has the higher claim. But with reference to Coetzee's essays and interviews, I am inclined, first, to respond this way: if there were simply a better, more entertaining, and freer way to say in the fiction what the critical essays say, why not scrap the essays? Secondly (with thoughts of the "countervoices" passage cited earlier), it is important to note that in his response to Attwell, Coetzee is stepping down from his monologic position of "subject supposed to know" with regard to his own writing. The countervoices for Coetzee are *in oneself*: the "embarking upon speech with them" is not a simple dialogue between two autonomous people. Instead, each word becomes a site of internal dialogic interaction for the writer — an "internal polemic," in Bakhtinian terms. Coetzee's allusive juxtaposition of Bakhtin and Lacan through the notion of countervoices provides the means for interrogating the supposed monologic authority of the writing self, and it is this misplaced demand for a monologic and summary answer in the interview, rather than the practice of literary criticism itself, that Coetzee resists.

The context of the "countervoices" passage is a conversation with David Attwell about the straitjacketing violence of interviews. The serious writer tries to raise countervoices, but "interviewers want speech, a flow of speech. That speech they record, take away, edit, censor, cutting away all its waywardness, till what is left conforms to a monologic ideal" (*DP*, 65).

The interviewer assumes that the writer is the one supposed to know what his writing means — and destroys its seriousness (in Coetzee's sense of the term) by asking for the potted version. This is the risk of a certain kind of criticism, too. But now I return to the paper with which I started out, "Die Skrywer en die Teorie," where Coetzee offers a subtle argument. It is problematic to assume in advance that criticism is always secondary to literature, and in his paper Coetzee summarizes two of these assumptions. The first is the metaphor of critical theory as a parasite on the literary text,[13] and further,

> dat letterkundige werke in mindere of meerdere mate kritiese ontleding weerstaan, dat die grootste werke die taaiste weerstand bied, en dat dié in 'n werk wat ontleding totaal weerstaan die kern van die werk uitmaak. (ST, 155)

> [that literary works resist analysis to a greater or lesser extent, that the greatest works offer the toughest resistance, and that *that* within a work which absolutely resists analysis, constitutes its kernel.]

The second assumption that Coetzee challenges is the idea that any literary work written with conscious theoretical principles in mind will be stillborn, since literature, by its very nature, avoids or escapes theory (ST, 155). Both these assumptions encourage antitheoretical judgments, and make it easy for the critic to resort to mystification: it presents criticism as being in its essence a derivative and uncreative industry. In *Doubling the Point*, Coetzee revisits this: "If I were a truly creative critic," he says, "I would work toward liberating that discourse — making it less monological, for instance." Coetzee goes on to add, "But the candid truth is that I don't have enough of an investment in criticism to try" (*DP*, 246).[14] Nevertheless, what I have been suggesting throughout my discussion is that Coetzee's critical essays are far from monologic, and perhaps best read as a palimpsestic writing-in-response to other writers. It is worth taking the trouble to track references and allusions in the essays, which then cast Coetzee's own discourses as texts "full of other people's words" (PDP, 195).

Yet there is a further sense in which I think Coetzee surely has liberated the discourse of criticism, made it less monologic. On the way to asking a few difficult questions in the closing paragraphs of this chapter, my first stop is at Coetzee's thesis on Beckett: "The author-narrator cannot of course be identified with the historical Beckett," writes Coetzee,

> But how sharply is it possible to draw a line between this author's sentences and those of his characters? Does each sentence in the text fall into one of these two classes, or are there also sentences of indeterminate origin or sentences which belong in both classes? In other words, can narrative point of view be treated as a small-scale matter, a matter of sentences? (SA, 61)

The same question could be asked of the characters in Coetzee's fiction, where it is also sometimes difficult to decide to whom a given sentence belongs. Here is JC in *Diary of a Bad Year* thinking about Dostoevsky's realization of his character's voice: "Far more powerful than the substance of his argument, which is not strong, are the accents of anguish, the personal anguish of a soul unable to bear the horrors of this world. It is the voice of Ivan, as realized by Dostoevsky, not his reasoning, that sweeps me along" (*BY*, 225).

Here is David Lurie in *Disgrace*, after spending an afternoon easing the deaths of neglected dogs in the animal clinic:

> he actually has to stop at the roadside to recover himself. Tears flow down his face that he cannot stop; his hands shake.
>
> He does not understand what is happening to him. . . .
>
> His whole being is gripped by what happens in the theatre. (*DG*, 143)

Here is the Coetzee of *Doubling the Point*:

(Let me add, *entirely* parenthetically, that I, as a person, as a personality, am overwhelmed, that my thinking is thrown into confusion and helplessness, by the fact of human suffering in the world, and not only human suffering. These fictional constructions of mine are paltry, ludicrous defenses against that being-overwhelmed, and, to me, transparently so.) (*DP*, 248)

And here is the Elizabeth Costello of *The Lives of Animals*: "And that, you see, is my dilemma this afternoon," she says,

Both reason and seven decades of life experience tell me that reason is neither the being of the universe nor the being of God. On the contrary, reason looks to me suspiciously like the being of human thought; worse than that, like the being of one tendency in human thought. Reason is the being of a certain spectrum of human thinking. And if this is so, if that is what I believe, then why should I bow to reason this afternoon and content myself with embroidering on the discourse of the old philosophers? (*LA*, 23)

This is not the place to speak about Coetzee's contribution to debates about reason and language, but I have juxtaposed these passages to broach a related question that extends beyond asking who the speaker is. In all these excerpts, the "accents of anguish" exceed what could be contained in a monologic authorial consciousness, or in the teleological development of a philosophical argument.

When Coetzee was invited to give the 1997–98 Tanner Lectures on Human Values at Princeton University, the expectation was surely that he would present a series of philosophical essays, but instead, under the title *The Lives of Animals*, he read the fictional stories about Elizabeth Costello and her being-overwhelmed by the suffering humans inflict on other animals. If the "discourse of the old philosophers" is inadequate to the task Costello has set for herself, Coetzee's radical decision to present fictions *as* the Tanner Lectures on Human Values, even before the thematic concerns of the work become apparent, raises questions about the presumption of philosophical reasoning as prior in the best of "human thinking." And this leads me to the question: Is it clearly the case that *The Lives of Animals* — and I would add, *Elizabeth Costello*, *Diary of a Bad Year* (and perhaps the three autobiographical novels, too, although this is surely a topic for another essay) — can best be considered as *fiction*? Would it not be more interesting to consider *The Lives of Animals* and other works as instances of Coetzee's rising to the challenge of being "a truly creative critic," of working toward "liberating that discourse — making it less monological" (*DP*, 246)? To consider these texts as dialogical and creative acts of criticism, rather than as fictions raising philosophical questions, is to consider Coetzee's oeuvre in an entirely different light; one could pay keener attention to developments in Coetzee's criticism (for example, reading the Jerusalem Prize Acceptance Speech[15] alongside the Nobel Prize Lecture), and to the *style* — with all that word's semantic freight — of the critical works up for discussion. Such a reading would begin to respond to an appeal Coetzee makes in "Die Skrywer en die Teorie": he envisages a scene in which "letterkundige teks en kritiese teks parallel en mede-afhanklik sou bestaan, saam met ander tekste van die letterkunde, die filosofie ens" (ST, 158; literary and critical texts would have a parallel and mutually dependent existence, alongside other texts in literature and philosophy, etc.). Perhaps it is worthwhile to ask, in as specific a way as possible, and perhaps with some skepticism: what is to be gained by drawing too sharp a line between authorial voice and character, between criticism and fiction, between the philosophers and the poets? These questions, it seems to me, are never very far from the surface of Coetzee's own writing. If, for the Roland Barthes of *Roland Barthes by Roland Barthes*, "Tout ceci doit être considéré comme dit par un personnage de roman" (All this must be considered as if spoken by a character in a novel — or rather by several characters),[16] it may be instructive to say of Coetzee's *writing*, "All this must be considered as if spoken by a truly creative critic."

Notes

[1] "Die Skrywer en die Teorie," *SAVAL Conference Proceedings* (Bloemfontein, 1980), 155–61; here, 60. Subsequent references appear as ST with the accompanying page number.

[2] J. M. Coetzee, "The Works of Ford Madox Ford with Particular Reference to the Novels" (Master's thesis, U of Cape Town, 1963). Subsequent references appear as FMF with the accompanying page number.

[3] J. M. Coetzee, "The English Fiction of Samuel Beckett: An Essay in Stylistic Analysis" (PhD diss., U of Texas at Austin, 1969). Subsequent references appear as SA with the accompanying page number.

[4] "The Novel Today" is an essay that is frequently cited in Coetzee scholarship, but not reprinted in any of the five collections of Coetzee's published essays. "The Novel Today," *Upstream* 6, no. 1 (1988): 2–5.

[5] Jean Sévry, "An Interview with J. M. Coetzee," *Commonwealth* 9 (Autumn 1986): 1–7; here, 1.

[6] "Linguistics at the Millennium," opening address at the conference held at the University of Cape Town, January 2000 (Photocopy UCT African Studies Library).

[7] Interview with Paul Bailey, *Third Ear*, BBC Radio 3, 18 December 1990, cited in Patrick Hayes, *J. M. Coetzee and the Novel: Writing and Politics after Beckett* (Oxford: Oxford UP, 2010), 1.

[8] David Attwell, "An Exclusive Interview with J. M. Coetzee," *Dagens Nyheter*, 8 December 2003, 1–4; here, 3; www.dn.se/kultur-noje/an-exclusive-interview-with-j-m-coetzee-1.227254 (accessed 31 March 2008). Subsequent references appear as EI with the accompanying page number.

[9] J. M. Coetzee, "Homage," *Threepenny Review* 53 (Spring 1993): 5–7; here, 7. Subsequent references appear as H with the accompanying page number.

[10] This is a leading argument in my book, *J. M. Coetzee: Countervoices* (Houndmills: Palgrave, 2009). The present essay draws on discussions that find fuller expression in my book.

[11] Bakhtin, *Problems of Dostoevsky's Poetics* ed. and trans. Caryl Emerson (Minneapolis: U of Minnesota P, 1984), 197. Subsequent references appear as PDP with the accompanying page number. Coetzee cites part of this passage within the context of a discussion about Breyten Breytenbach's prison writings and South African censorship (*GO*, 223–37).

[12] I have spoken in some detail about this essay in the chapter, "You," in *J. M. Coetzee: Countervoices.*

[13] Hillis Miller's groundbreaking "The Critic as Host" was first presented at the MLA conference in December 1976, in response to M. H. Abrams' paper, "The Deconstructive Angel." It seems to me helpful to think of Coetzee's "Die Skrywer en die Teorie" within the context of this debate.

[14] In the concluding, retrospective interview in *Doubling the Point*, Coetzee refers to his essay on Tolstoy, Rousseau, and Dostoevsky; in retrospect, Coetzee says, he perceives "a submerged dialogue between two persons. One is a person I desired to be and was feeling my way toward. The other is more shadowy: let us call him the person I then was, though he may be the person I still am" (*DP*, 392).

[15] Reprinted in *DP*, 96–99.

[16] *Roland Barthes by Roland Barthes*, trans. Richard Howard (New York: Hill and Wang). The quotation in French serves as the epigraph, and the English passage is from the section titled "*Le Livre du Moi* ~ The Book of the Self," 119.

Works Cited

Ackerley, C. J. *Obscure Locks, Simple Keys: The Annotated "Watt."* London: Faber and Faber, 2006.

Ackerley, C. J., and S. E. Gontarski. *The Grove Companion to Samuel Beckett: A Reader's Guide to His Works, Life, and Thought.* New York: Grove Press, 2004.

Adorno, Theodor. *Aesthetic Theory.* Translated by C. Lenhardt. Edited by Gretel Adorno and Rolf Tiedemann. London: Routledge, 1984.

———. "Commitment." In *Aesthetics and Politics,* translated by Francis McDonagh, edited by Ronald Taylor, 177–95. London: NLB, 1977.

———. *Minima Moralia: Reflections from Damaged Life.* Translated by E. F. N. Jephcott. London: Verso, 1978.

Anker, Elizabeth S. "Human Rights, Social Justice, and J. M. Coetzee's *Disgrace.*" *Modern Fiction Studies* 54, no. 2 (Winter 2008): 233–67.

Attridge, Derek. "Against Allegory: *Waiting for the Barbarians, Life & Times of Michael K,* and the Question of Literary Reading." In Poyner, *J. M. Coetzee and the Idea of the Public Intellectual,* 63–82.

———. Introduction to *Inner Workings: Literary Essays 2000–2005,* by J. M. Coetzee, ix–xiv. New York: Viking, 2007.

———. "J. M. Coetzee's *Disgrace*: Introduction." *Interventions* 4, no. 3 (2002): 315–20.

———, ed. *J. M. Coetzee and the Ethics of Reading: Literature in the Event.* Chicago: U of Chicago P, 2004.

———, ed. *Jacques Derrida: Acts of Literature.* London: Routledge, 1992.

———. "Oppressive Silence: J. M. Coetzee's *Foe* and the Politics of Canonisation." In Huggan and Watson, 168–90.

———. "Sex, Comedy and Influence: Coetzee's Beckett." In Boehmer, Iddiols, and Eaglestone, 71–90.

———. "Trusting the Other: Ethics and Politics in J. M. Coetzee's *Age of Iron.*" *The Writings of J. M. Coetzee,* edited by Michael Valdez Moses. Special issue of *South Atlantic Quarterly* 93, no. 1 (1994): 59–82.

Attridge, Derek, and Rosemary Jolly, eds. *Writing South Africa: Literature, Apartheid, and Democracy, 1970–1995.* Cambridge: Cambridge UP, 1998.

Attwell, David. "Coetzee's Estrangements." *Novel* 41, no. 2 (Spring/Summer 2008): 229–43.

———. "'Dialogue' and 'Fulfilment' in J. M. Coetzee's *Age of Iron.*" In Attridge and Jolly, 149–65.

———. "An Exclusive Interview with J. M. Coetzee." *Dagens Nyheter*, 8 December 2003. Available at: www.dn.se/kultur-noje/an-exclusive-interview-with-j-m-coetzee-1.227254. Accessed 31 March 2008.

———. *J. M. Coetzee: South Africa and the Politics of Writing*. Berkeley: U of California P and Cape Town: David Philip, 1993.

———. "The Life and Times of Elizabeth Costello: J. M. Coetzee and the Public Sphere." In Poyner, *J. M. Coetzee and the Idea of the Public Intellectual*, 25–41.

———. "The Problem of History in the Fiction of J. M. Coetzee." *Poetics Today* 11, no. 3 (1990): 579–615. Republished in *Rendering Things Visible: Essays on South African Literary Culture*, edited by Martin Trump, 94–133. Athens: Ohio UP, 1990.

———. "Race in Disgrace." *Interventions* 4, no. 3 (2002): 331–41.

Bailey, Paul. *Third Ear*, BBC Radio 3, 18 December 1990. Cited in Patrick Hayes, *J. M. Coetzee and the Novel: Writing and Politics after Beckett*.

Baker, Geoffrey. "The Limits of Sympathy: J. M. Coetzee's Evolving Ethics of Engagement." *Ariel* 36, nos. 1–2 (2005): 27–49.

Bakhtin, M. M. *The Dialogic Imagination: Four Essays*. Translated by Caryl Emerson and Michael Holquist. Austin: U of Texas P, 1981.

———. *Problems of Dostoevsky's Poetics*. Ed. and trans. Caryl Emerson. Minneapolis: U of Minnesota P, 1984.

Baldick, Chris. *The Oxford English Literary History, v*ol. 10, *1910–1940: The Modern Movement*. Oxford: Oxford UP, 2004.

Baral, Kailash, ed. *J. M. Coetzee: Critical Perspectives*. New Delhi: Pencraft International, 2008.

Barnard, Rita. *Apartheid and Beyond: South African Writers and the Politics of Place*. Oxford: Oxford UP, 2007.

———. "Coetzee's Country Ways." *Interventions* 4, no. 3 (2002): 384–94.

———. "J. M. Coetzee's *Disgrace* and the South African Pastoral." *Contemporary Literature* 44, no. 2 (2003): 199–224.

Bataille, Georges. "The Notion of Expenditure." Translated by Allan Stoekl, with Carl R. Lovitt and Donald M. Leslie Jr. In *Visions of Excess: Selected Writings, 1927–1939*, edited by Allan Stoekl, 116–29. Minneapolis: U of Minnesota P, 1985.

Beard, Margot. "Lessons from the Dead Masters: Wordsworth and Byron in J. M. Coetzee's *Disgrace*." *English in Africa* 34, no. 1 (2007): 59–77.

Beckett, Samuel. *Company*. London: John Calder, 1980.

———. *Lessness*. 1969, rpt. in *Samuel Beckett: The Complete Short Prose, 1929–1989*, edited by S. E. Gontarski. New York: Grove Press, 1995.

———. *Molloy*. 1955; rpt. in *Three Novels by Samuel Beckett: Molloy: Malone Dies: The Unnamable*. New York: Grove Press, 1959.

———. *Murphy*. 1938; rpt. New York: Grove Press, 1957.

———. *Waiting for Godot*. New York: Grove Press, 1954.

———. *Watt*. Paris: Olympia Press, 1953.

———. *Watt*. Edited by C. J. Ackerley. 1953; rpt. London: Faber and Faber, 2009.

———. *Watt*. In *Novels* (Grove Centenary Edition). Vol. 1. New York: Grove Press, 2006.

Begam, Richard. "The Pitfalls of a Postcolonial Poetics: J. M. Coetzee's *Foe* and the New Literatures in English." *Symbolism: An International Annual of Critical Aesthetics* 7 (2007): 299–315.

———. "Silence and Mut(e)ilation: White Writing in J. M. Coetzee's *Foe*." *South Atlantic Quarterly* 93, no. 1 (1994): 111–29.

Bell, David. "Goethe's Orientalism." In *Goethe and the English Speaking World*, edited by Nicholas Boyle and John Guthrie, 199–212. Rochester, NY: Camden House, 2002.

Benjamin, Walter. *Selected Writings*, vol. 2, *1927–1934*. Edited by Michael W. Jennings, Howard Eiland, and Gary Smith. Translated by Rodney Livingstone. Cambridge, MA: The Belknap Press, Harvard UP, 1990.

Berger, John. "The Hour of Poetry." In *Selected Essays: John Berger*, edited by Geoff Dyer, 445–52. New York: Vintage, 2001.

Bhabha, Homi. *The Location of Culture*. New York: Routledge, 1994.

Bishop, G. Scott. "J. M. Coetzee's *Foe*: A Culmination and a Solution to a Problem of White Identity." *World Literature Today* 64, no. 1 (1990): 54–57.

Blanchot, Maurice. "Orpheus' Gaze." Translated by Sacha Rabinovitch. In *The Sirens' Song: Selected Essays*, edited by Gabriel Josipovici. Brighton: Harvester Press, 1982.

Boehmer, Elleke. "Not Saying Sorry, Not Speaking Pain: Gender Implications in *Disgrace*." *Interventions* 4, no. 3 (2002): 342–51.

———. "Sorry, Sorrier, Sorriest: The Gendering of Contrition in J. M. Coetzee's *Disgrace*." In Poyner, *J. M. Coetzee and the Idea of the Public Intellectual*, 135–47.

Boehmer, Elleke, Katy Iddiols, and Robert Eaglestone, eds. *J. M. Coetzee in Context and Theory*. London: Continuum, 2009.

Bongie, Chris. "'Lost in the Maze of Doubting': J. M. Coetzee's *Foe* and the Politics of (Un)Likeness." *MFS: Modern Fiction Studies* 39, no. 2 (1993): 261–81.

Brooker, Peter. "Afterword: 'Newness' in Modernisms, Early and Late." In *The Oxford Handbook of Modernisms*, edited by Peter Brooker, Andrzej Gasiorek, Deborah Longworth, and Andrew Thacker, 1012–36. New York: Oxford UP, 2010.

Burnett, Paula. "The Ulyssean Crusoe and the Quest for Redemption in J. M. Coetzee's *Foe* and Derek Walcott's *Omeros*." In *Robinson Crusoe: Myths and Metamorphoses*, edited by Lieve Spaas and Brian Stimpson, 239–55. New York: St. Martin's, 1996.

Castillo, Debra. "Coetzee's *Dusklands*: The Mythic *Punctum*." *PMLA* 105, no. 5 (October 1990): 1108–22.

Clarkson, Carrol. *J. M. Coetzee: Countervoices*. Basingstoke: Palgrave Macmillan, 2009.

Coetzee, J. M. *Age of Iron*. 1990. Harmondsworth: Penguin, 1991.

———. *Boyhood: Scenes from Provincial Life*. London: Secker & Warburg, 1997.

———. *Diary of a Bad Year*. London: Harvell Secker, 2007.

———. "Die Skrywer en die Teorie," *SAVAL Conference Proceedings* (Bloemfontein, 1980), 155–61.

———. *Disgrace*. London: Secker & Warburg, 1999.

———. *Doubling the Point: Essays and Interviews*. Cambridge, MA: Harvard UP, 1992.

———. *Dusklands*. London: Vintage, 1974.

———. "Eight Ways of Looking at Samuel Beckett." In *Borderless Beckett / Beckett sans frontières: Tokyo 2006* [*Samuel Beckett Today / Aujourd'hui* 19], edited by Minako Okamuro, Naoya Mori, Bruno Clément, Sjef Houppermans, Angela Moorjani, and Anthony Uhlmann, 19–31. Amsterdam: Rodopi, 2008.

———. *Elizabeth Costello*. London: Secker & Warburg, 2003.

———. "The English Fiction of Samuel Beckett: An Essay in Stylistic Analysis." PhD dissertation, University of Texas at Austin, 1969 (unpublished; copy at the Beckett International Foundation, University of Reading).

———. "Fictions of the Truth." *The Age*, 13 May 2000, 12.

———. *Foe*. Harmondsworth: Penguin, 1987.

———. *Giving Offense: Essays on Censorship*. Chicago & London: U of Chicago P, 1996.

———. *He and His Man*. Nobel Lecture, 2003. New York: Penguin, 2004.

———. "He and His Man." The Nobel Prize Website, http://nobelprize. org/nobel_prizes/literature/laureates/2003/coetzee-lecture-e.html.

———. "Homage." *Threepenny Review* 53 (Spring 1993): 5–7.

———. *In the Heart of the Country*. Johannesburg: Ravan Press, 1977.

———. *Inner Workings: Literary Essays 2000–2005*. New York: Viking, 2007.

———. "An Interview with J. M. Coetzee." *World Literature Today* 70, no. 1 (1996): 107–10.

———. Introduction. In *Samuel Beckett: The Grove Centenary Edition*. Vol. 4, *Poems, Short Fiction, Criticism*, edited by Paul Auster, ix–xiv. New York: Grove Press, 2006.

———. *Life & Times of Michael K*. London: Random House, 1983.

———. "Linguistics at the Millennium." Opening address at the conference held at the University of Cape Town, January 2000 (photocopy UCT African Studies Library).

———. *The Lives of Animals*. Edited by Amy Gutmann. Princeton: Princeton UP, 1999.

———. "The Making of Samuel Beckett." *New York Review of Books* 56, no. 7 (30 April 2009). Available at: www.nybooks.com/articles/22612. Accessed 30 June 2011.

———. "The Manuscript Revisions of Beckett's *Watt*." *Journal of Modern Literature* 2 (1972): 472–80. Rpt. in abbreviated form in Attwell, *Doubling the Point*, 39–42.

————. *The Master of Petersburg*. Secker & Warburg, 1994. London: Vintage, 1999.

————. "Nobel Prize Lecture: He and His Man" (video). The Nobel Prize Website. http://nobelprize.org/mediaplayer/index.php?id=555. Accessed 28 February 2010.

————. "The Novel Today." *Upstream* 6, no. 1 (1988): 2–5.

————. "Remembering Texas (1984)." In *DP*, 50–54.

————. "Samuel Beckett in Cape Town: An Imaginary History." In *Beckett Remembering / Remembering Beckett*, edited by James and Elizabeth Knowlson, 74–77. London: Bloomsbury, 2006.

————. "Samuel Beckett's *Lessness*: An Exercise in Decomposition." *Computers and the Humanities* 7, no. 4 (1973): 195–98.

————. Seminar Notes from University of Cape Town, Master's in Literary Studies. 1993. NELM 2002.13.2.3.4 (Coetzee Collection). National English Literary Museum, Grahamstown, South Africa.

————. *Stranger Shores: Essays 1986–1999*. London: Random House, 2002.

————. "Truth in Autobiography." Unpublished inaugural lecture. Cape Town: University of Cape Town, 1984.

————. "Vorwort." In *Was ist ein Klassiker? Essays*. Translated by Reinhild Böhnke. Frankfurt am Main: S. Fischer, 2006.

————. *Waiting for the Barbarians*. Johannesburg: Ravan Press, 1981.

————. *White Writing: On the Culture of Letters in South Africa*. New Haven, CT: Yale UP, 1988.

————. "A Word from J. M. Coetzee." Opening address of exhibition, entitled Voiceless: I Feel therefore I Am, by Voiceless: The Animal Protection Institute, 22 February 2007, Sherman Galleries, Sydney, Australia, 26 April 2010. Available at: www.voiceless.org.au/About_Us/Misc/A_word_from_J.M._Coetzee_-_Voiceless_I_feel_therefore_I_am.html. Accessed 30 June 2011.

————. "The Works of Ford Madox Ford with Particular Reference to the Novels." MA thesis, University of Cape Town, 1963.

————. *Youth*. London: Secker & Warburg, 2002.

Connor, Steven. "Rewriting Wrong: On the Ethics of Literary Reversion." In *Liminal Postmodernisms: The Postmodern, the (Post-)colonial, and the (Post-)Feminist*, edited by Theo D'Haen and Johannes Willem Bertens, 79–97. Amsterdam: Rodopi, 1994.

Cornwell, Gareth. "Realism, Rape, and J. M. Coetzee's *Disgrace*." *Critique* 43, no. 4 (2002): 307–22.

Critchley, Simon. *The Ethics of Deconstruction: Derrida and Levinas*. 2nd ed. West Lafayette, IN: Purdue UP, 1999.

Currie, Mark. *Postmodern Narrative Theory*. London: Palgrave, 1998.

Deresiewicz, William. "Third-Person Singular." *New York Times*, 7 July 2002: 6.

Derrida, Jacques. *Acts of Religion*. Edited by Gil Anidjar. London: Routledge, 2002.

———. *Of Grammatology.* Translated by Gayatri Chakravorty Spivak. Baltimore: Johns Hopkins UP, 1976.

———. "On Forgiveness." Translated by Mark Dooley and Michael Hughes. In *On Cosmopolitanism and Forgiveness*, 25–60. London: Routledge, 2001.

———. *Writing and Difference.* Translated by Alan Bass. London: Routledge and Kegan Paul, 1978.

Donadio, Rachel. "Out of South Africa." Sunday Book Review, *New York Times*, 16 December 2007.

Donovan, Josephine. "'Miracles of Creation': Animals in J. M. Coetzee's Work." *Michigan Quarterly Review* 43, no. 1 (2004): 78–93.

Dostoevsky, Fyodor. "At Tikhon's." Translated by Avrham Yarmolinsky. In *Guilt and Shame*, edited by Herbert Morris, 6–39. Belmont, CA: Wadsworth, 1971.

———. *The Devils.* Translated by David Magarshack. Harmondsworth: Penguin, 1965.

Dovey, Teresa. "Coetzee and His Critics: The Case of *Dusklands.*" *English in Africa* 14, no. 2 (1987): 15–30.

———. *The Novels of J. M. Coetzee: Lacanian Allegories.* Johannesburg: Ad. Donker, 1988.

Du Plessis, Ménan. "Towards a True Materialism." Review of *Waiting for the Barbarians. Contrast* 13, no. 4 (1981): 77–78.

Dudiak, Jeffrey M. "Structures of Violence, Structures of Peace: Levinasian Reflections on Just War and Pacifism." In *Knowing Other-Wise: Philosophy at the Threshold of Spirituality*, edited by James H. Olthuis, 159–71. New York: Fordham UP, 1997.

Durrant, Sam. "Bearing Witness to Apartheid: J. M. Coetzee's Inconsolable Works of Mourning." *Contemporary Literature* 40, no. 3 (1999): 430–63.

———. "J. M. Coetzee, Elizabeth Costello, and the Limits of the Sympathetic Imagination." In Poyner, *J. M. Coetzee and the Idea of the Public Intellectual*, 118–34.

———. *Postcolonial Narrative and the Work of Mourning: J. M. Coetzee, Wilson Harris, and Toni Morrison.* Albany: State U of New York P, 2004.

Eckstein, Barbara. "Iconicity, Immersion and Otherness: The Hegelian 'Dive' of J. M. Coetzee and Adrienne Rich." *Mosaic: A Journal for the Interdisciplinary Study of Literature* 29, no. 1 (1996): 57–77.

Egerer, Claudia. "Hybridizing the Zero: Exploring Alternative Strategies of Empowerment in J. M. Coetzee's *Foe.*" In *Postcolonialism and Cultural Resistance*, edited by Jopi Nyman and John A. Stotesbury, 96–101. Joensuu, Finland: Faculty of Humanities, University of Joensuu, 1999.

Engdahl, Horace, "Nobel Lecture Presentation" (video), The Nobel Prize Website. http://nobelprize.org/mediaplayer/index.php?id=716. Accessed 28 February 2010.

Foucault, Michel. "What Is an Author?" Translated by Donald F. Bouchard and Sherry Simon. In *Language, Counter-Memory, Practice: Selected*

Essays and Interviews, edited by Donald F. Bouchard, 113–38. Ithaca: Cornell UP, 1977.

Frank, Joseph. *Dostoevsky: The Miraculous Years, 1865–1871*. Princeton, NJ: Princeton UP, 1995.

Friedman, Susan Stanford. "Planetarity: Musing Modernist Studies." *Modernism/Modernity* 17, no. 3 (September 2010): 471–99.

Gal, Noam. "A Note on the Use of Animals for Remapping Victimhood in J. M. Coetzee's *Disgrace*." *African Identities* 6, no. 3 (2008): 241–52.

Gikandi, Simon. "Modernism in the World." *Modernism/Modernity* 13, no. 3 (September 2006): 419–24.

Goffman, Erving. *Stigma: Notes of the Management of Spoiled Identity*. Great Britain: Penguin, 1981.

Gordimer, Nadine. *The Conservationist*. [1974] London: Penguin, 1978.

———. "The Idea of Gardening." In Kossew, *Critical Essays*, 139–44.

———. "The Idea of Gardening." *New York Review of Books* (2 February 1984): Available at: www.nybooks.com/articles/archives/1984/feb/02/the-idea-of-gardening. Accessed 30 June 2011.

Graham, Lucy Valerie. "'A Hidden Side to the Story': Reading Rape in Recent South African Literature." *Kunapipi* 24, nos. 1–2 (2002): 9–24.

———. "Textual Transvestism: The Female Voices of J. M. Coetzee." In Poyner, *J. M. Coetzee and the Idea of the Public Intellectual*, 217–35.

Hayes, Patrick. *J. M. Coetzee and the Novel: Writing and Politics after Beckett* (Oxford: Oxford UP, 2010). Available at: *Oxford Scholarship Online*. Oxford UP. http://dx.doi.org/10.1093/acprof:oso/9780199587957.001.0001. Accessed 16 January 2011.

———. "Literature, History and Folly." In Boehmer, Iddiols, and Eaglestone, 112–22.

Head, Dominic. "A Belief in Frogs: J. M. Coetzee's Enduring Faith in Fiction." In Poyner, *J. M. Coetzee and the Idea of the Public Intellectual*, 100–117.

———. *The Cambridge Introduction to J. M. Coetzee*. Cambridge: Cambridge UP, 2009.

———. *J. M. Coetzee*. Cambridge: Cambridge UP, 1997.

Herlitzius, Eva-Marie. *A Comparative Analysis of the South African and German Reception of Nadine Gordimer's, André Brink's and J. M. Coetzee's Works*. Munster: LIT VERLAG, 2005.

Herron, Tom. "The Dog Man: Becoming Animal in Coetzee's *Disgrace*." *Twentieth-Century Literature* 51, no. 4 (2005): 467–90.

Hitchcock, Peter. *The Long Space: Transnationalism and Postcolonial Form*. Stanford, CA: Stanford UP, 2010.

Hite, Molly. "Tonal Cues and Uncertain Values: Affect and Ethics in *Mrs. Dalloway*." *Narrative* 18, no. 3 (October 2010): 249–75.

Horrell, Georgina. "Postcolonial *Disgrace*: (White) Women and (White) Guilt in the 'New' South Africa." In *Bodies and Voices: The Force-Field of Representation and Discourse in Colonial and Postcolonial Studies*, edited by Merete Falck Borch, Eva Rask, Martin Leer, and Bruce Clunies Ross, 17–31. Amsterdam: Rodopi, 2008.

Huggan, Graham, and Stephen Watson, editors. *Critical Perspectives on J. M. Coetzee*. London: Macmillan, 1996.

Hughes, Robert. *The Shock of the New*. New York: Knopf 1981.

James, David. "By Thrifty Design: Ford's Bequest and Coetzee's Homage." *International Ford Madox Ford Studies* 7 (October 2008): 243–65.

Jolly, Rosemary. "Going to the Dogs: Humanity in J. M. Coetzee's *Disgrace*, *The Lives of Animals*, and South Africa's Truth and Reconciliation Commission." In Poyner, *J. M. Coetzee and the Idea of the Public Intellectual*, 148–71.

Jonas, Hans. *Gnosis und spätantiker Geist*. Göttingen: Vandenhock, 1934.

Jordaan, Eduard. "A White South African Liberal as Hostage to the Other: Reading J. M. Coetzee's *Age of Iron* through Levinas." *South African Journal of Philosophy* 24, no. 1 (2005): 22–32.

Joyce, James. "Daniel Defoe by James Joyce." Edited from Italian manuscripts and translated by Joseph Prescott. *Buffalo Studies* 1, no. 1 (December 1964): 5–25.

Kafka, Franz. "The Hunger-Artist." In *Metamorphosis and Other Stories*. Translated by Michael Hofmann, 252–63. London: Penguin, 2007.

———. "Vor dem Gesetz" ("Before the Law"). In *Franz Kafka: Short Stories*, edited by J. M. S. Pasley, 51–53. Oxford: Oxford UP, 1963.

Kehinde, Ayo. "Post-Colonial Literatures as Counter-Discourse: J. M. Coetzee's *Foe* and the Reworking of the Canon." *Journal of African Literature and Culture (JALC)* 4 (2007): 33–57.

Kellman, Stephen J. "J. M. Coetzee and Samuel Beckett: The Translingual Link." *Comparative Literature Studies* 33, no. 2 (1996): 161–72.

Kermode, Frank. "Fictioneering." Review of *Summertime*. *London Review of Books*, 8 October 2009: 9–10.

Khanna, Ranjana. "Indignity." *Ethnic and Racial Studies* 30, no. 2 (2007): 257–80.

———. "Indignity." *positions* 16, no. 1 (2008): 39–77.

Klopper, Dirk. "Critical Fictions in J. M. Coetzee's *Boyhood* and *Youth*." *scrutiny2: Issues in English Studies in South Africa* 11, no. 1 (2006): 22–31.

Kossew, Sue, ed. *Critical Essays on J. M. Coetzee*. London: Prentice Hall and New York: G. K. Hall & Co, 1998.

———. *Pen and Power. A Post-Colonial Reading of J. M. Coetzee and André Brink*. Amsterdam, Atlanta: Rodopi, 1996.

Lake, Carlton, ed. "No Symbols Where None Intended: A Catalogue of Books, Manuscripts, and Other Materials relating to Samuel Beckett in the Collections of the Harry Ransom Humanities Center." Austin: Harry Ransom Humanities Research Center, University of Texas at Austin, 1984.

Lane, Richard. "Embroiling Narratives: Appropriating the Signifier in J. M. Coetzee's *Foe*." *Commonwealth Essays and Studies* 13, no. 1 (1990): 106–11.

Lee, Hermione. "Heart of Stone: J. M. Coetzee." In *Body Parts: Essays on Life Writing*, 167–76. London: Chatto & Windus, 2005.

———. "Uneasy Guest." Review of *Youth*. *London Review of Books* 24, no. 13 (11 July 2002): 14–15.

Leist, Anton, and Peter Singer, eds. *J. M. Coetzee and Ethics: Philosophical Perspectives on Literature*. New York: Columbia UP, 2010.

Lenta, Margaret. "*Autre*biography: J. M. Coetzee's *Boyhood* and *Youth*." *English in Africa* 30, no. 1 (May 2003): 157–69.

Levinas, Emmanuel. *Basic Philosophical Writings*. Edited by Adriaan Peperzak, Simon Critchley, and Robert Bernasconi. Bloomington: Indiana UP, 1996.

———. *Collected Philosophical Papers*. Translated by Alphonso Lingis. Dordrecht, Boston and Lancaster: Martinus Nijhoff Publishers, 1987.

———. *Ethics and Infinity: Conversations with Phillipe Nemo*. Translated by Richard A. Cohen. Pittsburgh: Duquesne UP, 1985.

———. *Is It Righteous to Be? Interviews with Emmanuel Levinas*. Edited by Jill Robbins. Stanford: Stanford UP, 2001.

———. *The Levinas Reader*. Edited by Seán Hand. Oxford: Blackwell, 1989.

———. *Of God Who Comes to Mind*. 1986. Translated by Bettina Bergo. Stanford: Stanford UP, 1998.

———. *Otherwise Than Being, or, Beyond Essence*. [1978]. Translated by Alphonso Lingis. Pittsburgh: Duquesne UP, 1998.

———. *Totality and Infinity: An Essay on Exteriority*. Translated by Alphonso Lingis. Pittsburgh: Duquesne UP, 1969.

Macaskill, Brian. "Charting J. M. Coetzee's Middle Voice." *Contemporary Literature* 35, no. 3 (Autumn 1994): 441–75.

Madox Ford, Ford. *The Good Soldier*. Edited by Martin Stannard. New York: Norton, 1995.

———. "On Impressionism." *Poetry and Drama* 2, no. 6 (June–December 1914): 167–75.

Marais, Mike. "From the Standpoint of Redemption: Aesthetic Autonomy and Social Engagement in J. M. Coetzee's Fiction of the Late Apartheid Period." *Journal of Narrative Theory* 38, no. 2 (2008): 229–48.

———. "The Hermeneutics of Empire: Coetzee's Post-colonial Metafiction." In Huggan and Watson, 66–81.

———. "Impossible Possibilities: Ethics and Choice in J. M. Coetzee's *The Lives of Animals* and *Disgrace*." *English Academy Review* 18, no. 1 (2001): 1–20.

———. "Interpretative Authoritarianism: Reading/Colonizing Coetzee's *Foe*." *English in Africa* 16, no. 1 (May 1989): 9–16.

———. "Languages of Power: A Story of Reading Coetzee's *Michael K / Michael K*." *English in Africa* 16 (1989): 31–48.

———. "'Little Enough, Less than Little: Nothing': Ethics, Engagement, and Change in the Fiction of J. M. Coetzee." *Modern Fiction Studies* 46, no. 1 (2000): 159–82.

————. "The Novel as Ethical Command: J. M. Coetzee's *Foe*." *Journal of Literary Studies* 16, no. 2 (2000): 62–85.

————. "Places of Pigs: The Tension between Implication and Transcendence in J. M. Coetzee's *Age of Iron* and *The Master of Petersburg*." In Kossew, *Critical Essays*, 226–38.

————. "The Possibility of Ethical Action: J. M. Coetzee's *Disgrace*." *scrutiny2: Issues in English Studies in South Africa* 5, no. 1 (2000): 57–63.

————. "Reading against Race: J. M. Coetzee's *Disgrace*, Justin Cartwright's *White Lightning* and Ivan Vladislavić's *The Restless Supermarket*." *Journal of Literary Studies* 19, no. 3 (2003): 271–89.

————. *Secretary of the Invisible: The Idea of Hospitality in the Fiction of J. M. Coetzee*. Amsterdam: Rodopi, 2009.

————. "Very Morbid Phenomena: 'Liberal Funk,' the 'Lucy-Syndrome' and J. M. Coetzee's *Disgrace*." *scrutiny2: Issues in English Studies in South Africa* 6, no. 1 (2001): 32–38.

Marshall, David. "Friday's Writing Lesson: Reading *Foe*." In *Historical Boundaries, Narrative Forms: Essays on British Literature in the Long Eighteenth Century in Honor of Everett Zimmerman*, edited by Lorna Clymer and Robert Mayer, 225–51. Newark: U of Delaware P, 2007.

Mason, Travis. "Dog Gambit: Shifting the Species Boundary in J. M. Coetzee's Recent Fiction." *Mosaic* 39, no. 4 (2006): 129–44.

McDonald, Bill, ed. *Encountering* Disgrace: *Reading and Teaching Coetzee's Novel*. Rochester, New York: Camden House, 2009.

McDonald, Peter D. *The Literature Police: Apartheid Censorship and Its Cultural Consequences*. Oxford: Oxford UP, 2009.

————. "'Not Undesirable': How J. M. Coetzee Escaped the Censor." *TLS*, 19 May 2000: 14–15.

————. "The Writer, the Critic, and the Censor." *Book History* 7 (2004): 285–302.

————. "The Writer, the Critic, and the Censor: J. M. Coetzee and the Question of Literature." In Poyner, *J. M. Coetzee and the Idea of the Public Intellectual*, 42–62.

McEwan, Ian. "The State of Fiction: A Symposium." *The New Review* 5, no. 1 (1978): 50–51.

Meffan, James, and Kim L. Worthington. "Ethics before Politics: J. M. Coetzee's *Disgrace*." In *Mapping the Ethical Turn: A Reader in Ethics, Culture, and Literary Theory*, edited by Todd F. Davis and Kenneth Womack, 131–50. Charlottesville: UP of Virginia, 2001.

Memmi, Albert. *The Coloniser and the Colonised*. London: Souvenir, 1974.

Moses, Michael Valdez. "The Mark of Empire: Writing, History, and Torture in Coetzee's *Waiting for the Barbarians*." *Kenyon Review* 15, no. 1 (1993).

Mukherjee, Ankhi. "The Death of the Novel and Two Postcolonial Writers." *Modern Language Quarterly* 69, no. 4 (2008): 533–56.

Mulhall, Stephen. *The Wounded Animal: J. M. Coetzee and the Difficulty of Reality in Literature and Philosophy*. Princeton: Princeton UP, 2009.

Nashef, Hania A. M. *The Politics of Humiliation in the Novels of J. M. Coetzee*. New York: Routledge, 2009.

Neumann, Anne Waldron. "Escaping the 'Time of History'?: Present Tense and the Occasion of Narration in J. M. Coetzee's *Waiting for the Barbarians*." *Journal of Narrative Technique* 20, no. 1 (1990): 65–86.

Neumann, Gerhard. "Hungerkünstler und Menschenfresser. Zum Verhältnis von Kunst und kulturellem Ritual im Werk Franz Kafkas." In *Franz Kafka: Schriftverkehr*, edited by Wolf Kittler and Gerhard Neumann, 399–432. Freiburg: Rombach, 1990.

Newman, Judie. "Desperately Seeking Susan: J. M. Coetzee, *Robinson Crusoe* and *Roxana*." *Current Writing: Text and Reception in Southern Africa* 6, no. 1 (1994): 1–12.

Nicholson, Maureen. "'If I Make the Air Around Him Thick with Words': J. M. Coetzee's *Foe*." *West Coast Review* 21, no. 4 (1987): 52–58.

Parry, Benita. "Speech and Silence in the Fictions of J. M. Coetzee." In Huggan and Watson, 37–67.

Patton, Paul. "Becoming-Animal and Pure Life in Coetzee's *Disgrace*." *Ariel* 35, nos. 1–2 (2006): 101–19.

Pechey, Graham. "The Post-Apartheid Sublime: Rediscovering the Extraordinary." In Attridge and Jolly, 57–74.

Pellow, Kenneth. "Intertextuality and Other Analogues in J. M. Coetzee's *Slow Man*." *Contemporary Literature* 50, no. 3 (Fall 2009): 528–52.

Penner, Dick. *Countries of the Mind*. London: Greenwood Press, 1989.

Phelan, James. "Present Tense Narration, Mimesis, the Narrative Norm, and the Positioning of the Reader in *Waiting for the Barbarians*." In *Understanding Narrative*, edited by James Phelan and Peter J. Rabinowitz, 222–45. Columbus: Ohio UP, 1994.

Poyner, Jane, ed. *J. M. Coetzee and the Idea of the Public Intellectual*. Athens: Ohio UP, 2006.

———. *J. M. Coetzee and the Paradox of Postcolonial Authorship*. Farnham, UK: Ashgate, 2009.

———. "Truth and Reconciliation in JM Coetzee's *Disgrace*." *scrutiny2: Issues in English Studies in South Africa* 5, no. 2 (2000): 67–77.

Probyn, Fiona. "Cancerous Bodies and Apartheid in J. M. Coetzee's *Age of Iron*." In Kossew, *Critical Essays*, 214–25.

Probyn-Rapsey, Fiona. "Reconnaissance: The Role of the Feminine and Feminist Theory in the Novels of J. M. Coetzee." In Baral, 247–74.

Randall, Don. "The Community of Sentient Beings: J. M. Coetzee's Ecology in *Disgrace* and *Elizabeth Costello*." *English Studies in Canada* 33, nos. 1–2 (2007): 209–25.

Reinfandt, Christoph. "The Pitfalls of a Postcolonial Poetics: J. M. Coetzee's *Foe* and the New Literatures in English." *Symbolism: An International Annual of Critical Aesthetics* 7 (2007): 299–315.

Rich, Paul. "Apartheid and the Declines of the Civilization Idea: An Essay on Nadine Gordimer's *July's People* and J. M. Coetzee's *Waiting for the Barbarians*." *Research in African Literatures* 15, no. 3 (1984): 365–93.

Sachs, Albie. "Preparing Ourselves for Freedom." In *Spring Is Rebellious: Arguments about Cultural Freedom*, edited by Ingrid de Kok and Karen Press, 19–29. Cape Town: Buchu Books, 1990.

Said, Edward. *Culture and Imperialism*. 1993. London: Vintage, 1994.

Sanders, Mark. *"Disgrace."* *Interventions* 4, no. 3 (2002): 363–73.

Saunders, Rebecca. *"Disgrace* in the Time of a Truth Commission." *parallax* 11, no. 3 (2005): 99–106.

Sévry, Jean. "An Interview with J. M. Coetzee." *Commonwealth* 9 (Autumn 1986): 1–7.

Sheils, Colleen M. "Opera, Byron, and a South African Psyche in J. M. Coetzee's *Disgrace.*" *Current Writing* 15, no. 1 (2003): 38–50.

Sikorska, Liliana, ed. *A Universe of (Hi)Stories*. Frankfurt am Main: Peter Lang, 2006.

Silva, Denise Almeida. "Cartesianism Reviewed: The Logic of the Body in J. M. Coetzee's Fiction." *Stirrings Still: The International Journal of Existentialist Literature* 3, no. 1 (2006): 82–109.

———. "On Engendering Fiction: Authority and Authorship in *Foe, Elizabeth Costello* and *Slow Man*." In Baral, 221–46.

Soovik, Ene-Reet. "Prisoners of the Present: Tense and Agency in J. M. Coetzee's *Waiting for the Barbarians* and M. Atwood's *The Handmaid's Tale*." *Interlitteraria* 8 (2003): 259–75.

Spivak, Gayatri Chakravorty. "Can the Subaltern Speak?" In *Marxism and the Interpretation of Culture*, edited by Cary Nelson and Lawrence Grossberg. Urbana: U of Illinois P, 1988.

———. "Ethics and Politics in Tagore, Coetzee, and Certain Scenes of Teaching." *diacritics* 32, nos. 3–4 (2002): 17–31.

———. "Three Women's Texts and a Critique of Imperialism." *Critical Inquiry* 12, no. 1 (1985): 243–61.

Stanton, Katherine. *Cosmopolitan Fictions: Ethics, Politics, and Global Change in the Works of Kazuo Ishigur, Michael Ondaatje, Jamaica Kincaid, and J. M. Coetzee*. London and New York: Routledge, 2006.

Szczurek, Karina Magdelena. "Coetzee and Gordimer." In Boehmer, Iddiols, and Eaglestone, 36–46.

Taubes, Jacob. *Abendländische Eschatologie*. Berlin: Matthes & Seitz, 2007.

Taylor, Jane. "The Impossibility of Ethical Action. Review of *Disgrace*, by J. M. Coetzee." *Mail & Guardian*, 23–29 July 1999: 25.

Tiffin, Helen. "Post-Colonial Literatures and Counter-Discourse." *Kunapipi* 9, no. 3 (1987): 17–34.

Titlestad, Michael, and Mike Kissack. "The Persistent Castaway in South African Writing." *Postcolonial Studies* 10, no. 2 (2007): 191–218.

Tremaine, Louis. "The Embodied Soul: Animal Being in the Work of J. M. Coetzee." *Contemporary Literature* 44, no. 4 (2003): 587–612.

Tutu, Desmond. *No Future without Forgiveness*. London: Doubleday, 2000.

van Coller, H. P. "A Contextual Interpretation of J. M. Coetzee's Novel *Disgrace*." In Sikorska, 15–37.

Van der Elst, Jacques. "Guilt, Reconciliation and Redemption: *Disgrace* and its South African Context." In Sikorska, 39–44.

van der Vlies, Andrew. *J. M. Coetzee's Disgrace*. London: Continuum, 2010.

van Heerden, Adriaan. "Disgrace, Desire, and the Dark Side of the New South Africa." In Leist and Singer, 43–63.

VanZanten Gallagher, Susan. *A Story of South Africa: J. M. Coetzee's Fiction in Context*. Cambridge: Harvard UP, 1991.

Vaughan, Michael. "Literature and Politics: Currents in South African Writing in the Seventies." *Journal of Southern African Studies* 9, no. 1 (October 1982): 118–38.

Vice, Samantha. "Truth and Love Together at Last: Style, Form, and Moral Vision in *Age of Iron*." In Leist and Singer, 293–315.

Walkowitz, Rebecca L. "Comparison Literature." *Literary History* 40, no. 3 (Summer 2009): 567–82.

Walsh, Richard. "How to Explore a Field." *Modernism/Modernity* 14, no. 3 (2007): 569–72.

Watson, Stephen. "Colonialism and the Novels of J. M. Coetzee." In Huggan and Watson, 13–36.

Watt, Daniel. *Fragmentary Futures: Blanchot, Beckett, Coetzee*. Ashby-de-la-Zouch, UK: InkerMen Press, 2007.

Wenzel, Jennifer. "Keys to the Labyrinth: Writing, Torture, and Coetzee's Barbarian Girl." *Tulsa Studies in Women's Literature* 15, no. 1 (1996): 61–71.

Wicomb, Zoë. "Slow Man and the Real: A Lesson in Reading and Writing." *Journal of Literary Studies* 25, no. 4 (December 2009): 7–24.

Wilson, Angus. "Diversity and Depth." (1958). In *Diversity and Depth in Fiction: Selected Critical Writings*, edited by Kerry McSweeney, 130–34. London: Secker & Warburg, 1983.

Wimsatt, W. K. Jr., and Monroe C. Beardsley. *The Verbal Icon: Studies in the Meaning of Poetry*. Lexington: U of Kentucky P, 1954.

Worthington, Kim L. *Self as Narrative: Subjectivity and Community in Contemporary Fiction*. Oxford: Clarendon, 1996.

Wright, Laura. "Displacing the Voice: South African Feminism and J. M. Coetzee's Female Narrators." *African Studies* 67, no. 1 (2008): 11–31.

———. "'Does He Have It in Him to Be the Woman?': The Performance of Displacement in J. M. Coetzee's *Disgrace*." *Ariel* 37, no. 4 (2006): 83–102.

———. *Writing "Out of All the Camps": J. M. Coetzee's Narratives of Displacement*. New York: Routledge, 2006.

Yeoh, Gilbert. "J. M. Coetzee and Samuel Beckett: Ethics, Truth-Telling, and Self-Deception." *Critique: Studies in Contemporary Fiction* 44, no. 4 (June 2003).

Zimbler, Jarad. "Under Local Eyes: The South African Publishing Context of J. M. Coetzee's *Foe*." *English Studies in Africa: A Journal of the Humanities* 47, no. 1 (2004): 47–60.

Contributors

CHRIS ACKERLEY is professor and former head of English at the University of Otago. His research interest is annotation, particularly of the works of Malcolm Lowry and Samuel Beckett. He is coauthor of the Grove Press and Faber *Companion to Samuel Beckett* (2004), and has recently edited Beckett's *Watt* for Faber. His annotations of *Watt* and *Murphy* have been reissued by the University of Edinburgh Press. He is currently working on a study entitled *Samuel Beckett and Science* and annotating a newly discovered novel by Lowry.

DEREK ATTRIDGE is the author of, among other books, *J. M. Coetzee and the Ethics of Reading: Literature in the Event* (2004) and *The Singularity of Literature* (2004). He is the coeditor, with Rosemary Jolly, of *Writing South Africa: Literature, Apartheid, and Democracy, 1970–1995* (1998) and, with David Attwell, the forthcoming *Cambridge History of South African Literature*. He is professor of English at the University of York and a Fellow of the British Academy.

CARROL CLARKSON is the author of *J. M. Coetzee: Countervoices* (2009). Her research interests include language philosophy, law and literature, and postapartheid South African literature and art. Her next book, *Drawing the Line: Toward an Aesthetics of Transitional Justice* is forthcoming with Fordham University Press. She is head of the department of English at the University of Cape Town, where she also hosts the Coetzee Collective, an international network of Coetzee scholars. In 2009 she was the recipient of UCT's Distinguished Teacher's Award.

SIMONE DRICHEL is senior lecturer in the English Department at Otago University. She is the coeditor (with Jan Cronin) of *Frameworks: Contemporary Criticism on Janet Frame* (2009) and author of several articles on deconstructive postcolonial ethics. She is currently working on a monograph provisionally entitled "The Other Other: Postcolonialism and Ethics." She is a founding member of the Postcolonial Studies Research Network at Otago University and was the principal organizer of the network's 2010 event "Vulnerability: A Symposium." She is also a coeditor of *borderlands e-journal* and the New Zealand representative for the Australasian Society for Continental Philosophy.

JOHAN GEERTSEMA teaches in the University Scholars Programme of the National University of Singapore. His research focuses on the writing of J. M. Coetzee, a topic on which he has published widely. At present, he is preparing a book that considers Coetzee's late work as a set of ironic confrontations with the sublime. A number of essays that read novels such as *Disgrace, Slow Man,* and *Diary of a Bad Year* with reference to these issues are forthcoming in 2011 and 2012.

DAVID JAMES is lecturer in nineteenth- and twentieth-century literature in the School of English Studies at the University of Nottingham, UK. His work on the modern and contemporary novel is reflected in *Contemporary British Fiction and the Artistry of Space: Style, Landscape, Perception* (2008), and in articles in venues such as *Textual Practice, Modernism/ Modernity,* and *Journal of Modern Literature.* He is currently guest-editing a special issue of *Contemporary Literature* on "Post-Millennial Commitments" (Winter 2012). His most recent publication, of which he is sole editor, is *The Legacies of Modernism: Historicising Postwar and Contemporary Fiction* (2011).

MICHELLE KELLY is a teaching fellow in the Department of English and Related Literature at the University of York. Her research interests are in the field of postcolonial literature, especially South African literature, Irish literature, literature and the law, and literature and human rights. She is working on a book on confession in Coetzee's work, and has also written on Coetzee and the law.

SUE KOSSEW is professor of English at Monash University. She has published numerous journal articles and book chapters on postcolonial and South African literature. Her monographs include *Writing Woman, Writing Place: Contemporary Australian and South African Fiction* (2004) and *Pen and Power: A Post-Colonial Reading of J. M. Coetzee and André Brink* (1996). She has edited the volumes *Lighting Dark Places: Essays on Kate Grenville* (2010), *Re-Imagining Africa: New Critical Perspectives* (2001, with Dianne Schwerdt) and *Critical Essays in World Literature: J. M. Coetzee* (1998). She has also coedited a volume of essays entitled *Strong Opinions: J. M. Coetzee and the Authority of Contemporary Fiction.*

MIKE MARAIS teaches in the department of English at Rhodes University, Grahamstown. He has published widely on the fiction of J. M. Coetzee and other contemporary South African writers, such as Ivan Vladislavic and Zoë Wicomb.

JAMES MEFFAN lectures English literature at Victoria University of Wellington. His focus is on literary theory, particularly postcolonial and narrative theory.

TIM MEHIGAN has published widely on German literature and thought from Lessing to the present. He is the author of *Robert Musil* (2001), and of *The Critical Response to Musil's "The Man without Qualities"* (2003) and *Heinrich von Kleist: Writing after Kant* (2011). With Barry Empson he has recently issued the first English translation of K. L. Reinhold's *Essay on a New Theory of the Human Capacity for Representation* (2011). He is professor of languages at the University of Otago, honorary professor in the School of Languages and Comparative Cultural Studies at the University of Queensland, and a Fellow of the Australian Academy of Humanities.

CHRIS PRENTICE teaches New Zealand and postcolonial literatures and theory in the Department of English, University of Otago. Her research focuses on the cultural politics of settler postcolonial societies, and specifically on the implications of mobilizing culture as a basis for political intervention at the intersection of decolonization and globalization. She has published in such journals as *Ariel, Modern Fiction Studies, New Literatures Review*, and in numerous edited collections. She has coedited a volume of essays on textual, musical, and visual cultures entitled *Cultural Transformations: Perspectives on Translocation in a Global Age* (2010).

ENGELHARD WEIGL studied German literature and philosophy in Hamburg and Bochum, Germany. His principal research interests relate to eighteenth-century German literature and philosophy and the history of science. He is the author of *Schauplätze der deutschen Aufklärung* (1997), *Instrumente der Neuzeit: Die Entdeckung der modernen Wirklichkeit* (1990) and *Aufklärung und Skeptizismus: Untersuchungen zu Jean Pauls Frühwerk* (1982). He has also edited the first Japanese translation of Alexander von Humboldt's account of his travels during the years 1799–1804 (Iwanami Shoten). Until recently he taught at the University of Adelaide. He is now retired and living in Berlin.

KIM L. WORTHINGTON has published various articles on the work of J. M. Coetzee, notably in relation to questions about (narrative) ethics. She has a particular interest in issues concerning apology, confession, forgiveness and amnesty and their relationship to contemporary politics and literature. She is the author of *Self as Narrative: Subjectivity and Community and Contemporary Fiction* (1996) and was until recently editor of the New Literatures section of *The Year's Work in English Studies* (Oxford Journals). She teaches in the School of English and Media studies at Massey University.

Index